"McWorld is the universe of manufactured needs, mass consumption, and mass infotainment. It is motivated by profits and driven by the aggregate preferences of billions of consumers. Jihad is shorthand for the fierce politics of religious, tribal, and other zealots. In its most extreme manifestations—in the ultra nationalism of Vladimir Zhirinovsky's Russia, for example, or the balkanization of the Balkans—it counters McWorld's centrifugal pull and bloodless calculation.

Although some countries or parts of countries fit into one or the other category, Jihad and McWorld are not so much places as reactions to experience and attitudes of mind. As Mr. Barber provocatively puts it: 'Belonging by default to McWorld, everyone is a consumer; seeking a repository for identity, everyone belongs to some tribe. But no one is a citizen.' "

—The Economist

"*Jihad vs. McWorld* is that rare phenomenon—a book that is immensely readable, yet with a serious theme."

—Government & Opposition

"Challenging and instructive."

—San Francisco Chronicle

"Stimulating, tartly written."

—Publishers Weekly

A *BOOKLIST* EDITORS' CHOICE

BOOKS BY BENJAMIN R. BARBER

The Truth of Power (2001)

A Passion for Democracy (1998)

A Place for Us (1998)

Jihad vs. McWorld (1995)

An Aristocracy of Everyone (1992)

The Conquest of Politics (1988)

Strong Democracy (1984)

Marriage Voices (A Novel) (1981)

Liberating Feminism (1975)

The Death of Communal Liberty (1974)

Superman and Common Men (1971)

COLLABORATIONS

The Struggle for Democracy
with Patrick Watson (1989)

The Artist and Political Vision
edited with M. McGrath (1982)

Totalitarianism in Perspective
with C. J. Friedrich and M. Curtis (1969)

Jihad *vs.*
McWorld

Benjamin R. Barber

Ballantine Books • New York

A Ballantine Book
Published by The Ballantine Publishing Group

Copyright © 1995 by Benjamin Barber
2001 Introduction copyright © 2001 by Benjamin Barber

www.ballantinebooks.com

Library of Congress Catalog Card Number: 96-96061

ISBN: 0-345-38304-4

Manufactured in the United States of America
First Ballantine Trade Paper Edition: August 1996

21   22   23   24   25

To the Memory of Judith N. Shklar

Acknowledgments

I was given extraordinary support by two research assistants. Carolyn Nestor did extensive work preparing the empirical materials for the chapters on McWorld, and also reviewed and corrected the notes and bibliographic materials on a crash schedule whose deadlines she met with remarkable aplomb. She acted as a sounding board for ideas and contributed far more than would be expected from a research assistant. I am very much in her debt. Mark Button helped develop research materials, theoretic and empirical, for the Jihad chapters, and was particularly astute in getting to the heart of alternative historical readings. Although the errors remain my own doing, the work of Nestor and Button saved me from what I know would have been many more.

Kathleen Quinn gave the finished manuscript several ruthless readings and readers owe her much for whatever fluency and continuity the text now has. Had she had her way, the book would have been even shorter and more readable, but someone had to take a stand for prolixity and I managed in the end to ignore rather too many of her sound editorial judgments.

Steve Wasserman at Times Books called me in Paris not long after my article on Jihad and McWorld appeared in *The Atlantic* and initiated a process of persuasion and discussion that led to this book. I am grateful to him for his enthusiasm and commitment, without which I would not have written the book. The same can be said of my old friend at *The Atlantic*, Jack Beatty, who encouraged me in developing a provocative idea into a sustainable argument.

Many friends, colleagues, associates, and anonymous commentators—both in the United States and abroad—have responded to the original *Atlantic* article, scholarly and popular presentations of the argument as it developed, and sections of the manuscript as it was being written. I feel lucky to have had so many astute critics who were also friends, among them Michael Kustow, François D'Alancon, Bhikhu Parekh, Ivan Vitanyi, Jean Leca, Preston King, Michael Greven, Bruce Ackerman, Ghita Ionescu, Brian Barry, Chantal Mouffe, George Kateb, Nina Belyaeva, Harry Boyte, Richard Lehne, Seyla Benhabib, Alan Ryan, and the consummate scholar and dear friend to whom the book is dedicated, Judith N. Shklar—who feared Jihad, distrusted McWorld, and, ever so carefully, worked to clear a space for freedom and democracy.

Had I heeded these friendly critics more consistently, I would have certainly written a better book.

To my wife Leah and my daughter Nellie I owe an apology, though they have asked none of me. Without the labors of this project, I would have been better able to repay their indulgent tolerance. The guilt I feel arises not from complaint, but from how much too lovingly understanding they have been.

Contents

2001 Introduction
Terrorism's Challenge to Democracy

O N SEPTEMBER 11, Jihad's long war against McWorld culminated in a fearsomely unprecedented and altogether astonishing assault on the temple of free enterprise in New York City and the cathedral of American military might in Washington, D.C. In bringing down the twin towers of the World Trade Center and destroying a section of the Pentagon with diabolically contrived human bombs, Jihadic warriors reversed the momentum in the struggle between Jihad and McWorld, writing a new page in an ongoing story. Until that day, history's seemingly ineluctable march into a complacent postmodernity had appeared to favor McWorld's ultimate triumph— a historical victory for free-market institutions and McWorld's assiduously commercialized and ambitiously secularist materialism. Today, the outcome of the confrontation between the future and the radical reaction to it seems far less certain. As the world enters a novel stage of shadowed warfare against an invisible enemy, the clash between Jihad and McWorld is again poignantly relevant in understanding why the modern response to terror cannot be exclusively military or tactical, but rather must entail a commitment to democracy and justice even when they are in tension with the commitment to cultural expansionism and global markets. The war against terrorism also will have to be a war for justice if it is to succeed, and not just in the sense in which President George W. Bush used the term in his address to Congress.

A week after the trauma of the first large-scale assault on the American homeland, more successful than even its scheming perpetrators could possibly have hoped for, the president joined the abruptly renewed combat with Jihadic terrorists by deploying the rhetoric of retributive justice: "We will bring the terrorists to justice," he said gravely to a joint session of Congress, "or we will bring justice to the terrorists." The language of justice was surely the appropriate context for the American response, but it will remain appropriate only if the compass of its meaning is extended from retributive to distributive justice.

The collision between the forces of disintegral tribalism and reactionary fundamentalism I have called Jihad (Islam is not the issue) and the forces of integrative modernization and aggressive economic and cultural globalization I have called McWorld (for which America is not solely responsible) has been brutally exacerbated by the dialectical interdependence of these two seemingly oppositional sets of forces. In *Jihad vs. McWorld*, I warn that democracy is caught between a clash of movements, each of which for its own reasons seems indifferent to freedom's fate, and might suffer grievously. It is now apparent, as we mount a new military offense against Jihad (understood not as Islam but as militant fundamentalism) that democracy rather than terrorism may become the principal victim of the battle currently being waged.

Only the globalization of civic and democratic institutions is likely to offer a way out of the global war between modernity and its aggrieved critics, for democracy responds both to Jihad and to McWorld. It responds directly to the resentments and spiritual unease of those for whom the trivialization and homogenization of values is an affront to cultural diversity and spiritual and moral seriousness. But it also answers the complaints of those mired in poverty and despair as a consequence of unregulated global markets and of a capitalism run wild because it has been uprooted from the humanizing constraints of the democratic nation-state. By extending the

compass of democracy to the global market sector, civic globalization can promise opportunities for accountability, participation, and
governance to those wishing to join the modern world and take
advantage of its economic blessings; by securing cultural diversity
and a place for worship and faith insulated from the shallow ortho-
doxies of McWorld's cultural monism, it can address the anxieties of
those who fear secularist materialism and are fiercely committed to
preserving their cultural and religious distinctiveness. The outcome
of the cruel battle between Jihad and McWorld will depend on the
capacity of moderns to make the world safe for women and men in
search of both justice and faith, and can be won only if democracy
is the victor.

If democracy is to be the instrument by which the world avoids
the stark choice between a sterile cultural monism (McWorld) and a
raging cultural fundamentalism (Jihad), neither of which services
diversity or civic liberty, then America, Britain, and their allies will
have to open a crucial second civic and democratic front aimed not
against terrorism per se but against the anarchism and social
chaos—the economic reductionism and its commercializing homogeneity—that have created the climate of despair and hopelessness
that terrorism has so effectively exploited. A second democratic front
will be advanced not only in the name of retributive justice and secularist interests, but in the name of distributive justice and religious
pluralism.

The democratic front in the war on terrorism is not a battle to dissuade terrorists from their campaigns of annihilation. Their deeds
are unspeakable, and their purposes can be neither rationalized nor
negotiated. When they hijacked innocents and turned civilian air-
crafts into lethal weapons, these self-proclaimed "martyrs of faith" in
truth subjected others to a compulsory martyrdom indistinguishable
from mass murder. The terrorists offer no terms and can be given
none in exchange. When Jihad turns nihilistic, bringing it to justice
can only take the form of extirpation—root, trunk, and branch.
Eliminating terrorists will depend on professional military, intelligence, and diplomatic resources whose deployment will leave the
greater number of citizens in America and throughout the world sitting on the sidelines, anxious spectators to a battle in which they cannot participate, a battle in which the nausea that accompanies fear

will dull the appetite for revenge. The second front, however, engages every citizen with a stake in democracy and social justice, both within nation-states and in the relations between them. It transforms anxious and passive spectators into resolute and engaged participants—the perfect antidote to fear.

The first military front must be prosecuted, both because an outraged and wounded American nation demands it and because terrorists bent on annihilation will not yield to blandishments or inducements. They are looking not for bargains but for oblivion. Yet it will be the successful prosecution of a second civic front in the war rather than the strictly military campaign that will determine the outcome. It too, in President Bush's words, will be a war for justice, but a war defined by a new commitment to distributive justice: a readjudication of North-South responsibilities, a redefinition of the obligations of global capital to include global justice and comity, a repositioning of democratic institutions as they follow markets from the domestic to the international sector, a new recognition of the place and requirements of faith in an aggressively secular market society. The war against Jihad will not, in other words, succeed unless McWorld is also addressed.

To be sure, democratizing globalism and rendering McWorld less homogenizing and trivializing to religion and its accompanying ethical and spiritual values will not appease the terrorists, who are scarcely students of globalization's contractual insufficiencies. Jihadic warriors offer no quarter, whether they are the children of Islam, Christianity, or some blood tribalism, and they should be given none. I describe these warriors in *Jihad vs. McWorld* as people who detest modernity—the secular, scientific, rational, and commercial civilization created by the Enlightenment as it is defined by both its virtues (freedom, democracy, tolerance, and diversity) and its vices (inequality, hegemony, cultural imperialism, and materialism). What can these enemies of the modern do but seek to recover the dead past by annihilating the living present?

Terrorists, then, cannot themselves be the object of democratic struggle. They swim in a sea of tacit popular support and resentful acquiescence, however, and these waters—roiling with anger and resentment—prove buoyant to ideologies of violence and mayhem. Americans were themselves first enraged and then deeply puzzled by scenes from Islamic cities where ordinary men, women, and children who could hardly be counted as terrorists nonetheless manifested a kind of perverse jubilation in contemplating the wanton slaughter of American innocents. How could anyone cheer such acts? Yet an environment of despairing rage exists in too many places in the third world as well as in too many third-world neighborhoods of first-world cities, enabling terrorism by endowing it with a kind of quasi-legitimacy it does not deserve. It is not terrorism itself but this facilitating environment against which the second-front battle is directed. Its constituents are not terrorists, for they are terrified by modernity and its costs and, consequently, vulnerable to ameliorative actions if those who embrace democracy find the will to take such actions. What they seek is justice, not vengeance. Their quarrel is not with modernity but with the aggressive neoliberal ideology that has been prosecuted in its name in pursuit of a global market society more conducive to profits for some than to justice for all. They are not even particularly anti-American; rather, they suspect that what Americans understand as prudent unilateralism is really a form of arrogant imperialism, that what Americans take to be a kind of cynical aloofness is really self-absorbed isolationism, and that what Americans think of as pragmatic alliances with tyrannical rulers in Islamic nations such as Saudi Arabia and Pakistan are really a betrayal of the democratic principles to which Americans claim to subscribe.

Hyperbolic commentators such as Samuel Huntington have described the current divide in the world as a global clash of civilizations, and warn of a cultural war between democracy and Islam, perhaps even between "the West and the rest." But this is to ape the messianic rhetoric of Osama bin Laden, who has called for precisely such a war. The difference between bin Laden's terrorists and the poverty-stricken third-world constituents he tries to call to arms, however, is the difference between radical Jihadic fundamentalists and ordinary men and women concerned to feed their children and nurture their religious communities. Fundamentalists can be found among every religious sect and represent a tiny, aggravated minority whose ideology contradicts the very religions in whose names they act. The remarkable comments of the American fundamentalist preacher Jerry Falwell interpreting the attacks on New York and

Washington as the wrath of God being vented on abortionists, homosexuals, and the American Civil Liberties Union no more defines Protestantism than the Taliban defines Islam.

The struggle of Jihad against McWorld is not a clash of civilizations but a dialectical expression of tensions built into a single global civilization as it emerges against a backdrop of traditional ethnic and religious divisions, many of which are actually created by McWorld and its infotainment industries and technological innovations. Imagine bin Laden without modern media: He would be an unknown desert rat. Imagine terrorism without its reliance on credit cards, global financial systems, modern technology, and the Internet: Terrorists would be reduced to throwing stones at local sheiks. It is the argument of this study that what we face is not a war between civilizations but a war within civilization, a struggle that expresses the ambivalence within each culture as it faces a global, networked, material future and wonders whether cultural and national autonomy can be retained, and the ambivalence within each individual juggling the obvious benefits of modernity with its equally obvious costs.

From Seattle and Prague to Stockholm and Genoa, street demonstrators have been protesting the costs of this globalization. Yet though President Chirac of France acknowledged after the dissident violence of Genoa months before the attacks in New York and Washington that a hundred thousand protesters do not take to the streets unless something is amiss, they have mostly been written off as anarchists or know-nothings. More media attention has been paid to their theatrics than to the deep problems those theatrics are intended to highlight. After September 11, some critics even tried to lump the antiglobalization protesters in with the terrorists, casting them as irresponsible destablizers of world order. But the protesters mostly are the children of McWorld, and their objections are not Jihadic but merely democratic. Their grievances concern not world order but world disorder, and if the young demonstrators are a little foolish in their politics, a little naive in their analyses, and a little short on viable solutions, they understand with a sophistication their leaders apparently lack that globalization's current architecture breeds anarchy, nihilism, and violence. They know too that those in the third world who seem to welcome American suffering are at worst reluctant adversaries whose principal aim is to make clear that they too suffer from violence, even if it is less visible and destroys with greater stealth and over a longer period of time than the murderous schemes of the terrorists. They want not to belittle American suffering but to use its horrors to draw attention to their own. How many of these "enemies of McWorld," given the chance, would prefer to enjoy modernity and its blessings if they were not so often the victims of modernity's unevenly distributed costs? How many are really fanatic communists and how many are merely instinctive guardians of fairness who resent not capitalism's productivity but only the claim that, in the absence of global regulation and the democratic rule of law, capitalism can serve them? It is finally hypocrisy rather than democracy that is the target of their rage.

Too often for those living in the second and third worlds to the south of the United States, Europe, and Japan, globalization looks like an imperious strategy of a predominantly American economic behemoth; too often what we understand as the market-driven opportunities to secure liberty and prosperity at home seems to them nothing but a rationalization for exploitation and oppression in the international sphere; too often what we call the international order is for them an international disorder. Our neoliberal antagonism to all political regulation in the global sector, to all institutions of legal and political oversight, to all attempts at democratizing globalization and institutionalizing economic justice looks to them like brute indifference to their welfare and their claims for justice. Western beneficiaries of McWorld celebrate market ideology with its commitment to the privatization of all things public and the commercialization of all things private, and consequently insist on total freedom from government interference in the global economic sector (laissez-faire). Yet total freedom from interference—the rule of private power over public goods—is another name for anarchy. And terror is merely one of the many contagious diseases that anarchy spawns.

What was evident to those who, before September 11, suffered the economic consequences of an undemocratic international anarchy beyond the reach of democratic sovereignty was that while many in the first world benefit from free markets in capital, labor, and goods, these same anarchic markets leave ordinary people in the third world largely unprotected. What has become apparent to the rest of us after September 11 is that that same deregulated disorder from which financial and trade institutions imagine they benefit is the very disorder on which terrorism depends. Markets and globalized financial institutions, whether multinational corporations or individual currency speculators, are deeply averse to oversight by nation-states. McWorld seeks to overcome sovereignty and make its impact global. Jihad too makes war on sovereignty, using the interdependence of transportation, communication, and other modern technological systems to render borders porous and sovereign oversight irrelevant. Just as jobs defy borders, hemorrhaging from one country to another in a wage race to the bottom, and just as safety, health, and environmental standards lack an international benchmark against which states and regions might organize their employment, so too anarchistic terrorists loyal to no state and accountability to no people range freely across the world, knowing that no borders can detain them, no united global opinion can isolate them, no international police or juridical institutions can interdict them. The argument laid out in what follows proposes that both Jihad and McWorld undermine the sovereignty of nation-states, dismantling the democratic institutions that have been their finest achievement without discovering ways to extend democracy either downward to the subnational religious and ethnic entities that now lay claim to people's loyalty or upward to the international sector in which McWorld's pop culture and commercial markets operate without sovereign restraints.

Unlike America, which pretends to still enjoy sovereign independence, taking responsibility neither for the global reach of its popular culture (McWorld) nor for the secularizing and trivializing character of its adamant materialism, the terrorists acknowledge and exploit the actual interdependence that characterizes human relations in the twenty-first century. Theirs, however, is a perverse and malevolent interdependence, one in which they have learned to use McWorld's weight jujitsu-style against its massive power. Ironically, even as the United States fosters an anarchic absence of sovereignty at the global level, it has resisted even the slightest compromise of its national sovereignty at home. America has complained bitterly in recent years about the prospect of surrendering a scintilla of its own sovereignty, whether to NATO commanders, to supranational institutions such as the International Criminal Tribunal, or to international treaties such as those banning land mines or regulating emissions. Even as I write, with the United States launching a military campaign against terrorism surrounded by a prudently constructed coalition, it has made clear that it prefers "coalitions" to "alliances" because it wants to be free to target objectives, develop strategy, and wage war exactly as it wishes.

Yet terrorism has already made a mockery of sovereignty. What were the hijacking of airliners, the calamitous attack on the World Trade Center, and the brash attack on the Pentagon if not a profound obliteration of American sovereignty? Terrorism is the negative and depraved form of that interdependence, which in its positive and beneficial form we too often refuse to acknowledge. As if still in the nineteenth century, America has persuaded itself that its options today are either to preserve an ancient and blissfully secure independence that puts us in charge of American destiny, or to yield to a perverted and compulsory interdependence that puts foreigners and alien international bodies such as the United Nations or the World Court in charge of American destiny. In truth, however, Americans have not enjoyed genuine independence since sometime before the great wars of the last century— certainly not since the advent of AIDS and West Nile virus, global warming and an ever more porous ozone layer, job "mobility" that has decimated America's industrial economy, and restive speculators who have made capital flight more of a sovereign reality than any conceivable government oversight could be. Interdependence is not some foreign adversary against which citizens need to muster resistance. It is a domestic reality that already has compromised the efficacy of citizenship in scores of unacknowledged and uncharted ways.

It was the interdependence of America with the world and the interdependence of shared economic and technological systems everywhere on which the Jihadic warriors counted when they brought terror to the American homeland. They not only hijacked American airplanes, turning them into deadly missiles, but provoked the nation into closing down its air transportation system for nearly a week. They not only destroyed the temple of American capitalism at the World Trade Center but forced capitalism to shut down its markets and shocked the country into a recession, of which the stock market in free fall was only a leading indicator. How can any nation claim independence under these conditions?

In the world before McWorld, democratic sovereign nations could claim to be independent autonomous peoples exercising autonomous control over their lives. In Andrew Jackson's premodern, largely rural America, where communities existed in isolation, where there was no national system of transportation or communication, systematic terror was simply not an option, as there *was* no system. There was no way to bring America to its knees because in a crucial sense America did not exist, at least not as an integral collectivity of interdependent regions with a single interest, until after the Civil War and the Industrial Revolution that followed it. Today there is so much systemic interactivity, so highly integrated a global network, so finely tuned an integral communications technology, that it has become as easy to paralyze as to use the multiple systems and networks. Hence, the decision would-be sovereign peoples face today is not the felicitous choice between secure independence and unwanted interdependence. It is only the sobering choice between, on the one hand, a relatively legitimate, democratic, and useful interdependence (which, however, is still to be constructed and which leaves sovereignty in tatters) and, on the other hand, a radically illegitimate and undemocratic interdependence on the terms of criminals, anarchists, and terrorists (an interdependence that is already here and which will triumph in the absence of a democratizing political will). In short, either we can allow McWorld and Jihad—Hollywood cowboys and international desperadoes—to set the terms of our interdependence, or we can leave those terms to new transnational treaties, new global democratic bodies, and a new creative common will. We can have our interactivity dictated to us by violence and anarchy, or we can construct it on the model of our own democratic aspirations. We can have a democratic and useful interdependence on whatever common ground we can persuade others to stand on, or we can stand on the brink of anarchy and try to prevent criminals and terrorists from pushing us into the abyss.

It will be hard for defenders of modernity—whether of McWorld's markets or democracy's citizenship—to have it both ways. Terrorism turns out to be a depraved version of globalization, no less vigorous in its pursuit of its own special interests than are global markets, no less wedded to anarchist disorder than are speculators, no less averse to violence when it serves their ends than marketers are averse to inequality and injustice when they are conceptualized as the "costs of doing business." It is their instinctive reading of this equation that turns poor people abroad into cheering mobs when Americans experience grievous losses at home. It is their perception of overwhelming hypocrisy that leads them to exult where we would wish for them to grieve.

In his address to Congress, President Bush was speaking to the world at large when he said, "You are with us or you are with the terrorists." Americans may appreciate the impulse to divide the world into good and evil (though some will think that it smacks of the very Manicheanism for which Americans excoriate their fundamentalist adversaries), but America's enemies (and more than a few of its friends) are likely to find this discourse unfortunate and misleading if not hubristic. An America that comprehends the realities of interdependence and wishes to devise a democratic architecture to contain its global disorder cannot ask others to either join it or else "suffer the consequences." It is not that the world must join America: McWorld already operates on this premise, and the premise is precisely the problem. Rather, America must join the world on whatever terms it can negotiate on an equal footing with the world. Whether a product of arrogance or prudence, the demand that the world join the United States simply cannot secure results. It defies the very interdependence to which it is addressed. It assumes a sovereign autonomy the United States does not and cannot enjoy.

In *Jihad vs. McWorld*, I worry that a pervasive culture of fast food, fast computers, and fast music advanced by an infotainment industry rooted in the spread of brands tend to homogenize global markets and render taste not merely shallow but uniform. McWorld's culture represents a kind of soft imperialism in which those who are colonized are said to "choose" their commercial indenture. But real choice demands real diversity and civic freedom (public choice—a point explored below). It also requires a willingness by the United States to work multilaterally and internationally to build global democratic infrastructures that rise next to McWorld and offset its trivial and bottom-up but all-too-pervasive hegemonies.

Yet in the last ten years the United States has intensified its commitment to a political culture of unilateralism and faux autonomy that reinforces rather than attenuates the effects of McWorld. There is hardly a multilateral treaty of significance to which the United States has willingly subscribed in recent times, whether it is the Kyoto Protocol on global warming, the ban on land mines, or the Comprehensive Test Ban Treaty. Indeed, at the time of the terrorist attack the United States was threatening to unilaterally abrogate the ABM treaty in order to be able to develop and deploy its missile defense shield. There is hardly a single international institution that has not been questioned, undermined, or outright abandoned by the United States in the name of its need to protect its sovereign interests. Only the competing need to gather a coalition to underwrite its antiterrorist military strike compelled the American government finally to pay its UN dues and to commit to modest amounts of simple humanitarian aid that should have been a function of normalcy (the United States still devotes a smaller percentage of its GNP to foreign aid than any other developed nation in the world).

The Bretton Woods institutions such as the International Monetary Fund and the World Trade Organization (heir to the General Agreement on Tariffs and Trade) might have been of some succor in the effort to construct a more democratic globalism if they had been used for the kinds of developmental and democratic purposes for which they were designed in postwar Europe. Instead they have been cast by the democratic governments that control them as undemocratic instruments of private interest—seemingly the tools of banks, corporations, and investors that to an untoward degree also control the policies of the governments that nominally control them. Anarchism in the global sector is no accident: It has been assiduously cultivated.

Yet terrorism can be understood in part as a depraved version of this global anarchism—one that, for all its depravity, is as vigorous and self-justifying as the global markets. It too profits from the arrogant pretense of claims to national sovereignty that turn out to be indefensible. It too benefits by the absence of international executive police and juridical institutions. It too exploits global anarchy to ferment national anarchy and the further weakening of the capacity of nations to control their own destinies, either apart or together. In late-nineteenth-century America, when the federal government was markedly weaker than it is today, social relations looked rather like global relations do today. Lawlessness came easily, both to the robber barons of growing capitalist metropolises and to the robber desperadoes of the western prairies. Outlaws prospered in the suites as well as in the streets.

The global sector today seems driven by the same anarchy, in which burgeoning forces of what many American bankers have called wild capitalism spread both productivity, which we welcome, and injustice, which we try to ignore. But alongside wild capitalism rage the reactionary forces of wild terrorism. Against capitalism's modern message, Jihadic fundamentalism spreads its antimodern message, sowing fear and nurturing chaos, hoping to bring both democracy and capitalism to their knees. The war between Jihad and McWorld takes no prisoners. It cannot serve democracy, however it turns out.

The democratic project is to globalize democracy as we have globalized the economy—to democratize the globalism that has been so efficiently marketized. The issue is no longer the utopian longing for global democracy against the siren call of consumerism or the passionate war cries of Jihad; it is the securing of safety. Following September 11, global governance has become a sober mandate of political realism.

Mandate or not, it will not be easy for America to overcome the reassuring myth of national independence and innocence with which it has lived so comfortably for two hundred years. Before it began to trade in the international currency of McWorld that made it the global merchandiser, America had invented a simpler story about itself. In the Puritan myth of the city on the hill, in the Enlightenment conceit of a tabula rasa on which a new people would inscribe a fresh history, Americans embraced Tom Paine's quaint and revolutionary notion that on the new continent humankind could literally go back and start over again, as if at "the beginning of the world." Europe's cruel torments, its ancient prejudices and religious persecutions, would be left behind. Safeguarded by two immense oceans, at home on a bountiful and empty continent (the native inhabitants were part of the new world's flora and fauna), Americans would devise a new and experimental science of government, establish a new constitution fortified by rights, and with the innocence of a newborn people write a new history. Slavery, a great civil war, two world conflagrations, and totalitarian regimes abroad could not dissuade America from its precious self-definition. Even as the oceans became mere streams that could be crossed in an instant by invisible adversaries, even as the pressures of an impinging world grew too complex to yield to simplicity, America imagined that it could safeguard its autonomy, deploying its vaunted technology to re-create virtual oceans, fantasizing a magic missile shield that would ward off foreign evil.

Was America ever really a safe haven in the tainted streams of world history? Was it ever any more innocent than the children of every nation are innocent? Human nature is everywhere morally ambivalent, the better angels cooing into one ear, their demonic cousins crowing into the other. Americans know no evil, even when they do it. To others their claim to innocence is an assertion of hypocrisy—among the deadliest of sins for Muslims and others who watch America demonize others and exonerate itself.

Terrorism has brought the age of innocence, if there ever really was one, to a close. How could the myth of independence survive September 11? The Declaration of Independence, which announced a new coming, a new kind of society, has achieved its task of nation building. To build the new world that is now required calls for a new Declaration of Interdependence, a declaration recognizing the interdependence of a human race that can no longer survive in fragments—whether the pieces are called nations, tribes, peoples, or markets. There are no oceans wide enough to protect a nation from a tainted atmosphere or a spreading plague, no walls high enough to defend a people against a corrupt ideology or a vengeful prophet, no security strict enough to keep a determined martyr from his sacrificial rounds. Nor is any nation ever again likely to experience untroubled prosperity and plenty unless others are given the same opportunity. Suffering too has been democratized, and those most likely to experience it will find a way to compel those most remote from it to share the pain. If there cannot be equity of justice, there will be equity of injustice; if all cannot partake of plenty, impoverishment—both material and spiritual—will be the common lot. That is the hard lesson of interdependence, taught by terror's unsmiling pedagogues.

To declare interdependence, then, is in a sense merely to acknowledge what is already a reality. It is to embrace willingly and constructively a fate terrorists would like to shove down our throats.

Their message is: "Your sons want to live, ours are ready to die." Our response must be this: "We will create a world in which the seductions of death hold no allure because the bounties of life are accessible to everyone."

Such grand notions must start with the mundane, however. America is perhaps the most parochial empire that has ever existed, and Americans—though harbingers of McWorld's global culture—are the least cosmopolitan and traveled of peoples who husband such expansive power. Is there another democratic legislature that has so many members without passports? There is certainly no democratic nation that pays a smaller percentage of its GNP for foreign aid (a third of what other democracies pay). And for a remarkably multicultural nation, how is it that the American image is so monocultural, its inhabitants so averse to the study of foreign languages? Such a nation, even if it cultivates the will to a constructive and benevolent interdependence, will have a difficult time meeting its demands. Military strategists complain America does not speak the languages of its enemies. In America's universities, they no longer even teach the languages of its friends. Too many Ph.D. programs have given up language requirements, often allowing methods or statistics courses to take their place. Statistics may help us count the bodies, but it will do little to prevent the slaughter.

In the wake of two centuries of either isolationism or unilateralism, with only a few wartime pauses for coalition building and consultation, the United States is today inexperienced in the hard work of creative interdependence and international partnership. When America discerns problems in international treaties (the Kyoto Protocol, the land mine ban, the International Criminal Tribunal) and cannot negotiate its way in, it simply walks out. When international institutions such as UNESCO and the United Nations and international conferences such as the racism discussions in Durban resonate with hostility (as they often do), the United States withdraws in arrogant pique instead of participating with a view toward making its influence felt. The missile shield with its attendant requirement that we abandon the ABM treaty is a typically unilateral and hubristic instance of America's inclination to go it alone. Aside from its technological infeasibility—if we cannot keep terrorists off airplanes or individual "sleepers" from engaging in biological and chemical warfare, how can we imagine that we can intercept multiple warheads and their multiplying decoys without a hitch?—the missile shield once again isolates America from a world it ought to participate in in changing. In Ronald Reagan's vivid fantasies that resonated so powerfully with the American public, a virtual bubble would envelop the good nation and keep it safe from foreign nightmares. But the nightmares have come to our shores in the bright light of morning, and there is no shield against their terror except a confrontation with Jihad's complex global genealogy.

Technology is at best a tool. It is a peculiarly American conviction that engineering can take the place of human ingenuity and action in warding off trouble. Smart bombs are given preference over smart people, missiles that think take the place of policy makers who judge, electronic listening posts replace culturally and linguistically adept human agents. Technology is the last redoubt for our vanishing independence, the means by which America aspires to keep alive the fading dream of sovereign autonomy. Yet technology itself, like the science from which it arises, is a product of transnational communities and is a better symbol of interdependence than independence. McWorld itself, with it reliance on global communications technology, teaches that lesson.

When America finally turns from its mythic independence and acknowledges the real world of interdependence, it will face an irony it helped create: The international institutions available to those who wish to make interdependence a tool of democracy and comity are far and few between. McWorld is everywhere, CivWorld is nowhere. But Nike and McDonald's and Coke and MTV can contribute nothing to the search for democratic alternatives to criminal terrorism; instead, these corporations sometimes inadvertently contribute to the causes of terrorism. That is the melancholy dialectic of Jihad vs. McWorld that is at the heart of this book.

The encompassing practices of globalization we have nurtured under the archs of McWorld and the banner of global markets have in fact created a radical asymmetry: We have managed to globalize markets in goods, labor, currencies, and information without globalizing the civic and democratic institutions that have historically constituted the free market's indispensable context. Put simply, we have removed capitalism from the institutional box that has (quite literally) domesticated it and given its sometimes harsh practices a human face. To understand why taking capitalism out of the box has been so calamitous, we need to recall that the history of capitalism and free markets has been one of synergy with democratic institutions. Free economies have grown up within and been fostered, contained, and controlled by democratic states. Democracy has been a precondition for free markets—not, as economists try to argue today, the other way around. The freedom of the market that has helped sustain freedom in politics and a spirit of competition in the political domain has been nurtured in turn by democratic institutions. Contract law and regulation as well as cooperative civic relations have attenuated capitalism's Darwinism and contained its irregularities, contradictions, and tendencies toward self-destruction around monopoly and the eradication of competition that leads to uncapitalist monopolies. On the global plane today, the historical symmetry that paired democracy and capitalism has gone missing. We have globalized the marketplace willy-nilly, because markets can bleed through porous national boundaries and are not constrained by the logic of sovereignty. But we have not even begun to globalize democracy, which—precisely because it is political and is defined by sovereignty—is trapped inside the nation-state box.

The resulting global asymmetry, in which diminished states and augmented markets serve only private, economic interests, damages not only a well-functioning democratic civic order but a well-functioning international economic order as well. The continuing spread of the new globalization has only deepened the asymmetry between private vices and public goods. McWorld in tandem with the global market economy has globalized many of our vices and almost none of our virtues. We have globalized crime, the rogue weapons trade, and drugs; we have globalized prostitution and pornography, and the trade in women and children made possible by "porn tourism." Indeed, the most egregious globalization has been of the exploitation and abuse of children in war, pornography, poverty, and sex tourism. Children have been soldiers and victims in the raging ethnic and religious wars; children are the majority of the global cohort that suffers poverty, disease, and starvation. Children are our terrorists-to-be because they are so obviously not our citizens-to-come. How can this starkly asymmetrical globalization, one that entails such slow suffering, such deliberately paced violence, be anything other than fertile ground for recruiting terrorists? Indeed, it is terrorism itself along with its propaganda that has been most effectively globalized by the softening of sovereignty and the adjuration of democracy—sometimes (ironically) using the modern technologies of the World Wide Web and the worldwide media to promote ideologies hostile both to technology and to anything smacking of the worldwide or the modern. Following September 11, Osama bin Laden became a regular on CNN; the channels of McWorld transformed into conduits for an attack on it.

Privatized, marketized globalization lacks anything resembling a civic envelope. As a result, it cannot support the values and institutions associated with civic culture, religion, and the family. Nor can it enjoy their potentially softening, domesticating, and civilizing impact on raw market transactions. No wonder Pope John Paul said in his Apostolic Exhortation on the Mission of the Roman Catholic Church in the Americas: "If globalization is ruled merely by the laws of the market applied to suit the powerful, the consequences cannot but be negative."[1] Of course, one expects the pope to moralize in this fashion. More startling is a similar message from another, more powerful pope of the secular world, who wrote recently: "You hear talk about a new financial order, about an international bankruptcy law, about transparency, and more . . . but you don't hear a word about people. . . . Two billion people live on less than two dollars a day. . . . We live in a world that gradually is getting worse and worse and worse. It is not hopeless, but we must do something about it now." The moralist here is the hardheaded James Wolfensohn, president of the World Bank, who has begun to replace the bank's traditional energy and industrialization projects, thought to favor the interests of foreign investors, with environmental and health projects aimed at the interests of the populations being directly served.[2]

There are, of course, extant international institutions that might serve as building blocks for a global democratic box into which the economy could safely be put. The international financial institutions conceived at Bretton Woods after World War II to oversee the reconstruction of shattered European and Asian economies were intended originally to function as regulatory agencies to ensure peaceful, stable, and democratic redevelopment under the watchful eye of the victorious Allied powers. Though the World Bank and the International Monetary Fund (and later the General Agreement on Tariffs and Trade and the World Trade Organization, which grew out of GATT in 1995) were ostensibly forged as instruments of democratic sovereign nations designed to guide and regulate private-sector interests in the name of public sector reconstruction, over a period of time they became instruments of the very private-sector interests they were meant to channel and keep in check. Those who today call for their elimination in the name of transparency, accountability, and democracy might be surprised to learn that these norms were once regarded as among the postwar financial order's primary objectives. Given the role modern institutions representing this order play as potential pieces in a global regulatory infrastructure, one way to begin the process of global democratization would be to redemocratize them and subordinate them to the will of democratic peoples.

Globalization does not occur in a vacuum, of course. Its corrosive impact on democratic governance and our inability to put to real democratic use international financial institutions that are nominally already at the service of democracy is augmented by a cognate ideology of privatization that is prevalent both on the international scene and within the countries whose economies are being globalized. McWorld is accompanied by this ideology of privatization—what Europeans often call neoliberalism and George Soros has labeled market fundamentalism (an appropriate implicit comparison to Jihadic fundamentalism)—that saps democracy by attacking government and its culture of public power. By arguing that markets can do everything government once did, and better, with more freedom for citizens, privatization within nation-states opens the way for a deregulation of markets that in turn facilitates the globalization and hence privatization of the economy. It softens up citizens to accept the decline of political institutions and tries to persuade them that they will be better off—more "free"—when their collective democratic voice is stilled, when they think of themselves not as public citizens but as private consumers. Consumers are poor substitutes for citizens, however, just as corporate CEOs are poor substitutes for democratic statesmen. It is telling that on the morning of September 12, 2001, America did not call Bill Gates or Michael Eisner to ask for assistance in dealing with terrorism. A privatized airport security system turned out to be fallible because it was more attuned to costs than to safety. Long-neglected public institutions reacquired overnight their democratic legitimacy and their role as defenders of public goods.

Can this renewed legitimacy be employed on behalf of international institutions dedicated to public rather than private goods? If it can, new forms of civic interdependence can be quickly established.

The ideology of privatization has always confounded private and public modes of choosing. Consumer choice is always and necessarily private and personal choice. Private choices, autonomous or not, cannot affect public outcomes. Democratic governance is not just about choosing; rather, it is about public choosing, about dealing with the social consequences of private choices and behavior. In the global sector this is crucial, because only public and democratic decisions can establish social justice and equity. Private markets cannot, not because they are capitalist but because they are private. In the language of the great social contract theorist Jean-Jacques Rousseau, through participation in the general will, global citizens can regulate the private wills of global consumers and global corporations. They can tame Jihad and interdict terrorism even as they regulate markets and civilize their consequences.

It is both a noxious tribute to the power of privatization and a marker of our deep confusion about the difference between public and private goods in the new century that the question of "who should own the code of life" (as the headline of a recent *Newsweek* article had it)[3] is being asked. Currently, the inclination is to answer, "Private biotech companies"—a contradiction of everything we know about the public character of our species being. Under the rules of both democracy and morality, the code of life presumably belongs to some version of "us" rather than to some corporate "me." There is something comically childish about adult scientists arguing over who owns the human genome as if it were a stray Pokémon card found on the playground, just one more commercial product in McWorld's bag of tricks. If the genetic code of the species can be sold for profit, why shouldn't women and children be sold for profit? And if there is no rational answer to this question, how can we defeat the cold logic of terror, which evinces the same righteous devotion to anarchy.

This critique points to the crucial difference between public and private liberty, a difference that goes to the heart of Pope John Paul's warning that "the human race is facing forms of slavery that are new and more subtle than those of the past, and for far too many people, freedom remains a word without meaning." To think that shopping is what freedom means is to embrace the slavery against which the pope warns (though of course the pope is a thoroughly unmodern man, if not yet a Jihadic warrior).

There are many things government cannot do very well, but there are many others that *only* government can do, such as regulate and protect, and sometimes subsidize and redistribute—not because it does them particularly well, but because they are public things for which only we, the public, can be held accountable. These res publicae (literally, "public things") include education, culture, incarceration, transportation, defense, health care, social justice, and, yes, the human genome. They include the war on terrorism. And they include the construction of a fair and equitable international order that offers every person and every group equal access and equal opportunity. Put simply, the struggle against Jihad (which some claim it to be a holy struggle against us) can succeed only if it is also a struggle on behalf of genuine transnational public goods against the private interests manifest in McWorld.

Capitalism is an extraordinarily productive system. There is no better way to organize human labor for productivity than mobilizing a billion private wills motivated by self-interest. Capitalism fails miserably at distribution and hence at safety and justice, however, which are necessarily the objects of our public institutions, motivated by the search for common ground and ways to overcome the conflicts and inequalities that arise out of private production. Domestically, most nation-states have struck the balance that is the meaning of democratic capitalism. Internationally, there is only a raging asymmetry that is the first and last cause of an anarchism in which terror flourishes and terrorists make their perverse arguments about death to young men and women who have lost hope in the possibilities of life.

This book depicts a war then between Jihad and McWorld that cannot be won. Only a struggle of democracy against not solely Jihad but also against McWorld can achieve a just victory for the planet. A just, diverse, democratic world will put commerce and consumerism back in their place and make space for civil society religion; it will combat the terrors of Jihad not only by making war on it but by creating a world in which the practice of religion is as secure as the practice of consumption and the defense of cultural values is not in tension with the defense of liberty but part of how liberty is defined (the true meaning of multiculturalism). Terror feeds off the parasitic dialectics of Jihad and McWorld. In a democratic world order, there will be no need for militant Jihad because belief will have a significant place without the aid of self-serving warriors; and there will be no advantage to McWorld because cultural variety will confront it on every television station and at every mall the world over. When Jihad and McWorld have vanished as primary categories, terror may not wholly disappear (it is lodged in a small but impregnable crevice in the dark regions of the human soul), but we can hope it will become less relevant to the hopes and aspirations of women and men who will have learned to love life too much to confuse religion with the courtship of death.

Notes

[1] Pope John Paul's Apostolic Exhortation, cited in the *New York Times*, January 24, 1999.
[2] James D. Wolfensohn, cited by Jim Hoagland, "Richer and Poorer," *Washington Post National Weekly Edition*, May 3, 1999, p. 5.
[3] "The Code of Life," *Newsweek*.

Jihad *vs.*
McWorld

Introduction

HISTORY IS NOT OVER. Nor are we arrived in the wondrous land of techné promised by the futurologists. The collapse of state communism has not delivered people to a safe democratic haven, and the past, fratricide and civil discord perduring, still clouds the horizon just behind us. Those who look back see all of the horrors of the ancient slaughterbench reenacted in disintegral nations like Bosnia, Sri Lanka, Ossetia, and Rwanda and they declare that nothing has changed. Those who look forward prophesize commercial and technological interdependence—a virtual paradise made possible by spreading markets and global technology—and they proclaim that everything is or soon will be different. The rival observers seem to consult different almanacs drawn from the libraries of contrarian planets.

Yet anyone who reads the daily papers carefully, taking in the front page accounts of civil carnage as well as the business page stories on the mechanics of the information superhighway and the economics of communication mergers, anyone who turns deliberately to take in the whole 360-degree horizon, knows that our world and our lives are caught between what William Butler Yeats called the two eternities of race and soul: that of race reflecting the tribal past, that of soul anticipating the cosmopolitan future. Our secular eternities are corrupted, however, race reduced to an insignia of resentment, and soul sized down to fit the demanding body by which it now measures its needs. Neither race nor soul offers us a future that is other than bleak, neither promises a polity that is remotely democratic.

The first scenario rooted in race holds out the grim prospect of a retribalization of large swaths of humankind by war and bloodshed: a threatened balkanization of nation-states in which culture is pitted against culture, people against people, tribe against tribe, a Jihad in the name of a hundred narrowly conceived faiths against every kind of interdependence, every kind of artificial social cooperation and mutuality: against technology, against pop culture, and against integrated markets; against modernity itself as well as the future in which modernity issues. The second paints that future in shimmering pastels, a busy portrait of onrushing economic, technological, and ecological forces that demand integration and uniformity and that mesmerize peoples everywhere with fast music, fast computers, and fast food—MTV, Macintosh, and McDonald's—pressing nations into one homogenous global theme park, one McWorld tied together by communications, information, entertainment, and commerce. Caught between Babel and Disneyland, the planet is falling precipitously apart and coming reluctantly together at the very same moment.

Some stunned observers notice only Babel, complaining about the thousand newly sundered "peoples" who prefer to address their neighbors with sniper rifles and mortars; others—zealots in Disneyland—seize on futurological platitudes and the promise of virtuality, exclaiming "It's a small world after all!" Both are right, but how can that be?

We are compelled to choose between what passes as "the twilight of sovereignty" and an entropic end of all history;[1] or a return to the past's most fractious and demoralizing discord; to "the menace of global anarchy," to Milton's capital of hell, Pandaemonium; to a world totally "out of control."[2]

The apparent truth, which speaks to the paradox at the core of this book, is that the tendencies of both Jihad *and* McWorld are at work, both visible sometimes in the same country at the very same instant. Iranian zealots keep one ear tuned to the mullahs urging holy war and the other cocked to Rupert Murdoch's Star television beaming in *Dynasty, Donahue,* and *The Simpsons* from hovering satellites. Chinese entrepreneurs vie for the attention of party cadres in Beijing and simultaneously pursue KFC franchises in cities like Nanjing, Hangzhou, and Xian where twenty-eight outlets serve over 100,000 customers a day. The Russian Orthodox church, even as it struggles to renew the ancient faith, has entered a joint venture with California businessmen to bottle and sell natural waters under the rubric Saint Springs Water Company. Serbian assassins wear Adidas sneakers and listen to Madonna on Walkman headphones as they take aim through their gunscopes at scurrying Sarajevo civilians looking to fill family watercans. Orthodox Hasids and brooding neo-Nazis have both turned to rock music to get their traditional messages out to the new generation, while fundamentalists plot virtual conspiracies on the Internet.

Now neither Jihad nor McWorld is in itself novel. History ending in the triumph of science and reason or some monstrous perversion thereof (Mary Shelley's Doctor Frankenstein) has been the leitmotiv of every philosopher and poet who has regretted the Age of Reason since the Enlightenment. Yeats lamented "the center will not hold, mere anarchy is loosed upon the world," and observers of Jihad today have little but historical detail to add. The Christian parable of the Fall and of the possibilities of redemption that it makes possible captures the eighteenth-century ambivalence—and our own—about past and future. I want, however, to do more than dress up the central paradox of human history in modern clothes. It is not Jihad and McWorld but the relationship between them that most interests me. For, squeezed between their opposing forces, the world has been sent spinning out of control.[3] Can it be that what Jihad and McWorld have in common is anarchy: the absence of common will and that conscious and collective human control under the guidance of law we call democracy?

Progress moves in steps that sometimes lurch backwards; in history's twisting maze, Jihad not only revolts against but abets McWorld, while McWorld not only imperils but re-creates and reinforces Jihad. They produce their contraries and need one another.

My object here then is not simply to offer sequential portraits of McWorld and Jihad, but while examining McWorld, to keep Jihad in my field of vision, and while dissecting Jihad, never to forget the context of McWorld. Call it a dialectic of McWorld: a study in the cunning of reason that does honor to the radical differences that distinguish Jihad and McWorld yet that acknowledges their powerful and paradoxical interdependence.

There is a crucial difference, however, between my modest attempt at dialectic and that of the masters of the nineteenth century. Still seduced by the Enlightenment's faith in progress, both Hegel and Marx believed reason's cunning was on the side of progress. But it is harder to believe that the clash of Jihad and McWorld will issue in some overriding good. The outcome seems more likely to pervert than to nurture human liberty. The two may, in opposing each other, work to the same ends, work in apparent tension yet in covert harmony, but democracy is not their beneficiary. In East Berlin, tribal communism has yielded to capitalism. In Marx-Engelsplatz, the stolid, overbearing statues of Marx and Engels face east, as if seeking distant solace from Moscow: but now, circling them along the streets that surround the park that is their prison are chain eateries like T.G.I. Friday's, international hotels like the Radisson, and a circle of neon billboards mocking them with brand names like Panasonic, Coke, and GoldStar. New gods, yes, but more liberty?

What then does it mean in concrete terms to view Jihad and McWorld dialectically when the tendencies of the two sets of forces initially appear so intractably antithetical? After all, Jihad and McWorld operate with equal strength in opposite directions, the one driven by parochial hatreds, the other by universalizing markets, the one re-creating ancient subnational and ethnic borders from within, the other making national borders porous from without. Yet Jihad and McWorld have this in common: they both make war on the sovereign nation-state and thus undermine the nation-state's democratic institutions. Each eschews civil society and belittles democratic citizenship, neither seeks alternative democratic institutions. Their common thread is indifference to civil liberty. Jihad forges communities of blood rooted in exclusion and hatred, communities that slight democracy in favor of tyrannical paternalism or consensual tribalism. McWorld forges global markets rooted in consumption and profit, leaving to an untrustworthy, if not altogether fictitious, invisible hand issues of public interest and common good that once might have been nurtured by democratic citizenries and their watchful governments. Such governments, intimidated by market ideology, are actually pulling back at the very moment they ought to be aggressively intervening. What was once understood as protecting the public interest is now excoriated as heavy-handed regulatory browbeating.[4] Justice yields to markets, even though, as Felix Rohatyn has bluntly confessed, "there is a brutal Darwinian logic to these markets. They are nervous and greedy. They look for stability and transparency, but what they reward is not always our preferred form of democracy."[5] If the traditional conservators of freedom were democratic constitutions and Bills of Rights, "the new temples to liberty," George Steiner suggests, "will be McDonald's and Kentucky Fried Chicken."[6]

In being reduced to a choice between the market's universal church and a retribalizing politics of particularist identities, peoples around the globe are threatened with an atavistic return to medieval politics where local tribes and ambitious emperors together ruled the world entire, women and men united by the universal abstraction of Christianity even as they lived out isolated lives in warring fiefdoms defined by involuntary (ascriptive) forms of identity. This was a world in which princes and kings had little real power until they conceived the ideology of nationalism. Nationalism established government on a scale greater than the tribe yet less cosmopolitan than the universal church and in time gave birth to those intermediate, gradually more democratic institutions that would come to constitute the nation-state. Today, at the far end of this history, we seem intent on re-creating a world in which our only choices are the secular universalism of the cosmopolitan market and the everyday particularism of the fractious tribe.

In the tumult of the confrontation between global commerce and parochial ethnicity, the virtues of the democratic nation are lost and the instrumentalities by which it permitted peoples to transform themselves into nations and seize sovereign power in the name of liberty and the commonweal are put at risk. Neither Jihad nor McWorld aspires to resecure the civic virtues undermined by its denationalizing practices; neither global markets nor blood communities service public goods or pursue equality and justice. Impartial judiciaries and deliberative assemblies play no role in the roving killer bands that speak on behalf of newly liberated "peoples," and such democratic institutions have at best only marginal influence on the roving multinational corporations that speak on behalf of newly liberated markets. Jihad pursues a bloody politics of identity, McWorld a bloodless economics of profit. Belonging by default to McWorld, everyone is a consumer; seeking a repository for identity, everyone belongs to some tribe. But no one is a citizen. Without citizens, how can there be democracy?

From Self-Determination to Jihad

NOT LONG AGO, Daniel Patrick Moynihan predicted that the next half hundred states likely to come into existence over the next fifty years will all be defined by ethnic conflict: that is to say, by civil war.[7] The Soviet Union and Yugoslavia have together already produced twenty or more new (old) "nations" or national fragments. In the most egregious cases, the United Nations sends peacekeeping forces, although its member nations are increasingly loath to put their soldiers at risk. Currently, it has stationed troops in eighteen countries—in nearly every case, arrayed against forces of domestic insurrection and civil discord.[8] The Carter Center in Atlanta has a still more nuanced and thus expansive list that is more or less mirrored in the forty-eight trouble spots charted by *The New York Times* at the beginning of 1993.[9] Amnesty International reports political prisoners and political executions in more than sixty countries.

In this tumultuous world, the real players are not nations at all but tribes, many of them at war with one another. Their aim is precisely to redraw boundaries in order to divide—say in Kurdish Iraq or Muslim Sudan or Serbian-populated sections of Croatia. Countries like Afghanistan, recently fighting a foreign invader in the name of its national independence, have been effectively dismembered: divided among Panthans, Hazaras, Uzbeks, and Tajiks. This is ethnic membership enhanced via national dismemberment—or by expulsion or expunction of unwanted contaminators, as has occurred in slaughter-happy Rwanda. Is this pandaemonium just an extension of benign efforts at multiculturalism? A natural consequence of a centuries-old impulse to self-determination? Or the appearance of a new disease that has corrupted integral nationalism and opened the way to ethnic and religious Jihad?

Jihad is, I recognize, a strong term. In its mildest form, it betokens religious struggle on behalf of faith, a kind of Islamic zeal. In its strongest political manifestation, it means bloody holy war on behalf of partisan identity that is metaphysically defined and fanatically defended. Thus, while for many Muslims it may signify only ardor in the name of a religion that can properly be regarded as universalizing (if not quite ecumenical), I borrow its meaning from those militants who make the slaughter of the "other" a higher duty.[10] I use the term in its militant construction to suggest dogmatic and violent particularism of a kind known to Christians no less than Muslims, to Germans and Hindis as well as to Arabs. The phenomena to which I apply the phrase have innocent enough beginnings: identity politics and multicultural diversity can represent strategies of a free society trying to give expression to its diversity. What ends as Jihad may begin as a simple search for a local identity, some set of common personal attributes to hold out against the numbing and neutering uniformities of industrial modernization and the colonizing culture of McWorld.

America is often taken as the model for this kind of benign multiculturalism, although we too have our critics like Arthur Schlesinger, Jr., for whom multiculturalism is never benign and for whom it signals the inaugural logic of a long-term disintegration.[11] Indeed, I will have occasion below to write about an "American Jihad" being waged by the radical Right. The startling fact is that less than 10 percent (about twenty) of the modern world's states are truly homogenous and thus, like Denmark or the Netherlands, can't get smaller unless they fracture into tribes or clans.[12] In only half is there a single ethnic group that comprises even 75 percent of the population.[13] As in the United States, multiculturalism is the rule, homogeneity the exception. Nations like Japan or Spain that appear to the outside world as integral turn out to be remarkably multicultural. And even if language alone, the nation's essential attribute, is made the condition for self-determination, a count of the number of languages spoken around the world suggests the community of nations could grow to over six thousand members.

The modern nation-state has actually acted as a cultural integrator and has adapted well to pluralist ideals: civic ideologies and constitutional faiths around which their many clans and tribes can rally. It has not been too difficult to contrive a civil religion for Americans or French or Swiss, since these "peoples" actually contain multitudes of subnational factions and ethnic tribes earnestly seeking common ground. But for Basques and Normans? What need have they for anything but blood and memory? And what of Alsatians, Bavarians, and East Prussians? Kurds, Ossetians, East Timorese, Quebecois, Abkhazians, Catalonians, Tamils, Inkatha Zulus, Kurile Islander Japanese—peoples without countries inhabiting nations they cannot call their own? Peoples trying to seal themselves off not just from others but from modernity? These are frightened tribes running not to but from civic faith in search of something more palpable and electrifying. How will peoples who define themselves by the slaughter of tribal neighbors be persuaded to subscribe to some flimsy artificial faith organized around abstract civic ideals or commercial markets? Can advertising divert warriors of blood from the genocide required by their ancient grievances?

Like McWorld, Jihad can of course be painted in bright as well as dark colors. Just as McWorld's sometimes rapacious markets have been advanced in the name of democratic free choice, so Jihad's combative interests can be touted in the name of self-determination. Indeed, the ideology of self-determination may be the source of more than a few of Jihad's pathologies. President Woodrow Wilson's own secretary of state, Robert L. Lansing, failed to share his chief's enthusiasm for the idea, asking would not self-determination "breed discontent, disorder and rebellion? The phrase is simply loaded with dynamite. It will raise hopes which can never be realized. It will, I fear, cost thousands of lives. What a calamity that the phrase was ever uttered! What misery it will cause!"[14]

Lansing's anxieties seem well justified. In Wilson's own time, the politics of self-determination balkanized Europe, fanned nationalist wildfires, and created instabilities that contributed to the rise of fascism. Today there is no tribe, no faction or splinter group or neighborhood gang, that does not aspire to self-determination. "Don't dis me!" shouts the gangsta rapper, "I gotta get some respect." The futile Owen-Vance map for the partition of Bosnia, multiplying boundaries as it narrowed the compass of ethnic communities, finally seemed to give respectability to a gang logic, trying to write into law the absurdity of treating nearly each city block as a nation, almost every housing unit a potential sovereign. In other times, this bankrupt political arrangement, sanctioned for a considerable time by a desperate United Nations Security Council, would carry the name anarchy.[15]

One cannot really blame the cartographers or peacemakers for Jihad's absurdity, however. They do not rearrange the scene, they just take snapshots of it. Multiculturalism has in some places conjured anarchy. Self-determination has at times amounted to little more than other-extermination. Colonial masters did still worse in their time, drawing arbitrary lines across maps they could not read with consequences still being endured throughout the ex-colonial world, above all in Africa and the Middle East.[16] Jihad is then a rabid response to colonialism and imperialism and their economic children, capitalism and modernity; it is diversity run amok, multiculturalism turned cancerous so that the cells keep dividing long after their division has ceased to serve the healthy corpus.[17]

Even traditionally homogenous integral nations have reason to feel anxious about the prospect of Jihad. The rising economic and communications interdependence of the world means that such nations, however unified internally, must nonetheless operate in an increasingly multicultural global environment. Ironically, a world that is coming together pop culturally and commercially is a world whose discrete subnational ethnic and religious and racial parts are also far more in evidence, in no small part as a reaction to McWorld. Forced into incessant contact, postmodern nations cannot sequester their idiosyncrasies. Post-Maastricht Europe, while it falls well short of earlier ambitions, has become integrated enough to force a continent-wide multicultural awareness whose consequences have by no means been happy, let alone unifying. The more "Europe" hoves into view, the more reluctant and self-aware its national constituents become. What Günter Grass said of Germany—"unified, the Germans were more disunited than ever"—applies in spades to Europe and the world beyond: integrated, it is more disintegral than ever.[18]

Responding to McWorld, parochial forces defend and deny, reject and repel modernity wherever they find it. But they also absorb and assimilate, utilizing the native's strategy against every colonizer to have crossed a border since the Romans came to Gaul. When the Hilton came to the Hills of Buda, a local architect grafted the new structure onto a thirteenth-century monastery. When the French restored the Champs Élysées to its former glory, they banished the arch from McDonald's. When American music invaded the Caribbean, Orlando Patterson reminds us, the Caribbean reacted with enormous music production of its own, of which reggae is only one well-known example.[19] Yet to think that indigenization and globalization are entirely coequal forces that put Jihad and McWorld on an equal footing is to vastly underestimate the force of the new planetary markets. The Budapest Hilton's "monastery" houses a casino; Paris's McDonald's serves Big Macs and fries with or without the arch; reggae gets only a tiny percentage of MTV play time even in Latin markets. It's no contest.

A pattern of feudal relations does, however, persist. And so we are returned to the metaphor of feudalism, that puzzling world of fragments knit together by the abstraction of Christianity. Today's abstraction is the consumers' market, no less universal for all its insistent materialist secularism. Following McDonald's golden arch from country to country, the market traces a trajectory of dollars and bonds and ads and yen and stocks and currency transactions that reaches right around the globe. Grass's observation works the other way around as well: disunited, pulled apart by Jihad, the world is more united than ever. And more interdependent as well.

The Smalling World of McWorld

EVEN THE MOST DEVELOPED, supposedly self-sufficient nations can no longer pretend to genuine sovereignty. That is the meaning of *ecology*, a term that marks the final obsolescence of all man-made boundaries. When it comes to acid rain or oil spills or depleted fisheries or tainted groundwater or fluorocarbon propellants or radiation leaks or toxic wastes or sexually transmitted diseases, national frontiers are simply irrelevant. Toxins don't stop for customs inspections and microbes don't carry passports. North America became a water and air free-trade zone long before NAFTA loosened up the market in goods.

The environmental tocsin has been sounded, loudly and often, and there is little to add here to the prodigious literature warning of a biospherical Armageddon. We have learned well enough how easily the German forests can be devastated by Swiss and Italians driving gas-guzzling roadsters fueled by leaded gas (the Europeans are far behind the Americans in controlling lead). We know that the planet can be asphyxiated by greenhouse gases because Brazilian farmers want to be part of the twentieth century and are burning down their tropical rain forests to clear a little land to plow, and because many Indonesians make a living out of converting their lush jungles into toothpicks for fastidious Japanese diners, upsetting the delicate oxygen balance and puncturing our global lungs.

Ecological interdependence is, however, reactive: a consequence of natural forces we cannot predict or fully control. But McWorld's interdependence and the limits it places on sovereignty is more a matter of positive economic forces that have globalism as their conscious object. It is these economic and commercial forces—the latest round in capitalism's long-standing search for world markets and global consumers—that are the primary subject of this book.

Every demarcated national economy and every kind of public good is today vulnerable to the inroads of transnational commerce. Markets abhor frontiers as nature abhors a vacuum. Within their expansive and permeable domains, interests are private, trade is free, currencies are convertible, access to banking is open, contracts are enforceable (the state's sole legitimate economic function), and the laws of production and consumption are sovereign, trumping the laws of legislatures and courts. In Europe, Asia, and the Americas such markets have already eroded national sovereignty and given birth to a new class of institutions—international banks, trade associations, transnational lobbies like OPEC, world news services like CNN and the BBC, and multinational corporations—institutions that lack distinctive national identities and neither reflect nor respect nationhood as an organizing or a regulative principle. While mills and factories sit somewhere on sovereign territory under the eye and potential regulation of nation-states, currency markets and the Internet exist everywhere, but nowhere in particular. Without an address or a national affiliation, they are altogether beyond the devices of sovereignty.[20] Even products are becoming anonymous: whose national workforce do you fault on a defective integrated circuit labeled:

> Made in one or more of the following countries: Korea, Hong Kong, Malaysia, Singapore, Taiwan, Mauritius, Thailand, Indonesia, Mexico, Philippines. The exact country of origin is unknown.[21]

How are the social and political demands of responsibility preserved under such remarkable circumstances?

The market imperative has in fact reinforced the quest for international peace and stability, requisites of an efficient international economy, without improving the chances for civic responsibility, accountability, or democracy, which may or may not benefit from commerce and free markets and which, although it depends on peace, is not synonymous with it. The claim that democracy and markets are twins has become a commonplace of statesmanship, especially in light of the demise of state socialism, which has left capitalism's zealots free to regard themselves not only as victors in the Cold War but as the true champions of a democracy that (they are certain) markets alone make possible. Thus have they managed to parlay the already controversial claim that markets are free into the even more controversial claim that market freedom entails and even defines democracy. President Clinton employed the phrase *democratic markets* as a mantra during his historic visit to Eastern Europe and Russia at the beginning of 1994.[22] His foreign policy aides have consistently done the same.[23]

This stealth rhetoric that assumes capitalist interests are not only compatible with but actively advance democratic ideals, translated into policy, is difficult to reconcile with the international realities of the last fifty years. Market economies have shown a remarkable adaptability and have flourished in many tyrannical states from Chile to South Korea, from Panama to Singapore. Indeed, the state with one of the world's least democratic governments—the People's Republic of China—possesses one of the world's fastest-growing market economies. "Communist" Vietnam is not far behind, and was opened to American trade recently, presumably on the strength of the belief that markets ultimately defeat ideology.[24] Capitalism requires consumers with access to markets and a stable political climate in order to succeed: such conditions may or may not be fostered by democracy, which can be disorderly and even anarchic, especially in its early stages, and which often pursues public goods costly to or at odds with private-market imperatives—environmentalism or full employment for example. On the level of the individual, capitalism seeks consumers susceptible to the shaping of their needs and the manipulation of their wants while democracy needs citizens autonomous in their thoughts and independent in their deliberative judgments. Aleksandr Solzhenitsyn wishes to "tame savage capitalism," but capitalism wishes to tame anarchic democracy and appears to have little problem tolerating tyranny as long as it secures stability.[25]

Certainly the hurried pursuit of free markets regardless of social consequences has put democratic development in jeopardy in many nations recently liberated from communism.[26] Social insecurity and rampant unemployment for peoples accustomed to the cradle-to-the-grave ministrations of paternalistic socialist bureacracies are unlikely to convert them to a system of democracy for which they have otherwise had no preparation. This is perhaps why majorities in all but a handful of ex-Soviet lands have been busy reelecting former Communist officials (usually wearing new party labels and carrying new ideological doctrines) to their new democratic legislatures. In economist Robert McIntyre's blunt words: "Communists and former Communists are winning because the Western economic advice has led to pointless, dysfunctional pain, while failing to set the foundations for politically and socially viable future growth."[27] The right to choose between nine VCR models or a dozen automobile brands does not necessarily feel like freedom to workers whose monthly salaries can hardly keep up with the rising price of bread, let alone to women and men with no jobs at all. Capitalists may be democrats but capitalism does not need or entail democracy. And capitalism certainly does not need the nation-state that has been democracy's most promising host.

This is not to criticize capitalism in and of itself: joint-stock, limited-liability corporations are quite properly interested primarily in profits and pursue civic liberty and social justice only where they do not interfere with the bottom line. Indeed, they have certain conspicuous virtues beyond their intrinsic economic utilities like efficiency, productivity, elasticity, profitability. They are enemies of parochialism, isolation, fractiousness, and war and are hostile to constraints on economic choice and social mobility, although this hardly makes them friends of justice. Market psychology also can attenuate the psychology of ideological and religious cleavages and nurture concord among producers and consumers, identities that ill-suit Jihad's narrowly conceived ethnic or religious cultures. But it also undermines the psychology of skeptical inquiry upon which autonomous judgment and resistance to manipulation are founded. In the world of McWorld, the alternative to dogmatic traditionalism may turn out to be materialist consumerism or relativistic secularism or merely a profitable corruption.[28] Democracy's ties to McWorld are at best contingent. Shopping, it is true, has little tolerance for blue laws, whether dictated by pub-closing British paternalism, Sabbath-observing Jewish Orthodoxy, or no-Sunday-liquor-sales Massachusetts Puritanism; but intolerance for blue laws is hardly a condition for constitutional faith or a respect for due process. In the context of common markets, international law has largely ceased to be a vision of justice and has become a workaday framework for getting things done: enforcing contracts, certifying deals, regulating trade and currency relations, and supervising mergers or bankruptcies. Moralists used to complain that international law was impotent in curbing the injustices of nation-states, but it has shown even less capacity to rein in markets that, after all, do not even have an address to which subpoenas can be sent. As the product of a host of individual choices or singular corporate acts, markets offer no collective responsibility. Yet responsibility is the first obligation of both citizens and civic institutions.

While they produce neither common interests nor common law, common markets do demand, along with a common currency, a common language; moreover, they produce common behaviors of the kind bred by cosmopolitan city life everywhere. Commercial pilots, computer programmers, film directors, international bankers, media specialists, oil riggers, entertainment celebrities, ecology experts, movie producers, demographers, accountants, professors, lawyers, athletes—these compose a new breed of men and women for whom religion, culture, and ethnic nationality are marginal elements in a working identity. Although sociologists of everyday life will continue to distinguish a Japanese from an American mode, shopping has a common signature throughout the world. Cynics might even suggest that some of the recent revolutions in Eastern Europe had as their true goal not liberty and the right to vote but well-paying jobs and the right to shop. Shopping means consumption and consumption depends on the fabrication of needs as well as of goods in what I will call the infotainment telesector of the service economy.

McWorld is a product of popular culture driven by expansionist commerce. Its template is American, its form style. Its goods are as much images as matériel, an aesthetic as well as a product line. It is about culture as commodity, apparel as ideology. Its symbols are Harley-Davidson motorcycles and Cadillac motorcars hoisted from the roadways, where they once represented a mode of transportation, to the marquees of global market cafés like Harley-Davidson's and the Hard Rock where they become icons of lifestyle. You don't drive them, you feel their vibes and rock to the images they conjure up from old movies and new celebrities, whose personal appearances are the key to the wildly popular international café chain Planet Hollywood. Music, video, theater, books, and theme parks—the new churches of a commercial civilization in which malls are the public squares and suburbs the neighborless neighborhoods—are all constructed as image exports creating a common world taste around common logos, advertising slogans, stars, songs, brand names, jingles, and trademarks. Hard power yields to soft, while ideology is transmuted into a kind of videology that works through sound bites and film clips. Videology is fuzzier and less dogmatic than traditional political ideology: it may as a consequence be far more successful in instilling the novel values required for global markets to succeed.

McWorld's videology remains Jihad's most formidable rival, and in the long run it may attenuate the force of Jihad's recidivist tribalisms.[29] Yet the information revolution's instrumentalities are also Jihad's favored weapons. Hutu or Bosnian Serb identity was less a matter of real historical memory than of media propaganda by a leadership set on liquidating rival clans. In both Rwanda and Bosnia, radio broadcasts whipped listeners into a killing frenzy. As *New York Times* rock critic Jon Pareles has noticed, "regionalism in pop music has become as trendy as microbrewery beer and narrowcasting cable channels, and for the same reasons."[30] The global culture is what gives the local culture its medium, its audience, and its aspirations. Fascist pop and Hasid rock are not oxymorons; rather they manifest the dialectics of McWorld in particularly dramatic ways. Belgrade's radio includes stations that broadcast Western pop music as a rebuke to hard-liner Milosevic's supernationalist government and stations that broadcast native folk tunes laced with antiforeign and anti-Semitic sentiments. Even the Internet has its neo-Nazi bulletin boards and Turk-trashing Armenian "flamers" (who assail every use of the word *turkey*, fair and fowl alike, so to speak), so that the abstractions of cyberspace too are infected with a peculiar and rabid cultural territoriality all their own.

The dynamics of the Jihad-McWorld linkage are deeply dialectical. Japan has, for example, become more culturally insistent on its own traditions in recent years even as its people seek an ever greater purchase on McWorld. In 1992, the number-one restaurant in Japan measured by volume of customers was McDonald's, followed in the number-two spot by the Colonel's Kentucky Fried Chicken.[31] In France, where cultural purists complain bitterly of a looming Sixième République ("la République Américaine"), the government attacks "franglais" even as it funds EuroDisney park just outside of Paris. In the same spirit, the cinema industry makes war on American film imports while it bestows upon Sylvester Stallone one of France's highest honors, the Chevalier des arts et lettres.[32] Ambivalence also stalks India. Just outside of Bombay, cheek by jowl with villages still immersed in poverty and notorious for the informal execution of unwanted female babies or, even, wives, can be found a new town known as SCEEPZ—the Santa Cruz Electronic Export Processing Zone—where Hindi-, Tamil-, and Mahratti-speaking computer programmers write software for Swissair, AT&T, and other labor-cost-conscious multinationals. India is thus at once a major exemplar of ancient ethnic and religious tensions and "an emerging power in the international software industry."[33] To go to work at SCEEPZ, says an employee, is "like crossing an international border." Not into another country, but into the virtual nowhere-land of McWorld.

More dramatic even than in India, is the strange interplay of Jihad and McWorld in the remnants of Yugoslavia. In an affecting *New Republic* report, Slavenka Drakulic recently told the brief tragic love story of Admira and Bosko, two young star-crossed lovers from Sarajevo: "They were born in the late 1960's," she writes. "They watched Spielberg movies; they listened to Iggy Pop; they read John le Carré; they went to a disco every Saturday night and fantasized about traveling to Paris or London."[34] Longing for safety, it seems they finally negotiated with all sides for safe passage, and readied their departure from Sarajevo. Before they could cross the magical border that separates their impoverished land from the seeming sanctuary of McWorld, Jihad caught up to them. Their bodies lay along the riverbank, riddled with bullets from anonymous snipers for whom safe passage signaled an invitation to target practice. The murdered young lovers, as befits émigrés to McWorld, were clothed in jeans and sneakers. So too, one imagines, were their murderers.

Further east, tourists seeking a piece of old Russia that does not take them too far from MTV can find traditional Matryoshka nesting dolls (that fit one inside the other) featuring the nontraditional visages of (from largest to smallest) Bruce Springsteen, Madonna, Boy George, Dave Stewart, and Annie Lennox.[35]

In Russia, in India, in Bosnia, in Japan, and in France too, modern history then leans both ways: toward the meretricious inevitability of McWorld, but also into Jihad's stiff winds, heaving to and fro and giving heart both to the Panglossians and the Pandoras, sometimes for the very same reasons. The Panglossians bank on Euro-Disney and Microsoft, while the Pandoras await nihilism and a world in Pandaemonium. Yet McWorld and Jihad do not really force a choice between such polarized scenarios. Together, they are likely to produce some stifling amalgam of the two suspended in chaos. Antithetical in every detail, Jihad and McWorld nonetheless conspire to undermine our hard-won (if only half-won) civil liberties and the possibility of a global democratic future. In the short run the forces of Jihad, noisier and more obviously nihilistic than those of McWorld, are likely to dominate the near future, etching small stories of local tragedy and regional genocide on the face of our times and creating a climate of instability marked by multimicrowars inimical to global integration. But in the long run, the forces of McWorld are the forces underlying the slow certain thrust of Western civilization and as such may be unstoppable. Jihad's microwars will hold the headlines well into the next century, making predictions of the end of history look terminally dumb. But McWorld's homogenization is likely to establish a macropeace that favors the triumph of commerce and its markets and to give to those who control information, communication, and entertainment ultimate (if inadvertent) control over human destiny. Unless we can offer an alternative to the struggle between Jihad and McWorld, the epoch on whose threshold we stand—postcommunist, postindustrial, postnational, yet sectarian, fearful, and bigoted—is likely also to be terminally postdemocratic.

PART I

The New World of McWorld

I

The Old Economy and the Birth of a New McWorld

GILLETTE'S CHAIRMAN Alfred M. Zeien has said "I do not find foreign countries foreign."[1] Welcome to McWorld. There is no activity more intrinsically globalizing than trade, no ideology less interested in nations than capitalism, no challenge to frontiers more audacious than the market. By many measures, corporations are today more central players in global affairs than nations. We call them multinational but they are more accurately understood as transnational or postnational or even antinational. For they abjure the very idea of nations or any other parochialism that limits them in time or space. Their customers are not citizens of a particular nation or members of a parochial clan: they belong to the universal tribe of consumers defined by needs and wants that are ubiquitous, if not by nature then by the cunning of advertising. A consumer is a consumer is a consumer.

McDonald's serves 20 million customers around the world every day, drawing more customers daily than there are people in Greece, Ireland, and Switzerland together.[2] General Motors (still the world's largest company despite its uneven recent sales history) employs more people internationally than live in a number of the world's smaller nations.[3] With $2.4 billion worth of pizzas sold in 1991, the privately owned Domino's earned enough revenues to fund the collective government expenditures of Senegal, Uganda, Bolivia, and Iceland.[4] Toshiba, the General Electric of Japan, boasts in its 1992 annual report that "as good corporate citizens" they "do our part to ensure that progress continues within the world community," but its citizenship—whether Japanese or global—is hemmed in on every side by limits set by the demands of profitability, which in turn is driven by sales in 1992 of $25 billion, only slightly less than Argentina's recent government budget.[5] Globalism is mandated by profit not citizenship. Fast food goes upscale in the chic new chain Planet Hollywood. And "On planet Reebok," according to the successful ad campaign of an only nominally "American" athletic shoe company, "there are no boundaries."[6] Ralph Lauren's perfume for men, Safari, also boasted of "Living Without Boundaries" in its launch campaign in 1992.

A popular protectionist sticker appearing across the nation on American automobile bumpers reads "Real Americans Buy American." The trouble is, it is hard to know which car is really more "American": the Chevy built in Mexico from primarily imported parts and then reimported into the United States, the Ford built in German plants employing Turkish workers and sold on the Hong Kong and Nigerian markets, or the Toyota Camry designed by American Peter J. Hill at Toyota's Newport Beach California Calty Design Research Center, assembled at the Georgetown, Kentucky, Toyota plant by American workers, primarily from American-made parts, and test-driven at Toyota's twelve-thousand-acre Arizona proving ground.[7] These international "Japanese" cars are puzzling: for to remain truly Japanese, the whole must somehow become more than its American parts. Thus, in a fit of schizophrenic self-congratulation, Honda has been boasting about its "made-in-America" roots (that is, parts) even as it revels in its status as *Motor Trend*'s "Import of the Year."

So confusing has the question of automotive genealogy become that the United States government enacted an American Automobile Labeling Act that since October 1, 1994, has required that labels be affixed to new autos specifying their "domestic content," from their engines to their windshield wipers. The labels are unlikely to clarify the situation, however, since they reveal (to take just one example) that Chrysler Corporation's Dodge Stealth is built by Mitsubishi in Nagoya, Japan, while Mitsubishi's Eclipse RS is built in Normal, Illinois, and features Chrysler engines.[8] Labels can be confusing: the Nissan Altima assembled in America with mostly American parts does utilize radiator hoses manufactured in Paris . . . Paris, Tennessee.[9]

The authors of the North American Free Trade Agreement found it particularly cumbersome to decide which products could qualify for tariff-free status in the new zone since so many products "foreign" to North America were nonetheless assembled in the region with local parts. How about Japanese picture tubes installed in Mexican television chassis? Under traditional trade rules they were "domestic"; under NAFTA rules, the picture tubes and electron guns will also have to be domestic to qualify. But since Japanese companies own large shares of both of the "American" glass companies that manufacture tubes, "American" domestic television sets will still be substantially Japanese, even if they qualify as American under NAFTA rules.[10] American-made cars will have to have 50 percent of their parts (by value) as well as 50 percent of their labor contributed domestically (rising to 62.5 percent in 2002) but does this really make the cars "American"? Putting identity labels on products turns out to be even more challenging than establishing ethnic identities for people, for products have to be disassembled and labeled part by part, by origin of material, nationality of labor force, and cultural identity of designer to arrive at an *ad absurdum* conclusion about *their* ethnic identity.[11]

Historically, there is something prototypically American about the automobile: Henry Ford's commitment to a mass-produced motorized vehicle that would set every American family free has come to be associated with many of the virtues of American lifestyle and not a few of its vices. The internationalization of automobile culture—what George Ball once called "an ideology on four wheels"—as well as of automobile manufacturing is thus actually a globalization of America, no matter who is making the cars. The Chinese have recently committed to automobile manufacture as a foundation for economic modernization: more than any other decision they have made, this one may commit them to the Americanization they most fear.[12]

Yet however American cars are in concept, they are hardly American in their manufacture whether measured by parts, design, or even labor. Indeed, increasingly, corporations refuse to define themselves by reference to labor at all, let alone by reference to a particular parochial labor force with a local national character. Ignacio Ramonet argues that in the global economy neither capital nor work nor material is the determining factor, but rather the "optimal relationship between these three," which pushes us into the world of information, communication, and administration where traditional nation-states can exert little control and are bound to feel more and more uncomfortable.[13] Robert Kuttner reports that the state-of-the-art handle for the postindustrial company—which clearly is also the post–nation-state company—is "the virtual corporation" where "the company is no longer a physical entity with a stable mission or location, but a shifting set of temporary relationships connected by computer network, phone and fax."[14]

McWorld *is* a kind of virtual reality, created by invisible but omnipotent high-tech information networks and fluid transnational economic markets, so the *virtual corporation* is not just a provocative turn of phrase.[15] Without even trying, reporter Julie Edelson Halpert gives it concrete meaning in the portrait she draws of Ford Motor Company's Mondeo project:

> Seeking to shave months and millions of dollars from car design, Ford has consolidated management of its European, North American and Asian design operations into a single international network using powerful work stations based on Silicon Graphics Inc. technology linked by Ethernet networking software.
>
> . . . The Ford system . . . was brought under a single "electronic roof" . . . based in Dearborn, Michigan. The other main sites on the network are in Dunton, England; Cologne, Germany; Turin, Italy; Valencia, California; Hiroshima, Japan; and Melbourne, Australia. The circuits—satellite links, undersea cables and land lines—are purchased from telecommunications carriers.[16]

The virtual corporation also exists in the labor market as an employer of "virtual" rather than actual laborers. The ideal virtual laborer is a robot: an interactive, "intelligent," fully programmed worker capable of working twenty-four hours a day with no sustenance and minimal upkeep. What a poignant marriage: in McWorld's chilly new cyberspace, yesterday's invisible hand reaches out to grasp the invisible body of tomorrow's newly born virtual corporation to guide its spasmodic newborn movements toward an eternity of profits, almost entirely without the intervention of a visible human hand.

Many modern nation-states have generated national industrial policies aimed at strategic coordination of economic policy and domination of international markets by their business corporations on the theory that the nation's citizens will somehow be benefited by supporting corporations even if corporations decline to return the favor. Yet although full employment is a public good, it is not a corporate good. Business efficiency dictates downsizing, which means capital-intensive production, and capital-intensive production means labor-minimizing job policies. Translated into English this means firing as many permanent workers as possible and eliminating their costly benefit and pension packages. In their place appear machines, robots, and multiplying (so-called) "temporary" jobs, which are actually long-term jobs without long-term contracts, long-term security, or long-term benefits. Unemployment may eventually weaken the market by debilitating potential consumers (you can't buy unless you earn), but corporations taken one by one are necessarily rabid competitors with (at most) a quarterly earnings horizon. They must be "lean and mean" to prevail. The "fat" here is workers and a corporate diet spells permanent "structural" unemployment for increasing numbers of workers.

American agriculture remains a dominant producer for world markets, but where once it took 80 percent of the workforce to grow crops, today it takes 2 percent. Manufacturing is following agriculture. IBM sloughed off labor fat to the tune of sixty thousand workers in 1993 to the general applause of market analysts, and it secured private advantages in the international computer market whose public costs will not be seen for several years and whose consequences will in any case not be directly borne by IBM.[17] Nineteen ninety-three was the year of "downsizing" (a euphemism for layoffs and firings) for many larger corporations, including a number that were in the black and were acting "preemptively." The only thing labor-intensive about modern manufacturing is the cost-cutting. Fearing inroads by generic brand companies, Procter & Gamble announced plans in 1994 to eliminate 13,000 jobs (and to close 30 of 147 plants) over a three-year period, while Eastman Kodak intends to cut 10,000 jobs through 1995 as part of its "restructuring." In the Common Market, unemployment is over 11 percent and in France, with a declining Gross Domestic Product (GDP), it is higher. The global recession has eased but jobs are unlikely to reappear in prerecession plenitude, as the American recovery of the mid-nineties is already proving. Many of the new jobs are lower paying service positions, often without benefits or safety nets. Downsizing is after all a global market strategy responding to the new economics of the automation/electronic information age, and McWorld's labor market has little interest in employment per se and even less in protectionist governments monkeying with labor supply and demand.

There are of course timorous and weak businesses (they hardly meet the criteria of capitalist ventures at all) that, like the ailing unions, welcome the attention of an interventionist government. But they belong more to a vanishing mercantilist economy than to McWorld. In recent decades we have witnessed some of America's largest corporations seeking succor from the state—Chrysler or Amtrak or the savings and loan industry—demanding the socialization of their risk, so that public taxpayers can pay the costs of their business fiascos. In a world where socialism has disappeared, it can still be found lurking in the boardrooms of failing and bad-risk investment companies like those that misjudged the peso that yearn to spread their losses across the backs of long-suffering taxpayers.

Unions too hide behind protectionist policies, trying to insulate their members from the often unfair discipline of international markets like NAFTA. But as Robert J. Samuelson has said, "the drive of big companies to win world markets and maximize sales overwhelms all but the most draconian protectionism."[18] Social justice makes little more headway against market ideology than national self-interest. Markets are by their nature unfair, and when confronted with state-generated public interest issues like justice, full employment, and environmental protection they seek above all to be left alone. That is what a market *is:* an unobstructed set of exchange relationships among individual consumers and individual producers that is allowed to take its course; and McWorld is nothing if not a market. Market proponents insist that, like a river kept from its natural flood plain by engineers bent on containing its occasional rampages, a market hemmed in by government levees and regulatory dams will in the end create far more havoc than one left to follow its own cycles.

Government has a perfect right, indeed it has a duty, to intervene in the economy in the name of justice, ecology, strategic interests, full employment, or other public goods in which the market has and can have no interest. But it cannot expect the denizens of McWorld to welcome such intervention or to demur from trying to obstruct government through their own political interventions. This is the major reason why trade sanctions and embargoes generally fail. Market-driven profit has little tolerance for policy-driven punishment. With the rare exception of a country like Iraq with a leadership so obnoxious that it provokes unanimity among its adversaries and induces national governments to actually prosecute private companies that breach the cordon sanitaire, embargoes are little more than noisy nuisances. South Africa, Serbia, Iran, Israel, Chile, Argentina, and, until recently, even Cuba have at different times weathered embargoes with remarkable equanimity; many have sustained economic growth with the help of market exchanges that simply do not respond to coercive national policies or international law. Even Iraq managed to acquire a nuclear weapons capacity via secret trade well after it had become an outlaw country.[19]

Modern transnational corporations in quest of global markets cannot really comprehend "foreign policy" because the word *foreign* has no meaning to the ambitious global businessperson. Like Gillette Chairman Zeien, they do not find foreign countries foreign: as far as production and consumption are concerned, there is only one world and it is McWorld.[20] How can the physical distinction between domestic and foreign have resonance in a virtual world defined by electronic communications and intrinsically unbounded markets? World trade in 1950 stood at $308 billion. By 1968 it was over a trillion and today it has passed $3½ trillion; meanwhile, tariffs—as potent a symbol of national boundaries as there is—have declined from 40 percent of average product prices to about 5 percent.[21] If world trade is comprising an ever greater percentage of world GDP, currency exchanges are in turn outstripping trade—some say by as much as three to one.

During the 1980s, Japan scoffed at American companies that moved manufacturing facilities overseas to take advantage of cheaper labor, to get closer to markets, and to avoid dependency on an expensive dollar. In the nineties, the Japanese are themselves moving manufacturing outside of Japan. Seventy percent of "Japanese-made" televisions and 30 percent of VCRs are now manufactured overseas. And while General Motors produces over 40 percent of its cars beyond American shores, Toyota's extranational production is up to 20 percent of its total.[22] Mabuchi Motors, which controls a remarkable one-half of the world market in those tiny motors that power toothbrushes and zoom lenses and car windows, employs thirty-three thousand workers—but only one thousand of them work in Japan; the rest are offshore foreign laborers at plants in cheap labor markets like China.[23]

Likewise, while it makes sense for nation-states to create incentives for exports and tariff disincentives for imports, corporate producers and individual consumers start from a very different vantage point: literally speaking, producers are universal "exporters" (they export everything they make in their factories "out") and consumers are universal "importers" (they import from "outside" their home everything they consume); this universalism means in practice that the idea of imports and exports has little or no meaning for market players. The American textile company that moves its factory to Indonesia and, using cheaper labor, sends cheaper dresses back across the border incurs no trade deficit, only greater profitability. The American consumer who purchases that dress does not lose a job, she gains a bargain. Trade deficits belong to nation-states alone. Individual American workers may lose jobs and individual American citizens may have to deal with interest rate changes induced by their nation's trade deficit, but American consumers and American producers, qua consumers and producers, couldn't care less.

Of course nobody really intends to segment their being quite so schizophrenically: Americans are job holders as well as consumers, and even in the narrow terms of economic efficiency, their capacity to consume over the long haul depends on secure employment over the long term—and they know it. They are citizens no less than producers and need to consider the public space consequences of their private sector acts. Market identity is only one fractious piece of a person's whole identity, which also contains ethnic and civic dimensions that may rival or even be inimical to market identity. The consumer who welcomes lower prices may, as an employee of a textile firm, be hostile to the export of jobs that brought prices down. The producer who profits from the circumventing of environmental regulations may regret as a citizen the damage businesses like his cause to the environment and, as a citizen, support clean air legislation injurious to his business.

Yet full employment and environmental preservation are social goods rather than private-market goods; and the proponents of McWorld view markets and their impact strictly from the one-dimensional perspective of capitalist efficiency. From this constrained, short-term perspective, citizenship, ethnicity, and job status as well as other rival forms of identity are at best irrelevant, at worst, obstacles to be overcome. People and nations may shudder at corporate downsizing policies that result in massive job elimination, but the market will celebrate its players' new competitiveness.

Nations may have national economic policies but to the true capitalist, regulations, tariffs, bailouts, embargoes, wage restraints, employment quotas, environmentalist restrictions, and even putatively procapitalist incentives or price-fixing schemes are anathema—all equally to be disdained as statist attempts to distort a "natural" process that works properly only when left to itself. Thus the ancient war cry of old and new capitalists alike: *laissez-faire!* Leave us alone! Let us do what producers and consumers do: sell, buy, produce, consume.

These classical doctrines were conceived for a much simpler world and were pushed to the margins by Keynesianism and the welfare state. The modern democratic state is legitimated by the priority of the public over the private, where public goods trump private interests and the commonweal takes precedence over individual fortunes. But under conditions of internationalism—the world trade policies and global markets that constitute what I have called McWorld—old laissez-faire notions reemerge with a new force. For there is no international state and thus no guarantor or discoverer of an international good. The international dis-order remains a kind of state of nature among nations and it is marked by a "war of all against all"—the "quest for power after power that ceaseth only in death" portrayed by Thomas Hobbes in his *Leviathan* more than three hundred years ago.

The invisible hand thus takes on new significance in the setting of invisible cyberspace, where virtual corporations defeat real nations. Now the space in which they operate is as invisible as the market's phantom hands. I underscore the importance of these new market hyperrealities here for two reasons: because the free market ideology they rehabilitate is a battering ram against the walls of the nation-state, exposing McWorld's antagonism to nationalisms of every kind; and because they challenge and ultimately rewrite the traditional account of markets in terms of free trade in raw materials, manufactured goods, and services. For in the economics of McWorld, the traditional dominance of raw materials and goods yields to a novel and distinctive new realm of activity—what I call the infotainment telesector—that redefines the economic realities of McWorld and reorders the relations of nation-states in ways that neither Francis Fukuyama nor Paul Kennedy could anticipate.

2

The Resource Imperative: The Passing of Autarky and the Fall of the West

TRADE IN NATURAL resources and the fruits of the land, whether animal, vegetable, or mineral, is among the oldest and most prosperous and profitable sectors of the economy, dating back to the beginning of economic time. Slave/master societies as well as agricultural and feudal societies were grounded in the discovery, processing, and use of these primary goods. Agriculture and trade in natural resources represents the first rung on the economic ladder, and in the modern economy they have been the Third World's principal door to development. It is here we find those dozen or so corporations on the southern side of the North/South divide that have clawed their way onto the list of the world's five hundred largest industrial monoliths.[1]

Agriculture, the other subsector of the traditional resources category, also dominates the Third World in terms of labor investment (two-thirds of the labor force in many Third World nations work in agriculture), although not, unfortunately for such nations, in terms of production. For First World nations using advanced technology from the information/technology sector can produce goods efficiently while employing only a tiny fraction of their labor force.[2]

When we compare the percentage of GDP devoted to agriculture to the percentage devoted to goods and services in Third World nations, the First/Third World division is strongly reinforced. Organization for Economic Cooperation and Development (OECD) countries devote on average only 2.8 percent of their GDP to farming, 33 percent to manufacturing, and a whopping 57.6 percent to services while the percentage for agriculture rises to 17.2 percent in Eastern Europe, to 21.8 percent in sub-Saharan Africa, and to 34 percent in south Asia, with a corresponding decline in the service sector to 38.5 percent for Eastern Europe, and to 18 percent for sub-Saharan Africa and south Asia.[3] A number of impoverished nations lack not just manufacturing capacity but elementary natural resources and agricultural potential, and are likely to belong in perpetuity to what realistically should be called not the Third World but the Terminal World. Others are "Third World" only on the way to being Second and First World—much in the manner of the United States compared to Britain a couple of centuries ago.[4] The bleak prospects of many sub-Saharan countries is epitomized by Ghana. Paul Kennedy has noted that at the beginning of the sixties, it shared a per capita income of a little over $200 with a number of Asian countries, including South Korea. Today, South Korea's per capita income has increased twelvefold to over $3,000; Ghana's remains where it was, in the low 200's.[5]

Yet the most impressive new truth about natural resources in the era of McWorld is that even here debate about national interest or national independence is increasingly irrelevant. To be sure, economic self-sufficiency has been a dream of all peoples from the outset of their collective histories, especially those with democratic aspirations. Economic dependency meant political servitude internally as well as externally. In classical republican theory from Pericles to Machiavelli and Montesquieu, the free society was the society sufficient unto itself in food and resources. Democrats thus dreamed of utopias whose political autonomy rested firmly on economic independence, what they called autarky. It was not so much the free market but the independent market that would secure freedom for the city-state. However, the Athenians were not able to achieve autarky: human nature, it turns out, *is* dependency, perhaps because human needs and the escalating psychologies by which they are determined are by nature insatiable.

The dream of autarky had a brief reign in nineteenth-century America as well, when the underpopulated, endlessly bountiful land, the cornucopia of natural resources, and the natural barriers of an island continent walled in by two great seas together created a magical interlude in which many could believe that America might actually become a world unto itself. This has imprinted the American mind with an illusory sense of self-sufficiency and has nurtured a spirit of isolationism that has periodically led to a withdrawal from world affairs. For nations, however, no island is ever really an island. And though it has been hard for Americans to accept the inevitability of interdependence, not even our continental cornucopia has been immune to depletion. Elsewhere, the maldistribution of arable soil and mineral resources on an unjustly created planet leaves even the wealthiest societies ever more resource-dependent and relegates many other nations to the permanent despair of the Terminal World.

For nations like Japan and Switzerland, modernized and progressive but resource poor, autarky has never been an option. Either through military dominion over their better-endowed neighbors (Japan's "Greater East Asian Co-prosperity Sphere," as its iron-handed pre–World War II empire was known) or extensive trade and prudent foreign policy (Switzerland's neutrality is the preferred example), such nations have had to forge relationships with others that made a virtue of their dependency. Japan's military grip on East Asia was a stern discipline for the Japanese too, requiring a large imperial army, permanent occupation, and constant surveillance. Japan's postwar economic miracle, while it allowed it to reacquire dominion, has made it even more dependent on its trading partners than it once was on its colonies.

Nations whose geography is more promising have fared little better. Potential agricultural behemoths like Russia and India sometimes seem hard-pressed to feed themselves: certainly the Soviet Union failed to do so, compounding the circumstances that sealed its doom. Every nation, it turns out, needs something another nation has. Many nations have almost nothing they need. The erosion of American autarky in natural resources over the last one hundred years stands as an exemplar for dozens of progressive nations, its story more dramatic than most, but finally all too familiar.

As recently as 1960, the United States imported only a handful of minerals such as aluminum, manganese, nickel, and tin. Today we look abroad for zinc, chromium, tungsten, lead, and of course oil. And soon copper, potassium, sulfur, and even iron will become weighty items in our negative balance of trade. Domestic production of coal and shale will take us into the century after next, and the exhaustion of our agriculture will take even more stupidity and incompetence than the economic managers most amply endowed in these qualities are likely to be able to muster. But in most other respects, America—the eighteenth-century's second Eden and new found land—is looking more and more like Britain or Switzerland, if not Chad or Bangladesh, importing more and more of what it requires to survive.

Less than fifty years ago, there was no aggressor, however bold, that could hope to defeat in battle an America whose supply lines originated in such bounty. From the iron ore and bauxite and phosphate and petroleum reserves came an endless supply of airplane engines and battleships and mortar shells and hand grenades; from the aboriginal fertility of the great plains came food and clothing for as many armies as the nation saw fit to field. Yet by the 1980s the vestiges of this prized autarky were gone and America was as dependent on imports as most of its trading partners. America's success in World War II had in fact endangered the very resource autarky on which victory rested. The United States drew heavily on its resource banks to acquire global leadership, and would draw even more heavily on them to retain it into the heady years following the war when its relations with the Soviet Union were freezing down at the very moment its domestic economic growth was heating up.

The sharp and sudden deterioration in America's resource independence produced by this juxtaposition is evident from U.S. bauxite figures. Bauxite is the source of aluminum and a crucial element in industrialization, not least of all in its war-making moment. America was less favorably endowed by nature in bauxite than in other minerals, yet through the end of World War I, America produced nearly 50 percent of the world's bauxite.[6] More important, through 1920 it imported less than 10 percent of its domestic consumption, and at the end of World War II was still producing 57 percent of what it needed.[7] Yet within five years (by 1950), imports were up to 65 percent of consumption, with a rapid increase in dependency to 87 percent in 1960, 90 percent in 1980, and 94 percent in 1988.[8] Moreover, U.S. bauxite production has continued to plummet as consumption has continued to soar. While in 1945 America was still producing 27 percent of the world's ore and more than half of what it needed domestically, by 1950 domestic production had dropped to 16 percent of world supply. Ten years later (1960) it was at 7 percent, by 1970 it was half of that (3.4 percent), and in 1989 it was approaching nil—0.5 percent.[9]

In the fifty years since the end of World War II, then, America has become crucially dependent for the aluminum on which its world leadership is in part based, on the very Third World nations its leadership was meant to subordinate.[10] Nearly identical stories can be recounted about other mineral resources as well as about other nations. America's global rivals, the Common Market and Japan, for example, are 85 to 100 percent dependent on imports for columbium, strontium, manganese, cobalt, tantalum, platinum, chromium, nickel, tin, antimony, iron ore, gold, copper, molybdenum, and phosphate.[11] Like America, Europe increasingly depends on potential adversaries for the strategic metals on which its military capacity to confront such adversaries depends.

Although new discoveries of copper, lead, and zinc (as well as aluminum) increased overall world reserves faster than world consumption reduced them through the 1980s, the patterns of production, refining, and distribution have increased dependency for all nations involved in the process—particularly for those like France, Russia, and America that once enjoyed the illusion of autarky. Moreover, as the developable (non-Terminal) Third World evinces a growing First World appetite for consumption to fuel its developing industrialization, global consumption is clearly going to outstrip global production by ever greater margins, increasing the urgency of resource dependency and bringing Malthusian imperatives into dramatic play once again: who will get how much of a vanishing supply of irreplaceable resources? Will China really pursue an automotive economy for everyman as it proposed it would do in 1994? A billion more cars will do in China's independence as surely as it will exhaust global mineral and fossil fuel supplies (not to mention the environment). If the Chinese were to drive as many per capita passenger miles as Americans currently do each year, it would take only five years to use up all the earth's known energy reserves.

Technology will of course continue to do battle with nature in the endless clash of hope and despair that defines human life. Manufacturers have found replacements for ozone-layer-damaging propellants and introduced them with such alacrity—outstripping legislated requirements—that estimates of damage are now being gratefully revised downwards. Government manipulation of market incentives can make a difference. In the domain of minerals, technological innovation in recycling suggests a strategy that can mitigate both resource depletion and the dependency it produces. In 1987, waste stockpiles from American mining, mineral processing, and metallurgical industries were estimated at almost 2 billion tons, and while the varying mineral content of such wastes makes recycling expensive, we are nevertheless doing more and more of it.[12] The environmental savings are considerable: the amount of energy required to produce a ton of a given metal by mining, extraction, and refining is anywhere from double to tenfold the energy required to produce the same ton from recycling. Reusing things may not do much for corporate profits but it spares mother earth and leaves more for the generations still to come.[13] In the brave new epoch of McWorld, we may yet find a way to refashion our garbage into liberty and wring from our waste products a semblance of our lost independence.[14]

Technology also holds out the promise of a new age alchemy: contriving from synthetics strange new substitutes for natural metals that eliminate dependency on natural resources while improving performance. It also promises new ways of getting to and processing mineral resources once too low-grade or too far underground or undersea to warrant recovery.[15] The Pacific floor is strewn with manganese nodules—a wealth of small nuggets that contain far more cobalt, nickel, and copper than all the world's known land reserves. They are currently at depths where their recovery is unfeasible but the science of submersibles marches on while robotic vacuums capable of sucking up the treasure are already on the drawing board.[16]

Yet ultimately, even where technology offsets resource depletion through new discovery techniques and more economical extraction methods or through recycling and substitution, the long-term trends spell ineluctable interdependence for just about everyone in just about everything. Promethean hope may ultimately overcome Malthusian doubt, but Prometheus's theft of technology's fire can be exploited only through collaboration. Science and technology, like Prometheus, cannot be bounded: not by frontiers, not by national sovereignty. They are made possible by cooperation and they command interdependence. The world's nations, having exhausted their natural bounty one by one, may still find a way to survive on the wings of artifice, but they will do so interdependently and together: globally or not at all. The nation-state's days are numbered.

Petroleum: The Same Old Story, Only Worse

MANY MINERAL RESOURCES can be recycled or replaced by technological surrogates, but energy resources—above all fossil fuels—on the scale they are currently being consumed around the globe surely cannot. There is a little hope to be had from renewable resources. These include solar power obtained from photovoltaic cells, whose production grew an average of 15 percent a year from 1981–91 even as their price fell dramatically; geothermal power—the tapping of the earth's hot fluids and gases—which in 1950 produced only 239 megawatts of electricity but today produces nearly 10,000 megawatts or enough to meet the energy needs of 6 million energy-guzzling Americans; wind power, which in just eleven years has gone from 15 to 2,652 megawatts; hydroelectric power, which satisfies as much as a third of the power needs of many developing countries and has grown from under 50,000 to well over a half million megawatts since 1950; and nuclear power—although the environmental dangers have brought it to a virtual standstill in the last few years after reaching a high in 1990 of 328,000 megawatts or less than half of hydroelectric.[17] Yet all of these resources together have made only a small dent in world petroleum consumption—considerably less than the dent made by the oil crises and recessions of the seventies and eighties.[18] Global production after peaking in 1979 at almost 63 million barrels a day has settled at between 59 and 60 million barrels a day since 1989: this represents a full 40 percent of the total energy globally consumed each day, and while production is well under its peak potential today, long-term prospects grow dimmer as the time frame grows longer. The advanced economies that are creating McWorld depend on the automobile, a zealously petroleum-dependent mode of transportation that symbolizes both prosperity and the individualism and mobility associated with liberal democratic societies: how then can developing countries be dissuaded from striving to automobilize their societies as China now wishes to do?[19]

The world still spins on the energy of fossil fuels—nonrecyclable and irreplaceable. The United States represents an especially foreboding case study, for here is one of the world's richest fossil fuel producers using up its own resources in an orgy of consumption that is reflected neither in elevated living standards nor in a proportionately larger GDP. Nor have we learned much from two major crises in supply and our ever more debilitating dependency on foreign oil: gas prices remain absurdly low, taxes (even after the Clinton administration's budget initiative added 4.3 cents) are insignificant, and strategic stockpiles unimpressive.

Even more than with minerals, energy resources represent a form of power that seems to shrink as it grows. That is the irony of modernization, described by modernity's first incisive critic, Jean-Jacques Rousseau. Rousseau had seen that the power given us by science and technology to gratify our needs actually compounds and multiplies them so that as our power increases our satisfaction diminishes. If happiness is a function of needs in harmony with our capacity to satisfy them, "progress" will always mean that power, however fast it grows, will be outstripped by needs, which grow faster. Hence, modern man's conundrum: the more powerful he becomes, the more miserable he feels. All that we have only serves to make us "need" more, and the more we have the more we need in order to protect what we have. Like the proverbial landowner who yearns only for the land adjacent to his, our modern consumer needs only products that are proximate to products he already possesses. The TV "needs" the VCR, which "needs" a laser disc player, which "needs" a computer, which "needs" endless software. The automobile first "needs" theft protectors and radar detectors and cassette players and onboard computers, and then it needs places to go and drive-in facilities, then parking lots and strip malls and pretty soon it needs all of what passes for modern civilization—goods that a person must slave for over a lifetime to begin to be able to afford. And then of course she will complain that she has no leisure to enjoy the "possessions" that turn out to feel more like her owners than her property.

What Hobbes called the quest for power after power that ends only in death has become the quest for oil wellhead after oil wellhead that ends only in economic and environmental bankruptcy. In America, it hardly seemed possible that supply could ever be overtaken by demand. From the discovery of oil in western Pennsylvania just before the Civil War—a discovery that would make John D. Rockefeller's fortune—right down to the 1930s, exploration seemed to uncover new reserves far faster than an industrializing world used them up. Yet within a few years of the end of World War II, America found itself sliding into dependency, though reliance on imports was at first thought to be nothing more than a matter of convenience and efficiency.

Why pump expensive domestic petroleum when foreign oil was so cheap? In the century's first three quarters, oil use in America had grown by about 3 percent a year, while real Gross National Product (GNP) was growing at an average 4 percent a year.[20] Domestic production, peaking in 1970, managed to keep up to need, with 88 percent of consumption still being met from domestic American sources in 1970.[21] But as a result of the 1973 Mideast War and oil embargo, the one-tenth or less of our fuel needs that depended on foreign imports in the sixties nearly tripled by 1974, creating for the first time a vivid sense of national jeopardy. Imports in 1974 had grown to 28 percent of consumption while oil prices had spiraled up from $1.73 a barrel in 1970 to $10.89 at the end of 1974.[22] By 1980, imports had risen to 38 percent of domestic consumption and by 1990 to 42 percent.[23] Today, despite a lingering business turndown and roller-coaster consumption patterns that have kept world oil production under the peak production levels reached in the seventies, American import dependency has remained well above 40 percent and in 1994 went, for the first time, above 50 percent.

These long-term rising figures for imports reflect both a very gradual decline in domestic production and an appetite for energy that, though it moderated in the late seventies as prices rose, has continued to grow. While domestic energy consumption fell from an all-time high of 11.30 million barrels per day in 1970 (for crude oil and natural gas), to around 9 million barrels per day in 1990, consumption rose from less than 15 million barrels per day to an all-time high of nearly 18 million barrels in the late seventies (although since then consumption has fallen, risen, and fallen again, leaving it only slightly higher today than it was fifteen years ago). If prices stay low, experts at the Energy Information Administration predict that domestic production may fall to about 6 million barrels per day by 2010, while consumption could rise to nearly 24 million barrels per day, a deficit of 17 or 18 million barrels that could add up to a dependency on imports of nearly 75 percent of consumption by 2010.

The American story is every developed nation's energy nightmare. If we exclude those OPEC nations like Qatar and Bahrain with minuscule populations and gargantuan production surpluses,[24] almost all of the industrial nations are import-dependent, in many cases almost completely so. With roughly one-half of the world's GDP between them (27 percent for the United States, 16 percent for Japan, and 7 percent for Germany), America, Japan, and Germany import far more than half of their energy—under 50 percent for the United States but more than 90 percent for Japan and somewhere in between for Germany.[25] Because it has gone nuclear, France produces most of its own energy, but when we look at consumption rather than production, it too remains import-dependent.[26] Among OECD nations, only Canada and Australia, and with their North Sea oil, Norway and the United Kingdom, turn out to be net energy producers—which has allowed Norway to stay out of Europe. On the other hand, the world's five largest economies are the world's largest energy importers. The stronger the nation, the more fragile its independence.

There also lurks in this welter of statistics a powerful element of injustice that illuminates a darker side of McWorld. Even as nations are superseded by transnational markets, their populations remain the producers and consumers of the global market. The unequal distribution of world resources skews and unbalances affairs, and turns McWorld—its virtues and its vices—into a playground for some and a cemetery for others. If we look at energy consumption in the rich nations where America is again the archetype we get a disturbing take on fairness. Not only is there less and less to go around, but what is left is being more and more unfairly and inefficiently allocated. Unfairness thus turns out to be a crucial trait of McWorld, and although it is not our primary focus here it cannot be ignored.[27] (See Appendix A.)

Mineral and Energy Resources: Jihad or McWorld?

WITH RESPECT TO McWorld, the clearest conclusion that can be drawn from this review is that the integrating forces of interdependence associated with globalism actually reinforce the fragmenting tendencies of Jihad they seem to combat. For mineral and energy use patterns seem both to enhance interdependence by reinforcing the imperative for global cooperation *and* to underscore divisiveness, injustice, and weakness, disclosing the susceptibility of the new world economy to the forces of Jihad. The vulnerability of the developed countries' emerging McWorld is thrown into sharp relief by asking how many of the world's primary energy producers outside the OECD are likely candidates for Jihad and its associated pathologies: that is, how many seem ripe for episodes of internal turmoil, political instability, civil war, or tribal fragmentation. (See risk tables, pp. 44–45.) Among Jihad-prone producers, we can surely count Iran, Iraq, Algeria, Libya, Nigeria, and ex-Yugoslavia as high-risk; moderate-risk nations—would you invest your children's savings in any of the following?—include Argentina, Brazil, Peru, Venezuela, Albania, Romania, the republics of the former USSR, Angola, Cameroon, the Congo, Gabon, China, India, Malaysia, and Mexico, and of course the rest of the Middle East including Saudi Arabia, Kuwait, Oman, Qatar, Egypt, Syria, and the United Arab Emirates. In 1991, the high-risk group accounted for almost 8 million barrels per day of 60 million worldwide; that is about 13 percent of the world's oil production.

JIHAD AND OIL PRODUCTION: RISKS

High- and moderate-risk oil-producing nations and Jihad. These are final numbers for world oil production for 1992.

Numbers are in 1,000 barrels/day. Total world production: 60,029.4 (thousand barrels/day).

High Risk	
Algeria	771.3
Iran	3,415.3
Iraq	417.3
Libya	1,468.7
Nigeria	1,887.0
Yugoslavia	22.2
TOTAL	7,981.8 (thousand barrels/day)

13.30 percent of the total world production of oil is occurring in nations that are either currently involved in an ethnic conflict or are at a high risk for future conflicts.

Moderate Risk	
Albania	30.0
Angola	553.2
Argentina	554.3
Brazil	640.7
Cameroon	139.0
China	2,833.6
Commonwealth of Independent States*	8,898.8
Congo	182.7
Egypt	870.7
Gabon	302.7
India	573.8

(continued)

Kuwait	845.3
Malaysia	661.0
Mexico	2,775.7
Oman	729.0
Peru	115.7
Romania	140.0
Saudi Arabia	8,206.7
United Arab Emirates**	2,337.2
Venezuela	2,328.7
TOTAL	33,718.8 (thousand barrels/day)

56.17 percent of the total world production of oil is occurring in nations that are at a moderate risk for future ethnic conflicts.

GRAND TOTAL   **41,700.6 (thousand barrels/day)**

69.47 percent of the total world production of oil is occurring in nations that are at a high and moderate risk for current or future ethnic conflicts.

Source: *The International Petroleum Encyclopedia* (Tulsa: PennWell Publishing Company, 1993), pp. 350–354.

*Commonwealth of Independent States
Azerbaijan, Belarus, Georgia, Kazakhstan, Kirgizstan, Russia, Tajikistan, Turkmenistan, Ukraine, Uzbekistan

**United Arab Emirates
Abu Dhabi, Ajman, Dubai, Osujara, Ras al-Khaimah, Sharjah, Umm al-Quaiwain

JIHAD AND OIL RESERVES: RISKS

A worldwide look at proven oil reserves. (Proven oil reserves = amount of oil recoverable at current prices with current technology.) These are final numbers for January 1, 1993.

Numbers are in billion barrels. Total world oil reserves: 997.04 billion barrels.

High Risk

	Oil Reserves	Percentage of World Oil Reserves
Algeria	9.20	0.92
Iran	92.86	9.31
Iraq	100.00	10.03
Libya	22.80	2.29
Nigeria	17.90	1.80
Yugoslavia	0.08	0.008
TOTAL	242.84 billion barrels	24.36

24.36 percent of the total proven oil reserves are located in nations either currently involved in an ethnic conflict or at a high risk for future conflicts.

Moderate Risk

	Oil Reserves	Percentage of World Oil Reserves
Albania	0.17	0.012
Angola	1.50	0.15
Argentina	1.57	0.16
Brazil	3.03	0.30
Cameroon	0.40	0.04
China	24.00	2.41
Commonwealth of Independent States*	57.00	5.72

(continued)

Congo	0.83	0.08
Egypt	6.20	0.62
Gabon	0.73	0.07
India	6.05	0.61
Kuwait	94.00	9.43
Malaysia	3.70	0.37
Mexico	51.30	5.15
Oman	4.48	0.45
Peru	0.38	0.04
Romania	1.57	0.16
Saudi Arabia	257.84	25.86
United Arab Emirates**	98.10	9.84
Venezuela	62.65	6.28
TOTAL	675.50 billion barrels	67.75

67.75 percent of the total proven oil reserves is located in nations that are at a high and moderate risk for current or future ethnic conflict.

GRAND TOTAL   **918.34 billion barrels of oil**

92.11 percent of the total proven oil reserves is located in nations that are at a high or moderate risk for current or future ethnic conflict.

Source: *The International Petroleum Encyclopedia* (Tulsa: PennWell Publishing Company, 1993), pp. 284–285.

In the moderate-risk group, non-Arab nations account for about 21 million barrels a day (better than a third of global production), while the Middle East tinderbox (not including high-risk-category Iraq and Iran) accounts for nearly 13 million more barrels a day, or another fifth of world production. Add it up: better than three-fifths of the world's current oil production (and almost 93 percent of its potential production reserves) are controlled by the nations least likely to be at home in McWorld and most likely to be afflicted with political, social, and thus economic instability.[28]

The results are equally disconcerting when we rate energy exporters in the high- and moderate-risk categories on a democracy scale. Since democracy is correlated with continuity of government and thus stability and since democratic nations are less likely to make war on other democracies than nondemocratic nations, oil-producing democracies make safer partners in McWorld's trade relations. Yet the Western powers were content to return Kuwait to oil production without inducing it to become more democratic.

The most rigorous standards would put the Latin American group and India on the democratic margin, at best, giving them only 7 of the 42 million barrels produced by nations in the high- and moderate-risk group, and leaving over four-fifths of production in these two groups in non-democratic hands. If all of the oil-producing ex-USSR republics actually become democratic, another 10 million barrels will be "safe," but nearly one-half of world production will still remain at risk. Indeed, the subdivision of once-extensive federations like Yugoslavia and the Soviet Union into smaller fragments has turned once-producing exporters into net importers. As part of the Soviet Union, the Ukraine could think of itself as part of a powerful fossil-fuel and lumber producer. But though it has now acquired the illusion of independence, it has become a needy importer desperately negotiating with Russia for oil, gas, and wood. Yuri Byelomestnov, director of the Ukraine's October Mine, says bitterly: "Ukrainian independence, it's a mistake. . . . [N]ationalism blinds intelligence. We used to get 8,000 pieces of equipment—conveyor belts, lumber—from Russia a month. Now we can't get them."[29]

The logic is spare and fearful: both Jihad and McWorld weaken nations. Jihad splinters them but increases their dependency on McWorld; McWorld draws nations out of their isolation and autarky, but in making them dependent, reduces their power. Democracy suffers either way, especially if, as I will argue below, democracy historically has rooted its liberties in nation-state institutions. Even as we secure the macropeace through trade, treaties, law, cooperation, and common force, the microwars occasioned by Jihad's fractious parochialisms become of ever greater global significance. Interdependence makes boundaries permeable not just for the good but for the bad, for Jihad no less than for McWorld.

3

The Industrial Sector and
the Rise of the East

How different is the story when we move from the domain of raw resources to manufactured goods—supposedly the foundation of any national economy? Manufactured durable goods constitute the traditional industrial sector by which the rise of capitalism has generally been measured. Until recently this sector has been regarded as the engine of all developed economies. The decline of American manufacturing in traditional domains like steel and automobiles has thus been closely associated with a putative erosion in world economic leadership. America's "rust belt" has turned America into a vast rust bucket. The "American Century" celebrated by *Life*'s Henry Luce in 1941 ended without ceremony sometime in the 1970s when America crossed the midway point on its sad journey from being the world's largest creditor nation to being its largest debtor nation and when Europe and Japan, well recovered from the war, began to eat away at America's leadership in automobile, home appliance, electronics, and computer manufacturing. Paul Kennedy, David Calleo, and other pessimists have concluded that the American epoch, scarcely half a century long, is over.[1]

By the same logic, the emerging economic powers to whom the future supposedly will belong have been identified in recent decades by their emerging industrial manufacturing potential. The multiplying "tigers" on the Asian side of the Pacific Rim like Japan, the Koreas, Taiwan, Singapore, and China (with Hong Kong) have thus caught up to and even surpassed European powers like Germany and France as major economic players. Smaller and less noticed specialists in manufacturing like Israel, Iraq, Cuba (before the demise of their Communist patrons), Botswana, Kuwait, and Libya have also come to exercise an economic influence disproportionate to their size while Chile, Turkey, and even Mexico may yet achieve extraordinary rates of growth in this decade.[2] All of the above countries devote over half of their GDP to industry.[3] Yet these trends prove little. Projections based on manufacturing capacity are fundamentally flawed because they miss the direction in which the evolving economy is moving. Economic strength in the era of McWorld has passed to the domain of services, and here new and distinctive measures of leadership have emerged quite separate from the traditional industrial sector.

Joseph Nye has written persuasively about the shift from the kind of "hard power" that is rooted in the coerciveness of command structures—military and machine power—to a novel form of "soft power" that leads by consent and is rooted in "the universalism of a country's culture and its ability to establish a set of favorable rules and institutions that govern areas of international activity."[4] He suggests that politically soft power is supplanting hard in the modern world, and I will argue that there has been a parallel evolution in the economy from the hard manufacturing to the soft service (information and communication) sector, and that economic power is likely to follow this evolution in the coming decades, upsetting the grim predictions of the declinists about the United States.[5] The United States, no longer the dominant manufacturing entity it once was, nonetheless has a sure command of the softer powers that are forging McWorld, which positions it to recapture global leadership. What this suggests is that the story of America's rise and decline as a manufacturing power is only part of a larger, not yet finished, journey.

In 1950 not long after the end of World War II and before the burgeoning Cold War began to challenge American strength and divert its attention from rebuilding a demobilized peacetime economy to restarting a cold wartime economy, the United States had already overtaken England and Germany as *the* global power. Military and political factors seemed primary, but underlying them was demonstrated economic power. This unprecedented strategic hegemony rested almost entirely on the American industrial economy as it emerged from World War II—an economy that was driven by the largest and most productive manufacturing and banking companies in the world.[6]

In that postwar moment when America dominated the world economically, the world it dominated was a far more diversified place culturally. While America exercised hard power hegemony, soft power was scattered and insubstantial, a matter of many different insular local cultures. Semiotic systems were fragmented, while cultural symbols were the possessions of parochial peoples with colorfully distinctive self-images. In the fifties and sixties, there was no "Europe" in Europe. In the world before McWorld, the Swedes drove, ate, and consumed Swedish; the English drove, ate, and consumed English, and the rest of the world's inhabitants either mirrored their colonial masters or developed domestic consumption economies around native products and native cultures. In France one ate nonpasteurized Brie and drank vin de Provence in cafés and brasseries that were archetypically French; one listened to Edith Piaf and Jacqueline Françoise on French national radio stations and drove 2CV Citroëns and Renault sedans without ever leaving French roadways—two-lane, tree-cordoned affairs that took you through half the villages in France on the way from, say, Paris to Marseille. An American in Paris crossed the waters to get away from Tastee-Freez, White Castle, and Chevrolet pickup trucks and once in France could be certain they would vanish. A German studied in Italy to imbibe Mediterranean, not Atlantic, culture. Americans dominated the economic world in the abstract, but the French dominated France, the English England, and the Italians Italy.

Yet two rival worlds of industrial power evolved inside and outside of the Cold War. While the United States and the Soviet Union focused their energies on defense- and aerospace-related heavy industry, Germany and Japan homed in on consumer products where, ironically, the ideal American mobile, autonomous, choosing consumer who would define the future economy was the natural target. Where defense and aerospace industry were closely associated with hard power and state command structures, the new consumer economies privileged the private sector and pointed toward soft power.

America's postwar economic hegemony was reinforced by its decision to focus on automobiles. The choice of roadway over railway and the construction of the huge interstate highway system meant that the industries on which automobiles depended (steel, aluminum, chrome, petroleum, rubber, concrete, asphalt, and electronics) would be continually nurtured not just for public sector defense spending but for private sector consumer spending. Automobiles facilitated the suburbanization of America and thus had a vital impact on the housing and construction industry as well. Suburbanization required improved communications and home entertainment and gave television a new role as the national medium. This domestic productivity combined with heavy industrial production in the defense sector sent the economy surging and secured America's global economic leadership. The arms race allowed (forced) the Soviet Union and suppliers like East Germany to build powerfully competitive industrial economies as well, but it was to those nations that could concentrate on consumer goods that the future really belonged. The United States and the Soviet Union were in effect arms-racing themselves right out of the leadership. The USSR would eventually bankrupt itself in the competition, and America would survive economically only by securing an elephantine national debt, a wrenching trade deficit, and the unwanted status of the world's largest debtor nation, uneasy in the 1990s with the McWorld its postwar economy has created.

Innovations in electronic and computer technology that had originated in American defense research facilitated developments in consumer goods that the new manufacturing powers in Europe and the Pacific Rim could take advantage of. The smaller throw capacity of America's underpowered rockets spurred miniaturization, while the demands of high-tech weaponry induced advances in electronics and computers that were quickly translated into consumer technology. Radios, cameras, telephones, video equipment, kitchen and household appliances, as well as home computers—all the things needed to fill up America's multiplying private cars and private homes—were the new frontier of manufacturing. Despite America's leadership in research and development, it quickly lost its competitive edge to the nations it had defeated in the war.[7]

Yet despite attrition, the United States remained a formidable industrial power, gradually building a base for its new ventures in the service economy. Its GDP approached $5 trillion in 1993—better than one-fifth of gross world product, produced by only one-twentieth of its population. Of the world's 500 leading industrial corporations in 1992, 161 were still American, including five of the top nine and all of the top three (General Motors, Exxon, and Ford).[8] But a surprising number of the nation's leading corporations are newcomers. Founded in 1968, Intel Corporation had sales of $8.8 billion and thirty thousand employees in 1993. Nike was born in 1972, Microsoft in 1975, Apple Computer and Gene Tech in 1976. These corporations are not only new, they represent a new form of economic power.

The real story of America's vicissitudes as *the* global manufacturing nation is in fact not the story of power shifting from one country to another, but of the gradual erosion of the very meaning of national predominance in industries that year by year are becoming ever more transnational in their corporate makeup, multinational in their parts acquisition, international in their job allocation, and global in their consumer marketing strategies. Just look at Nike or Intel or Apple. American manufacturing leadership simply is not any longer American, anymore than Japanese manufacturing leadership is Japanese. Manufacturing corporations have become as global as the markets they ply. This is why Paul Kennedy's book on the rise and fall of the great powers might more appropriately have been titled "On the Rise and Fall of the Very Idea of a Great Power."

Of course in speaking of global companies and global markets, the globe encompasses only designated players in the game. The geography of the whole planet is not at issue. Excluding oil and mining concerns, there is not a single African, South American, Middle Eastern, or Indian company among the top five hundred corporations, and the story is not much better with respect to patterns of consumption since the primary producers turn out to be the primary consumers as well. In 1991, for example, the United States exported $85 billion in goods to Canada, $48 billion to Japan, $33.3 billion to

Mexico, $22 billion to the United Kingdom, and $21.3 billion to Germany. These top five export markets comprised almost $210 billion in exports or way over half of America's 1991 exports globally.[9] Of America's top five supplier countries, four are also top five export markets. Of the top ten importers, eight comprising over 77 percent of America's total are top export markets.

Country	Ranking as Supplier (U.S. imports from)	Ranking as Export Market (U.S. exports to)
Japan	1	2
Canada	2	1
Mexico	3	3
Germany	4	5
China	6	16
United Kingdom	7	4
South Korea	8	6
France	9	6
Italy	10	12

Americans worry about their trade deficit: the United States runs significant deficits with seven of the ten on the list, all save France, the United Kingdom, and Mexico. Nonetheless, its deficit trading partners are also its export partners. The only non-European, non–Pacific Rim countries among the top twenty-five U.S. export markets are its Latin American neighbors (with whom America also runs trade deficits): Brazil at number 17 and Venezuela at number 20. Nearly half of the world's exporters or nearly seventy of the world's nations listed America as the first, second, or third largest destination for their exports in 1987–88. Forty put America first including all of Latin America but also South Korea, Japan, Nigeria, Mozambique, Iraq, Uganda, Pakistan, Sri Lanka, India, and poor Bangladesh.[10] In short, America buys from and sells to its rivals, and they do the same with one another when they are not trading with America. Within the club there may be differentials in import/export ratios that stir up domestic passions (as with NAFTA), but belonging to the club is what really counts.[11]

Third World countries are marginalized coming and going while Terminal World nations fall off the planet. There may be radical trade deficits among trading partners but only a handful of nations are even part of the calculation. The North/South split overshadows the East/West split. It is reflected in almost every economic report available on central Asia, the Middle East, and—most dauntingly—sub-Saharan Africa, which as a "human and environmental disaster area" totally "peripheral to the rest of the world" can hardly be thought of as occupying "the same historical time."[12]

Ironically, global economic forces weaken the nation-state in developed areas where it is most democratic and strengthen it in the Third World where it is least democratic, imperiling liberty in both cases. Democracy loses at both ends of the developmental spectrum. Free societies with expansive economies gradually sever the ties that hold a people to traditional religion and nationhood and corrode the state institutions that make democracy and a free economy possible in the first place. Despotic nations offer no such solvent to nationality and religion, which are strengthened in ways obstructive to modernization and democratization. Not only do the rich get richer and the poor poorer, but the rich get freer while the poor are enslaved.

Of course in the long term, democracy is served by these ironies in neither the First nor the Third Worlds. In the Third World too much state coercion steals liberty from peoples poised potentially for economic takeoff; and in the First World too little state coercion leaves individuals unprotected from market forces over which they have no rational or collective control. Dependency on global markets by virtue of global largesse may be a better deal than dependency by virtue of poverty on local despots, but both constitute a kind of subjugation and neither staves off that common servitude in which disparities are increased as common liberty is diminished.

These manifold ironies, while contributing powerfully to the story of growing global injustice and shrinking the prospects for global democracy, are only footnotes to our primary focus here: the internationalization of markets and the companies that serve them. In the developed world that "counts," where liberty has (at least in theory) been minimally secured, the erosion of nationality as a significant conditioner of corporate business remains the most important feature of the manufacturing sector. For the decline of democratic control over markets at the level of the nation endangers both justice and social policy *and* the prospects for global democratic control over the economy. Among the top twenty-five U.S. companies (for 1992) with the largest non-U.S. sales can be found not only energy giants like Exxon (77 percent of sales outside America), Mobil (68 percent), and Texaco (53 percent), and chemical companies like Dow (50 percent) and DuPont (47 percent), but Philip Morris, Coca-Cola, Johnson & Johnson, and Eastman Kodak.[13] Dow Chemical earns nearly $4 of every $10 in sales overseas and has nearly twice as many plants abroad as in the United States. Goodyear Tire and Rubber earns 43 percent of its income from abroad and sites more than half of its eighty-three plants outside the United States in twenty-five different foreign countries.

One need knock on only a few doors of corporate entities that carry the name "American" in their company titles to hear how hollow their patriotism rings. Consider American Greetings Corporation (cards and gift items), which earns 14 percent of its sales revenues abroad; American Express, which gets over 20 percent of its earnings beyond America; American Home Products, which earns 24 percent of sales far away from home; the American International Insurance group, which gets 46 percent of its revenue from its international rather than its American side; American Standard (plumbing), which earns 49 percent of revenue on someone else's currency standard; American Cynamid, which like most American chemical companies earns more than half its revenue (51 percent) abroad; and finally American President (shipping), which derives two thirds of its income from foreign port sailings.[14]

Twenty or more years ago, many of the American companies now deriving majority revenue abroad were almost exclusively focused on the domestic market. A "French" company like Michelin (tires), with 20 percent of world tire sales, earns only 19 percent of its revenues in France, while Sony earns less than a quarter of its nearly $30 billion in annual income from Japan, deriving over half from the United States and Europe (28 percent of its total sales in each). Smaller countries have also lost even nominal sovereignty over their businesses. Sweden's cheap furniture retail giant IKEA sells better than four-fifths of its products ($3.2 billion in sales in 1992) beyond Swedish frontiers and founder Anders Moberg (like Wal-Mart's Sam Walton, a billionaire) recently transferred total ownership of IKEA to a foundation he established in Amsterdam, while company headquarters went to Denmark (Moberg himself moved to Switzerland).[15] With a style called "Danish modern," how Swedish can IKEA really be?

As manufacturing is internationalized, and traditional industrial powers cede dominion to new markets with cheaper labor, the industrial sector is itself being transformed. The internationalization of companies is only one part of this change; for the goods companies make—the very idea of what a consumer good is—are evolving. From hard to soft goods, from soft goods to services, which are themselves becoming goods. We turn now to that part of the story.

4

From Hard Goods to Soft Goods

WHILE MAKING AND selling goods is still the dominant form of economic activity in the international markets of McWorld, the goods are increasingly associated with or defined by symbolic interactions that belong to the service sector in its postmodern, virtual economy manifestations. The move from heavy defense-related industrial production to consumer goods that has been a continuing feature of economic development has in the last decade moved into another phase in which hard consumer goods are increasingly becoming associated with soft technologies rooted in information, entertainment, and lifestyle, and in which products are emerging that blur the line between goods and services. The ancient capitalist economy in which products are manufactured and sold for profit to meet the demand of consumers who make their unmediated needs known through the market is gradually yielding to a postmodern capitalist economy in which needs are manufactured to meet the supply of producers who make their unmediated products marketable through promotion, spin, packaging, and advertising. Whereas the old economy, mirroring hard power, dealt in hard goods aimed at the body, the new economy, mirroring soft power, depends on soft services aimed at the mind and spirit (or aimed at undoing the mind and spirit). This wedding of telecommunications technologies with information and entertainment software can be called for short the infotainment telesector. The goods sector is captured by the infotainment telesector, whose object is nothing less than the human soul.

Hyperbole? The long dormant language of the soul, until just recently quite unfashionable, at least in corporate capitalism's domain, is making a secular comeback. As it assimilates and transforms so many other ideologies, postmodernist capitalism has not shied away from assimilating and transforming religion. If Madonna can play erotic games with a crucifix, why shouldn't Mazda and American Express work to acquire some commercial purchase on the Holy Spirit? "Trucks," intones a gravelly-voiced consumer in a 1993 Mazda television ad, "are a spiritual thing for me." The new Mazda pickup is "like a friend"—a friend, that is, "with a new V-6 and a soul to match." In another ad campaign, American Express teams up with Anita Roddick's Body Shop to exploit environmentalism, human rights, and what it calls "trading honorably." The print ad ends with a spiritual pitch: "American Express knows a lot of stores that are good for your body. And Anita knows one that's good for your soul."

For America's largest brand-name consumer goods corporations like Coca-Cola, Marlboro, KFC, Nike, Hershey, Levi's, Pepsi, Wrigley, or McDonald's, selling American products means selling America: its popular culture, its putative prosperity, its ubiquitous imagery and software, and thus its very soul. Merchandising is as much about symbols as about goods and sells not life's necessities but life's styles—which is the modern pathway that takes us from the body to the soul. AMERICAN CULTURE (AND GOODS) THRIVE IN SOUTH AFRICA, reads the *New York Times* headline about new investment possibilities in a nation where, as it prepared for its first interracial free elections, black South Africans were sitting around in "a Kentucky Fried Chicken restaurant, sipping Coca-Cola and listening to a Whitney Houston tape" and where seven of the top ten television programs were American.[1] Meanwhile, Marlboro announces Marlboro Gear, merchandising the style it has invented ("Marlboro Country") to sustain tobacco sales in an anti-smoking era.

The style marketed is uniquely American yet potentially global since, for the corporations in a quite literal sense, we *are* the world. To the world, America offers an incoherent and contradictory but seductive style that is less "democratic" than physical culture: youthful, rich urban, austere cowboy, Hollywood glamorous, Garden of Eden unbounded, goodwilled to a fault, socially aware, politically correct, mall pervaded, and, ironically, often dominated by images of black ghetto life—black, however, as in hip and cool rather than in crime-ridden and squalid, "baaaad" but not bad. PepsiCo's 1992 Annual Report features mostly black dancers from the Martha Graham Company and the School of American Ballet on its front and back covers, and the Pepsi Generation, multicolored and multicultured, is nothing if not American. The Michaels (Jordan and Jackson), the Jacksons (Michael, La Toya, and Jesse), the King (Martin Luther) and Prince too; and the Simpson (not the Simpsons): thus does white America use an indiscriminate selection of heroes from black America to capture heroically conceived global markets. Heroes fall—Michael Jackson and O. J. Simpson have tumbled— but living on the edge is part of what makes American ghetto culture thrilling to outside observers.

In the selling of America as a means to selling American goods, advertising has itself become big business on a global scale. Of the twenty-five largest advertising companies, fifteen are American. Total world advertising revenues are estimated to be anywhere from $150 billion to $250, nearly one half of which are American.[2] The largest firm, Britain's Saatchi & Saatchi, operates in over eighty countries and, according to media expert Ben Bagdikian, buys 20 percent of all commercial time in world television; its Pepsi-Cola account developed an advertisement to be placed in forty different national markets that could be seen by one-fifth of the human race.[3] Coca-Cola's new subsidiaries include China and, in a manner of speaking, Rutgers University. In China it must share its market with PepsiCo and other companies but at Rutgers University it has outbid the competition and, for $10 million, has secured a market monopoly for its products along with the right to advertise its association with the school. Late capitalism is no longer about either products or competition. Image is everything and the "it" that Coke is, is now education—as image rather than substance. Such recent victories, including its sponsorship of recent Olympic games, are perhaps fruits of the link Coke forged a few years earlier with Creative Artists Agency, the powerful talent agency and image spinner run by Michael Ovitz, to "help mold its marketing and media strategies around the world." Coke understands the link between its drink and American culture: according to an executive, "American culture broadly defined—music, film, fashion, and food—has become the culture worldwide."[4] The Coca-Cola company has discovered McWorld—which, without knowing it, it had actually helped invent over the previous half century.

Meanwhile, Creative Artists has figured out that if it wants to spin McWorld for the likes of Coke it needs to increase its synergy with the information and communications sector. In the summer of 1994 Ovitz brought aboard at C.A.A. the former chief financial officer of AT&T, Robert Kavner. His job was to "seek opportunities for directors, writers and performers in the rapidly expanding arena linking personal computers to on-line services involving, at the outset, education, shopping, films and video games"; Mr. Kavner allowed as to how "we're in the equivalent of the industrial revolution."[5]

The story of McWorld's rise is the story of the advertising industry's explosive growth in the same period. Global advertising expenditures have climbed a third faster than the world economy and three times faster than world population, rising sevenfold from 1950 to 1990 from a modest $39 billion to $256 billion.[6] Per capita global spending has gone from $15 per person in 1950 to nearly $50 per person today. While the United States leads the pack at nearly $500 per person, countries like South Korea (whose advertising industry had an annual rate of growth of 35 to 40 percent in the late eighties) and India (where billings increased fivefold during the eighties) are racing to catch up.[7] Advertising both reflects and reinforces the importance of brand over product in the global market. Brand names like Marlboro, Bud beer, Barbie doll, and Nescafé often carry their parent companies (Philip Morris, Anheuser-Busch, Mattel, and Nestlé), and both corporate names and product lines have brand values worth billions of dollars.[8]

Brand names are ciphers for associations and images carefully cultivated by advertising and marketing because they are what generate market demand. In defending his striking and deeply nihilistic

Benetton campaign that displays AIDS victims and crime scenes rather than sexy models and pastel sweaters, Luciano Benetton insists "we are forging a new art of communication . . . we spread no lies. We say, in this world there is sickness, war and death."[9] What exactly is a picture of a naked male torso sporting a tattoo that reads HIV POSITIVE meant to communicate to potential apparel purchasers? Social commitment? A subtle warning against stereotyping or an unsubtle example of it? A political provocation? Or just some creative director's notion of a subliminally hot hip-hop amalgam of flesh, disease, and gay politics that makes green the dominant hue in the Colors of Benetton and turns death into one more attractive lifestyle?[10]

American Express has also been running an ad campaign with selected retailers that tries to make shopping socially responsible but actually subordinates social responsibility to shopping. One ad in the series enthuses, "customers come into The Body Shop to buy a hair conditioner and find a story about the Xingu Reserve and the Kayapo Indians who collect Brazil nuts for us." It turns out that The Body Shop is less interested in "selling soap" than in saving the rain forest. How? By paying Kayapo Indians to extract nut oil and get them out of logging so they will leave the tropical rain forest alone! Body Shop founder Anita Roddick repays American Express for the alchemy by which they turn a soap seller into a conservation society by mentioning at the end of the ad that "the travel I do is often dangerous. I am in bizarre places, remote places. What I use for that is the American Express Card." The Xingu Reserve—certainly remote, also bizarre?—apparently takes the American Express Card.[11]

In 1995, following its "triumph" over communism, few would want to risk saying that capitalism is imperialist; but markets must grow and advertising has a natural tendency to seep like rising groundwater into every cellar of a commercial culture's multiple dwellings. Advertisers talk about the need to fill empty or "dead" space wherever they find it, by which they mean space not yet put to commercial use. Schoolrooms are now being used as video billboards by Channel One (sold by Chris Whittle to K-III in 1994). And the technology is in place to send audio ads your way while you wait for the telephone call you have dialed to go through,[12] and to put electronic billboards in space that would blot out the stars with earthly logos and put an end once and for all to the epiphanal dead space of the night.[13] The CEO of the company prepared to orbit ads enthused about the "tremendous opportunity for a global-oriented company to have its logo and message seen by billions of people on a history-making high-profile advertising vehicle."[14] "Living Without Boundaries," which is how Ralph Lauren sells his Safari perfume for men, is also how advertising colonizes empty space—space, that is to say, empty of advertising.

Helped along by the Reagan administration's 1984 decision to lift limits on television advertising time, advertising bleeds across various entertainment and information formats, blurring boundaries. Advertisements simulate independent editorial judgments and become advertorials; they infest news programming and turn into infomercials where the public cannot be quite sure whether they are watching a television magazine show about a product or a soft sell for the product. They move into storytelling so that ads look more and more like soap operas, with characters and plots that carry over from one ad to the next as in MCI's "Gramercy Press" series or the Taster's Choice love story that follows an affair to (where else?) Paris. But then the "soaps" were always about selling soap by telling stories just as the entire MTV network, the ads quite aside, is one interminable commercial for the music industry and its products—as well as for commercial culture in general.[15]

Today's corporate synergy does not permit storytelling to stand alone. Nike offers readers of an advertisement as passion play a phone number where they can order Nike's "Women's Source Book," printed on recyclable paper.[16] MCI is discussing a book sale of the silly "Gramercy Press" melodrama cited above about a publishing house being hardwired for the new age; it has also made "Gramercy Press" characters accessible to fans via the Internet—as the ad agency handling the MCI account says, "anything is possible in cyberspace."[17]

Infomercials merchandise even more subtly. The National Association of Broadcasters actually told the F.C.C. that these half-hour slow-mo ads "advanced the public interest by providing consumers with more information about product choices than other types of advertising." Stuart Elliot, who covers advertising for *The New York Times* and has presumably heard just about everything, was nonetheless astonished: "Who could have imagined that the motley crew of shills, hucksters and impersonators peddling spray-on hair, plastic exercise equipment and overpriced cosmetics were advancing the public interest? Not even one of Dionne Warwick's 'psychic friends' could have predicted that."[18] *Time* magazine, no stranger to hucksterism, acknowledges frankly that what infomercials actually do is to get "messages across to audiences that don't fully realize they are receiving them."[19]

Licensing offers advertisers another kind of colonization. Names carefully cultivated in a narrow business like high fashion can become global marketing devices when licensed for use on products that bear no relationship to the original designer and that the designer may have never even seen. Pierre Cardin pioneered the low-end licensing of a high-end fashion name when in the 1960s he licensed over eight hundred products from colognes to sunglasses.[20] Perfumes are sold almost entirely via designer labels. Calvin Klein nearly went bust selling fashion apparel, but his three consecutive lines of perfume—each reflecting its time—were commercial triumphs. Obsession, mirroring the hedonistic eighties; Eternity, following the new family values; and most recently, Escape, echoing tired yuppies in search of a way out, all earned major success in a market crowded with newcomers (over 120 new perfumes each year). Here is the case where a rose is *not* as sweet by any other name, where it is the brand and not the scent that brings in the profits.

Tie-ins and the licensing of spin-off merchandise from blockbuster films like *Jurassic Park* and *The Lion King* (as well as Oscar winners like *Forrest Gump*) not only make fortunes for the companies that own them (Disney expects a billion dollars from *Lion King* licensing) but blur the lines between domains once thought to be distinct. The Disney marketing program "connects its book, movie, recording and theme park units" with a synergy no other company can rival.[21]

Disney is the obvious champion of synergy, but the footwear business also offers an altogether apt, if rather less explicit, example of the power of name and trademark over product and of the associational psychology that attaches the chic glamor of the woman's movement and youth volunteerism to for-profit merchandising. Sneakers are apparel items and Nike is a novice in the shoe business (here only since 1972), so it has had to capture its $4 billion share of the market not by selling shoes but by cultivating trademark and brand loyalty that depends on lifestyle choices and the images associated with them. In search of effective wholistic marketing strategies, Nike has consulted Ovitz's Creative Artists Agency dream factory. Ovitz told Nike CEO Phil Knight something Knight presumably already knew: that "sports is bigger than entertainment now."[22] Humankind walked the globe for millennia without the specialty items developed in the last few decades for professional athletes. Today when 40 percent of all shoes sold are already athletic shoes, if Nike, Adidas, and Reebok have their way, no one will walk at all without their products; and this will be a consequence of a lifestyle choice arising out of the manipulation of emotions linked to sports and winning rather than to the satisfaction of needs linked to walking and shoes.

Nike started up just over twenty years ago and sold a little over $3 million in sneakers to Oregon consumers, many of whom (Nike now gleefully reports) thought the logo said "Mike." Today the company does better than $3.5 billion in sales worldwide. "We are not a shoe company," explains Liz Dolan, Nike's corporate communications vice president, "we are a sports company."[23] Nike CEO Phillip H. Knight is even more forthright: "How do we expect to conquer foreign lands?" he asks in the 1992 Annual Report. "The same way we did here. We will simply export sports, the world's best economy."[24] Well, not exactly sports and not just sports, but the image and ideology of sports: health, victory, wealth, sex, money, energy—don't name it, "just do it."

If actual athletes were the only consumers of athletic shoes, there would be far too few of them to keep sales perking in the billions round the world, so the object becomes to make those who watch athletics believe that in wearing Nikes they too are athletes, even if they never get up out of the armchairs from which they watch the world's most famous Michael sail across the heavens in his Air Jordans. Mr. Knight is pretty blunt about it: "Our target consumers have been watching John McEnroe and Charles Barkley for years. The emotional ties are in place." Watching, not doing. Emotional ties, not real needs. Nike is not trying to export sneakers (a limited market, the corporation acknowledges), it is trying to export Michael Jordan who, Chairman Knight assures us, is tied for first place in

China as the world's greatest man with Chou En-lai (an astonishing comparison that, from the viewpoint of sales, is apparently nonetheless worth flaunting!).

In the new McWorld of global sales, the trademark has surpassed the sales item and the image has overtaken the product as the key to earned income. Michael Jordan himself, until his temporary retirement into a mediocre minor league baseball career, earned $3 million a year for playing basketball and $36 million a year selling his name.[25] In a section titled simply "The Nike Image," Nike's corporate report notes that while "early advertising and promotional efforts focused on the shoe, its features and benefits . . . in the years since, corporate communication has broadened to make Nike one of the few global leaders with an actual personality." The new virtual reality corporation, even as it sheds its traditional character as a concrete corporate person, acquires an "actual" personality.[26] Nike wants customers not simply to buy its goods but to believe in Nike; not only to assess the quality of the products but to believe in the "motivations" of the producers. This rhetoric suggests the corporation is acting more like a civil state or a state religion than like a shoe company. It aspires to "the development of strong Pan-European, Asian and Latin American media channels" that will "allow Nike to communicate its message and personality to consumers in every corner of the world—an integral part of ensuring a consistent global brand image."

In communicating messages and conveying a personality, Nike is shaping the affective and behavioral contours of McWorld. Attesting to the sincerity of its globalism, the Nike chairman's letter in the Annual Report in which these excerpts are found is presented in Japanese, French, German, and Spanish where those prized "emotional ties already in place" appear multilingually as "les liens émotionnels . . . déjà en-place" and "die gefühlsmässige Bindung . . . bereits vorhanden" and "los lazos sentimentales . . . en el lugar apropiado." The Japanese version I will leave to the reader's imagination. Nike's new virtual reality defined by information and communication cyberspace, a full remove from any reality you and I know, is reified and brought back to earth in new stores like its multiplying "Nike Towns," the template for which in suburban Beaverton (Portland), Oregon, has been described as "part Disneyland, part

MTV," outfitted with video screens, exotic fish, flute choruses, and the dum-dum-dum sounds of an epiphanal dribbling basketball. The Nike Towns have become tourist attractions that draw overflow crowds looking not for shoes but for "fun."[27] These stores stand to traditional stores as the new marketing of images stands to the traditional selling of products. They are sneaker theme parks in which sports (winning? exercising? just doing it?) suffuse reality. That reality, corporate public affairs officials being quick studies, is as well attuned to fashionable political attitudes as to fashionable footwear. Nike has thus acquired a conscience. Having marketed shoes to inner city kids whose tough urban image is crucial to international sales but who are themselves unlikely to be able to buy the shoes, Nike is pushing a volunteer program called P.L.A.Y. (Participation in the Lives of American Youth). It hopes a little of its own money will leverage a lot of customer effort on behalf of urban kids, some of whom are robbing and killing one another to secure a pair of Nike's pricey high-tops.[28]

Nike is perhaps the most aggressive promoter of itself as a brand rather than a product in this consumer sector, but Reebok is not far behind. Its corporate self-definition portrays it as a "leading worldwide designer, marketer and distributor of sports, fitness and lifestyle products, including footwear and apparel" and its advertising features "Planet Reebok" (which it apparently cohabits with Ralph Lauren) where there are also "no boundaries." In the late eighties, after successfully exploiting the American domestic market, both Nike and Reebok went after the European market, dominated by the German firms Adidas and Puma, and have recently moved aggressively into other world markets.

In almost any soft consumer-sector one looks at, the pitch is at once ever more American and ever more global: there is less tension than meets the eye, because global pop culture *is* American. The two elephantine cola war rivals Coca-Cola and Pepsi are typical.[29] Coke remains the global soft-drink leader with more than two-thirds of its 1992 revenues coming from abroad (compared with only 20 percent of Pepsi's). Yet (in its own unparaphrasable words), "as huge as our world of Coca-Cola is today, it is just a tiny sliver of the world we can create."[30] Coke has had global ambitions for a long time.[31] But nowadays an ambitious company cannot simply capture global consumer markets by aping their ideologies and accommodating their tastes: it must also be prepared to create global markets by careful planning and control. The new technologies are more powerful than the old, and Coke has now manufactured its own soft-drink ideology that assimilates the ideals of the Olympics, the fall of the Berlin Wall, and Rutgers University into a theme-park ideal existence for Coke drinkers. McWorld's innovative virtual industries generate virtual need factories (advertising agencies, corporate public relations and communications divisions, business foundations) where emotions are identified and manipulated with images that forge new wants.[32]

Now thirst cannot be manufactured but taste can. The world's thirsty can drink water (just as the world's footloose walkers can wear ordinary old shoes): if they are to drink beverages that earn someone else an income, consumption has to be associated with new "needs," new tastes, new status. You must drink because it makes you feel (your choice): young, sexy, important, "in," strong, sporty, smart, with it, cool, hot (as in cool), athletic, right on, part of the world as in we-are-the-world as in we-Americans-are-the-world: in sum, like a winner, like a hero, like a champion, like an American, which is to say, above all, fun-loving (as in blondes have more). The one reason you must not consume soft drinks is to quench your thirst in any decisive way. Water would accomplish that. In fact, if you're going to buy another soda, the ideal soft drink should give you the feeling your thirst has been quenched while actually leaving you metabolically thirstier after you finish than before you began. Within the right informational nexus, even H_2O can be sold for profit, as it is with so-called designer waters like Perrier. And if a potable salted beverage could only be found . . .

"How long can a company of our scope keep doubling its size?" asks Coca-Cola CEO Roberto C. Goizueta. "Where will the next 10 billion unit cases come from? And the 20 billion after that?"[33] Goizueta has an answer, which to him seems obvious. "The fact is," he observes, "that we are just now seriously entering and developing soft drink markets that account for the majority of the world's population. These new worlds of opportunity are not only heavily populated, but also culturally and climatically ripe for significant soft drink consumption." Climatically ripe, that's pretty obvious: where it is hot, people are thirsty, and if we can only get them off of water. . . . But culturally ripe? What can this mean? Coke is anything but disingenuous: in Indonesia (whose Boy Scouts and Girl Scouts, Cokes in hand, are featured on the 1992 Annual Report's cover), "aggressive investment" can defeat local culture and force the nation to follow those "societies that have traditionally consumed beverages like tea" but have been brought to make "the transition to sweeter beverages like Coca-Cola." Getting people off of water is a matter of economics (water is free), but getting them off of tea entails a cultural campaign. The "decline in tea consumption," which might for cultural anthropologists signal a foreboding onset of erosion in a dominant local culture, is welcomed as a door ajar for sweet beverage sales. If only every Indonesian could switch from tea to Coke—and from sandals to Nikes and from rice to chicken McNuggets and from saris to Laura Ashley dresses and from oxen to Grand Cherokees and from indigenously produced movies to Arnold Schwarzenegger videos and from Buddhism to consumerism—imagine what "worlds of opportunity" would be thrown open to McWorld's bold corporate adventurers; and imagine what kind of homogenous and profitable McWorld-wide market those once distinctive regions would constitute.

Even Africa, although it is falling off the world's economic charts, is to be gathered into McWorld's fold. For in the gunsight of Coke's ambitions, it is not the home of endless poverty, rampant AIDS, and ongoing authoritarianism, but rather a 568-million-person soft-drink market featuring "warm climates, youthful populations and governments moving toward market economies." The same is true of Slovenia, Croatia, and Bosnia-Herzegovina in ex-Yugoslavia where a "successful bottling system (is) in place." Where ordinary observers see hell in the making, Coke sees a 24-million-person market, which surely can be "targeted for more investment when territorial/political tension subsides." After all, when Coke trucks first appeared in Warsaw, crowds lined the sidewalks and cheered.

Creating the world in its own image also lets Coke redefine political and social reality. Uncontrolled, economy-wrenching birthrates modified only slightly by the plague of AIDS become "youthful populations" ripe for consumer exploitation. Ethnic cleansing, rape as policy, and genocide become "territorial tensions" that, though they may diminish the market by a couple of million consumers, give or take a million Muslims (less likely prospects for Western-style consumption in any case), will eventually yield to less tumultuous, more profitable forces of globalization. From this perspective, the journey from AIDS, starvation, and genocide to just plain fun American-style seems far shorter than anyone could have imagined.

It is perhaps unfair to hold corporate companies chasing maximum sales, bottom-line profits, and shareholder satisfaction to some vision of global diversity or international justice or world democracy. Yet their strictly economic ambitions turn out to be anything but strictly neutral. As we have seen, they themselves wade into Big Social Issues, if only to stroke a new age middle class they want to target for the same old little economic reasons. And even where multinational companies claim to be interested exclusively in production and consumption figures, increasingly they can maximize those figures only by intervening actively in the very social, cultural, and political domains about which they affect agnosticism. Their political ambitions may not be politically motivated and their cultural ambitions may not be the product of cultural animus, but this only makes such ambitions the more irresponsible and culturally subversive.

Consumer sales depend on the habits and behaviors of consumers, and those who manipulate consumer markets cannot but address behavior and attitude. That is presumably the object of the multibillion-dollar global advertising industry. Tea drinkers are improbable prospects for Coke sales. Long-lunch traditions obstruct the development of fast-food franchises and successful fast-food franchises inevitably undermine Mediterranean home-at-noon-for-dinner rituals—whether intentionally or not hardly matters. Highly developed public transportation systems lessen the opportunity for automobile sales and depress steel, rubber, and petroleum production. Agricultural lifestyles (rise at daylight, work all day, to bed at dusk) are inhospitable to television watching. People uninterested in sports buy fewer athletic shoes. Health campaigns hurt tobacco sales. The moral logic of austerity contradicts the economic logic of consumption. Can responsible corporate managers then afford to be anything other than immoral advocates of sybaritism? Or to act as irresponsible citizens in these new, mostly less developed, worlds of opportunity? Are they not bound as good businesspeople to emerge from the cocoon of the free market and to try to influence cultural and lifestyle habits, some of which may be political as well? A *New York Times Magazine* fashion spread is only punning when it runs the title "Party Line" across photos of a half-dozen New Year's celebrants, but it reveals a darker side when it speaks mischievously of being "committed to the ideology of fun."[34]

Elaborating on Marx's offhand assumption about the political idiocy of rural life, Edward C. Banfield, examining rural Italy after World War II, associated the agrarian lifestyle with a morally backward set of political attitudes.[35] Whether he was right or not about agriculture, it seems likely that lifestyles are increasingly relevant to the postmodern political economy. They make a difference: a leisure society may afford more time for civil society, volunteer service, and politics than a work society; suburban lifestyles diminish public and common space of the kind found in towns and cities; twenty-four-hour-a-day global markets linked by electronic telecommunications, and global business communities linked by international flights interfere with schedules and routines rooted in traditional diurnal clocks. Markets demand freedom from public-sector regulation and interference, but increasingly they are themselves engaged in activities that impinge directly on civic culture and public goods. Political agnostics, they nonetheless borrow and warp political ideas and political terms. A Western fast-food chain that sells varieties of baked potatoes thus advertises that it "empowers" customers because it gives them the right to "choose toppings." Brand choice and, within brands, item choice (Crest blue and Crest regular), have been widely taken to constitute the essence of freedom in market societies and has even been sold to "new democracies" as such. But it turns out to be something less than real liberty. The ideology of having fun actually *is* an ideology.

This is most evident in what has perhaps been the greatest growth area for consumer goods qua services, the information and entertainment industries that both drive and are driven by the hardware but depend ultimately on the software. This infotainment telesector is supported by hard goods, which in fact have soft entailments that help obliterate the hard/soft distinction itself.

5

From Soft Goods to Service

THE WALKMAN IS a perfect exemplar of the impact of new hard
technologies on choice and liberty, appearing to expand each,
yet in truth contracting both. By one measure the Walkman is not
new at all: it is just the latest version of a very old modern technology: the phonograph. But the Walkman's portability, its suitability to
solitary listening, and its supermobility make it a ten-ounce fifth column for McWorld that insinuates lifestyle preferences directly into
the inner ear while modifying traditional behaviors in socially significant ways. The Walkman technology transforms listening from a
social into a solitary occupation; it takes a foreground end-in-itself
activity and turns it into background for other consumer-society-
desirable behaviors like jogging (Walkmans sell athletic shoes and
athletic shoes sell Walkmans!); and it permits a sometime music listening activity to become an all-the-time habit that demands the
production and sale of ever more music software.

Computer technology has equally momentous (equally invisible)
social entailments. A computer not only conveys information to users
but draws them into new forms of interaction that more or less leave

their bodies behind, abandoned in front of screens that are the entry to new and peculiar kinds of virtual community that (unlike, say, books) reconstructs their bodies as cyberspace members and thus suggests some kind of virtual politics. Just what kind of politics remains altogether problematic—albeit we can be sure there *will* be a politics of one kind or another. Even the form that information takes—video-textual, digital, programmed, time-shifted, technology-dependent—will inevitably impact culture and politics and the attitudes that constitute them. It has been speculated that video-game players acquire hand-eye skills critical to certain professions—fighter pilots, for example, or laboratory technicians handling dangerous materials by remote control; it has also been speculated that players may develop diminished capacities in other domains such as imagination or human sympathy. There have been no decisive empirical studies of such linkages, but it certainly seems likely that linkages exist and will have important political implications. Those interested in democracy, culture, and civic life cannot afford to leave the discovery of their character to chance.

With these considerations in mind, it is difficult to treat the electronics and computers sector of the hard goods economy as discrete from the high-tech service sector or from the social attitudes that sector mediates. To act as general contractor for the information superhighway but yield control over the nature and content of the traffic for which it will act as a conduit is to misconceive where power lies in McWorld. Industry leaders like IBM, Sony, Toshiba, Matshui, and Nintendo have not fallen prey to such a misconception. They are busy seeking ways through mergers, acquisitions, and buyouts to extend their hardware business (high-tech paving) into the software sector (traffic control and governance over who or what rides in the vehicles). Telephone companies (the Baby Bells), cable corporations, and software producers (film studios) and distributors (Blockbuster Video) are eyeing one another with appetites whetted by social Darwinism and the belief that ultimately capitalism is about monopoly and that only a few of them can emerge from the coming software struggle as winners.

Seen from the perspective of this intra-American competition, this shift from products to services mirrors an economy-wide trend and corrects the impression given by high-tech manufacturing that America is in a steep decline. In hardware, to be sure, what were once American monopolies have given way to intense rivalry with the Europeans and the Japanese. For example, in 1974 the United States exercised a complete monopoly over the production of sophisticated DRAM memory chips essential to computers. By 1980, the U.S. share had fallen to 56 percent while Japan's share had risen to 40 percent. Seven years later, the United States produced less than a fifth and the Japanese more than three-quarters of DRAM chips.[1] Similar stories can be told about semiconductors, where the American share has fallen from double Japan's in 1980 to less than Japan's today, and telecommunications equipment where Japan rose from fourth place among producers in 1980 to first today, while the United States languishes in third place barely ahead of Sweden.[2] Even research and development spending—a longtime American virtue—has plateaued and after peaking at $94 billion in 1989 has fallen back to under $90 billion.[3] There are many explanations for these trends including the absence of an American state effort to match Japan's industrial policy, unfair trade practices, and the costs of maintaining a defense from whose responsibilities the Japanese have been largely exempted.

Yet services and soft goods are where the action is, and in this domain the American story is rather different. Services have gone from being the poor cousin of the global economy to being its first citizen. In the year 1990, *Fortune* magazine, which had been tracking hard corporations for decades, finally noticed that service no longer meant just food and travel but included finance, information, and telecommunications and that it comprised over 60 percent of GDP and accounted for eight out of every ten American workers.[4] The result: a new annual list surveying "The World's Largest Service Companies." On the 1990 list of top five hundred service corporations, the United States led with 150 (Japan followed with 106, with Britain, 49, and Germany, 41, trailing). In 1992, America remained the leader with 135, although with its prominence diminished in commercial banks (8 of the top 10 and 31 of the top 100 were Japanese versus 8 of the top 100 for the United States, with Citicorp as the first American bank on the list at number 27!) and life insurance companies (where 7 of the top 10 were Japanese). With 128 companies on the top 500, Japan seemed to be closing in on the American lead.[5] In software, information, and entertainment, however, America is pulling away.

The extraordinary significance of this new infotainment service sector to the new world economy can be seen by its impact on the often lamented American trade deficit. The 1992 deficit of 40 billion dollars is actually a mean average of a far worse $96 billion *goods deficit,* offset by a $56-billion *service surplus.* In the service sector, the United States has a powerhouse surplus economy. And with world trade in services now estimated at over $600 billion annually, the edge is of growing importance. Advertising exports now rival automobile exports in revenues. Moreover, all these figures are on the conservative side: the Commerce Department admits its traditional "merchandise bias" probably means exports in services are being radically underestimated.[6]

Now critics will point out that even in the service sector where America seems dominant, it leads the world only in the retail sector where Sears and Wal-Mart remain the indisputable giants. In banking and insurance it has been overtaken by others in the top ten category. However, not all service sectors are equal with respect to the emerging postmodern economy of McWorld. From the point of view of the hard economy, banks and insurance companies may seem crucial, but from the perspective of the virtual economy, telecommunications and information along with entertainment predominate; indeed, the first two, if not the third, undergird the real power of the banks and insurance companies. Here the United States maintains an unrivaled and largely unnoticed superiority— with consequences for global democracy that demand careful examination.

On *Fortune*'s key 1992 list of the one hundred largest "diversified service companies," eleven specialize in entertainment, telecommunications and information services: of these, eight are American, while only one each is Japanese, British, and Canadian. Of the top one hundred American diversified service companies, only seventeen are entertainment, telecommunications, or information related but these seventeen comprise $140 billion in sales or one-third of the total sales of $421.5 billion for all one hundred companies.[7] One-sixth of the top one hundred companies earn one-third of the revenues. In the following section, the predominance of these companies will be shown to be a matter of much more than just revenues.

Our brief journey from the postwar to the postmodern economy tells a fairly plain story that moves from goods to services, low-tech to high-tech, hard to soft, real to virtual, body to soul. Its lesson for today is that tomorrow's McWorld will be less about resources than about goods, less about manufactured goods than about goods tied to telecommunication and information; less about goods than about services; less about services in general than about information, telecommunication, and entertainment services; less about software per se than about cultural software of the kind found in images and sound bites being manufactured in advertising agencies and film studios. As we follow this logic and move along the economic spectrum it describes, the United States looks better and better and bigger and bigger and the story of the fall of America from economic grace looks more and more suspect. More important, the consequences of the logic, although good for American economic leadership, are bad for democracy. Nation-state capitalism once contributed to democracy's founding: today McWorld's global capitalism may signal its demise.

Yet the full story remains to be told. Because the new information service economy shapes global marketing and sales, it shapes and indeed constitutes the new ideology of McWorld. Capitalism once had to capture political institutions and elites in order to control politics, philosophy, and religion so that through them it could nurture an ideology conducive to its profits. Today it manufactures as among its chief and most profitable products that very ideology itself. Communism collapsed for internal political and economic reasons, but there were external pressures on it as well. Hollywood and Madison Avenue have made the bourgeois revolution practically unnecessary and the proletarian revolution nearly impossible: there are no "workers," only consumers, no class interests, only a global pop culture that flattens economic contours and levels the spiritual playing field. Television, photocopy and fax machines, international travel, and the ideology of fun guaranteed that failing Communist regimes would expire even more expeditiously. These hard goods are, however, only so many vehicles. What they carry is McWorld's videology, which belongs not to the goods sector at all but to the service sector.

The Service Sector: Overview

THE SERVICE ECONOMY is a strange hybrid, including the oldest and most elementary industries like food delivery, education, and health care but also encompassing new age information and communication technologies that are being invented and introduced almost faster than they can be described. The catch-all service category thus lumps badly paid, nonunion hospital workers and no-future fast-food employees together with computer programmers, airline pilots, and information technicians. It includes commercial banks where Japan has long since seized the advantage from America and Europe as well as entertainment companies where American global leadership is actually growing and seems secure well into the next century. Examining the service sector affords an opportunity to make good on my rhetorical amalgamation of McDonald's, Macintosh, and MTV—fast food, computer software, and video—by showing how in this sector McWorld manufactures its own specially tailored twenty-first-century videology. When McDonald's sells *Dances with Wolves* and *Jurassic Park* videos and sundry movie tie-ins in a vague celebration of multiculturalism or environmentalism or extinct reptile preservation, or hires Michael Jordan to link its products to celebrity sport, simple service to the body, I have suggested, is displaced by complex service to the soul. McWorld is a product above all of popular culture driven by expansionist commerce. Its template is American, its form is style, its goods are images. It is a new world of global franchises where, in place of the old cry, "Workers of the world unite! You have nothing to lose but your chains!" is heard the new cry, "Consumers of the world unite! We have everything you need in our chains!"

In order to focus on McWorld, however, I must first sort out the odd bedfellows who cohabit the generic service sector. There are in fact three powerfully distinctive service subsectors that in many ways are more different from one another than they are as a whole from the natural resource and industrial manufacturing sectors. By the measure of training, income, prospects, and self-worth, a Burger King "cook" hand-grilling mass-produced preformed frozen meat patties has a good deal more in common with a sweatshop seamstress machine-stitching cheap frocks than she does with a computer programmer developing virtual reality arcade games, even though the cook and the programmer are in the service sector while the seamstress is in the manufacturing sector. Distinguished by their varying constituencies, my three candidates for subservice sectors are:

The traditional service sector, comprising those who serve people directly with traditional food, transportation, health, and housing services, including food preparers and servers, hoteliers and their helpers, airline pilots and train conductors, doctors and social workers, and all others who deliver services directly to the *individual human body;*

The systems facilitation sector, comprising those who serve the infrastructure—the political, economic, and social systems that make modern society possible; these include lawyers, accountants, economists, bankers, insurance people, computer operators, telephone operators, policy specialists, and anyone else who facilitates the operation and interaction of our national and global systems, all those who serve the *corporate body;* and

The new information sector, what I will dub the infotainment telesector, comprising those who create and control the world of signs and symbols through which all information, communication, and entertainment are mediated, including wordsmiths and image-spinners like advertisers, moviemakers, journalists, intellectuals, writers, and even computer programmers, as well as—to the degree they are in the sign/image business also—teachers, preachers, politicians and pundits, and others who minister to the *individual human and collective corporate soul.*

These three subsectors, each with its own professional (or not so professional) class of employees, stand to each other roughly as the three basic economic sectors (natural resources, industry, and service) stand to each other—in a hierarchy that is also an economic ladder. The new information subsector is on the frontier of economic development and corporations or nations that control it are prospective world leaders likely to dominate the next century. The traditional service subsector is the third world of the services domain, with its dependency at the lower end on relatively unskilled labor and uncomplicated work. It is a first but also quite possibly a terminal step on the stairway to power; it is certainly no ticket to global dominion. Doctors and transportation experts, though part of this first subsector by virtue of the direct consumer services they deliver, are also information technicians who, by the measure of their training and the science on which their service is premised, belong at least in part to the most advanced information subsector as well—just as fast-food workers can be seen as low-skilled manufacturing laborers (they "make" hamburgers). Between the two subsectors that define the parameters is the powerful new world of bankers, accountants, lawyers, and programmers who serve the great corporate entity, part real, part virtual, that is McWorld's global market. Although highly profitable and professionally rewarding, this sector can be overrated. For it neither delivers services directly to the mass of the world's people nor controls the crucial information and telecommunications services on which it wholly depends and that potentially can govern their minds and souls. It is global business's janitor and while it is well paid and makes the machine go it can tell it neither where nor how. That is the task of the infotainment telesector, from which McWorld draws its informal and mostly unarticulated governing norms.

Old-fashioned class analysis associated modes of production with class structure: Marx thus suggested that the ancient slave-master relationship was founded on the sovereignty of human labor (he who mastered labor was master of his world and eventually the political master as well), that the feudal relationship was rooted in sovereignty over land (he who owned the land ruled the world), and that the capitalist relationship rested on sovereignty over capital (he who capitalized machinery and bought labor bought into the ruling class). To the extent there *is* such a relationship between control over the economic mode of production and access to political power (and surely, though it is not as neat as Marx would have it, there is *some* relationship), it is the infotainment telesector of the service economy that is acquiring a certain postmodern sovereignty. She who controls global information and communications is potentially mistress of the planet. Sovereignty here is exceedingly soft, however, entailing rule by persuasion rather than by command, influence via insinuation rather than via coercion. This form of power, scarcely visible, is not easily rendered accountable. Its implications for democracy are in some ways far more disturbing than those that can be inferred from the anarchy bred by Jihad (see Part III).

Since, as the commercial with which MCI sponsored the 1994 Orange Bowl proclaimed, "the universe *is* information," the new semisovereign of this universe is the class of information and communication specialists who make, own, and control the software of our global civilization—the books, movies, computer programs, magazines, videos, theme parks, advertising pages, songs, software, newspapers, and television programs. Ted Turner and Jane Fonda are this new age's model couple, while creators like Disney CEO Michael Eisner and filmmaker Steven Spielberg and superagent Michael Ovitz and communications czar Michael Malone are its true captains of industry. What they control are not the artifacts (the cassette tapes or bound manuscripts or arcade game machines or celluloid that may belong to diverse "American" or "Japanese" multinationals) but the actual words and pictures and sounds and tastes that make up the ideational/affective realm by which our physical world of material things is interpreted, controlled, and directed. The very idea of what constitutes a product putatively serving a "need" is up for grabs—subject to *their* imagination—and those who work the infotainment telesector, in the absence of conscious political will, will inevitably become its default heirs. They may neither actively seek nor even passively wish to exercise power, but inevitably they will have it.

I see no conspirators here, no stealth tyrants using information to secure hegemony. This is rather a politics of inadvertence and unintended consequences in which the seemingly innocuous market quest for fun, creativity, and profits puts whole cultures in harm's way and undermines autonomy in individuals and nations alike. As reality catches up to science fiction, the literary metaphors committed by cyberspace fiction writers look ever less hyperbolic: "First," writes Pat Cadigan in the cyberspace novel *Synners,* "you see video. Then you wear video. Then you eat video. Then you be [*sic*] video."[8] The players understand the economic stakes of seeing, wearing, eating, and being video well enough, which is why Hollywood as the home of Columbia Pictures outranks Tokyo, the home of Columbia's parent company Sony, so that (as we shall see in some detail below) though Sony moved mountains to acquire CBS Records in 1988 and Columbia Pictures in 1989 for a total of nearly $7 billion, they purchased what they cannot possess.

Sony hoped to control and profit from what was being played in its Walkman and Watchman products on which it had built its early economic empire, but the film always owns the camera even when the camera pays for and houses the film. The crux is the live-action images, not the metal-cold, plastic-smooth hardware. McWorld's software underbelly is Hollyworld and it digests those who think they are swallowing it up. Tokyo can buy but will never own Hollywood. American director Robert Altman predicts that "the Japanese will disappear from Hollywood. They infused a lot of money in here. They'll eventually sell that interest out. The Japanese have been made kind of fools of here, and I think they're beginning to get it. They say they don't have any artistic or cultural inputs. So what are they doing here? They're just bankers, and they're being treated like that, and eventually they won't like it."[9] They don't. In 1995 Matsushita sold MCA back to a North American firm (Edgar Bronfman's Seagram). Whether Japanese money stays or goes, it will only be able to lease and take a profit from American pop culture: it can neither create it nor replace it; nor would it wish to do so. To the French, the ideological implications of American hegemony in the infotainment domain are not so subtle: "Of course the U.S. movie industry is a big business," says Marin Karmitz, a French film producer, "but behind the industrial aspect, there is also an ideological one. Sound and pictures have always been used for propaganda, and the real battle at the moment is over who is going to be allowed to control the world's images, and so sell a certain lifestyle, a certain culture, certain products and certain ideas."[10]

There is an irony in the infotainment telesector's primacy today. Of the three traditional economic sectors surveyed and the three service subsectors under review here, none has a greater global ideological and political impact on the nation-state and its democratic institutions. Yet none is less susceptible to national constraints or democratic regulatory public goods; none is more wedded to global market imperatives. Indeed, my prediction that Jihad will eventually (if not any time soon) be defeated by McWorld rests almost entirely on the long-term capacity of global information and global culture to overpower parochialism and to integrate or obliterate partial identities. If the choice is ultimately to be (as the French writer Debray has argued) "between the local ayatollah and Coca-cola"[11]—if "the satellite [TV dish] is exactly against the honorable Prophet, exactly against the Koran"[12]—the mullahs will lose, because against satellite television and videocassettes they have no long-term defense. Over the long haul, would you bet on Serbian nationalism or Paramount Pictures? Sheik Omar Abdul Rahman or Shaquille O'Neal? Islam or Disneyland? Can religion as a fundamentalist driving force survive its domestication and commodification and trivialization as something akin to a fun fiction? A consumer fairy tale? Religion can of course itself have recourse to television and the zealots of Jihad have not always eschewed modern technology. But the conundrum of televangelism usually resolves itself at the expense of religion: the medium here really is the message and its currency is measured by dollar donations rather than souls saved.

Finally, the new telecommunications and entertainment industries do not ignore or destroy but rather absorb and deconstruct and then reassemble the soul. In their hands, it becomes a more apt engine of consumption than the physically limited body. Thirst and hunger are too easily quenched: the yearnings of the soul know no limits at all. When the soul is enlisted on behalf of plastic—even protean—bodily wants, it can guarantee a market without bounds.[13] If the ardent quest for blood community and eternal redemption can be redirected toward the search for satisfaction of an artificially agitated itch, Jihad itself can be commodified.

The remaining task in the extended working examination of McWorld's global markets that makes up Part II is then to scrutinize the information subsector of the service economy. To confront this sector is to portray a certain American monocultural (or pop monocultural) hegemony. Some will want to deny that what we have here is really "culture" at all. When asked to characterize EuroDisney, Ariane Mnouchkine of Paris's Théâtre du Soleil dismissed it as a "cultural Chernobyl." But corrupt culture, commercial culture, even radioactive culture is still culture: that is to say, a pervasive set of common symbols and images that bind together and indeed may even constitute a community.

Others will insist global pop culture is not really American, not really a monoculture at all, that it has been internationalized thanks to English pop music, French high fashion, Italian style, Scandinavian minimalism, and Japanese technology; and of course they will be right. But if "international" means no more than a collection of Western Euro/Anglo/American images packaged and marketed in New York and committed to tape and celluloid in Memphis and Hollywood, "international" is just another way of saying global-American and thus monocultural after all.

Most important, the global culture speaks English—or, better, American.[14] In McWorld's terms, the queen's English is little more today than a highfalutin dialect used by advertisers who want to reach affected upscale American consumers. American English has become the world's primary transnational language in culture and the arts as well as in science, technology, commerce, transportation, and banking. The debate over whether America or Japan has seized global leadership is conducted in English. Music television sings, shouts, and raps in English. French cinema ads are now frequently in English (where American English is to the French as British English is to Americans). New Information Age critics attack the hegemony of CNN and the BBC World Service but they attack it in English. Somalian clan leaders and Haitian attachés curse America, for the benefit of the media, in English. The war against the hard hegemony of American colonialism, political sovereignty, and economic empire is fought in a way that advances the soft hegemony of American pop culture and the English language.

McWorld's culture speaks English first but it possesses an even more elementary Esperanto to which it can turn when English fails. Is there a locale so remote in today's world that a traveler will fail to be understood if he resorts to the brand name–trademark lexicon? "Marlboro? Adidas . . . Madonna . . . Coca-Cola . . . Big Mac . . . CNN . . . BBC . . . MTV . . . IBM!" he will say, and Babel recedes. Not too long ago, asked about what had turned him into a random killer, a sniper overlooking Sarajevo replied: "I am protecting you against Islamic fundamentalism, someone has to do the dirty work. And by the way, how is Michael Jordan doing?" McWorld's integrating Esperanto trumps the divisive hatred of Jihad's killing fields.

The soft hegemony of American pop culture is not just anecdotal. It is everywhere visible in hard data about four key elements of that culture: film, television, books, and theme parks. But it is not limited to such elements, for they are but pieces of a mesmerizing global mediology that suffuses consciousness everywhere. This mediology uses advertorials and infomercials, faction as well as fiction, myth-making and myth-making's modern cousin image-mongering, to make over life into consumption, consumption into meaning, meaning into fantasy, fantasy into reality, reality into virtual reality, and, completing the circle, virtual reality back into actual life again so that the distinction between reality and virtual reality vanishes. Indeed, distinctions of every kind are fudged: ABC places its news and sports departments under a single corporate division; television news-magazines blend into entertainment programs, creating new teletabloids that (in the new parlance) are reality-challenged; films parade corporate logos (for a price), presidents play themselves in films (President Ford in a television special), while dethroned governors (Cuomo and Richards) do Super Bowl commercials for snack food in which they joke about their electoral defeat, Hollywood stars run for office (Sonny Bono, no Ronald Reagan, was elected to Congress in 1994), and television pundits become practicing politicians (David Gergen and Pat Buchanan have crossed and recrossed the street to only mild chastisement from peers). Politicians can do no right, celebrities can do no wrong—homocide included. Nothing is quite what it seems.

Recognizing the power inherent in these forces, corporations from the parallel worlds of publishing, of telecommunication hardware, transmission and software, and of entertainment are fighting for the right to swallow one another up, converging, merging, and buying each other out as fast as financing can be found and stockholders bribed. The courts step in not to preserve a public good nor to impede a developing monopoly but only to assure that stockholder profitability will be the only criterion of a deal (as happened when the Delaware high court insisted Paramount reject a lower "friendly" bid from Viacom and entertain a higher unfriendly bid from QVC). Under the banner of synergy, which is how Mickey Mouse strong-arms the competition, they are doing and spending whatever it takes to secure monopolistic control over what they now see as a single, integrated high-tech mediological package that can dominate the global economy and all of its once diversified markets. While the megacorporations fight, governments (including the government of the United States) sit it out making small clucking noises about free markets, as if no public interests were involved or as if the radically skewed markets of McWorld would resolve matters judiciously all on their own. They cannot and they will not.

Who exactly is to represent the public interest or the common good in this Darwinian world of corporate predators that just happen to control the defining symbolic essentials of civilization remains moot. Few even raise the question. The multiplicity of broadcast and cable spectra has made the old fairness doctrine obsolete and just about put the F.C.C. out of business. A modest regulatory bill cognizant of the new technologies was left twisting in the wind (along with a lot of other legislation) in the 1994 Congress. Even that bill, sponsored by Senator Ernest F. Hollings, was as much about curtailing as initiating regulations pertinent to the establishment of the new information highway and even the Baby Bells (local phone companies) who would have been subject to its regulations were disappointed in its failure since they were depending on it to legitimize their entry into the cable television and long-distance business.

Yet legislating on behalf of the public weal in telecommunications has become almost impossible. The change from earlier years is palpable. When New York's classic music radio station WNCN tried to convert to rock in the 1970s, enraged listeners found a friend in the F.C.C. and the station was constrained to retain its classical format. When in 1993 it again jettisoned the classics, the F.C.C. was nowhere to be found, and WNCN's proprietors were able to make the absurd argument that two classical stations in a city with scores of stations and millions of listeners "saturated" the market, and that one alone would serve. What then will take the place of the F.C.C. or government oversight or democratic regulation and accountability?[15] Is there any hope for what Fred Friendly a dozen years ago called an "electronic bill of rights" in an era where a new Republican Congress is moving to abolish or privatize public broadcasting and dismantle what remains of the federal regulatory apparatus? How can the public be represented by markets that privilege individual consumption, taken consumer by consumer, but have no way of representing public goods—what individuals share and thus what makes them more than consumers? Where are the market incentives to protect public interests?[16]

These questions suggest that, after looking at the four distinctive elements of film, television, books, and theme parks and how they have become at once both internationalized and Americanized, we will need to take notice of the new merger and acquisitions frenzy in the information sector—a vertical integration frenzy in the name of free choice and free markets that could result in a monopoly more perilous to liberty than any dreamed of by mineral and durable goods megamonopolists like John Rockefeller, Sr., or Andrew Carnegie.[17]

6

Hollyworld: McWorld's Videology

To whom or to what belongs this expiring century? Is it the American century? Perhaps. The century of world wars and holocaust? Certainly. The science century? Undoubtedly. But I nominate celluloid and its baby cousin videotape: for more than anything else this has been the Movie Century, an epoch in which film and video and the images they mediate have replaced print and books and the words they once brokered as the chief instrumentalities of human communication, persuasion, and entertainment. Information has been digitalized and computerized and the pace of communication has been accelerated, but sound and pictures are how what passes as "knowledge" gets "communicated" to most people around the globe. The news has moved from print to video so that even newspapers emulate television formats. *USA Today*, for example, is television in tabloid form while even the venerable *New York Times* has gone to color in its advertisement-laden Sunday edition. And many magazines today are available on the Internet.

The table for McWorld has been set by Hollywood. If movable type (along with gunpowder and navigation) brought the medieval world of status, hierarchy, and popular ignorance crashing down in a colossal Re-formation of the human condition and propelled humankind over the threshold of modernity, movable photographic frames (and, in time, scanning ion beams) have challenged the world of print, propelling us out of the modern and into the postmodern. The formats and packaging have changed (television, videos, and computer screens), the content has evolved (music videos, advertorials, and infomercials), and the conduits have developed (cables, satellites, switched phone lines, and fiber optics), but the payoff still comes as moving images that pass before human eyes. These images, reinforced by recorded sound, take the place of words, numbers, and other ciphers with which humans have traditionally communicated. The abstraction of language is superseded by the literalness of pictures—at a yet to be determined cost to imagination, which languishes as its work is done for it; to community, which is bound together by words; and to public goods, which demand the interactive deliberation of rational citizens armed with literacy.

As with the other contributing elements to the culture of McWorld, movies and videos are ever more unitary in content as they become ever more global in distribution. More and more people around the world watch films that are less and less varied. Nowhere is American monoculture more evident or more feared than in its movies and videos. Moreover, as distinctions between phone companies, cable carriers, broadcast media, and software producers melt and elephantine communication corporations mix and merge, monoculture is enhanced, diversity yielding to uniformity and competition giving way to monopoly. With a few global conglomerates controlling what is created, who distributes it, where it is shown, and how it is subsequently licensed for further use, the very idea of a genuinely competitive market in ideas or images disappears and the singular virtue that markets indisputably have over democratic command structures—the virtue of that cohort of values associated with pluralism and variety, contingency and accident, diversity and spontaneity—is vitiated.

Technology experts like Jeff Miller who ask "Should Phone Companies Make Films?" and then, on grounds of efficiency or specialization, answer no, miss the point.[1] Mergers are driven not by coequal interdependency but by the reality of the absolute primacy of programming: the sovereignty of content over the manifold forms it can take in the age of McWorld. Rockefeller bought up the railroads and the distribution network in order to guarantee the flow of oil, the black gold of its time. McWorld's black gold is information and those who own the information "pipes" are rightly drawn to bid for the stuff the pipes deliver. This is no small matter in an economy where the audiovisual industry is the second largest export sector after aerospace—$3.7 billion to Europe alone in 1992, which may hint at why the Europeans (especially the French) were sufficiently alarmed to put the 1993 GATT agreement at risk in order to get audiovisual materials exempted from the new free-trade regulations.[2] "Cinema used to be side salad in world commerce," comments a French observer, "now it's the beef."[3]

With or without resistance, nations with proud traditions of filmmaking independence like France, England, Sweden, India, Indonesia, and Japan are in fact gradually succumbing to the irresistible lure of product that is not only predominately American but, even when still indigenous, is rooted in the glamour of the seductive lifestyle trinity sex, violence, and money, set to a harmonizing score of American rock and roll. Where it survives in other countries, domestic filmmaking is thus mainly devoted to low-budget imitations or blockbuster replicas of Hollywood fare. The new universalism turns out to be little more than an omnipresent American parochialism dubbed into various languages and funded by multinational coproducers. Privatization diminishes state support for filmmakers and leaves them more vulnerable to foreign films at the very moment that free trade leaves fragile domestic film industries unprotected. Local filmmakers cannot begin to compete with the monopolistic international giants that have control over production, distribution, and movie houses (the new multiplex theaters) throughout the world. Coproduction, which permits financial and creative forces from several nations to work together, was once seen as a savior of local film industries. In fact, it has only hastened the liquidation of truly indigenous films. Financing of *The Piano* by French television independent CIBY 2000 hardly makes Jane Campion's award-winning film French.

The Hungarian film industry, traditionally Eastern Europe's most fecund market and still active even in the financially pinched post-

Communist era, has discovered that Hungarian audiences will not support local filmmakers. Dozens of domestic films are made but only a handful are shown in a few small "art" houses in Budapest; the main screens in the large houses are entirely devoted to American product; hence, in Hungary the top eight grossing films of 1991 (as in the preceding several years) were all American (see Appendix B). American filmmakers conveniently conclude that the market has spoken; competitors fear they have been silenced by money and market muscle and the way in which markets and money privilege universal (read: bad) taste.

Even countries with aggressively protectionist cultural policies like Indonesia or France have been unable to stem the American tide. For both political and cultural reasons, Indonesia has tried to protect its cinema. The film industry has been a pawn in wider trade negotiations, however, and was recently sold down the river (or out into the Pacific Ocean) by the government in Jakarta in order to assure continued textile exports to America.[4]

The French have been driven to distraction by American inroads into French cinema audiences, their ire boiling over in 1991 when American films not only led domestic fare in the mass cinema sweepstakes, but—led by the Coen brothers' *Barton Fink*—also managed to completely dominate the Cannes Film Festival, adding the high-culture critics' sublimest prizes to their spoils. In desperation, the French film industry successfully campaigned to have films placed in the same category as fruit and vegetables as a vital national industry in the hope that, as with agriculture, it might be exempted from the free-trade provisions being forced on it both by the Uruguay round of GATT talks and by the Common Market. Former Culture Minister Jack Lang proclaimed all-out "war" against Hollyworld's cultural depredations and rules were established in the early nineties requiring that 60 percent of all video programming on French television be European and 40 percent of music played on French radio and television be of French origin. Why the protectionist panic? Almost into the eighties, American films had managed to secure a purchase of no more than a third of French cinema revenues and were actually lionized by auteur critics who still revered the black tones of earlier gangster melodramas and the vaudeville antics of comedians like Jerry Lewis.

Today although the French still make 150 films a year (versus about 450 for Hollywood) almost 60 percent of revenues go to America and there is little tolerance left. America now controls well over 80 percent of the European market, while Europe has less than 2 percent of the American market.[5] On its opening weekend, the American blockbuster *Jurassic Park* took over nearly a quarter of France's eighteen hundred movie screens in larger towns and cities, provoking an outcry from defenders of local culture such as Lang's successor, Culture Minister Jacques Toubon.[6] Lang had prohibited non–French-language films from competing for the French Oscars (the "Césars") even though this had meant that many French directors who made English-speaking films were shut out (including Jean-Jacques Annaud with his film of Duras's *The Lover* and Louis Malle, with *Damage*). He declared war on American trade representatives and again got audiovisual "products" into the GATT round at the end of 1993. France won the GATT skirmish at the eleventh hour, preserving its quotas and its state film subsidies of $350 million a year. However, with EuroDisney settling into a long run just outside of Paris (despite a very shaky financial start) and with American films and television programs the staple of powerful new "French" pay networks like CANAL PLUS and CIBY 2000, there is unlikely to be an easy way back to the glory years of the fifties and sixties for French filmmakers.

With its 150 films a year, of which perhaps two dozen are exportable, France still has one of the world's great cinema cultures; indeed, it still controls nearly half of what appears on its own screens, and still makes films that are both parochially French and globally distributed as well as universally acclaimed. Compared with Berlin or Budapest, where Hollywood rules, Paris cinemas still screen a great many French films.[7] But major studios are closing and for all the rancorous expletives no one knows how to stop the American tidal wave. A group of European directors wrote an open letter to "Martin" (Scorsese) and "Steven" (Spielberg) imploring them to recognize that the Europeans were "only desperately trying to protect European cinema against its complete annihilation." If films are not exempted from free trade, they predicted, "there will be no more European film industry by the year 2000."[8] Jack Lang must have seen the writing on the screen, however, because even while he was doing battle in the name of culture against the American celluloid colossus, he was decorating Sylvester Stallone with a Legion of Honor.

Vincent Malle, Louis Malle's brother and a producer, has also seen the future: surveying the success in France of the juvenile film that turns Beethoven into a pet Saint Bernard, he sighs: "What works in Chattanooga now works in the Sixth Arrondissement of Paris; it's a little sad."[9] It may be as Charles Grassot, another French producer, says, that "one has to admit that American movie audiences are infantile."[10] But as a potential audience for American pop culture, the rest of the world seems bent on growing backwards into the universal childhood of Hollywood and Vine.[11] Infantilism is a state of mind dear to McWorld, for it is defined by "I want, I want, I want" and "Gimme, gimme, gimme," favorites from the Consumers Book of Nursery Rhymes. And that is not just "a little sad," it is a lot sad.

Surveying the wreckage of Europe's once proudly independent cinema, critic David Stratton observed bitterly that the excitement and discovery of the 1960s, when Bergman, Antonioni, Visconti, Truffaut, Godard, and Buñuel were busy at their craft in nations that possessed vibrant indigenous film industries, were gone with the wind.[12] He lamented that "although probably just as many people are going to the world's cinemas today, they're more likely to be seeing mainstream American films than attending new works by the descendants of Bergman, Godard and the rest."[13] What remains is "the American juggernaut," which manages to overwhelm not only local film industry but rival competitors from abroad. Thus while in 1972 only 86 or one-third of the 255 foreign films shown in West Germany were American, by 1991, 162 or nearly two-thirds of 262 foreign films were American.[14] In Europe today, American films account for about 85 percent of the revenue—about $1.7 billion of the $2 billion in box office receipts.[15] Europe tries as best it can: with French leadership, it passed an E.E.C. regulation requiring all national television stations to maintain 50 percent domestic programming (including movies and series). Pay TV and satellite television has paid little attention, however, and while the measure survived the 1993 GATT round it will eventually yield to market forces via satellite or home video or other new technologies. The time is not so far off when there will be one single image—an American image of America, something like Ronald Reagan's opening shot in his celebrated *It's Morning in America* video, or a burger sizzling on the desert-baked enamel of a Chevy V-8—an image so generic, so affecting, so ubiquitous, and so empty that it will no longer be recognized as American, it will just be.[16]

The dismal story of film in Europe can be duplicated over and over again around the world. In India in 1991, despite its stalwart local film industry, 78 of 124 imported films were American.[17] In revolutionary Iran, where zealous censors banish most imports and encourage "banal, opportunistic, psuedo-revolutionary films, full of pompous political language," *Dances with Wolves* and *Driving Miss Daisy* nevertheless were admitted and found a large audience.[18] Innocuous enough, one might surmise, but in a country where "even the people in charge were confused about what Islamic cinema is" (according to Iranian director Bahram Bayxai), a foot in the door may be the beginning of a kick in the rear end for an insular Islamic culture trying to preserve itself politically and culturally against the West.[19]

These general trends are confirmed in almost every country around the world that makes and shows films in theaters or on television. They define major markets like Japan and Germany that have strong indigenous cultural traditions and define markets that remain closed to Western films like China and Cuba where, although unable to import American trash, they produce trash of their own that imitates the very American obsession with sex, violence, and soap opera, which their own propaganda condemns and their censorship is designed to exclude. Americans notice talented films like Chen Kaige's *Farewell My Concubine* (the first Chinese film to win the Palme d'Or in Cannes, 1993) and Zhang Yimou's *Raise the Red Lantern*. But neither of these films was seen in China in its original cut, and the censors seem harder on serious local fare than on Hong Kong kickboxing films or bloody American suspense melodramas, which are being reproduced and sold in pirated versions in collusion with a Chinese government that has risked heavy American trade sanctions rather than acknowledge the practice. Chinese filmmaker Chen is not optimistic: "A quarter of a century ago, we were crazy about politics. Now we are crazy about making money. Our thinking has not really changed. I am afraid one day we will become money hooligans, without culture."[20] Since McWorld follows economic prosperity, they are unlikely to be entirely without culture: only without their own culture. In its place will be the culture of the money hooligans.

American films dominate the world market in a manner that far outpaces its leadership in any other area. In the new Russia, complains Peter Shepotinik, the editor of a leading Moscow film journal, "it's cheaper to buy and distribute some unknown third-rate American film than it is to make a Russian film these days."[21] The table of top-grossing films in twenty-two countries for 1991, which is reproduced in Appendix B, speaks for itself. Either *Dances with Wolves* (nine first-place slots) or *Terminator 2* (six first-place slots) are in first place in fifteen of the twenty-two countries surveyed. One or the other is in second place in another eight countries. Five other first-place films are also American, including *Robin Hood* and *Home Alone,* which also are favorite second- and third-place choices in many countries. Of the top three grossing films in each of the twenty-two countries (66 films in all), fifty-eight are American. Of the 222 top ten slots in the survey, 191 are American.

Nothing changed in 1992, when *Basic Instinct, Beauty and the Beast,* and sequels like *Lethal Weapon 3* and *Home Alone 2* were (in different slots) in the top five places in all the same countries where anywhere from seven or eight to all of the top ten were Hollywood productions.[22] In monopolizing local markets, America has helped annihilate other exporters and hence has contributed to the troubles of competitors in their domestic industries. Coproductions are supposed to have blunted the American impact, but have had the opposite effect.[23] Would anyone really be expected to think of *Total Recall,* the Arnold Schwarzenegger vehicle of a few years back, as a French-financed movie made by a Dutch director and an Austrian star? Foreign money, immigrant talent, a non-American distribution company are invisible threads in a garment that, to the wearer, looks and feels wholly American.[24] Hollywood on the Seine may bring Europe some California-scale megaprofits, but it will extend rather than contain the ambit of McWorld.[25]

In general, American filmmakers do not leave home to make movies. Rather, the best and most successful of filmmakers elsewhere traditionally emigrate to Hollywood.[26] Chen Kaige, for example, the celebrated Chinese director of *Farewell My Concubine* who is often referred to as an example of how filmmaking can thrive outside Hollywood, followed his film to America where he said in an interview that making an American film is "what I want to do," and cited *The Godfather* as the sort of film he could make.[27] Paul Verhoeven should be a model for Kaige: a foreign auteur gone Hollywood big time with an assiduously nonauteur corpus that includes *Robocop, Total Recall,* and *Basic Instinct.* And so Michel Ciment complains in vain about the "moronic/sophomoric movies churned out by Hollywood for their teenage audiences and tossed like garbage on hundreds of French screens in the dry summer season,"[28] while European auteurs journey to Hollywood to get rich and famous.[29]

There are apparent exceptions to the growing American hegemony. Mexico is enjoying a modest film renaissance for which the success of *Like Water for Chocolate* serves as a token. But much of its industry is occupied with making soft-porn violence for East L.A. barrios and soap operas for the private network TELEVISA as well as for the burgeoning Spanish-language outlets on American cable. And, as in France and other nations that have preserved a local industry, Mexico's film business depends on strong government support (from the Instituto Mexicana de Cinematográfica [IMCINE])—an innovation of President Gortari that may or may not survive and presumably goes against the ethos of free trade. But among strong national film industries, Indonesia's rather than Mexico's is the norm. There, the local industry is dying, "squeezed out," according to critic Philip Shenon, "by the U.S. giant."[30] In October 1992, sixty-six of eighty-one Jakarta movie theaters were showing foreign films. Domestic gems like *My Sky, My Home,* which won awards in Germany and France and (ironically) even in America, cannot find a domestic outlet in Indonesia. "The presence of so many American films," writes Shenon, "has led an entire generation to believe that Indonesia is incapable of producing great movies." According to one twenty-nine-year-old Indonesian (Franky Boyoh), "my friends and I always see American films. There are no good Indonesian movies."[31]

To demonstrate that American films exercise an increasingly mortal hold on the world market's cinema jugular is of course not yet to predict a particular set of cultural consequences: market omnipresence is not the same as determinative influence. Still, American films are everywhere—on global television even more overwhelmingly than on the world's movie screens.[32] They have the status of amusements but they are also likely to inspire a vision of life and to affect habits and attitudes.[33] Hollywood is McWorld's storyteller, and it inculcates secularism, passivity, consumerism, vicariousness, impulse buying, and an accelerated pace of life, not as a result of its overt themes and explicit story-lines but by virtue of what Hollywood is and how its products are consumed. Stories told to a tribe around the campfire, whatever their content, knit people together and reflect a common heritage. Stories that pass through the magic lantern and reappear on a movie or television screen are conditioned by their own particular media context. Disney movies and Disneyland are tied together by gossamer threads that weave mythic stories around cartoon identities that seem to celebrate multiculturalism even as they eradicate real difference; seem to turn active engagement into a new kind of virtual spectator sport; seem to transmute what is supposed to be sharp curiosity into blunt and reactive consumption. At the end of 1993, with great promotion, Warner Brothers Films opened a New York Warner Brothers Studio Store where one could "discover New York's newest entertainment shopping experience." Now studio stores are everywhere. McWorld *is* an entertainment shopping experience that brings together malls, multiplex movie theaters, theme parks, spectator sports arenas, fast-food chains (with their endless movie tie-ins), and television (with its burgeoning shopping networks) into a single vast enterprise that, on the way to maximizing its profits, transforms human beings.

Many people, the great majority in developed countries, a minority climbing toward the majority in developing countries, spend far too much of their time each day in one of the commercial habitations of the new world being "imagineered" (as the Disney people like to say) in Hollywood and its satellites—in front of a TV screen or at a mall or in a movie theater or chewing on fast food while contemplating a promotion for a tie-in movie or buying some licensed piece of bric-a-brac; much more time than they spend in school, church, the library, a community service center, a political back room, a volunteer house, or a playing field. Yet only these latter environments elicit active and engaged public behavior and ask us to define ourselves as autonomous members of civic communities marked by culture or religion or other public values. As wordsmiths yield to imagineers, literate private readers and deliberative public citizens alike are made to feel like endangered species. Speaker Gingrich is working hard to get government off the back of the private sector, but who will get the private sector off the back of civil society?

McWorld calls on us to see ourselves as private and solitary, interacting primarily via commercial transactions where "me" displaces "we"; and it permits private corporations whose only interest is their revenue stream to define by default the public goods of the individuals and communities they serve. NAFTA—McWorld's global strategy in its North American guise—serves American business as well as world markets and is unquestionably a policy geared to the future: but it does not and cannot serve American or global public interests such as full employment, the dignity of work, the creative civic use of forced leisure, environmental protection, social safety nets, and pension protection. McWorld's advocates will argue that the "market" does "serve" individuals by empowering them to "choose" but the choice is always about which items to buy and consume, never about *whether* to buy and consume anything at all; or about the right to earn an income that makes consumption possible; or about how to regulate and contain consumption so that it does not swallow up other larger public goods that cannot be advanced in the absence of democratic public institutions. In McWorld's global market, empowerment lies in the choice of toppings on a baked potato: the rest is passive consumption. When profit becomes the sole criterion by which we measure every good, every activity, every attitude, every cultural product, there is soon nothing but profit. In the empire of the market, the money hooligans are princes and largesse is king.

Films are central to market ideology. Watching them reveals a sameness pervading McWorld that seems as suffocating as the invisible "ether" that was once thought to have suffused the entire cosmos and to have given it the invisible infrastructure that made Newtonian physics plausible. Go into a Protestant church in a Swiss village, a mosque in Damascus, the cathedral at Reims, a Buddhist temple in Bangkok, and though in every case you are visiting a place of worship with a common aura of piety, you know from one pious site to the next you are in a distinctive culture. Then sit in a multiplex movie box—or, much the same thing, visit a spectator sports arena or a mall or a modern hotel or a fast-food establishment in any city around the world—and try to figure out where you are. You are nowhere. You are everywhere. Inhabiting an abstraction. Lost in cyberspace. You are chasing pixels on a Nintendo: the world surrounding you vanishes. You are in front of or in or on MTV: universal images assault the eyes and global dissonances assault the ears in a heart-pounding tumult that tells you everything except which country you are in. Where are you? You are in McWorld.

Go to a live theater and within a few seconds of the curtain rising you will know exactly which region, which city, which culture you are in. Watch television for days at a time and you still may not have a clue as to what planet you are on—unless it is Planet Reebok. There are stylistic differences between McDonald's in Moscow, in Budapest, in Paris, and in London by which they can be distinguished from the original McDonald's franchise opened by Ray Kroc in Des Plaines, Illinois, back in 1955. But squint a little and all the small differences vanish and the Golden Arch is all that remains, a virtual ghost haunting our retinas even on the Champs Élysées in Paris, where its actual display is no longer permitted. Director Alain Corneau's prophetic "world in which there is only one image" has come to pass.

Of course inside a fast-food establishment or even a movie theater, cyberspace is a metaphor. But when it comes to television, cyberspace is virtually the reality—that is to say, is virtual reality.

7

Television and MTV:
McWorld's Noisy Soul

Films are McWorld's preferred software, but television rather than the cinema is its preferred medium; for with television, McWorld goes one on one, the solitary individual and cyberspace confronting one another in exquisite immediacy—with the screen as the perfect nonmediated (im-mediate) medium.[1] Where cinema is limited in time and place, television is a permanent ticket to ceaseless film watching anytime, anywhere. It is a private window on McWorld—providing personal access via computers, satellites, cable, and phone lines to information sources, data collections, shopping centers, banking facilities, and the now almost notorious Internet—that welter of interlinked computers and interactive bulletin boards and video games and information banks and video-marketers and ordinary users that will one day (we are told) replace more or less every other kind of interaction in our lives. We think of the information highway as a way to get from one place to another. But the industry aims at displacing the rigidity of electronic trains with the versatility of cars. Bell Atlantic President Ray Smith thus told reporters at the news conference announcing his failed takeover of T.C.I., America's largest cable operator, "We are providing the flexibility of the automobile. You will be able to go anywhere you want when you want."[2] But like vagrants and adventurers and robbers of old, many of us may not know exactly where we want to go and may end up living on the road, content to ride the highway like solitary bikers once rode Route 1, crisscrossing America to nowhere in particular. Or, to take an adjacent metaphor, a movie screen is to a computer monitor hooked up to the electronic highway as an airplane is to a bird. The airplane does one thing well: it flies from point A to point B and you have to know exactly where and when you want to go. The bird does that too but it can also build a nest, sit on eggs, search for food and feed its young, alight on any surface anywhere, soar, dive, chirp, peck, and scratch. And it doesn't have to have a particular destination. Movie screens show films, period. Television is a portal on the information superhighway and in its own peculiarly electronic manner it soars, dives, chirps, pecks, and scratches.

Projected onto a movie-house big screen, films reach only a small percentage of the world's population for specified and quite limited periods of time. The new interactive systems will permit users to dial up films—entertainment and informational, hard data and hardcore, funny and functional—all on demand so that anyone can watch anything, and buy anything, any time she chooses. Through television, films thus speak potentially to every person on earth twenty-four hours a day.[3]

As movies and television have pursued common programming strategies, Hollywood's creative monopoly over material has increased: indeed, the Americanization of global television is proceeding even faster than the globalization of American films. In England, where football (soccer) and cricket once dominated weekend sports broadcasting, viewers can now watch the NFL Game of the Week, and even in France there is an American football *jeu de semaine*, complete with an American-born announcer whose breathless French description of plays, rendered in an intentionally atrocious American accent, runs on with a gritty Yankee charm along the lines of "alors, quelle finesse! Regardez le quarterbacksneak de Dan Marino, ça marche vraiment parfaitment, n'est-ce pas?! Tiens! Touchdown! Eh, oui, je suis étonné! Quelle jeu! Quel grand show!"

The Anglophilia that characterizes so much of American high culture is reciprocated by the British in low culture. On the tube, Hollywood is the template, with imitations of *Gladiators* and Oprah (in the person of Crystal Rose) joining *Brighton Belles* (a licensed version of *Golden Girls*) and the goofily Amerocentric youth magazine show *The Word*, which features personalities like basketball superstar Shaquille O'Neal, the porn star Jeff Stryker, and a policeman from Albuquerque who had his penis enlarged (though, regrettably, not on camera).[4]

Eastern Europe is chasing its neighbors to the West in the race to catch America in television along with everything else. According to Miklos Vamos, a Hungarian journalist, "Hungarians, Czechoslovaks and Bulgarians try to imitate everything that is American—and I mean *everything*. . . . [T]he state-run financing system of culture doesn't exist any longer, but neither does any network of foundations and other private funds that can be used, as in the West, to support the arts. East European films and literature cannot compete with their American counterparts. If we keep going on like this, our small countries will gradually lose their national cultures."[5] In Budapest they are watching *The Cosby Show* on reruns—though in a German dub since Magyar dubbing is not yet available. In Yeltsin's Russia, TV viewers can watch a rip-off of *Wheel of Fortune* called *Field of Wonders* on which lucky winners receive Sony VCRs into which they can load their pirated cassette versions of wildly popular American films.[6]

Poland does still better, having access to *Wheel of Fortune* itself (dubbed in Polish) along with its own licensed version *Kolo Fortuna*, which plays to 70 percent of Polish households on Thursday evenings. Twenty-five percent of Polish households have access to cable or satellite at relatively moderate cost.[7] Where Jihad and McWorld collide on television there is little doubt about who wins: the Catholic Church may be reasserting itself in areas like abortion (banned in Poland in 1992) and the Communists may be making a political comeback, but the cultural wars are being won hands down by American television. The Church has conceded as much, and elsewhere in Europe is advertising on VH1 and MTV for converts to the priesthood, which is rendered as a kind of new, AIDS-safe form of cool.

In Asia, where wiring homes with cable or fiber optics is not yet financially feasible, satellite is making major inroads. Asian (now

Murdoch's) Star satellite network reaches hundreds of thousands of upscale Indians pining for Western fare. Satellite dishes are showing up in China as well, in flagrant disregard of state laws banning their use in keeping with the war on "spiritual pollution." In 1993, State Council Proclamation 129 prohibited both purchase and possession of dishes. Yet millions of electronic outlaws have installed them and current estimates suggest over a half million "heavenly threads" (the literal translation of satellite antenna into Mandarin) tie 15 million viewers to a side of capitalism the regime is not anxious to promote. Prime Minister Li Peng talks a tough line, but so far no dishes have been removed and it is hard to imagine him winning a war against McWorld, particularly since in other domains of the economy he is working so hard to join it.[8] He has good reason to worry, however, for what the Chinese are seeing courtesy of their dishes is unadulterated Western fare including the BBC, CNN, MTV, and an English-language sports network. The communications firms that serve Asia have not been seduced into diversification by the daunting prospects of trying to find appropriate programs for India and China. On the contrary, as the spectator venues and the distribution conduits keep evolving and multiplying and the markets keep expanding, the messages and the products being churned out get ever more homogeneous. The commercial purveyors of satellite TV are in any case interested in profits not politics, and Rupert Murdoch was not averse to pulling BBC news-programming from Star Television to placate the Chinese government.

The Hong Kong–based Star satellite network originally appeared as an independent Asian rival to Western companies, but four of its five channels are English-language broadcasts and toward the end of 1993 it sold out to Rupert Murdoch's News Corporation for a little more than a half billion dollars. The Australian-born naturalized American Murdoch owns, in America alone, Fox Television, Twentieth Century Fox Film, *TV Guide*, HarperCollins Publishers, and the *New York Post*. In addition to his global newspaper-and-magazine empire, he also controls Fox Television as well as a 50 percent share in British Sky Broadcasting (Europe's dominant satellite broadcaster): with Star TV in his pocket, he adds another thirty-eight nations with a potential audience of two-thirds of the world's population.[9] That means that several billion Asian ears are cocked in his direction. Yet the only thing we know for sure about Murdoch's intentions is that they include neither the preservation of indigenous cultures nor the democratic and civic uses of media and telecommunication networks. He might seem a threat in China, where—as in Singapore—satellite dishes are forbidden (but manufactured by the army and widely used). But Murdoch agreed to withdraw the BBC World News from Star in return for less Chinese resistance, knowing perhaps that it is not CNN or the BBC but MTV that is McWorld's real Trojan horse in alien cultures and hostile states.

Music Videos—McWorld's Noisy Soul

MTV OFFERS A fascinating picture of the rapid changes that have given American television and music a global grip on audiences. The music television video was born only in 1981, an offspring (ironically) of performance art and experimental television on the cultural margin; the kind of work presented at innovative performance studios like the Kitchen in New York. Within five years, the MTV network had become a mainstream colossus, propelling its owner Viacom into a media limelight from which it has preyed ever since on a widening spectrum of rival media outlets. When its owner, Sumner Redstone's Viacom, snatched victory in the war for Paramount from Barry Diller's QVC teleshopping network, Viacom emerged as one of the world's most powerful media monoliths. Meanwhile, though mauled by Viacom, QVC has continued to mall television. But the world's largest electronic mall is neither network television nor the shopping network, but MTV itself that exists exclusively as a marketing tool for the music industry. As John Seabrook has written, "one of the reasons MTV is a landmark in the history of media is that the boundary between entertainment and advertising has completely disappeared."[10]

By the mid-1980s when the group Dire Straits used MTV to launch its megahit "Money for Nothing" (with its own backhanded commercial tie-ins), MTV had gone international. In early 1993, its global audience stood at nearly a quarter of a billion households (60 million in the United States) with over a half billion viewers in seventy-one countries (see map, pages 106–107). The numbers escalate day by day, eclipsing CNN, which, though it is in 130 countries, boasts far fewer viewing households and speaks to yesterday's generation of the over-forty's rather than tomorrow's of the under-thirty's. MTV Europe began broadcasting in East Germany two days before the Wall came down, which, in a certain perverse sense, almost rendered the latter event superfluous.[11]

Indigenous-language MTV programming is available in most countries, but although Orlando Patterson would like to think that "world musical homogenization" is simply "not occurring," young watchers often prefer American, which is, after all, what MTV is promoting. Sumner Redstone, the owner of MTV and three times the average age of his employees there, sounds like Gillette chairman Zeien when he insists that "kids on the streets in Tokyo have more in common with kids on the streets in London than they do with their parents."[12] In Belgium, a Flemish-language MTV program was canceled and replaced by English as a result of complaints from local Flemish viewers.[13] Anglo-American pop accounts for most of MTV's music, and where local groups get airtime they generally imitate the Americans. Critic Helmut Fest complains that local European groups appearing on MTV are consigned to the "ghetto slot—a kind of 'look-how-curious-and-quaint-these-continentals-are' approach."[14] In Berlin, if you get tired of MTV, you can also get the best bands on David Letterman's *Late Night* on another channel.

Asia affects to go its own way, and then marches in lockstep with America. The new Asia Television Network (ATN) is nominally pursuing cultural preservation, and it has started the first all-Hindi network on the subcontinent, but it is simultaneously broadcasting MTV-Europe in order to compete with its rival, Star.[15] Star has its own Asian version of MTV (with plenty of American hits), so Indians and Malaysians and Pakistanis can now choose from two "indigenous" MTV channels that offer the same bland pop American musical fare—or local imitations thereof. Once new media are in place, however conservative the cultural intentions of users, the door is wide open to the outside world.[16]

MTV's audience, united for all its ideological differences and cultural reluctance by satellite and the United Colors of Benetton, includes not just Taiwan but China, not only Israel but Iran and Saudi Arabia, secessionist Georgia as well as progressive Hungary,

Music Television's Reach Around the World

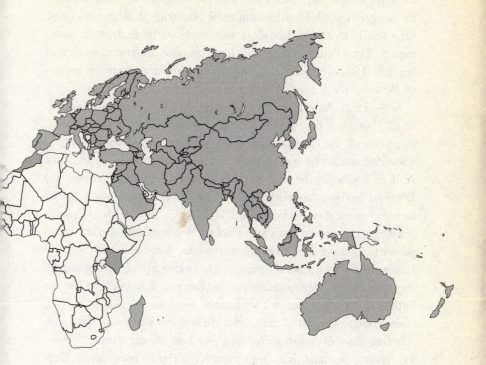

■ Countries that receive Music Television
□ Countries that do not currently receive Music Television

J. Sinclair, 1995

Brazil no less than Mexico, Bangladesh and Vietnam as well as India and Hong Kong, and, along with South Korea, North Korea too (see map, pages 106–107). Satellites have little regard for Jihad and are messengers for McWorld in the most obstinate of ethnic enclaves. One nearly hysterical Islamic youth confesses to an Iranian newspaper, "I can't study anymore, I have become impatient, weak and nervous. I feel crippled . . . so vulgar and stimulating" are the images of Western TV and MTV being beamed down from satellites.[17]

Self-critical Americans worry about MTV's "cultural colonialism,"[18] but when the supposed targets in Eastern Europe are warned, they wave off the caveats insisting that rock music is about freedom— a weapon against both the old Communists and the new nationalists. And, of course, in the near run they are right: in today's reactionary Beograd (Serbia), dissident radio stations like B-92 play Western rock music to signal their disdain for ethnic parochialism, much as Russian dissidents once wore jeans and smoked Winstons and spoke rock to power to unnerve their Communist masters. Just a few years ago, Bill Roedy, MTV's European director, was writing about "being part of the process of democratization in Eastern Europe." MTV, he enthused, "is more than a TV channel. For some audiences, we're a connection to the rest of the world. We're a window to the West with our free flow of information and freedom of expression."[19] Free expression, perhaps, but "information"? "Democratization"? German hate groups also groove to pop music, and supporters of Vladimir Zhirinovsky, the leader of Russia's hard-line nationalist Liberal Democratic Party (which is anything but liberal democratic), established "Zhirinovsky's Rock Store" for "hard-rock fans who have taken up the cause of Russian nationalism."[20]

McWorld's videology churns out an elusive rhetoric. The old masters were tyrants as visible as they were surly, tyrants about whose illegitimacy there could be no question; the new masters are invisible, and sing a siren song of markets in which the name of liberty is invoked in every chorus. Perhaps that is why the authorities in Serbia not only tolerate B-92 but give it a favorable broadcast slot on the official radio station. The station managers insist the station is left alone so the authorities can prove their "liberalism" to the West. But perhaps those authorities recognize how little damage rock music can do to their political policies and imperialist programs. MTV succors liberty . . . of a kind. It is certainly good for the kind of choice entailed by consumption; but whether it is of any use to civic liberty is quite another question. It runs interviews with President Clinton, it sponsors a periodic "Rock the Vote" registration and voting campaign for young people, and like other hip advertisers, plays a game that cynics might mistake for an insincere version of political correctness.

Others argue that this debate takes MTV far too seriously: they dismiss the network as "empty-V"—the mindless music of a generation of preadolescents who will in time move on and up to the BBC, CNN, and NBC. Yet MTV not only shares but helps generate McWorld's videology. A Russian producer, wondering whether cultural life in Hollywood is really an improvement on life under a repressive Stalinism, observes: "Before I had to deceive the censor; then I could shoot my film; now I am forced to look for all the money and materials myself. . . . Instead of being a revered and dominant influence in society, the writer or artist has become a mere creator of cultural values."[21]

To create the cultural values necessary to material consumption is McWorld's first operating imperative. Thirty years ago Disney's little sales-creatures crooned to theme park visitors, "It's a small world, after all." The smalling world is being dumbed down by Beavis and Butt-head and heavy metal music. Cop killer rap is hissing to restive teenage audiences around the globe that to "off" (kill) policemen is necessary, to despise women is cool, and to grow up is unnecessary—even as P.C. recording executives assure us nobody really means any of it. To be sure, MTV is a complex medium with a variety of messages: subliminally, it offers blips savoring freedom and disdaining authority (thus the appeal to resistance movements), it catalyzes consumption (thus the attraction to advertisers), it reinforces identity (we *are* the world!) even as it underscores differences (the Dis-United Colors of Benetton), flirts with violence and makes a (sometimes brutal) sport of sex (women are "ho's and bitches" and men are fucking machines). It celebrates youth, encouraging a forever-infantile obliviousness that defines life in the default mode as passive consumerism. More liminally, it engages in shallow but pervasive political campaigns that are vaguely liberal and empowering though often countercultural and sometimes even scandalizing (as with black rap and hip-hop), but finally as vapid as the vacuously tendentious lyrics of its most scandalous songs.[22] "Rock the vote," it shouts, wrapping Madonna in a flag and urging youth to register. Live Aid, Free Your Mind, Choose or Lose—rock musicians flexing underdeveloped political muscles in the name of causes so safe and universal that the campaigns can do little harm though scarcely much good either.

Political content, to be sure, is hardly a matter of carefully deliberated principle on MTV; more a question of aesthetics, taste—call it hip-hop whimsy. When in the summer of 1993, unruly New York youngsters started sexually harassing girls in the city's overcrowded pools, Mayor David Dinkins talked rap groups into mouthing namby-pamby lyrics like "Don't dis your sis."[23] The lyrics can sell love or hate, can preach neighborliness or urge slaughter, can call for one world, which "we are," and can instigate paranoid fear of foreigners or cops or blacks or whites or even (the old favorite) Jews. At the very moment Madonna was wearing a flag to rock the vote, a well-known Caribbean rapper was urging listeners to off homosexuals while German skinhead groups were swaying to the rhythms of a syncopated xenophobia. The popular rapper Dr. Dre sings to rapt listeners: "Rat-a-tat-tat and a tat like that/Never hesitate to put a nigga on his back." Just-Ice, as popular as Dr. Dre, chants about "faggots" and "bitches," and how when they see "Just-Ice" approach "they move before they get stitches . . . A bullet or a bat,/Just pick it."

Yet the lyrics are not finally the point (just try following them): gangsta rappers think they are using rock to take on the official culture. But of course the official culture owns them rock, stock, and barrel and it is they who are being used. The point is neither the words nor even the music, but the pictures as they image the music and the big sell that goes with the pictures. MTV is about the sound of American hot and American cool, about style and affect where nothing is quite as it seems, where "bad" is good and lovers are bitches and killing is enlivening and where politics doesn't count but pictures are politics. Frank Biondi, the CEO of Viacom, Redstone's company that won the battle for Paramount in 1994 and that owns MTV, tries to explain: "There will be MTV movies, MTV products. Why not? You see Disney going into the cruise business. Maybe there will be MTV cruises and MTV special events. MTV's mission is connecting to the audience, to the MTV Generation. . . . We want to provide a point of view for the MTV Generation. Why do you read the *Times* when you can get almost all the same information on-line? Because you want a point of view, a sensibility. That is what we are selling."[24] It is hard to know exactly what, beyond simple consumption, the impact of selling ambience by promoting rock music will be either in America or on the hundred cultures whose youth are now tuned in to it. It is easy to condemn lyrics weighted with hate, but while plenty of musicians end up with assault, rape, and even murder charges on their rap sheets (rep sheets!), such lyrics are hardly the cause of the brutal realities they mirror or caricature, and breeding anarchy and brutality is clearly not what MTV executives who talk about promoting "freedom, liberation, personal creativity, unbridled fun and hope for a radically better future" think they are doing.[25]

Sharp musicological investigations are desperately needed, for though we cannot perhaps guess what the ultimate impact will be, it is clear that there *will* be an impact unconnected to specific lyrics; and that it is likely to play havoc with the conscious wishes and willed public policies of traditional nation-states trying to secure the common welfare or to conserve their national cultures. MTV wears neither lederhosen nor peasant blouses, and speaks neither Serbo-Croat nor Chinese, and worships neither Buddha nor Jesus, and cares neither for the family nor the state. Finally it trades in dollars, and profit is its only judge. The rockers and rappers may end up in jail, but the record companies and cable stations keep raking in the dough.[26] As Robert Scheer has said in discussing Michael Jackson's recent agon, "what is clear is that (Jackson) is neither a boy nor a man but rather a product. Throughout all but five of his thirty-five years he has been marketed energetically by avaricious adults who condoned his weirdness as long as it was marketable."[27]

Some observers have expressed a naïve confidence in the essentially populist character of television. Michael J. O'Neill is fairly ardent in his belief that television is a form of "people power." He is persuaded that "It is no longer statesmen who control the theater of politics but the theater which controls the statesmen," and in that he is right.[28] But to think that because states have lost control of television, the "people" have acquired it is a dangerous illusion. In Italy, Silvio Berlusconi came to power through control of a media monopoly through which he could sell "dreams and miracles" and pretend to be a populist.[29] But the lines were clear: the people did not control Berlusconi, Berlusconi controlled the people; and Berlusconi did not control television, television controlled Berlusconi. Indeed, it finally brought him down as disinterestedly as it had raised him up. In America, it is often television that makes policy. A single picture of the abused body of an American soldier in Somalia provoked American withdrawal there, and the Pentagon is loath to take casualties nowadays not only because of the ongoing trauma of Vietnam but because of fear of the media. There is no abstract doctrine, not containment, not democracy, not anticommunism, not even imperialism, that can hold out against a video snapshot of a dying American boy.

Some might argue this is a good thing for peace or at least for ordinary people since it is *their* perspective that television purveys. Television, however, purveys no images but its own. If, as Gore Vidal wrote in his brilliant odyssey through film, "he who screens the history makes the history," it is not those whose history is up on the screen but those screening it who will be in the drivers' seat.[30] The medium has its own program driven by Hollyworld's videology and McWorld's corporate balance sheets and it displays American corpses neither in order to influence history nor to condition American foreign policy but to sell advertising and keep viewers glued to their sofas. "TV's basic purpose," writes media critic Mark Crispin Miller, "is to keep you watching," and so the medium moves to "box in" viewers, in and out of the home, displacing their reality with its own.[31] Television spreads a modest flood tide on a flat plain: its waters are everywhere, and though it makes a shallow-bedded sea, and though there are traditional landmarks—newspaper trees and book steeples and many a beckoning print rooftop—millions lose their way and slip under the shimmering images without anyone quite noticing, least of all they themselves. Children have been known to drown in just a few inches of water: television's shallows are more perilous still.

States once did recognize the significance of television as an instrument of propaganda, socialization, and civic education. (The Berlusconis and Murdochs and Turners of McWorld still do.) In the early days, legislators spoke about the "public airwaves" and essayed to regulate "public broadcasting." Television was a state monopoly not only in Communist countries, but in many Western democracies as well, where its potential influence, educational or corrupting, was deemed too important to leave to the private sector—which has displayed little other than a monomaniacal concern for profits and an abysmally bad taste that it passes off as responsiveness to popular will. In the United States, a Federal Communications Act was passed in 1934 establishing the Federal Communications Commission and developing doctrines of fairness, access, and social responsibility (mandatory news programming, for example). The legislation called for the F.C.C. to "study new uses for radio, provide for experimental uses of frequencies, and generally encourage the larger and more effective uses of radio in the public interest."

Today there are few signs that anyone, least of all the federal government, is looking to encourage the larger and more effective civic uses of cable, satellites, fiber optics, computers, and data banks in the public interest. The supposed explosion of media outlets via cable and fiber optics has created an incentive for government to excuse itself from the messy business of regulation. Although Vice President Gore has tried to focus civic attention on the new technologies, new media monopolies (described below) are coming into existence without so much as a glance from federal authorities who once upon a time would have been screaming for antitrust action. Since earlier regulation depended on "spectrum scarcity" (the seemingly finite character of available broadcast wavelengths and delivery conduits), the explosion of media outlets and delivery vehicles—fiber optic communications that can carry millions of digitalized information and picture bytes, cable systems with a five-hundred-plus channel capacity, and satellites—coupled with our current passion for markets and for privatization have delegitimized the very idea of public regulation. They make it impossible for us to use McWorld's chief invention—television—to preserve our public goods and identity against McWorld's values. We cannot even use the public airwaves for public political purpose (elections) without paying the private companies to whom we have licensed those airwaves millions and millions of dollars. Kenichi Ohmae, Japan's most celebrated management guru, captures the spirit of videology perfectly when he puts his faith in the power of "customers to triumph over man as regulator," since "it's the regulators we have to fear."[32]

A few countries still try to maintain some control, if not monopoly control, over the traditional broadcast media, but with diminishing success against the diversifying technologies that undergird new media. As communication shifts from broadcast spectra and cable to computer faxes, telephone lines, and satellites the very idea of governmental regulation—let alone "totalitarian" control—loses its credibility. Congress is currently threatening to privatize or abolish public broadcasting. In theory, this might seem to be a good thing: in dismantling state monopolies, the market puts an end to monopoly altogether. In practice it merely eliminates public monopolies and with them accountability and civic responsibility and leaves the field to new, relatively invisible, private monopolies that, unlike government, are not even accountable in theory, let alone in practice. These monopolies are today becoming ever more visible as companies from the once distinct realms of program creation (software), program distribution (networks and broadcast companies), delivery systems (cable, telephone, satellite), and hardware (the people who make the television receivers and computers) gobble one another up. Rupert Murdoch's News Corporation is headquartered in Sydney, Australia, but it owns a global array of media-interlinked companies and services including, in the United States: Fox Television; Fox Video; *New York* magazine; *TV Guide;* HarperCollins Publishers; Delphi Internet Services; Scott Foresman educational publishers; News and Electronic Data information services; Kesmai video game development corporation; Etak, Inc., the Digital map data company; *Mirabella,* the fashion magazine; and literally dozens of newspapers and independent television stations; and elsewhere, *The Times* of London along with the tabloid *The Sun;* Ansett Transport, an air cargo carrier; B Sky B, the English satellite broadcaster; Star TV, which is the Asian satellite network described above; Geographia Ltd., the cartography company; and Fox Video companies in Spain, Japan, France, Germany, New Zealand, and Australia. Murdoch's News Corporation is a one-company, one-man infotainment telesector unto itself.

The elementary theory of markets argues that with the dismantling of state communication monopolies, monopoly will go while the public interest stays; in fact, the public interest has gone and monopoly has persisted, in new privatized and thus unaccountable forms. There is nothing wrong with profit. As the engine of capitalism, it is a good thing for shareholders, consumers, and society at large. But it has turned out to exercise a sovereignty no less coercive but far less public-spirited than the state's. It imposes a uniformity all its own, but one hidden behind the screen of free-market competition. Murdoch's global influence may be scarcely recognized, let alone felt. Hollywood's hegemony may feel good—certainly it feels better than Stalin's or Deng's or Honnecker's—but it may be as depressingly uniform in its formula hits as Socialist Realism was in its heroic monuments. The common currency of sex and violence may be minted by an uncoerced (if arduously manipulated) private market, but it depreciates as quickly as greenbacks minted by a state that has gone off the gold standard. Under Soviet communism, dissident poetry could be published only surreptitiously and read only in private. Under Russian capitalism, dissident poetry isn't published at all, in part because there is nothing obvious to dissent from, but mainly because poetry doesn't make a profit and cannot compete with Stephen King. French policy scientist Dominique Moisi's lament about France applies around the world: "There is less and less of France abroad, and more that is foreign in France."[33]

As television and computer information takes to the telephone wires, which in turn either become fiber optic or get tied in to the new "switched" networking capabilities that let old-fashioned phone wires carry much heavier two-way traffic, software producers will have ever greater access to the world's population.[34] From their point of view, the goal is an instantaneous, interactive, holographic, enhanced sound/real picture virtual network in which every human on earth can be accessed by every other human being and everyone is linked to every company with something to tell or to sell, whether a durable good, a service, some species of information or entertainment, or an explicit political message—albeit in McWorld's videology entertainment *is* the political message. Will this increase real choice? Multiplying the access routes and diversifying the delivery systems will not necessarily increase product pluralism or program diversity. It could mean a thousand different new ways to promote and sell just one universal product—Coke, the Simpsons (either ones, the Barts or the O.J.s—you choose), Michael Jackson, or a candidate for political office.

The distance between Paramount Pictures and the Home Shopping Network was shrinking long before QVC tried in vain to acquire Paramount or the Internet offered computer shopping services. Five hundred channels will not necessarily make viewers feel freer than fifty or even five, and in any case, with the same old handful of cultural providers offering the programming, there will not necessarily be greater variety: only a different and far more effective monopoly and a radical segmentation of what will remain the same old markets: American pop culture instead of Indonesian pop culture; a global political policy forged by markets rather than French state policy forged by technocrats; an unofficial MTV aesthetic rather than an official Hindi cultural line. And such differences as are built into special "narrowcast" programming of the kind the multiplication of channels will facilitate are likely only to divide viewers into horizontally segmented consumer markets—a sportsman's channel and a couch potato's channel, a Latino mutual fund holders' channel and a Jewish gold standard channel, a gay Republicans' channel and a Democratic smokers' channel.

Choosers are made, not born. For free markets to offer real choice, consumers must be educated choosers and programming must proffer real variety rather than just shopping alternatives. Much of McWorld's strategy for creating global markets depends on a systematic rejection of any genuine consumer autonomy or any costly program variety—deftly coupled, however, with the appearance of infinite variety. Selling depends on fixed tastes (tastes fixed by sellers) and focused desires (desires focused by merchandisers). Cola companies, we have seen, can no more afford to encourage the drinking of tea in Indonesia than Fox Television can encourage people to spend evenings at the library reading books they borrow rather than buy; and Paramount, even though it owns Simon & Schuster, cannot really afford to have people read books at all unless they are reading novelizations of Paramount movies. By the same logic, for all its plastic cathedrals, Disneyland cannot afford to encourage teenagers to spend weekends in a synagogue or church or mosque praying for the strength to lead a less materialistic, theme-park-avoiding, film-free life. Variety means at best someone else's product or someone else's profit, but cannot be permitted to become no product at all and thus no profit for anyone.

When Channel One brings television advertising into the classroom, teachers can be sure it is not in order to provide an audiovisual tool for teaching critical thinking.[35] Without a concerted pedagogical effort, television is unlikely to enhance learning: it is better at annihilating than at nurturing the critical faculties. Private consumption cannot help youngsters develop an empowering sense of the need for public goods—something that might throw the very premises of McWorld into doubt. Television enmeshed in commerce cannot but view schoolchildren as prospective consumers rather than prospective critics and citizens.[36]

Education is unlikely ever to win an "open market" competition with entertainment because "easy" and "hard" can never compete on equal ground, and for those not yet disciplined in the rites of learning, "freedom" will always mean easy. Perhaps that is why Tocqueville thought that liberty was the most "arduous of all apprenticeships." To grow into our mature better selves, we need the help of our nascent better selves, which is what common standards, authoritative education, and a sense of the public good can offer. Consumption takes us as it finds us, the more impulsive and greedy, the better. Education challenges our impulses and informs our greediness with lessons drawn from our mutuality and the higher goods we share in our communities of hope. Government, federal and local, with responsibility for public education once took it upon itself (back when "itself" was "us") to even up the market and lend a hand to our better selves. Now via vouchers the market threatens to get even with public education. This sorry state of affairs is not the work of villains or boors. It arises all too naturally out of the culture of McWorld in a transnational era where governments no longer act to conceive or defend the common good.

8

Teleliterature and the Theme Parking of McWorld

As SURVIVORS OF aging print technologies, books are relics of a slowly vanishing culture of the word—democracy's indispensable currency and a faltering bulwark against the new world of images and pictures flashed across screens at a speed that thwarts all deliberation. Democracy, like a good book, takes time. Patience is its least noticed yet perhaps most indispensable virtue. Television and computers are fast, fast, faster, and thus by definition hostile to the ponderous pace of careful deliberation upon which all public conversation and decision making on behalf of the common good is premised. One reason it is hard to use the speed-of-light medium of television for civic education is that while television wants to fly, education lumbers along with all the ponderous tedium of a deliberate and prudent pedagogy. It is unwatchable—unless the aim is to learn and to grow. Finally, educational television is a contradiction in terms.[1] Where then do books belong in our videoland helter-skelter? They belong not at all—unless they acquiesce to assimilation and takeover and become one more genre in the infotainment service telesector's commercial culture, what we can call teleliterature.

Assimilation of the new for publishers entails modification (read: adulteration) by the very technologies by which they are being supplanted, and the book format is particularly vulnerable to computer technology. TECHNOLOGY THREATENS TO SHATTER THE WORLD OF COLLEGE TEXTBOOKS, screams a *Wall Street Journal* article, which features the somber warning, "If textbook publishers don't wake up and learn how to make, market and distribute something other than a book, the rug will be pulled right out from under us."[2] The Authors Guild is sufficiently impressed to have alerted its members. In a "Position Statement on Electronic Publishing Rights," it announces that "publishing technology is changing fast, and a writer's work can now be made available in many forms—on databases, CD-ROM discs, and CD-Interactive (Cd-I) discs, among others. New technologies make it easy to combine works of journalism, literature, art, photography, music, and film and video in multimedia and interactive formats." Costs for publishers for these formats are "far lower than for traditional publishing," it adds.[3]

Disc manufacturers would rather not pay royalties, of course. A company called Bureau Development has gathered together hundreds of excerpts from antique public domain (i.e., no royalty) editions of classic works, thus often of lesser quality, sometimes bowdlerized, and put them on a "Great Literature" CD-ROM disc. The postmodern reader's ticket to the classics requires "a PC or a PS/2 compatible computer, a CD-ROM drive that supports the ISO-9660 standard, with interface card, cable and software, Microsoft Extensions version 2.0 or later, a minimum of 640K RAM, with 500K available, and DOS 3.1 or later." It's a little more complicated than opening a book, but once you have the equipment "you can run Great Literature directly from CD-ROM drive. Simply log onto the CD-ROM drive and type LIT."[4] New-format great literature may be as little read and innocuous as faux leather "Great Literature" sets of the kind that have decorated the homes of television-watching nonreaders for decades, and CD-ROM formatting certainly need not directly alter literary content any more than textbooks re-created as videotext communicate in anything other than words.

Once they are on CD-ROM discs, however, allied technologies press in on old and new books alike. Meg Cox reports in the *Wall Street Journal* that as the new computer technologies displace textbooks, "assignments will routinely include multimedia projects, mixing words with sound and video."[5] Bureau Development's Personal Library on disc comes with pictures and sound that turn some of the great works into virtual *son et lumière* shows. When books become subordinate to multimedia projects and words are tied to pretty pictures, print culture is put at risk.

The status of books in McWorld today teaches lugubrious lessons about the corrupting reach of the image makers into the world of print and via that world, into the world of democracy. When we allow Chris Whittle to insert advertisements into books and television (with ads intact) into public school classrooms, literacy and literary pleasure clearly are no longer our aim. When a single picture of a brutally abused soldier's corpse takes the place of careful debate and the reasoned discourse of words in forging political foreign policy priorities, democracy itself as a deliberative practice is jeopardized.

Television and film do not, to be sure, wholly displace books. Rather, they are parasitic on them. Rather than making television literate, television tends to make books illiterate. Howard Stern and Rush Limbaugh "write" best-sellers that are extensions of their radio and television personalities. Reading becomes another form of gossip—as in the O. J. Simpson "book," published in conjunction with his televised murder trial. Given the scarcity of readers, the trick is to publish books that people who do not read books will nevertheless buy, whether or not they actually read them: for in McWorld, consumption demands only that we purchase but not that we actually utilize products, many of which we do not actually "need" in the first place. An avalanche of embarrassingly huge-selling how-to books finally led *The New York Times Book Review* to remove them from the regular best-seller list, for they had come so thoroughly to dominate it that "real" books had ceased to be competitive. But the how-to's were quickly replaced not by real books but by genre novels designed explicitly to meet the imperatives of a quick and lucrative film sale. In the fall of 1993, of the top ten "fiction" listings on *The New York Times* list, seven were filmic suspense thrillers by just two authors: Michael Crichton and John Grisham, whose previous books included the recent film megahits *The Firm* (Grisham) and *Jurassic Park* (Crichton). Indeed, in 1994 both authors sold future books—then not yet written, let alone published—to Hollywood for millions of dollars.

To be sure, suspense and mystery novels geared to movie adaptation have topped best-seller lists for a long time. Media incest has been spreading, however, and now dominates the nonfiction list as well. *The New York Times* nonfiction best-seller list for November 28, 1993, listed five media-linked best-sellers in the top fifteen, with "books" by TV conservative Rush Limbaugh, trash-radio star Howard Stern, and comedian Jerry Seinfeld in first, second, and fourth place. William Shatner's *Star Trek Memories* followed in ninth place with Michael Jordan's NBA memoir *Rare Air* in fifteenth on the hardback lists and simultaneously in second place on the nonfiction softcover list, right behind an earlier book by Limbaugh that was first among paperbacks—giving Limbaugh the top place on both lists. During the same week, *MTV's Beavis and Butt-head,* a cartoon book based on the MTV series (whose banal cruelty and teenage knownothingness had forced producers to move it out of prime time to a later time slot), was fourth on the "Advice and How-To" list. The fastidious *New York Times* not only reported on but contributed to this dazzling mediocratic spectacle, offering both daily and Sunday reviews of Howard Stern's exercise in confessional porn (over a million books in print within a few weeks of publication and possibly the fastest selling book in publishing history) by reviewers who were astonishingly polite and respectful, as if they had before them a slightly puzzling but not unpleasing work of postmodern skepticism from a delightful cultural eccentric—an FM Oscar Wilde for our own radio times.[6] Howard Stern himself recognized how pusillanimous the "literary" marketplace was. On the air, he confided to listeners that he was already the master of radio, and everything he knew about books and publishers persuaded him that they were an easy mark. So they proved to be. When literature becomes an outpost of McWorld, laying siege to it presents little challenge to commercial hustlers of Stern's audacity or Limbaugh's hubris.

The chief importance of writers and celebrities in McWorld (and of course the point here is precisely that the distinction between the two is fading),[7] is as food for the endless appetite of television and film for "story" and "story lines," for plot and character, and for perverse personalities and salably scandalous "real-life" happenings. This is why the pursuit of Paramount by Viacom and QVC was also a hunt for Simon & Schuster and why the German publishing colossus Bertelsmann bought itself a new skyscraper in New York's image and entertainment center, Times Square. It is why political films starring not just elected officials but the backroom operators who spin their careers—films like *The War Room* (about colorful James Carville's role in Clinton's presidential election victory)—become establishment cult hits. Norman Ornstein, a careful and moderate conservative Washington political analyst, comments: "Recently, there's been a real blurring of the lines between Hollywood, New York and Washington about who the celebrities are. We have actors playing public-policy figures and public-policy figures playing actors, and I can't believe that any of this is particularly healthy for the republic."[8]

American books are making inroads on global book publishing that parallel the story of films and television. Best-selling books in Russia, Switzerland, Brazil, England, and Holland nowadays mimic best-selling films: they are strictly American. Der Boekerij, a leading Dutch publisher, carries a list on which 90 percent of the books are foreign translations and almost all of those translations are of American books. They have made the long journey from Anne Frank to Amy Fisher without a hint of embarrassment, scoring at the end of 1993 with their best-selling translation of Fisher's memoir.[9]

In Eastern Europe and Russia, the prospects for literature are even more dismal. Socialist realism was a challenge that sparked a powerful literature of resistance. Commercial realism attests only to the irresistible power of the market. A Russian commentator reports that "publishers—both the old ones who have been freed from the party line yoke, and the new private or joint-stock ones—are not looking for bright and original texts. They are looking for marketable merchandise."[10] Pirated translations of science fiction, detective stories, and erotica flood the bookstalls, driving out local fare other than tepid imitations such as *A Book on Delicious and Healthy Food* and *Sex and a Woman's Life*. In the anarchic Russian economic climate, publishers spring up everywhere (four hundred new ones in the last few years), but reading is in a decline and readers' tastes are plummeting in almost perfect consonance with the rise of the market. Commerce offers incentives that are even more damaging to literature than the defunct censor's erstwhile prohibitions. Russia under the tsars and the commissars alike oppressed the body, yet oppression also seemed to feed the soul. Jean-Paul Sartre once remarked that he had never felt so free as under the Nazi occupation. In opposition, literature has a purpose; in the market, it must vie for dollars, appease popular taste, and guarantee profits to publishers. What was the Ministry of Culture under the Soviets has become the Ministry of Culture and Tourism under Yeltsin.

In what was formerly East Germany, a Leipzig distributor responded to the arrival of the free market by burning 10 million inexpensive volumes printed under the old regime, including works by dissident literary figures such as Stefan Heym and Christa Wolf (who fled to Malibu thinking perhaps that it was better to embrace McWorld voluntarily than to be ravished by it against her will). By the lights of McWorld's videology, commercial book-burnings to raise prices (like the shredding of unsold paperbacks in the West) have nothing in common with book burnings to repress literature (such as the Nazi bonfires of the thirties); but for authors and readers the difference may be hard to discern, and for literary culture, what happened in Leipzig in 1991 may be more fateful than what happened in Leipzig in 1934. In a typically ironic lyric in his poem "The Book Burning," Bertolt Brecht, finding that he has been left out of the bonfire, implores the incendiaries, "Burn my books too! What is wrong with my books that you are not burning them?!" But what modern author would think that his integrity depended on the demand that his works be relegated to a fire whose object was to raise book prices? In a sad postscript to the Leipzig funeral pyre, the Göttingen Literary Society awarded its "Göttingen Laurels" to the Reverend Martin Weskott for his efforts to save a half million books from "dumpsters and garbage cans" and put them to "the use for which they were intended" by selling them at charity auctions and donating the proceeds to "Bread for the World."[11] Swords into plowshares and words into bread.

If publishing mimics the film industry after which it panders in its globalizing distribution patterns, it also imitates it in its zest for internal monopoly. A free and democratic society depends on competition of ideas and heterogeneity of outlets; yet the number and variety of book, magazine, and newspaper publishing firms has undergone persistent contraction at least since the 1960s while the reach of the remaining monopolies has been globally extended. Ben

Bagdikian has been tracking the conglomerating tendencies of media for a number of years, and his statistics point unwaveringly to ever-increasing concentration.[12] Bagdikian notes that after World War II, 80 percent of American newspapers were independent; by 1989, 80 percent were owned by chains. In 1981, twenty corporations controlled over half of the nation's eleven thousand magazines; by 1988 those twenty corporations had become three.[13] Bagdikian estimates that just twenty-three corporations control "most of the business in daily newspapers, magazines, television, books and motion pictures."[14]

Bagdikian's dominant twenty-three corporations:
1. Bertelsmann, A.G. (books)
2. Capital Cities/ABC (newspapers, broadcasting)
3. Cox Communications (newspapers)
4. CBS (broadcasting)
5. Buena Vista Films (Disney; motion pictures)
6. Dow Jones (newspapers)
7. Gannett (newspapers)
8. General Electric (television)
9. Paramount Communications (books, motion pictures)
10. Harcourt Brace Jovanovich (books)
11. Hearst (newspapers, magazines)
12. Ingersoll (newspapers)
13. International Thomson (newspapers)
14. Knight Ridder (newspapers)
15. Media News Group (Singleton; newspapers)
16. Newhouse (newspapers, books, magazines)
17. News Corporation Ltd. (Murdoch; newspapers, magazines, motion pictures)
18. New York Times (newspapers)
19. Reader's Digest Association (books)
20. Scripps-Howard (newspapers)
21. Time Warner (magazines, books, motion pictures)
22. Times Mirror (newspapers)
23. Tribune Company (magazines)

Vertical integration and horizontal integration go hand in hand: the imperative is to own deep and own wide. If you own movies, buy book companies and theme parks and sports teams (Paramount acquiring Simon & Schuster, Viacom buying Paramount). If you own hardware, buy software (Sony swallowing Columbia). If you own television stations, buy film libraries (Turner imbibing MGM's library). If you own telephone wires, buy software. It is not just a matter of eliminating the competitors who are trying to profit by doing the same thing you do; it is a matter of buying up all the people who do what you don't do, but what nevertheless impacts on your business. If you own wires, get programming to push through the wires. If you own a film studio, get a satellite station so you can control subsidiary broadcasting rights. If you are into newspapers, buy cable and satellite systems and then you will own the news in every medium. If you make movies, buy publishers and leverage the writers. If you are on your own, create a new leviathan: imitate Steven Spielberg, the world's most successful director; Jeffrey Katzenberg, a rich and powerful producer recently cut loose from Disney; and David Geffen, billionaire recording executive. And join up, conjure a little synergy: make a deal with Bill Gates, chairman of Microsoft, to produce interactive, multimedia entertainment products. Get a half-billion-dollar investment from Gates and call the joint venture (what else?) Dreamworks. The newspapers compared the deal projected by this triumvirate to the founding of United Artists by Mary Pickford and her friends sixty years ago, but that would be to compare a flotilla of battleships to a couple of cap-gun-toting kids in a rowboat. Steven Spielberg was closer to the mark when he apparently misspoke himself and declared he was founding a "new country."[15]

Skeptics will insist, looking at the haplessness of Sony and Matsushita in the moving-picture business, that ownership does not touch artistic independence and that who owns publishers does not really matter. Certainly that is what Richard Snyder, the longtime chief of Simon & Schuster, dutifully said when Viacom took over Simon & Schuster's parent company Paramount. Regarded as both invulnerable and indispensable, too entrenched and too invaluable to fire, Snyder was gone within a year of the takeover, leaving stunned observers like agent Mort Janklow saying that Viacom must think selling books is like selling popcorn.[16] What Viacom knows is that in McWorld's global markets selling books *is* like selling popcorn: that's the whole point. Otherwise, why buy Paramount? Under Viacom, Paramount has also taken over Macmillan Publishing Co., Inc., another major publisher. Before the merger was even completed, Paramount announced it would "reorganize divisions, reduce the number of imprints and published titles and lay off up to ten percent" of the ten thousand employees of the firm.[17]

In fact, far from being the exception to merger mania, the book business follows the rule. As early as the 1960s, major corporations, many of them defense contractors including IBM, ITT, Litton, RCA, Raytheon, Xerox, General Electric, and Westinghouse, invaded the textbook business. Since then film and telecommunications companies, even as they fell prey to larger industrial corporations, had themselves been feeding on publishers. Bowker's *Books in Print* lists nearly 26,000 publishers but Bagdikian estimates that there are 2,500 or so that actually publish a book or more a year. Yet just six companies take in over half of the total book-sales revenues—Paramount (what was Snyder's Simon & Schuster; Ginn & Company); Harcourt Brace Jovanovich (Academic Press); Time Warner (Little, Brown; Scott Foresman); Bertelsmann, A.G. (Doubleday, Bantam, as well as RCA Records and Arista); Readers Digest Association; and Newhouse (Random House, *The New Yorker*).[18] Five of these are involved in other media including television, two in filmmaking directly; one—Time Warner—is simply the largest media corporation in the world, as well as the second largest cable company and among the largest publishing companies.

The trends are similar across the Atlantic where Bertelsmann in Germany, Murdoch's News Corporation in Australia and England, and Hachette in France have become planetary Goliaths in a world without many prospective publishing Davids. Bertelsmann once was a German publisher, much as Honda was a Japanese motorcycle manufacturer. Now, with its formidable megalith marker in New York's Times Square, it runs book clubs in England, publishes American magazines like *Parents,* owns Doubleday, Bantam, and Dell, has taken over the Literary Guild, and is active in records through its RCA and Arista labels. Along with seventy-four magazines around the world, France's Hachette (which controls nearly a third of French-language books published along with *Paris Match*) publishes the *Encyclopedia Americana,* controls the largest distributor in the Spanish-speaking world, and distributes newspapers and magazines in Germany, Britain, Belgium, and the United States.[19] I have already described the one-man media octopus that is Rupert Murdoch's News Corporation, Ltd., and will only add that in the context of print, in addition to HarperCollins and partial interests in Viking, Penguin, and Reuters, it controls two-thirds of Australia's newspaper circulation, one-half of New Zealand's, and a third of Britain's. Murdoch also happens to be the world's largest distributor of video-cassettes—from which an increasing majority of film profits derive and on which the viability of his publishing interests increasingly depend.

When books become a niche category for media octopi like Murdoch or Viacom with commercial entertainment tentacles and political information (news) tentacles and television tentacles and publishing tentacles, but no civic or literary torso, the future of the word and the civic and literary cultures it supports becomes extremely uncertain. When words are subordinated to pictures (film, television, or videocassette) whose producers are indentured to profit, democracy is unlikely to be a beneficiary. Imagine (not hard today) a court in which pictures are the only arguments: will there be the possibility of justice? Imagine a debate conducted in the flash-card imagery of MTV: can there be deliberation? Imagine imagination without words: does it ennoble or debase? Or simply cease to exist? Imagine an ontology, a science of the real, conceived in cyberspace: reality itself is transmuted into a virtual cousin, a species of the extant consisting in equal parts of pretense, illusion, and deception. Virtuality displaces reality, and Plato's Cave, where flickering shadows dancing on a smoky wall are our only clue to the "real," becomes the whole of our world. Words open the soul's window to ideas and the discourse of words is how we grope our way to conversation and, when conversation can be stripped of its inequalities and hidden hegemonies, how we eventually become capable of cooperation, of common life with others, and even of justice. Where democracy thrives on words—conditioners of rationality and commonality and equality—commerce prefers pictures. For pictures are drivers, even conjurers, of need. As need trumps reason, so pictures trump words, at least in the absence of education and hard work. Books into pictures is a devastating development for literature. Image factories in control of books is a devastating development for democracy.

McWorld as a Theme Park

THERE IS NO better emblem of the transformation of reality by commerce and the displacement of the actively imaginative reader by the passively receptive spectator than the commercial theme parks that increasingly dot our landscape. They are temples to modernity, our secular churches in which the values of play, health, fun, travel, leisure, and the American way are sanctified in a painless liturgy that draws together entertainment, information, and an effortless hint of instruction. The themes in McWorld's theme parks are the themes of McWorld.

I mean to use *theme park* generically, not just to allude to the Six Flags parks and Walt Disney Worlds and MGM Studios, but to highway commercial strips, malls, and chain eateries. There is a sense in which McDonald's is a theme park: a food chain featuring its own Mickey Mouse (Ronald McDonald), its miniature nonmechanical rides in the "playlands" outside, its commercial tie-ins with celebrities like Michael Jordan and Larry Bird and with hit films like *Dances with Wolves, Batman Returns,* and *Jurassic Park,* and its pervasive claim on American lifestyle—all of which make it far more than just a fast food restaurant chain.[20] Its annual report rightly focuses on the role of "one of the strongest brand names in the world, with instant recognition" as it seeks to position itself as "the leading foodservice retailer in the global consumer marketplace."[21] It opens as many as one thousand new franchises each year,[22] and can boast that one of its newer branches overlooks the intersection in Tiananmen Square where a seeming eon ago a young man captured the imagination of the world by stopping a column of tanks dead in its clanking tracks. It spends $1.4 billion a year on advertising, and projects a planetary capacity of forty-two thousand restaurants (only fifteen thousand built so far).[23]

Jim Cantalupo, president of international operations, explains how McDonald's "is more than just price. It's the whole experience which our customers have come to expect from McDonald's. It's the drive-thrus . . . it's the Playlands . . . it's the smile at the front counter . . . it's all those things . . . the experience."[24] Brand names sell an experience, and the experience becomes the defining attribute of a food marketplace that is also a theater of consumption and a theme park of lifestyles. The experience sold must be more than just a quick lunch. Fast food fits life in the computer world's fast lane, the bites and the bytes propelling our bodies and minds through the day at breakneck pace, not a second to lose. Eat fast and serve the business world's god of efficiency. Serve yourself and reduce the number of jobs available. Stand up and eat or take it with you, and transform eating from a social into a solitary activity. Switch (in Eastern countries) from rice or vegetables to meat and increase fat intake, medical costs, and the pressure on agriculture (growing grain to feed cattle that go into the beef we eat is radically inefficient, using up to ten times more grain than is consumed by humans who make grain their diet). The McDonald's way of eating is a way of life: an ideology as theme park more intrusive (if much more subtle) than any Marx or Mao ever contrived.[25] The theme park metaphor rests on the theme park reality.

Theme parks have their origin in the great world's fairs and industrial expositions that, in the nineteenth and early twentieth centuries, were intended as Enlightenment advertisements for a better future by the people who were converting science into industry and technology into commerce for an already globalizing market. In his vivid essay "See You in Disneyland," Michael Sorkin cites Prince Albert's address at the opening of the 1851 London Exposition. Speaker Gingrich has nothing on Prince Albert, who is remarkably up-to-date in his futurological enthusiasm:

"[W]e are living at a period of most wonderful transition which tends rapidly to accomplish that great end to which indeed all history points—the realization of the unity of mankind. . . . The distances which separated the different nations and parts of the globe are rapidly vanishing before the achievements of modern invention, and we can traverse them with incredible ease. . . . [T]hought is communicated with the rapidity, and even by the power, of lightning. . . . The products of all quarters of the globe are placed at our disposal, and we have only to choose which is the best and cheapest for our purposes, and the powers of production are entrusted to the stimulus of competition and capitalism."[26]

If, as Sorkin suggests, "the Prince Consort's evocation of a world shrunk by technology and the division of labor is the ur-theme of the theme park," then it is also the leitmotiv of McWorld and Prince Albert is the natural progenitor of Ronald McDonald (Sorkin calls the Prince a "mouseketeer avant la lettre") as well as of cyber-enthusiast Gingrich.

Whatever the genealogy of the theme park, it finds its most common outlet nowadays not in the specialty fairgrounds in Anaheim and Orlando but in shopping malls all across the country. For these malls are entertainment plazas built around the multifaceted pleasures of shopping. Once upon a time, stores found a home in downtown neighborhoods among workshops, churches, restaurants, theaters, schools, and town halls as elements in an architecture of public space that integrated shopping into other public activities and at the same time gave to commerce an appropriately complementary and utilitarian role. The isolation of commercial space from every other kind of public space hinted at by the world's fairs and certified by mall development has allowed commercial consumption to dominate public space, transmuting every other human activity into a variation on buying and selling. Margaret Crawford, an astute student of mall culture, has noticed that the express aim of the developers is to contain the entire world within the shopping plaza. She cites one of the builders of the world's largest mall, who at the opening ceremony boasted: "What we have done means you don't have to go to New York or Paris or Disneyland or Hawaii. WE have it all here for you in one place, in Edmonton, Alberta, Canada!"[27] Joan Didion has suggested that malls are actually addictive, a space where "one moves for a while in an aqueous suspension, not only of light, but of judgment, not only of judgment, but of personality."[28] The boundaries that separate the mall from the world are intended to remove every boundary between what goes on inside the mall and in the world: very few exits, no clocks. As fast food energizes consumers to shop ("dining" takes time away from shopping) and movie multiplexes provide entertainment incentives to consumption, so the architecture of mall space—

the placement of stairways, the grouping of shops by income level, the theming of stores, the funneling of pedestrian traffic—has as its sole object the facilitation of consumption.[29]

The mall is not so much part of the suburbs as their essence, for suburbs themselves strive to take on the aspect of a theme park. A pamphlet from the California Office of Tourism invites readers to take a fresh look at Orange County (this was before the county went belly-up bankrupt, which gives the following an even more affecting comic poignancy):

It's a theme park—a seven-hundred-and-eighty-six-square-mile theme park—and the theme is "you can have anything you want."

It's the most California-looking of all the Californias: the most like the movies, the most like the stories, the most like the dream.

Orange County is Tomorrowland and Frontierland, merged and inseparable. . . .

Come to Orange County. It's no place like home.[30]

Malls are theme parks; theme parks are whole suburban counties; suburban counties are malls. And of course mall stores sport "themes" of their own and specialize in impulse shopping. Necessitarian outlets for everyday items like hardware, stamps, and pharmaceuticals and traditional five-and-dime variety stores are almost entirely absent. In their place spring up nature stores, museum shops, new age boutiques, game and music box studios, and consumption mini-marts such as The Sharper Image and Brookstone that sell nothing you need but everything you want—once you enter the store. Alongside the mini-marts are brand-name stores and commercial offshoots of the big-time theme parks. Hundreds of Disney stores, early entrants in the mall sweeps, now face competition from other studio shops like Warner Brothers and MGM's. The grand opening of the Manhattan Warner Studio store displayed Mickey's competitors Bugs Bunny and Tweetie Bird inviting sundry New York sophisticates (animal and human) wearing silk top hats to "Discover New York's Newest Entertainment Shopping Experience," thereby offering the question "When is a store a theme park?" a simple answer: "When it is an 'entertainment shopping experience.' "

To ensure that malls are fun, many developers are installing high-tech virtual reality arcade games at very considerable cost (up to $2 million) and thereby further collapsing the distinction between Disneyland, McDonald's (which is also experimenting with the games), and the suburban mall. An investment analyst predicts "malls may find it necessary to have that kind of amusement to keep up as a destination point."[31] Malling neighborhoods and then theme-parking neighborhood malls makes them sure destination points for everyman and everywoman too, especially since in the suburbs (where well over half of America lives today), the mall *is* the "neighborhood" and commercial space is the only community space in sight.

Theme parks that are really shopping malls and malls that are actually theme parks are everywhere. Movie studios build them as real-world monuments to their other-world fantasies, durable goods producers establish them as entertainment arms of their sales strategies (Nike Town, for example—see above), and governments and states sponsor them in hopes of burnishing an image or commemorating a past or turning a profit. The same French government that successfully exempted the French audiovisual industry from the last GATT round played a major role a few years earlier (along with leading French financial institutions) in assembling the property and building the hotels for EuroDisney. They even financed a stop on the express train service that is France's pride. The French private sector retains a 51 percent holding in EuroDisney today, though its poor performance in its first years has left investors with a bad taste and Disney with its first prospective fiasco.

In the self-effacing spirit of government under assault, the state has mostly stayed on the sidelines. Local authorities have the right to demand concessions from developers to allow curb cuts and building permits, but they have played the zealous suitor to, rather than the public regulator of, the developers and have asked little. Indeed, H. Wayne Huizenga, the Blockbuster video magnate who also owns a group of professional sports clubs and recently merged Blockbuster with Viacom, Paramount's successful buyer, has also persuaded the Florida legislature to allow him to build "Blockbuster Park" on twenty-five hundred acres of swampland north of Miami as a kind of sixty-eighth Florida county. The enabling legislation calls it a "Multi-Jurisdictional Tourism, Sports and Entertainment Special

District," while locals call it "Wayne's World." A five-member council representing district landowners will govern. There is only one landowner, however: Blockbuster. The pro-park chairman of the Dade County Commission explains, "We're tinkering with the outer edges of democracy as we know it—the privatization of government."[32] Not so very long ago, this pungent phrase might have been deemed oxymoronic or perhaps just moronic. If any institution is irreducibly public by its very definition, it is government. But state sovereignty apparently ends at the gates of the theme park. To be without boundaries, unaccountable to any public authority whatsoever, is no longer just a metaphor on Planet Reebok.

The theme-parking of reality has many overseas zealots. Led by Berlin concert manager Frank Georgi (who had fled the German Democratic Republic in 1989), businessmen from the eastern states of Germany are currently discussing an "Ossi Park" theme fair on a five-hundred-acre army base near Wandlitz in Brandenburg that sits astride what was once East German leader Eric Honnecker's nuclear shelter. According to the planners, visitors to Ossi Park (the attraction is named for the slang term for Easterners during the Cold War) will:

> experience a condensed "typical year" in the [Communist era] German Democratic Republic, including state-organized mass celebrations, such as May 1. One-day visitors will be required to leave by midnight, as they were in the GDR; guards will patrol the border; attempts to escape will lead to hour(s)-long imprisonment. All visitors will be required to exchange a minimum of hard currency for eastern marks. . . . Political commentary will be available through a reconstructed "black channel" as it was in the GDR; there will also be static-ridden transmissions of western German television (and) blackmarketeers and an underground opposition. [The whole park will be surrounded by barbed wire and a wall and will] include badly stocked stores, snooping state secret police (*Stasi*) and scratchy toilet paper known as "Stalin's Revenge," whose texture, according to an old GDR joke, ensured that "every last ass is red."[33]

Whether the plan, goofy to be sure but hardly goofier than some of Disney's projects now under way, will come to fruition is uncertain in Germany's troubled fiscal condition. That it could even be conceived suggests how far the theme park ideology has come from its inception in London in 1851 or its second coming (with Disney) at Anaheim in 1955.[34]

Walt Disney World is McWorld's front parlor. The cartooning of reality with which Walt Disney established his first theme park at Anaheim nearly half a century ago foreshadowed McWorld's seductive blend of commerce, illusion, manipulated desire, and vicarious satisfaction. According to an early promotional piece:

> Disneyland will be based upon and dedicated to the ideals, the dreams, and the hard facts that have created America. And it will be uniquely equipped to dramatize these dreams and facts and send them forth as a source of courage and inspiration to all the world.
>
> Disneyland will be something of a fair, an exhibition, a playground, a community center, a museum of living facts, and a showplace of beauty and magic. It will be filled with the accomplishments, the joys, the hopes of the world we live in. And it will remind us and show us how to make those wonders part of our lives.[35]

Not really the "hard facts" and not quite a part of our lives, as things turn out. Eileen Orgintz writes in what is presumably intended as high praise (in the *Los Angeles Times*), "Disney World is an unreal place, and don't expect reality to intrude. Everyone is happy and well-fed. Everything is clean. Everyone is courteous. Don't be suspicious. Wait until you get home to feel guilty about all the world's problems."[36]

As once the sun never set on the British empire, so today, Disney can boast, "the fun now follows the sun around the globe."[37] Disneyland in Anaheim, template for all the models that followed, is approaching the half-century mark, Walt Disney World is over twenty years old, Tokyo Disneyland (with its new Splash Mountain), is over ten and in 1992 added another 16 million visitors to its 100 million plus in the nine previous years. Japanese couples are among those that select Disney theme parks for their postmodern nuptials. EuroDisney outside Paris has been the exception to the rule: even if it avoids becoming the first Disney Bankruptcyland, it will have a hard time denting the tough European market. For Europe is where dreams die; the dreamers have all emigrated to America's warmer climes. Florida, America's playground, has been a natural Disney venue: even at a moment when to some wary European tourists it has the feel of Murderland, it holds out the promise of Walt Disney World, the Disney-MGM Studios theme park, Disney's Dixie Landings Resort and Bonnet Creek Gold Club, the Disney Vacation Club Resort, the Epcot Center, and the projected new Disney town of Celebration. The Disney theme parks around the world earn $3.3 billion of Disney's annual $7.5 billion a year, with films accounting for another $3.1 billion and consumer products (with theme park and film tie-ins) representing another $1.1 billion. All three divisions of Disney derive inspiration from a single set of cartoon images spun out in endless variations by an Imagineering Department responsible for redefining our reality.

In recent years, the Disney Company has set about virtualizing American history and cartooning its politics. Walt Disney World in Florida recently added Bill Clinton to its popular Hall of Presidents. Like Abraham Lincoln before him, President Clinton has been "imagineered" as an Audio-Animatronic robot who can walk and talk—and unburden himself of some surprisingly terse oratory.[38] The company also nearly succeeded in building a "Disney's America" Civil War theme park at Manassas where America's bloodiest war was to have been reconsecrated as a pay-per-view spectacle rendered (in accord with the dourly correct realism expected of our times) in all its fratricidal mayhem. Political opposition in Virginia and the District of Columbia along with a national publicity campaign by indignant historians scotched the Manassas venture at the eleventh hour, but the Disney people are still seeking an Americana theme park. For the failed Civil War theme park, "with fake Indian villages, a replica farm, mock Civil War battles and a faux fair" all "within hailing distance of real Indian trails, actual farms, a county fairgrounds and a town that was sacked and burned by Union troops," was certified by reputable historians.[39] Scholars debate the preservationist merits of these new theme parks while the Disney company tries to approximate their exacting standards, but the issue is not preservation and there was something comical about securing scholastic certification for a virtual reality being raised up right next to the Civil War actuality it was reproducing.

Disney's creations, however, aspire not to truth but to verisimilitude: the metatruth of virtuality. The whole point of virtual reality is that it is just *like* the reality that it assiduously is not and cannot be. You cannot have sex in Pirate's Cove or get to Germany on a ride through a Disney Bavarian castle or assassinate Lincoln in the Hall of Presidents. All you can do is buy a ticket to watch: watch without consequences, watch without engagement, watch without responsibility. That is perhaps why Dexter King (Martin Luther King's youngest son) has met such resistance to his plan to turn his father's Atlanta memorial into a Disney-like theme park to be known as the Martin Luther King, Jr. Time Machine and Interactive Museum.[40]

The King family is one thing, but Disney is another; one should not ask Disney to bear a greater burden than the responsibilities of an entertainment company warrant. The company's aim is innocent enough, even endearing: not reality modification but a few hours or days (or ideally, if its hotels are to remain full, weeks) of escapist relaxation for the tired masses. Theme parks are not just shaping but are being shaped by the larger McWorld whose values they manifest. In one sense, McWorld itself *is* a theme park—a park called Marketland where everything is for sale and someone else is always responsible and there are no common goods or public interests and where everyone is equal as long as they can afford the price of admission and are content to watch and to consume.

McWorld as Marketland is, however, not a natural entity imagineered by some benevolent deity. It is fabricated and it is owned, and how it is owned tells us a great deal about its nature.

9

Who Owns McWorld?
The Media Merger Frenzy

THE INFOTAINMENT TELESECTOR is the heart of McWorld and increasingly has the look of a wholly owned subsidiary of a small handful of powerful corporations that, by the month, grow fewer in number and more encompassing in ambition. The concept that drives the new media merger frenzy carries the fashionable name "synergy," which describes what is supposed to be the cultural creativity and economic productivity that arise out of conglomerating the disparate industries that once, quite separately, controlled all three segments of the infotainment telesector: the software programming, the conduits and pipes that distribute it, and the hardware on which it is displayed. The production companies turning out product, the phone and cable and satellite companies, and the companies manufacturing or controlling television sets and computers and multiplexes all, in McWorld's ideal economy, belong in the hands of one global company. *Synergy* turns out to be a polite way of saying monopoly. And in the domain of information, *monopoly* is a polite word for uniformity, which is a polite word for virtual censorship—censorship not as a consequence of political choices but as a consequence of inelastic markets, imperfect competition, and economies of scale—the quest for a single product that can be owned by a single proprietor and sold to every living soul on the planet.

Traditional corporate ambitions that aimed at monopoly within a particular medium have been displaced by the drive for monopoly across media. By the 1990s, according to Bagdikian, seventeen intermedia conglomerates were earning half the total revenues "from all media" including recordings, cable, and videocassettes.[1] Conglomeration had reduced the number of players from forty-six in 1981 to twenty-three in 1991, of which a handful are genuinely intermedia.[2] Moreover, Bagdikian was describing the situation just before the Japanese buy-in and the very recent erosion of boundaries between telephone, cable, and broadcast transmission that has accelerated the conglomeration process even more radically.

Corporations are aiming at control over each step of the image-making process from source to consumer. Where once an author wrote a book and (perhaps via an agent) sold it to a publisher who then printed it, sold serial rights to an independent magazine, and then found still other independent distributors and booksellers to sell it; and where once the author or agent or publisher marketed it to Hollywood, where an independent film studio bought it and turned it into a film, and then found an autonomous distributor to release it and an independent movie-house owner or chain to show it; and where once the film studio sold rights to an independent broadcaster to show the film on television—so that when the full commercial cycle was completed perhaps a few dozen different independent entities participated in a complex, competitive process to bring a creative work to an extended multimedia public by means that allowed both entry and exit for many different creative and financial forces, and maximized choice and opportunity for cultural creators and cultural consumers alike—today the wonders of synergy permit one entity to control the entire process. Not only is the corporate proprietor of a conglomerate likely to own a stable of publishers, one of which will publish a given book, but it can also own the agency that sells the book, the magazine that serializes it, the movie studio that buys and films it, the distributor that purveys it, the cinema chain that screens it, the video export firm that brings it to the global market, and perhaps even the satellite pods or wires through which it is broadcast and the television set and VCR on which it is finally screened somewhere in, say, Indonesia or Nigeria. This is not synergy: this is commercial totalitarianism—a single value (profit) and a single owner (the monopoly holder) submerging all distinctions and rendering all choice tenuous and all diversity sham. No wonder even partisan Republicans were nervous about the meeting between Newt Gingrich and Rupert Murdoch. No wonder other critics faulted not just the $4.5 million deal (now set aside) for an unwritten book by the Speaker but the meeting itself.

The process that leads to conglomeration seems natural enough: carriers want to control and profit from what they carry; cultural creators want to control and profit from the entities (stations and networks) that carry what they create; software purveyors want to control and profit from the hardware on which their wares are purveyed. Everyone wants a piece of the creative core, where the "content" that drives everything else is manufactured. Why be a pipe for someone else's music, when you can own composer and composition alike? But the consequences are to obliterate the conceptual distinctions by which the key elements of this section were sorted out—films, television, books, and theme parks—as government looks passively on. "The idea," reports *Newsweek*, "is to get a piece of every pie in the business. Sony now brings you Mariah Carey on your Sony Walkman, *Wheel of Fortune* on your Trinitron and *Sleepless in Seattle* in its Loews theaters with Sony sound systems."[3] Or, as Alex J. Mandl (chief executive officer of AT&T's Communications Services Group) says in explaining AT&T's $12.6 billion projected buyout of McCaw Cellular Communications Inc. (it didn't quite come to pass), "we'd like to see the AT&T brand on a national basis. We can offer end-to-end service."[4] The key to it all remains the informational/creative core, the software. In the terse words of Sumner Redstone, "software is the name of the game."[5]

The vertical integration of media is a relatively new phenomenon. Bagdikian's careful record-keeping suggests that most newspapers and magazines remained independent from the end of World War II into the 1970s. The early mergers occurred within sectors, creating newspaper empires, book conglomerates, and movie studio mergers—an unwelcome intrusion of monopoly but one that respected the boundaries separating different kinds of information and entertainment and that studiously avoided the durable-goods production domains on which spectators and consumers depended. As recently as the 1970s there were hundreds of independent newspaper, magazine, and book publishers each with their own print niche, scores of independent film production studios (and viable film industries in several dozen countries around the world), three big networks along with a large number of independent stations, one nationwide phone company responsible for universal phone service and nothing else, and dozens of hardware companies that produced the durable goods through which the public received the competing soft goods of all the entertainment and information producers—TVs, phone wire, cassette recorders, tuners, computers, and so on.

Yet at the beginning of the eighties, partly in response to the more general merger mania but primarily as a result of ambitious and visionary media empire builders like Robert Maxwell and Rupert Murdoch—their vision was possessive, their ambition absolute—boundaries of every kind were crossed. Mimicking Gulf & Western's precedent-setting takeover of Paramount back in 1966 for $125 million, Murdoch's News Corporation, Matsushita, and Sony targeted entertainment companies not simply as another vehicle of diversification but as a way into the ruling house of McWorld's emerging civilization. By the middle of the 1990s relatively new companies like the Home Shopping Network, Viacom, and Blockbuster Video were engaged in rivalry and reciprocal takeovers and were positioning themselves as the dominant entertainment/selling conglomerates of the new millennium.

This takeover mania began in the early 1980s, with quite literally hundreds of media mergers and buyouts, of which I have listed only a representative sample on the accompanying table of media mergers (see p. 141).

While everyone chatters about synergy, the arrows all point one way: nearly all of the mergers targeted companies controlling creative product, without which neither the hardware manufacturers nor the delivery system owners had anything to show or deliver. Margo L. Vignola, a media analyst at Salomon Brothers, smartly noticed that it was a "paucity of creative talent and product available and an enormous amount of technology chasing it" that ultimately

MEDIA MERGERS

Date	Target	Buyer	Price (in billions)
1966	Paramount (first round)	Gulf & Western (changed name to Paramount in 1989)	$.125
1982	Columbia Pictures	Coca-Cola	$.750
1985	Fox Broadcasting	Murdoch's News Corp. (20th Century Fox, Fox Television, Fox Broadcasting Co.)	$.575
1985	MGM/United Artists	Turner Broadcasting (keeps MGM's 3,000 film library but sells off the rest for $.800)	$1.5
1986	NBC Network (RCA)	General Electric	$6.5
1988	CBS Records	Sony (as prelude to bid for Columbia)	$2
1989	Columbia Pictures	Sony (price—in cash—does not include $1.3 debt assumption and buyout of Coke's 49 percent holding)	$3.8
1989	Warner Communications (Warner Bros. Pictures)	Time Inc. creates Time Warner (Paramount tried to interdict this deal via hostile offer for Time, Inc.!)	$14
1990	MCA (first round) (Universal Pictures and Music), including MCA Records, Geffen Records, Motown;	Matsushita (Panasonic) (Panasonic: Japanese electronics giant)	$6.1

Date	Target	Buyer	Price (in billions)
	publishers group including Putnam, Berkley, Jove, Grosset & Dunlap, Coward-McCann; theme parks including Universal City Studios, Hollywood, Florida		
1992	Videoland (video rental chain)	Philips (Dutch electronics giant, chip maker)	$.148
1992	MGM (film studio)	Crédit Lyonnais (French bank takes over from bankrupt Italian buyer; must resell within 5 years)	$1.3
1993	Time Warner	U.S. West (a Baby Bell) buys 1/4 share	$2.5
1993	McCaw Cellular Communications	AT&T	$12.6
1993	Hauser Communications (cable company)	Southwestern Bell	$.650
1993	Grupo Iusacell (Mexico's second largest cellular company)	Bell Atlantic	$1.04
1993	MCI (long distance company)	British Telecom (buys 1/5 stake)	$4.3
1993	Sprint	France Telecom Deutsche Telekom	$2.1 $2.1
1994	Wometco & Georgia Cable TV	U.S. West	$1.2
1993	Castle Rock Films and New Line Cinema	Turner Broadcasting	$.672
1993	Republic Pictures (distribution company)	Blockbuster Video (video chain and	$.100

Date	Target	Buyer	Price (in billions)
		supporter of Viacom bid for Paramount)	
1993	Liberty Media	Tele-Communications, Inc. as prelude to Bell-Atlantic merger, repurchases Liberty after earlier spin-off	$8.3
1993	T.C.I. (Tele-Communications, Inc., the largest cable company in the world with 25 percent of U.S.)	Bell Atlantic (deal in jeopardy)	$26
1994	Nextel	Motorola	$1.76
1994	Times Mirror Cable	Cox Cable	$2.3
1994	Paramount (second round)	Viacom, Redstone's cable empire, after a long bidding war with Barry Diller's Home Shopping Network (QVC)	$10
1994	Blockbuster	Viacom, adding to its Paramount property	$7.6
1995	Houston Industries	Time Warner	$2.3
1995	Cablevision Industries	Time Warner	$2.2

fueled the mania for acquisitions and mergers. Surveying the war between Viacom and QVC for Paramount, she concludes "companies like the regional Bells and cable providers are hobbled by the fact that they don't have product, and a company that has very mixed results like Paramount becomes the jewel of Madonna. Everyone wants it."[6]

See for yourself: although many of the deals are mergers rather than takeovers, in almost every case the target is a company that controls creative product for McWorld—a movie studio, a film library, a video distributor, or a broadcast network or cable company. And these represent only a select number of the largest deals. Each of the companies in play already was involved in smaller acquisitions and mergers, which accounts for the variety of entities owned by what is technically a movie studio like Paramount. Paramount is a veritable festival of McWorld's goods and products. Back in 1989 when it tried to prevent Time's merger with Warner Communications via a $10.7 billion hostile bid for Time, it already had added to its extensive film and video properties the publisher Simon & Schuster (itself a publishing conglomerate including Prentice-Hall), as well as Madison Square Garden along with the basketball and hockey teams that play there (the Knicks and Rangers now spun off by new owner Viacom to still another infotainment company, Chuck Dolan's Cablevision Systems, with financial backing from ITT). Time, Inc., on which Paramount was mounting an unsuccessful raid, meanwhile controlled along with its traditional magazines (including *Life, People, Sports Illustrated, Fortune,* and *Money*), the Home Box Office cable network, Cinemax, the American Television and Communication Corporation cable operating company, Time-Life Books, and Little, Brown and Company. By the time Paramount was in play at the end of 1993, by then itself the target of a bidding battle between friendly (and ultimately victorious) suitor Viacom and unfriendly raider QVC, its properties also included the Trans-Lux Theater Corporation, USA network, Famous Music Corporation, the Miss Universe organization, and Paramount Theme Parks. No conglomerate is complete without its signature theme parks.

In the midst of its trials with Viacom and QVC, Paramount stopped to acquire still another major publisher—Macmillan Publishing Co., Inc.—and to contemplate a deal with Chris-Craft to start a fifth television network (Fox's being the fourth). Paramount's holdings are mirrored by the properties owned by its half-score of competitors, including Time Warner, Sony-Columbia, Matsushita-MCA, Murdoch's News Corporation, S. I. Newhouse's Advance Publications/Newhouse Broadcasting, and Capital Cities/ABC. Throw in the remaining independents (MGM/United Artists under the temporary financial tutelage of Crédit Lyonnais, and Disney, the last of the true independents) along with the seven regional Bells and their new cable and foreign acquisitions who are pursuing soft-product production companies themselves, and a handful of strictly publishing giants like Bertelsmann (which recently acquired Bantam Books and RCA Records along with a New York City skyscraper), Dow Jones and the New York Times Company, as well as computer chip and software powers like Intel and Microsoft, and there are still only about two dozen companies dominating nearly every pixel of the vast infotainment telesector. We will talk a great deal about free markets and their virtues and vices in the last part of the book, but there is not much of a free market in the infotainment telesector. The absence of government regulation has not and apparently will not produce anything like true competition or real diversity of product and ownership. Here, as in so many other sectors, deregulation in the name of competition has meant conglomeration and monopoly in practice.

The complicated, interlocking corporate structures of these companies cannot eclipse the powerful light cast by the handful of luminous personalities who have followed Cecil B. DeMille and Sam Goldwyn up Hollywood's Mt. Olympus. Michael Eisner, Ted Turner, Rupert Murdoch, Sumner Redstone, Barry Diller, Martin S. Davis, David Geffen, George Lucas, Michael Ovitz, Bill Gates, Jeffrey Katzenberg, H. Wayne Huizenga, John C. Malone, and Steven Spielberg currently stand at the summit, far above the uncertain corporate tides. They are (changing metaphors) sharks in a Gulf (& Western, now Paramount) Stream who dream of a world they alone imagine and image.[7] The alliances shift, the tides sweep in, but the players do not change: disappointed by Eisner, Katzenberg has joined Geffen and Spielberg; having digested Paramount, Redstone looks to dine with Huizenga; maltreated by Davis, Diller joins with Murdoch, only to cut himself loose and eventually go after Davis's Paramount.

The story of this last figure, QVC's Barry Diller, can stand as a symbol of the new media monopolies' predatory politics, which, though they may serve shareholders' interests in the short run (apparently the only public interest for which the courts have any concern), serve neither competition, nor choice, nor creativity, nor the public good in the short or long term. Barry Diller has been a force in Hollywood for many years, and in the early eighties, after an apprenticeship in film production, ended up at Paramount, quickly rising to a production post where he was a mentor to young producers like Scott Rudin. Tensions with Martin Davis, head of Paramount then and now, led to Diller's ouster. Diller went on to Fox where he established the Fox Television Network and prospered until Fox was purchased by Rupert Murdoch in 1992. Though invited to stay, Diller wanted a financial stake in Fox that Murdoch would not give him, so he moved on and into what many observers thought would be a career-ending cul de sac—QVC, the home-shopping network. QVC had stumbled on to one of McWorld's simplest and profoundest truths earlier than most players: television *is* consumption and commercials constitute its most popular programming. Let consumers buy what they watch, and you have united television and mall-dom—McWorld's two most powerful domains. As MTV and the newer and highly popular and profitable half-hour and one-hour infomercials demonstrate, the public scarcely can tell where commercial programming ends and programmed commercials begin. And, to the extent they can tell the difference, viewers may actually prefer the latter to the former. For Diller, QVC not only embodied the corporate philosophy of the bottom line that was driving mergers, it gave him a platform from which to create his own empire. When Sumner Redstone made a friendly offer to buy Paramount in the summer of 1993, Barry Diller saw an opportunity to parlay his emblematic company into genuine Hollyworld power and at the same time to even accounts with Martin Davis, his earlier nemesis at Paramount. Personal ambition enhanced by communications synergy yielded a still higher synergy that, with the help of court decisions critical of Paramount's favoritism toward Viacom, nearly enabled Barry Diller to complete the unfriendly deal that would have let him annex the last major independent studio save Disney.

In Hollywood, where no man is an island and every takeover demands at least a corporate archipelago, Diller had help. Viacom's Redstone was lining up financial support to the tune of $600 million from Blockbuster Video under H. Wayne Huizenga (with whom he eventually merged and who was already in control of Republic Pictures and Spelling Entertainment as well as three Miami sports franchises); and $1.2 billion from NYNEX, which had just struck another synergistic deal with the Tomem Corporation in Japan to develop cable and interactive television there—the Baby Bells were looking for product to pump through their telephone wires and cellular systems. So Diller called on Cox Enterprises and S. I. Newhouse's Advance Publications (which controls twenty-six newspapers, a cable system, and Random House, Inc., inter alia) for an initial pledge of $500 million each. Diller also was moved, if a little reluctantly, to rely on John C. Malone, one of the richest men in America and the acknowledged "King of Cable," a controlling force in the country's largest cable system, Tele-Communications (itself later involved in a gargantuan plan to merge with Bell Atlantic for $33 billion, although that deal may fall through), and in Liberty Media, a television programmer that owns Black Entertainment Television and the Family Channel and is itself a 22.5 percent owner of QVC. With Time Warner (which has a 25 percent share), Malone's Tele-Communications (with a 23 percent share) also controls the Turner Broadcasting System, which was forced to turn to outside funding when Turner's own burgeoning acquisitions outran his pocketbook. QVC, as the hostile would-be buyer of Paramount, is itself then owned not only by Barry Diller himself (12.6 percent) but also by John C. Malone (via Malone's Liberty Media, which owns 22.2 percent of QVC), and Brian Robert's Comcast Cable, which owns another 12.5 percent. Time Warner, which with Malone's Tele-Communications owns Turner Broadcasting, controls another 9 percent. Nothing is quite as it seems. Everybody owns a piece of somebody and nobody is really on the outside. As with the shopping malls, the outside is all on the inside.

The details of the linkages and relationships are not the point here. A year from now, the mergers and alliances will have again shifted and some successful owners will be some other corporations' prey. The players will not have changed, however, only the line score on their current game. There will still be a great many interlocking corporate structures shifting precariously on uncertain turf. Among the interstices of those structures just a few powerful individuals will continue to circulate—and only a tiny handful of them will be critical players on either the management or the creative side. Malone is a monied manager ("billionaire flunkey," as he terms himself in his new role as Bell Atlantic vice chairman), Diller is a putative creative genius.[8] In the bidding war between QVC and Viacom, Diller and Malone were bested and Sumner Redstone and Martin Davis have a temporary advantage. But in the process, the compass of players has narrowed again, and the interest that the public at large has in full access to the information highway, in maximum variety of fare and cultural diversity, and in real freedom of choice and expression, has in each case been further diminished.

The victory of the dollar over every other conceivable interest, public or private, entails not just a crass commercialism in the place where quality information and diversified entertainment should be, but also a monopoly antipathetic to democratic society and free civilization, if not also to capitalism itself. That "creative geniuses" like Spielberg, Katzenberg, and Geffen join up gives their rivals nightmares, but will not necessarily enhance competition—or even creativity, though observers will once again celebrate synergy. Yet how can an Edgar Bronfman (Seagram) take on a Matsushita/MCA/Universal Pictures without creating his own megamonopoly? Whatever else McWorld's mergers may serve in the vital infotainment telesector, they serve neither culture nor liberty nor democracy.

This lugubrious conclusion brings us back to the same questions raised in the previous section by the impact of economic markets generally in McWorld. Spectators can vote with their dollars as well as with their private viewing and purchasing prejudices, but who speaks in the Hollyworld domain of McWorld for the public? Is there a global equivalent of even so weak an institution as the F.C.C.? If theme parks are now talking about "privatizing government," and taking over many of the functions of a state, is there a way for citizens to do the opposite and "publicize private markets," compelling them to be accountable, and demanding from them at least some degree of public-interestedness? Which institutions can exert countervailing pressures on malls or theme parks or media monopolies in the name of quality or diversity or community?

The nations that have tried a modest dose of regulation in recent years are regarded as mercantilist bogeys, and find themselves under duress from free traders and market zealots to let go—in the ancient phrase, *laisser-faire*. There are few democratic governments around today, certainly not in America or England, that display much taste for regulation or control in the name of the public weal. Governments have become the targets of alienated and disaffected clients and are not likely to be regarded as the instruments by which citizens can tame wild capitalism for some time. Markets have emerged triumphant from a war against the nation-state and the public interests they represent that has been waged at least since Adam Smith. Kenichi Ohmae of Japan, Herbert Henzler of West Germany, and Fred Gluck of the United States—three competitors in search of consensus—agreed back in 1990 on a "Declaration of Interdependence Toward the World in 2005." Its paramount innovation was a call for the role of central governments to "change, so as to: allow individuals access to the best and cheapest goods and services from anywhere in the world; help corporations provide stable and rewarding jobs anywhere in the world regardless of the corporation's national identity; coordinate activities with other governments to minimize conflicts arising from narrow interest; avoid abrupt changes in economic and social fundamentals."[9] Abrupt changes like democratization? Narrow interest like national environmental or employment policies? The declaration calls on the nation-state to participate in its own liquidation. In many regions of the Western world, the state seems to be obliging, with the complicity of outraged women and men who clearly prefer their rights as clients and consumers to their responsibilities and freedoms as citizens.

Perhaps they are making a virtue of necessity. For where governments still try to regulate or censor or subsidize or intervene, their efforts are increasingly futile, because the market for entertainment and information has become so global, the technologies so impervious to local control, and the ideology of free trade so pervasive. In the United States, regulatory advocates like Vice President Gore have pushed for "universal service" on the new information superhighway, urging that the "schoolchild in Carthage, Tennessee" should "be able to plug into the Library of Congress and work at home at his own pace . . . regardless of [his] income."[10] Speaker Gingrich has even proposed ways of getting computers into the hands of the poor. Pretty thoughts, but about as unlikely as anything imaginable in the hostile climate of antigovernment sentiment and transnational markets that dominates our times.

And so the original question reappears: in a world where the nation-state and its democratic institutions are being fractured and weakened by the divisive forces of Jihad at the same moment they are being rendered antiquated and superfluous by the integrating forces of McWorld, how is democracy to survive? Where on the vaunted information highway are the roads that will lead to justice or the pipes that will convey the vox populi? Now that they have dismantled the empire of despots and statist political ideologies, including democracy, how can communities defend their common goods against the empire of profits and cultural monopoly? Which democratic ideology can contend with the pretense to "choice" of "free" markets so that we can regain the power to choose public goods in common and thereby free ourselves from the inadvertent public consequences of all the private market choices that masquerade as the whole of freedom? Is deliberative public debate on such questions even possible where McWorld's communication systems secret preferences that, without any discussion at all, modify public attitudes and precipitate private behaviors?

It would be silly to suggest that conspiracy or some ruthless political ambitions are at work here. McWorld runs on automatic pilot: that is the whole point of the market. The influences it brings to bear are not mandated by the imperative to control, only by the imperative to sell. The *ad absurdum* logic of sales is one corporation that makes one product that satisfies every need: an athletic shoe equipped with a nutrition patch linked to sunglasses that inject Coca-Cola directly into the veins of the inner ear while flashing videos directly into wide-irised eyeballs. The political entailments of this logic are inadvertent: a kind of default totalitarianism without a totalistic government: everyone a subject, no one a ruler. Women and men governed by their appetites rather than by those lesser tyrants traditionally feared as "dictators" or "monolithic parties."

The very idea of the public has become so closely associated with nation-states that the idea of a global public potent enough to take on McWorld's global privates seems inconceivable, especially given the further fracturing of local public entities by Jihad's many neo-tribalisms. In the solipsistic virtual reality of cyberspace, commonality itself seems to be in jeopardy. How can there be common ground when the ground itself vanishes and women and men inhabit abstractions? There may be some new form of community developing among the myriad solitaries perched in front of their screens and connected only by their fingertips to the new virtual web defined by the Internet. But the politics of that "community" has yet to be invented, and it is hardly likely to be democratic. People on the Net do prattle on about the community, but when have they last spoken to a neighbor? If good fences make good neighbors, virtual neighbors make good fences—against real neighbors.

In celebration of the potential commonality of America, Woody Guthrie once sang, less out of conviction than in burning hope, "This land is your land, this land is my land." Whose land is Disneyland? Or Steven Spielberg's "new country"? To whom ought McWorld to belong, and will they be able to wrest it away from the irresponsible and wholly random individuals or irresponsible and wholly monopolistic corporations that are its current proprietors? Poets less gifted than Guthrie have more recently proffered their own answer: "*We* are the world," they sing. But whose world are we? Where is the "we" in McWorld? It acknowledges welters of me's operating impulsively in an anonymous market, but it provides not a single clue to common identity or to the place of community in the market. No wonder the new tribes pummeling the nation-state see in McWorld only the destruction of everything that constitutes their common identity. Democracy seems to be the loser coming and going. Jihad has other virtues to pursue, McWorld's priorities omit it altogether. Under these circumstances, can it find new expressions, new institutions, new attitudes, that will permit it to survive?

These questions are, in a quite technical sense, questions of political theory and political science. They point toward the final section of our portrait of Jihad and McWorld by raising the question: is democracy possible under the conditions of either Jihad or McWorld? However, before they can be answered, we need to scrutinize what I have called the forces of Jihad with the same care we have spent on McWorld. For Jihad is the other challenge facing democracy in our third millennium and in the short run its peril to free institutions may be still greater.

PART II

The Old World of Jihad

10

Jihad vs. McWorld or
Jihad via McWorld?

HUMAN BEINGS are so psychologically needy, so dependent on community, so full of yearning for a blood brotherhood commercial consumption disallows, so inclined to a sisterhood that the requisites of personhood cannot tolerate, that McWorld has no choice but to service, even to package and market Jihad. We have seen how athletic shoe salesmanship revolves around selling American black subculture; how American Express treats global travel (a privilege of McWorld) as a safari to exotic cultures still somehow intact in spite of the visitations and depredations made possible by American Express; how McDonald's "adapts" to foreign climes with wine in France and local beef in Russia even as it imposes a way of life that makes domestic wines and local beef irrelevant. McWorld cannot then do without Jihad: it needs cultural parochialism to feed its endless appetites. Yet neither can Jihad do without McWorld: for where would culture be without the commercial producers who market it and the information and communication systems that make it known? *Modern* Christian fundamentalists (no longer an oxymoron) can thus access Religion Forum on CompuServe Information Service while Muslims can surf the Internet until they find Mas'ood Cajee's Cybermuslim document. That is not a computer error: "Cybermuslim" *is* the title.[1] Religion and culture alike need McWorld's technologies and McWorld's markets. Without them, they are unlikely to survive in the long run.

Now to be sure, I have identified McWorld with crucial developments made possible by innovations in technology and communications that appear only toward the end of the twentieth century. In a way, however, McWorld is merely the natural culmination of a modernization process—some would call it Westernization—that has gone on since the Renaissance birth of modern science and its accompanying paradigm of knowledge construed as power. On inspection, there is little in McWorld that was not philosophically adumbrated by, if not the Renaissance, the Enlightenment: its trust in reason, its passion for liberty, and (not unrelated to that passion) its fascination with control, its image of the human mind as a tabula rasa to be written on and thus encoded by governing technical and educational elites, its confidence in the market, its skepticism about faith and habit, and its cosmopolitan disdain for parochial culture. Voltaire despised history, dismissing it as little more than a catalog of humankind's errors and follies while Enlightenment psychology assumed a single universal human nature rooted in right reason and set down in the greater harmony of the chain of being. In Alexander Pope's ripe imagery in his *Essay on Man*:

> *All are but parts of one stupendous whole,*
> *Whose body, Nature is, and God the soul. . . .*

> *Look round our World; behold the chain of Love*
> *Combining all below and all above.*
> *See plastic Nature working to this end,*
> *The single atoms each to other tend . . .*

> *Nothing is foreign: Parts relate to whole;*
> *One all-extending all-preserving Soul*
> *Connects each being, greatest with the least;*
> *Made Beast in aid of Man, and Man of Beast;*
> *All serv'd, all serving! nothing stands alone;*
> *The chain holds on, and where it ends, unknown.*

McWorld's advertent meretriciousness and its numbing commercialism along with the fabulous curiosities of virtuality that have problematized the very meaning of reality may seem novel. They raise questions of whether, for example, virtual communities organized around the Internet are political or public communities in any meaningful sense, and whether information networks improve or corrupt public access and civic capacity. But novelty or no, there is little in our postmodernity that would surprise modernity's Enlightenment and post-Enlightenment champions like Pope, Voltaire, J. S. Mill, and Max Weber or, for that matter, that would cheer up its Cassandras like Rousseau and Nietzsche who had more than an inkling of how the Enlightenment would also write its own dark counterpoint. Allan Bloom was thus able to make the greater part of his complaint about our tarnished world today by rehearsing the spirited grievances of the ancients against their world then.[2]

What I have called the forces of Jihad may seem then to be a throwback to premodern times: an attempt to recapture a world that existed prior to cosmopolitan capitalism and was defined by religious mysteries, hierarchical communities, spellbinding traditions, and historical torpor. As such, they may appear to be directly adversarial to the forces of McWorld. Yet Jihad stands not so much in stark opposition as in subtle counterpoint to McWorld and is itself a dialectical response to modernity whose features both reflect and reinforce the modern world's virtues and vices—Jihad *via* McWorld rather than Jihad *versus* McWorld. The forces of Jihad are not only remembered and retrieved by the enemies of McWorld but imagined and contrived by its friends and proponents.

Modernity precedes and thus sponsors and conditions its critics. And though those critics, on the way to combatting the modern, may try to resuscitate ancient usages and classical norms, such usages and norms—ethnicity, fundamentalist religion, nationalism, and culture for example—are themselves at least in part inventions of the agitated modern mind.[3] Jihad is not only McWorld's adversary, it is its child. The two are thus locked together in a kind of Freudian moment of the ongoing cultural struggle, neither willing to coexist with the other, neither complete without the other. Benedict Anderson gets it exactly right when he conceives of that driving engine of Jihad, the nation, as "an imagined political community."[4] Which brings us to the crucial question of nationalism, and its role in the struggle of Jihad versus McWorld.

The Meaning(s) of Nationalism

AMONG THE FORCES that animate modern Jihad, religion may be at once the most noble and the most toxic, but none is so prominent as nationalism, according to Walter Russell Mead and many others "the most powerful political force on earth today."[5] The trouble is, those who agree on nationalism's potency do not agree on its meaning. There is old nationalism and new nationalism, good nationalism and bad nationalism, civic nationalism and ethnic nationalism, nationalism as the forge of great states and nationalism as their coffin, East European nationalism (arrayed against external empires [Turkish, Russian, Austrian]) and West European nationalism (arrayed against parochial forces inhibiting nation building), the nationalism of the liberal nation-state and the nationalism of *ethnie:* of parochial politics and tribalism.[6]

As a moment in the antimodern life of Jihad, nationalism suggests narrowness, antagonism, and divisiveness and seems to exist in a primarily negative form—ethnic and cultural particularism that aims at busting up the nation-state and flinging aside multicultural wholes in the name of monocultural fragments. Free traders and One McWorlders use nationalism as a scathing pejorative denoting a fractious and anticosmopolitan tribalism, reeking of bloody fraternalism and equally toxic doses of the parochial and the primitive.

Yet this is to distort what is in fact a far more dialectical conception of the nationalist idea in history. While it may seem to undermine integral states today, nationalism once helped fashion the states that forged the Enlightenment. As a consequence, it gained considerable momentum and a modernizing cachet of its own with the rationalistic (if often irrational) revolutions spawned by the Enlightenment in France, America, and Germany. The aspiration to a "liberal nationalism" that united the cosmopolitan ideals of liberty and equality with the communitarian ideals of fraternity and solidarity motivated the Jacobins and the American founders alike, and permitted peoples bound by culture and history nonetheless to fashion constitutions founded on rights and reason. The Greek revolt against Ottoman rule that drew Lord Byron to his epiphanic demise in 1824, for example, gained decisive support from English romantics and English liberals because national self-determination was perceived as the condition for the progress of liberty and liberty was understood to be nationalism's noblest aspiration. No less a liberal than J. S. Mill had established what he saw as a necessary linkage between liberty and national identity, echoing Rousseau's assertion that only an integral nation could sustain a republican constitution.[7] Liberal and romantic nationalists from Herder to Mazzini subscribed at once to a religion of humanity deifying a single, cosmopolitan conception of human nature *and* a vigorous nationality: in Mazzini's arching rhetoric "nationality is the role assigned by God to each people in the work of humanity."[8]

During a brief grace period (in the French Revolution and its aftermath) when *patriotism* meant love of fellow citizens no less than love of country (Rousseau), and *la patrie* referred to the democratic republic no less than to the nation, this splendid amalgam of individualist ideals and communitarian identity politics—a synthesis of the religion of humanity and the secular story of nations—appeared to make it possible for reason to set down roots and thereby secure legal personhood in a grounded identity of nationalist flesh and cultural blood. Particularism and cosmopolitanism were joined in a French ideology of progress and revolution, and the true cosmopolitan was, as Paul Hazard recognized, "someone who thought à la française."[9] This understanding of the nation made possible the creation of a constitutional state under the sovereignty of a "people" (*Volk, gens, peuple,* or *nation*)—the nation-state—which in turn offered the legal groundwork for democracy. To the extent our modern democratic institutions are tied to the idea of the nation-state, it has been a legacy of precisely this alliance between nationalism and liberalism.

The marriage was, however, a peculiar one, a partnership defined from the outset by disequilibrium. And if, initially, history played along and the first half of the nineteenth century witnessed the stabilization of aspiring liberal nation-states in Canada and America (and in a certain manner France) as well as their rise in Italy and Prussia, by the end of the century liberalism and nationalism were becoming unstuck. Although the marriage was premised on the essential compatibility of freedom and parochial identity, in the cases of America, France, and Canada, pluralism was built into national identity, providing the indispensable glue. But in Italy, Germany, Greece, and the Balkans, it was not, and in time the marriage failed with particularly disastrous consequences. In Eric Hobsbawm's description, toward the end of the nineteenth century, nationalism had "mutated from a concept associated with liberalism and the left, into a chauvinist, imperialist and xenophobic movement of the right . . . the radical right."[10]

The passing of liberal nationalism as a historical experiment was not the end of its career as social theory, however. The argument for the inclusionist liberal ideal of nationalism is made to this day by idealists who find in legal personhood too thin and abstract a basis for identity yet regard the actual record of historicist nationalism as too bloody and exclusionist to be made a basis for equal citizenship. Ortega y Gasset pointed out in the 1920s during a period of empire busting and "nationalist" aspirations that preceded the balkanization of the East—a period not unlike our own—that nationalism, having won its integrating national victories, was bound to change its strategy: "In periods of consolidation," Ortega observed, "nationalism has a positive value, and is a lofty standard. But in Europe everything is more than consolidated, and nationalism is nothing but a mania."[11] In our own well-consolidated era, while the new nationalism does seem to have become a kind of toxic mania for deconstructing states, there are still voices urging the inclusionist model. Yael Tamir thus believes that "the liberal tradition, with its respect for personal autonomy, reflection and choice, and the national tradition, with its emphasis on belonging, loyalty and solidarity, although generally seen as mutually exclusive, can indeed accommodate one another"; for, she is sure, history notwithstanding, "embeddedness and choice are not necessarily antithetical."[12]

Not perhaps necessarily: but in history all too frequently. The aspiration to dialectic has in this century more often than not been contradicted by the reality. Liberty and fraternity were brother constructs of the French revolution, but like Cain and Abel were born to strife. Embeddedness means, if not exactly subjugation to an extended communal identity, membership in entities that constrain choice. J. S. Mill to the contrary, sturdy old oaks don't fly—as Edmund Burke might have reminded him; for Burke knew that "men are not tied together to one another by papers and seals. They are led to associate by resemblances, by conformities, by sympathies."[13] Rousseau to the contrary, butterflies cannot grow roots any more than contractually bound legal persons can nurture affection. As any naturalized citizen can attest, to choose one's roots is not the same as being rooted by birth or blood. A voluntary membership may bring with it a special sense of appreciation—"I have become an American!"—but it cannot provide the sense of ascriptive identity that belongs to the native: "I *am* an American." If "the nation is always conceived as a deep, horizontal comradeship" centered in a common language that permits the imagining of a common past, liberty and inclusiveness are at best likely to be contingent features of its landscape, and are at worst likely to be seen as inimical.[14]

In his seminal study in social anthropology *Community and Society (Gemeinschaft und Gesellschaft),* the nineteenth-century sociologist Ferdinand Toennies concluded that the requisites of traditional blood and clan communities tended inevitably to yield to the requisites of voluntary and contractual societies in an evolution that pointed only forward; an evolution away from tradition, religion, and mystery toward contract, secularism, and rationality whose final destination could only be what Max Weber called the disenchantment of the world. The yearning for a reconstructed and remystified community was both fostered and contradicted by modern society's cold rationalism, just as more recently Jihad has been both fostered and contradicted by McWorld's postmodernity.

Indeed, by the end of the last century the experiment with liberal nationalism, though it perdured in France and America, had largely failed elsewhere, displaced by Ortega's "mania" for fragmentation. Empire had made nationalism more rabid and parochially oppositional and capitalism had driven it away from liberal individuals— agents of the bourgeois market—toward blood brothers: heirs to imagined ancient clans. Modernity meant modernization, which meant the aggressive expansion of practical mentalities of rationalization, bureaucratization, and secularization. These conditions in turn not only disenchanted and demythologized the world, but increasingly created a psychology of being in which individual self-determination and commercial consumption displaced community identity and group belonging. The consumer is perhaps modernity's most notable achievement and the consumer is finally a solitary being. While Joel Kotkin—stretching metaphor to the breaking point—has pretended to find newfangled "tribes" in the peoples who run McWorld's economic infrastructure (e.g., Jews, Japanese, Indians, Brits, and Americans [*sic!*]), buyers and sellers are not particularly well understood by being cast as blood-brother parochials.[15]

Many postmoderns have tried to reinvent community in the pallid face of contract relations. They all use history, but as Eric Hobsbawm noticed, "history is the raw material for nationalist or ethnic or fundamentalist ideologies, as poppies are the raw material for heroin-addiction," and since "in the nature of things there is usually no entirely suitable past," where necessary "it can always be invented."[16] Community too is often a contrivance of willed grievances, drawing on an invented past. "Most Hungarians," Tony Judt suggests, "did not know that their nation had been born in AD 896 until late-nineteenth-century patriots told them so."[17] That version of multiculturalism that infiltrates the pluralist "many" with a new ideology of, say, white Protestant or African-American monoculture offers one example of fictive historical communities—Max Weber's myths of common descent—invented to serve the need for a modern political base for group identity. Ethnic "nationalism" offers another far more toxic instance. Polish editor and social theorist Adam Michnik notes wryly that in Poland, putatively free of ethnic problems, "we can produce a Polish-Lithuanian conflict, a Polish-Belorussian conflict and a Polish-Ukrainian conflict, to say nothing of a Polish-German quarrel in Oppeln, a pogrom against the gypsies in Mlawa and an anti-Semitic campaign in a country which has virtually no Jews."[18] In matters of nationalism, necessity apparently remains the mother of invention.

More than a hundred years ago, Marx had observed that the breaking of feudal bonds by modern capitalism had decisively fragmented traditional community. He spoke of the sundering of all bonds and prophesied ongoing cultural meltdown: "All that is solid," he warned, "melts into air."[19] A half century later modernist anxieties had become popularized, so that one of American playwright William Saroyan's characters could repeat over and over again in the prewar stage classic *The Time of Your Life*, "no foundation, all the way down the line," and expect full sympathy from audiences already exasperated by modernity even before it had produced the Holocaust and the atomic bomb.

In Germany they did not just whine about it: reacting against what they took to be the stultifying leveling (*gleichschaltung*) of bourgeois society, the Nazi party revived medieval myths of Teuton morality (a feudal version of family values) and of Germanic identity (ironically reaching back not just to a second Empire of the German Nation but a first quite non-German Roman Empire). Eventually, it rode to power on a reactive ideology of grievance dressed up in the claims of an invented past in a manner not so different from the one currently being fashioned by the far Right in France, Italy, and the United States as well as, once again, in Germany. That the Nazis managed only to further the annihilation of intermediate associations of the kind that had once made genuine community feasible was an ironic compliment to their own unintentional complicity in the modernization they reviled. The irony is repeated today in the stellar rise and rapid fall of Silvio Berlusconi in Italian politics: a global corporate media mogul who owns Italy's premier AC Milan soccer team, using his media-made preeminence to give demagogic voice to the very parochial constituencies his media world is systematically destroying; and then being brought down by media-driven charges of corruption that make him look like any other politician. The same irony is visible in the startling juxtaposition in the new reunified Germany of heavy metal rock rhythms that are MTV's specialty and punk lyrics of which the young Goebbels might have been proud. Here is a piece of reactionary Jihad all decked out in the metered hip-hop of McWorld, as written by the German band Final Stage:

> *Times are tough for the German people*
> *Foreign troops still occupy our land*
> *Forty years of calamity and corruption . . .*

> *It's winter in the F.R.G.*
> *Will there ever be a Germany again*
> *Worth living in?*

German culture—where is it these days?
We meet at a dump called McDonald's
Lust for profits and power poisons our environment . . .

This state is ashamed of German history . . .

We've got as many foreigners as grains of sand
Pimps, junkies—it's all forbidden
Believe me, Christians, praying won't do any good

> *It's winter in the F.R.G.*
> *Will there ever be a Germany again*
> *Worth living in?*[20]

Today, the forces I identify with Jihad are impetuously demanding to know whether there will ever be a Serbia again, a Flanders again, a Quebec again, an Ossetia or Tsutsiland or Catalonia again, that is worth living in. Immigrants from old to New Orleans, from old to New England, from old to New Zealand, want to know whether the lands of origin that fire their imagination can be made real. And they gather, in isolation from one another but in common struggle against commerce and cosmopolitanism, around a variety of dimly remembered but sharply imagined ethnic, religious, and racial identities meant to root the wandering postmodern soul and prepare it to do battle with its counterparts in McWorld. "Let's slip the fighting dog's leash" and loose the "savage beast of German blood" on all the "scum," sings the band Stoerkraft (Destructive Force).[21] Not every partisan of Jihad is so menacing (or so blunt), and this particular band subsequently betrayed the Right and today sings songs urging tolerance and social comity.[22] But if democracy does not always necessarily appear as an adversary it is rarely deemed an ally. Even among new nationalists who proclaim no animus against it, the bargain has been struck: if to overcome modernity, the modern liberal nation state must be jettisoned along with its democratic institutions, that will be a justifiable cost of the war to revive community and insulate it from McWorld.

The language most commonly used to address the ends of the reinvented and self-described tribes waging Jihad—whether they call themselves Christian fundamentalists or Rwandan rebels or Islamic holy warriors—remains the language of nationalism. Religion may represent a more profound force in the human psyche, but as politics it finds its vessel in nationalism.[23] Yet nationalism can be elusive and its many usages are so variously inflected that it is not clear if a common language is actually being spoken. If, as Michael Ignatieff suggests, "the key narrative of the new world order is the disintegration of states" and the "key language" of that dissolution is ethnic nationalism, are we to assume that this is the nationalism of Mazzini and Yael Tamir?[24] Or the nationalism of the Nazis and Vladimir Zhirinovsky? Ignatieff speaks cautiously of a "new" nationalism, but strictly speaking, the sundry opponents of McWorld appear to be neither nationalists nor religious zealots. Their rhetoric is too worldly for true religion and far too sectarian and exclusive to be nationalist. The Crusades were murderous in their fanaticism but universalist and expansionist in aspiration—more imperialist than reactionary—which indeed accounts for their bloodiness. Universal ideals can create universal mayhem while the effects of parochial ardor are often far more modest. Our new tribes are murderous and fanatical but small-minded and defensive: trying to secure islands of parochial brotherhood in a sea that relentlessly leaches away essence and washes away fraternal bonds.

The critical question is whether postmodern "new" nationalism, with the nation-state as its target, is assimilable to traditional nationalism, on which the nation-state was founded. Rather than offer either a phenomenological answer (*both* varieties count as nationalism) or an essentialist answer (only *this* one or only *that* one counts as nationalism), I want to suggest here a more dialectical response. Nationalism clearly has now and has perhaps always had two moments: one of group identity and exclusion but another, equally important, of integration and inclusion. Today's "nationalists" boast about their deconstructive potential and revel in hostility to the state and other constituencies that make up the state. In its early modern manifestation, however, nationalism permitted Europe to emerge from feudalism and facilitated the architecture of the nation-state. Early European atlases like the sixteenth-century *Cosmography* show Macedonians and Bulgarians, Danes and Vandals, Sicilians and Hungarians, both as constituent pieces of a larger body (a feudal empire) and inclusionary national wholes that assembled parochial tribes into national entities like Italia and Germania.

Thus it is that the two moments of nationalism reflect the two moments of the feudalism against which early nationalism reacted.[25] The political entities that brought down and succeeded feudalism had at once to divide and to integrate old Europe: at one and the same time to dismantle the empire of the church and to weld together the provincial neighborhoods. Clannish loyalty and blood oaths were too narrow a basis for new national states, imperial contract and theological fealty too broad a basis. The nation seemed a perfect integer, holding together the tribes in larger entities that nonetheless permitted something resembling common culture and civic reciprocity.[26] The new relationship was one not of fealty but contract, one that in the novel language of Thomas Hobbes of Malmesbury pictured the king's power as embodying the wills of people understood as individuals rather than as blood brothers. The sovereign's authority derived directly from a contract among his subjects, who thus become his authors, his obedient but ultimately sovereign subjects. Emancipated from parochial fealty to kin and clan as well as from ascriptive subservience to vassal lords, newly created subjects of the British realm or of the French nation were little by little able to transform themselves from individual subjects into individual freemen whose obedience to the crown and responsibility to others grew out of rights they now understood themselves as possessing by birth and liberties they conceived as belonging to them by nature. Essex defined a parochial brotherhood: England defined the liberties of Englishmen. The feudal towns of Burgandy and Basque were walled: France was an idea that opened out to the cosmopolis. Feudal vassalage had created an intricate network of obligations in which birth inexorably controlled identity and identity in turn conditioned freedom (liberty being a hereditary characteristic of a single class). The new nation-state turned bondsmen into nationals and, in putting men on an equal footing, set the stage for a political theory of rights, resistance, and social contract, and thus for a political practice that would eventually become both egalitarian and democratic.

Nationalism is a kind of group remembering of ancient stories of founding, and foundings were often midwifed by fratricide. But, as the historian Michelet had learned from the bloody lessons of the St.

Bartholomew's Night Massacre (in which Protestant Huguenots were slaughtered in their beds), it also requires self-conscious group obliviousness: not just common remembering but common forgetting.[27] Differences are held in suspension in successful communities of difference—what civic nations are when they succeed—and that entails a certain amount of studied historical absentmindedness. Injuries too well remembered cannot heal. The greatest peril to American civic culture today is the memory of slavery, kept alive by ongoing prejudice and persistent institutional racism. Without an opportunity to forget slavery, there can never be a chance for racial harmony. The burden, of course, is on the heirs to the slaveholders, not the heirs to slavery.

In the peculiar transformation of nationalism in the nineteenth century, imperialism played a special mollifying role. The great empires spawned by Austro-Hungary, Russia, and the Ottomans (and to a lesser degree, the overseas empires of France, Spain, Britain, and the Netherlands) repressed the political expression of cultural identity and enforced a mutuality that made possible a more inclusive solidarity. Yet the empires afforded culture its own zone, and seemed to neutralize its toxicity without quashing its tastes. Ignatieff and others have perhaps overstressed the ways in which empire kept Kulturkampf under wraps and ethnicity at bay, yet there is little question that they contained Jihad.

Whether the ideological empire of the Communists or the economic empire of the capitalists can be said to have done the same is more controversial. Certainly under communism the nationalities question that had so perplexed Lenin and frightened Stalin was kept under control, if only by propaganda and brute force.[28] As the collapse of the great European empires of the nineteenth century following World War I catalyzed the balkanization that had so worried Ortega, so the collapse of the Communist empire seems to have unleashed the new forces of Jihad we see at work in Eastern Europe and European Asia. Whether that is because Communist repression worsened things (repression leading ineluctably to explosion) or contained forces in a fashion that might ultimately have eliminated them is a contentious question we cannot settle. What is clear is that even communism's version of empire deferred the issue for several generations, sparing parents and grandparents the bloodshed being visited today on their grandchildren (though communism certainly exacted its own price in blood).

Capitalist empire was less successful as a governor on the whirling dervishes of ethnic nationalism since its hold was less explicitly coercive and since, as we have seen here, commerce and markets can arouse as well as placate ethnicity and its countermaterialist zeal. That is precisely what Jihad is all about.

Yet times change quickly. Just a few years ago, astute commentators like Conor Cruise O'Brien pointed a warning finger at the Middle East, South Africa, and Ireland as the world's leading flash points; who would want to make that claim now? Yesterday, Libya was Europe's prime headache; today, Algeria causes more concern though just yesterday it was France's most "successful" ex-colony. The devil may be in the details, but in world politics the devil is a chameleon and no theory that dwells on one or another particular case is likely to survive the next political surprise.[29]

Hence, I hope in what follows to sketch a typology of Jihad with at best what can only claim to be transient illustrative evidence. The data are too protean to be definitive and the events too vulnerable to distortion by the very probes that affect to explain them to be detachable from the normative frames by which we try to capture them. This is the general problem with pretending that social and political theory can be "scientific." Although I can give neither the case studies I sketch nor the conundrums they raise anything like their full due, I focus then, without pretending to science, on four different versions of the reaction to modernity representing four distinct perspectives on Jihad.

11

Jihad Within McWorld:
The "Democracies"

IN THE WELL-ESTABLISHED European democracies, the temptation to resist modernity is modernity's nervous commentary on itself. Europe's rather pallid version of Jihad takes two intersecting forms: provincialism, which sets the periphery against the center; and parochialism, which disdains the cosmopolitan. Both are hostile to the capital city and all it stands for. Both understand decentralized power as less threatening to liberty and more susceptible to control than central power. Provincialism shares the democratic spirit of Jefferson. It prizes the sanctity of town or ward government and, with Tocqueville, understands liberty to be an essentially local or municipal notion unlikely to thrive under the pressures of large-scale governance and wholly contractual social relations. By this logic, Barcelona and Lyons are more likely to be free than Madrid or Paris, and the villages at their doorstep will in turn feel even freer than Barcelona and Lyons.

Parochialism adds to provincialism a cultural critique, descrying in the cosmopolitanism and commercialism of capital cities forces deeply corrupting to human association: atomism, agnosticism, anarchy, and anomie—a series of terms whose "a" prefix stresses the deracination or "withoutness" of a modern society reduced to its slightest particles and thus without communal coherence because it is without God and without order, without law and without justice. Rousseau's acerb portrait of eighteenth-century capital cities captures the visceral force of the parochial critique: "In a big city," thunders Rousseau, "full of scheming, idle people without religion or principle, whose imagination, depraved by sloth, inactivity, the love of pleasure, and great needs, engenders only monsters and inspires only crimes."[1]

Occitan France

THE FRANCE THAT is Paris and the France that is the provinces ("la France profonde") have been at odds for most of the nation's history, the regional *parlements* against the Bourbon monarchy, the landed aristocracy and their supported church against the Jacobins. When in World War II the French national center collapsed and Paris and the north were occupied by the army of the Third Reich, it was the periphery under the collaborationist Vichy regime that took on the tasks of conservator for France, redefining its spirit along the way. With agriculture the only honest culture the French could afford to recognize under Nazi occupation, Parisians who in the 1920s and 1930s had despised village life, in the 1940s suddenly discovered long-lost relatives in the provinces, country cousins with whom a newly unearthed cultural identity could be affirmed.

Even today, Parisians seek second homes in peripheral villages where they can escape not just French modernity, but McWorld's tawdry intrusions into Paris or the grinning visage of Mickey mocking them from EuroDisney just a few miles to the east. The irony is that the fast trains and superhighways by which these weekend traditionalists render the periphery accessible to Paris are destroying the rural landscape they wish to honor, just as their ex-urban occupation of quiet farm villages infects these hamlets with a corrosive cosmopolitanism even as it gives the cosmopolitans the illusion of a respite from McWorld. Here Jihad and McWorld intersect:

McWorld's spent consumers, who cannot do for more than a long weekend without the twin fixes of twentieth-century consumerism and twenty-first-century technology, periodically excuse themselves from the city and its suburbs to inhabit Jihad's contrived ethnic identities "dans la compagne" or "auf das Land."

To provide the illusion of a cultural identity, McWorld goes slumming in Jihad while its rootless denizens play at being "locals" in a manner that is almost entirely spurious, vicarious, unearned. In Europe, where they coexist cheek by jowl with centralized national power, such local identities as have been preserved are predominantly linguistic and the trade-off with McWorld still under negotiation. If, as Ignatieff has it, "the key language of our age is ethnic nationalism," then the key to ethnic nationalism is language.[2] In Western Europe's gentle Jihad, language is how the parts detach themselves from the whole. It is not only Americans who worry about a primary or mother language. In France, as elsewhere in Europe, provincials have rediscovered language (dialect) and made it the talisman of their reawakened cultural subnationalism, leaving modern French patriots to wonder what will be left of France if it is carved back up into its Norman and Breton and Basque parts.

The irony is that French itself is under siege and the National Cultural Ministry in Paris has actually prevailed upon the legislature to outlaw popular foreign terms, in particular, the multiplying Americanisms of McWorld. *Talk show, chewing gum, software, prime time,* and *cheeseburgers* inter alia will now be denoted by the terms *causerie, gomme à mâcher, logiciels, heures de grande écoute,* and . . . well, *quelque chose* (something or other) *"à la fromage"* (the equivalent will have to be invented) or such commodities will be mute (not an acceptable mode for a commodity). Ads using fashionable anglicisms will have to be translated, and scientific terms from the new global technology will have to find French neologisms if French scientists want to write or speak about them.[3] In this mini-Jihad of the French government against McWorld's bold Esperanto (recently softened by compromise) can be seen at the national level the parochial spirit of provincial efforts to hold a regional line against French. Two lines in the sand: one drawn by France to keep out McWorld; the other drawn by France's provinces to keep the French at bay.

The Basque region is the best known separatist entity (it exists on both sides of the Spanish/French border, where until very recently campaigns of terror have been conducted). But there are other less notorious and thus more telling instances of cultural and linguistic Jihad. In Brittany, though the old separatist bomb-throwers are gone and secession is no longer an issue, Breton cultural nationalism is probably running "stronger today than at any other time this century."[4] *French* bagpipes? Well hardly: but there are *Breton* bagpipes in the little Celtic town of Quimper, and Brittany, which immediately after World War II had only one hundred bagpipers, today boasts five thousand.[5]

In Provence, the story is much the same. Modern purveyors of gentle Jihad are trying to undo at least certain features of a four-hundred-year-old French history and relegitimize the dialects and cultures of the ancient region of Occitan. Occitan encompassed the Provençal, the Catalan, and the Basque regions of southern France along the Pyrenees and the Mediterranean, and featured "*oc*" ("yes") dialects quite distinctive from the "*oui*" ("yes") version of French spoken in the north. The French government, like so many harried denizens of McWorld trying to prove their traditionally parochial multicultural credentials without actually giving up their place at modernity's banquet table, now supports indigenous languages. Perhaps it does so because it appreciates that McWorld's global American-speak can use all the enemies it can get.

Provincial dialects may threaten French centralist culture but they also constitute multicultural France and so are at once a weapon of French nationalism and a weapon pointed at integral nationalism's heart. Europe, France's rival for the affection of the newly legitimized localities, is also supportive. The Western European Language Bureau, created in 1982, encourages the provinces in their cultural conceits, supporting not only Provençal and other Oc dialects in France but also, in the Netherlands, Frisian, in Ireland, Gaelic, and in other places, the linguistic flavor of the day.[6] Its activities and the realities they acknowledge have led some critics to refer to the new Europe as "a new tower of Babel."[7] Others see in its work a subtle strategy of national deconstruction by which the European whole nurtures the subnational fragments, all the better to undercut the resistance to wholeness on the part of the nation-states. In holding French centralists at bay, Provence may thus welcome support from Europe.

Whatever strategies are at work, parochial culture is not much enhanced. Despite support, and the opening of new bilingual schools in Nîmes and elsewhere, Provençal has hardly become a living language. Less than fifty thousand speak Breton and only half of those can write it. The model, unfortunately, is not the Flemish spoken at Dunkirk nor the French version of Catalan nor the German spoken in Italy's Alto Adige, France's Alsace, or Russia's Kaliningrad; in each of these cases, a local language survives because it is spoken by a substantial population across a proximate border. Breton and Provençal, on the other hand, like Corsican and Ladin, exist in splendid isolation, fragments of an otherwise vanished cultural legacy. Whether or not there are as many as 3 million, as some claim, who speak some words of one of the six dialects of Occitan, and whether or not the nominal Occitan dialect news programs being broadcast from Toulouse and Marseille really have listeners, the focus on Occitan revival is part of a larger campaign to vitalize and legitimize the provinces against McWorld's Parisian center, and parallels similar efforts in Belgium and in Switzerland. In the Alps, for example, there are fewer than forty thousand speakers of Raeto-Romantsch and Ladin left in the canton of Graubünden, and despite official efforts on behalf of pluralism, surviving latinate dialects seem unlikely ever to be more than a cantonal museum culture.[8]

Spanish (?) Catalonia

THE INTELLECTUALS INVOLVED in the Western European local cultural revival are deeply ambiguous about what they are doing. On the one hand, they do not necessarily see themselves as enemies of cosmopolitanism and they deny that there is any relationship between what they advocate and the kinds of ethnic warfare being conducted further to the east. Some see themselves as securing bastions of local democracy, seedbeds for real participation in the all-European federation that will presumably emerge, if not immediately, sometime in the next millennium. Catalonia boasts that it is a "country in Europe," and thereby can claim to serve both Jihad and McWorld: for it integrates itself into Europe precisely by segregating itself from Spain. We are not Spaniards, we are Catalonians; but Catalonians *are* Europeans—better Europeans than the Spanish!

In an ongoing advertising campaign that began before the 1992 Barcelona summer Olympics and continues into the present, the provincial government of Catalonia managed to have it both ways, outraging Madrid by printing maps that highlight Catalonia as part of Europe but omit Spain altogether. It would be as if California ran ads in Japan portraying itself as a vital appendage of the Pacific Rim installed by inadvertence on a nameless North American continent.[9] Catalan nationalist leader and provincial president Jordi Pujol has played a noisy role in Spanish politics and created pressures that moved Spain's crafty King Juan Carlos to address the opening ceremonies of the 1992 Olympic games in Catalan dialect. Courtesy of Señor Pujol, the well-liked monarch had been booed only three years earlier at the Barcelona Olympic stadium dedication, and many Catalonians had demanded that their athletes be permitted to compete separately from the Spanish team![10] Pujol himself is a viperous nationalist who not only helped make Catalan the official language of schools and universities (non-Catalans must use it if they wish to teach in Catalonia) but insisted "Catalonia is as much a nation as Slovenia or Estonia."[11] As happens with so many of Western Europe subnationalists, the Catalonian's nominal bow toward Europe and McWorld is accompanied by a withdrawal from national sovereignty—in this case, Spain's. Far from resisting McWorld's markets, Catalonia seeks a special relationship with them.

Unlike Catalonia, the Occitan regions have not yet quite realized they can blockade the capital without turning their backs on McWorld. Gerard Gouiran, a professor of Occitan at Montpellier University, insists his concern with local language is free of exclusivist animus. But, he explains, "the strengthening of the local language [is] vital to preserving the region's character because the south of France is changing so rapidly. New high-technology industries are settling in France's version of the sun-belt; outsiders are buying up entire villages as vacation spots, and television is barraging young people with images in which their own world never appears."[12]

Gouiran does not quite specify that the enemy is McWorld, but he is explicit about "containing" the Americanization of France and of Europe. Unlike Pujol, he has not yet grasped that "sun-belt" industries rooting in France's southwest can actually catalyze local pride and give economic sustenance to parochial pretensions to autonomy. Nonetheless, like partisans of local culture elsewhere, Gouiran does confront McWorld with a profound ambivalence that is evident in Switzerland as well as in North America's most dramatic case of separatism, Quebec.

German-Switzerland

SWITZERLAND EXEMPLIFIES THE problems Europe faces as a whole, for as a nation it has chosen to defy Europe and the supposedly irreversible pressures of McWorld's markets from the contradictory stance of a highly successful practitioner of market economics. In doing so it has also managed to open up deep inner fissures that threaten to destabilize Switzerland's own confederal equilibrium. Long a loosely federated neutral nation forged from German, French, and Italian (and Raeto-Romantsch) fragments, the Swiss (like the Americans) have seen themselves as an exceptionalist country—*Sonderfall Schweiz!*—and on the basis of their unique geographical position astride Europe and their long-standing armed neutrality, have resisted efforts at integration into a greater Europe, and refused entry into the United Nations in a 1967 national referendum. At the end of 1992, following an unnerving Danish "no" to the Maastricht Treaty, the Swiss also voted no on membership in the European Free Trade Association (as a preamble to membership in the Common Market). Their negative vote followed cultural fault lines with the French Swiss voting overwhelmingly for Europe and the German Swiss overwhelmingly against.[13] It had been hard enough for the German Swiss to surrender their precious semisovereignty to a new federal government back in 1848 when the "modern" constitution eroded certain crucial cantonal privileges. In 1992 it was not so much Switzerland, whose elites—the federal government, the major parties both conservative and liberal, as well as corporate, banking, and even many union leaders—fully supported Europe, but rather the cantons and communes that led the obstinate resistance. The elites spent millions trying to prod the citizenry out of its democratic parochialism, warning them that a "no" vote could put the Swiss multinationals out of business (or at least out of Switzerland) and turn Switzerland into "the Nepal of Europe."[14]

Europhile observers, that is to say the greater part of the European press, were utterly befuddled, muttering darkly about Switzerland's "reflexive traditionalism" and its self-defeating "neo-isolationism," and predicting that unless it permitted itself to be awoken by Europe's economic "electroshock" it was doomed to become a "third-world country."[15] Yet the Swiss have one of the highest standards of living in the world (higher than the United States), are committed free traders, and have been participants in the building of the financial ectoskeleton of McWorld. They are not stupid. What was at stake for Switzerland's reluctant "Europeans" was not a reactionary Jihad against modernity. Rather, the German Swiss in particular, but also the Italian Swiss who in the canton of Ticino voted nearly 62 percent no, were struggling against Europe in the name of cultural autonomy and regional democracy—two frequently disjunctive values that for unique historical reasons have intersected in Switzerland. Indeed, in Europe's oldest and most decentralized democracy, not just the cantons but the communes enjoy prerogatives few other constitutions in the world afford to people locally. *Gemeindefreiheit* (communal liberty) and *kantönligeist* (the local spirit of the canton) apparently remain values worth fighting for, even at the cost of the rewards of economic integration. But the tradition to which the Swiss cling is local democracy, and their loyalty may in part be due to the powerful impression left by Euro-technocrats and McWorld marketeers that democracy is simply not part of the global game they are playing.

In Switzerland, then, the struggle against McWorld is to a degree a self-conscious struggle on behalf of a parochial culture that happens to be generically associated with self-government and regional liberty. Perhaps alone among the partisans of Jihad, the Swiss are struggling to preserve a traditional culture against modernity in the name of democracy. Where elsewhere isolationists fight against both markets and democracy as twin products of a homogenizing modernity they fear, in the Alps they oppose homogeneity because it imperils democracy. Since it came to Switzerland long before the

Enlightenment, even the Enlightenment's most savage critics can count democracy as their ally rather than their enemy.

The refusal of the Swiss to buy into the McWorld for which their economic success has prepared them was again underscored in February 1994 when, in still another display of referendum obstinacy, they voted to ban all heavy cargo truck traffic through the Alps, ruling that by the year 2004 cargo must be carried exclusively by rail. In doing so, they turned the clock back nearly a century to the time when the citizens of the canton of Graubünden legislated a ban on all automobile traffic from that canton's extensive and still virgin territory (a quarter of Switzerland's land mass). The automobile, the denizens of Davos and St. Moritz and Chur had agreed, was a threat to regional autonomy and local liberty.[16] Switzerland remains to most Europeans an inexplicable maverick: a rich nation that seems prepared to put its wealth at risk for principle; a stubborn nation whose obstinacy sometimes looks like prescience, and whose prescience is often written off as obstinacy.

For all their brave pre-Enlightenment wisdom in resisting McWorld, however, along the way the Swiss are jeopardizing their prudent multicultural equilibrium. The francophone Swiss are far less attached to German Swiss localist traditions and far more anxious to follow France into a greater Europe than their German, Italian, or Ladin cousins. With only some of the parts willing to fight for the continuing national autonomy of the whole, the whole risks disintegration—a development that would defeat Switzerland's confederal democracy as surely as abject surrender to Europe.

A Sovereign Quebec Inside Canada?

MUCH THE SAME ambivalence can be found across the Atlantic among the Quebecois separatists, where federal Canada faces a Quebec province whose separatist leanings have actually been magnified by its recent economic successes. If anything, the resistant part of the whole here is actually as much or even more in tune with McWorld than the whole represented by the Canadian government that Quebec resists.[17] Quebec would seem to want it both ways: "a sovereign Quebec inside a united Canada," as the telling quip goes.

Perhaps this is because the Quebecois can be seen (and sometimes see themselves) less as nearly 7 million francophone Canadians (with another million in Canada outside Quebec Province), but as a French diaspora in North America. The struggle for cultural autonomy on the part of diaspora—communities that define themselves by reference to a distant homeland from which they once originated—looks rather different than the struggle of indigenous peoples conquered by or absorbed into a larger entity.

Minority diasporas like the French in Canada, the overseas Indian or Chinese populations, and Jews outside of Israel have forged a friendlier and more economically progressive relationship to McWorld than others, perhaps because they depend on trade for their sustenance and foreign lifelines for their continuing cultural identity. A Quebecois who tries to pretend France does not matter, like a Polish Jew who lives as if there were no Israel, is vulnerable. Security lies in embracing an interdependent McWorld within which the mother cultures can root their legitimacy.[18] Quebec thus favors its francophone cultural roots at the same time it celebrates its emerging economic status as a highly productive economic partner—no longer just of Canada's other provinces, but of the behemoth to the south and multiple overseas partners as well. "Quebec libre" is no longer a francophone entity caught up in poverty and backwardness compelled to retreat from an economically prosperous anglophone Canada into a new isolationism; rather it is a proud French enclave on an English continent deploying a vigorous and growing economy on behalf of its burgeoning linkages to the world beyond Canada. Jihad here embraces economic modernism even as it rejects the multicultural nation-state.

Quebec's place in Jihad is complicated by the dilemmas it creates for two related peoples: its own native Cree Indian population, and a million or so nonseparatist, non-Quebecois Canadian French who rely on Quebec for their status in Canada as Quebec relies on France. Native American Crees have made their own case for separatism within Quebec, although in the language of a people who see themselves more as guests on the land than its "owners." They have been greeted with an intensely hypocritical lack of sympathy by Quebecois who somehow cannot grasp the connection between their own suit against Canada and that of the Cree against them.

The case of the million or so francophone Canadians living outside of Quebec is perhaps even more embarrassing. To the 300,000 Acadians of New Brunswick Province, for example, Quebec as part of Canada secures equal treatment for all francophones. Acadians have lived successfully along the shores of the Gulf of Saint Lawrence for nearly four hundred years, and survived their dispersal by the English following the defeat of France by English armies in North America in 1763 (when many Acadians found their way to New Orleans where, as "Cajuns," they established another sanctuary). Now they face a paradox: Quebec's tribalism imperils their own.[19]

Jihad, even in its most pacific manifestations, almost always turns out to be not simply a struggle on behalf of an ethnic fragment for self-determination, but a compound struggle within that fragment that risks still greater fragmentation and plenty of confusion as well. Once the parts feel justified in jettisoning the whole, the logic of Jihad does not necessarily stop with the first and primary layer of fragments. If Quebec leaves Canada, non-Quebecois francophones may lose their equal place in New Brunswick. And if Quebec leaves Canada, why should not the Cree leave Quebec? And why then should not anglophone villages leave Quebec or opt out of a self-determining Cree nation if it is such they find themselves inhabiting? And if a few francophones reside in the predominantly English villages in the predominantly Cree region of predominantly French Quebec, what about their status? It was to such absurdities as these that the multicultural, civic constitutional nation-state addressed itself. Dismantle it and all the paradoxes come crashing back with an ardor commensurate to their centuries-long repression.

Germans: East and West, Old and New, Right and Red, Guilty and True

GERMANY WOULD SEEM a poor candidate for Jihad. It is still caught up in historical guilt and, more than any other nation in the world, has had reason to hold nationalism at bay; for nationalism is a concept that, as the source for so many of the historical catastrophes that have befallen Germany, remains forever suspect. Moreover, Germany is newly reunited, it is democratic, and it is as heavily invested in McWorld and the American pop culture that promotes McWorld as any country. Yet Jihad, perhaps because it is McWorld's ally and twin as well as its adversary, stalks the new Germany with astonishing ferocity.[20] Those in today's Germany who want Deutschland to retrieve *echt Deutschland* yearn to rip down all the foreign, all the commercial, all the materialist banners; and in their place:

> *Give Adolf Hitler the Nobel Prize*
> *Raise the red flag, raise the red flag,*
> *Raise the red flag with the swastika . . .*
>
> *As on the German flags of old*
> *It leads me down the right roads*
> *For me, what matters hasn't changed:*
> *Race and pride and swastika!*[21]

The new nationalists are not daunted by the official shame associated with taking Germany too seriously, dead seriously. Rather, such pusillanimity incites them to feel ashamed of feeling ashamed. Where else, they ask, are the most innocuous displays of national sentiment to be treated as provocations worthy only of banishment? Why must the recent past be taboo? Even the Japanese are permitted their emperor and their cultural superiority and their celebration of a mostly decensored history including their own version of the "Day of Infamy." So the skinhead punk rockers offer a crude but searingly frank version of views framed more diplomatically by Franz Schoenhuber's far right-wing Republican Party, singing "This state is ashamed of German history. . . ."[22] Many of the far right groups like National Alternative have been outlawed, but this only succors them in their sense of resistant alienation.

Poverty, I have suggested, deepens the rage of holy warriors and makes them more desperate enemies of a McWorld that has refused to succor them. German enragees are often if not always unemployed or underemployed in lower-paying jobs, often if not always young people with little education and few prospects, often if not always Ossi's or Easterners from the old German Democratic Republic, deprived overnight both of jobs and the social safety nets that might cushion their joblessness.[23] They would perhaps join

McWorld if they could, and they are happy enough to use its instrumentalities (whether these take the form of British fashion statements, commercially rewarding rock bands, or Internet bulletin boards like The Thule Network) as weapons in their struggle.[24]

In a sense, the German neo-fascists are a counterreaction to reunification that filled the void when the primary anti-Communist revolution failed. Had the indigenous political movements that helped bring down first the iron curtain and then the Berlin Wall survived the traumatic passage to German reunification and been even a little successful in the West-dominated elections that came soon afterwards, Ossi extremism might have been averted. But the citizens' movement that constituted itself as Neues Forum (New Forum) and the intellectuals and workers who had sought a "third way," some version of civil society between state-coercive communism and private market capitalism, drown in what we might call liberty's second wave.[25] Privatization quickly displaced democratization on the German agenda, which for East Germans meant that the price they had to pay for individual liberty was a total loss of regional autonomy. After four years of this experience, it is not so surprising that many East Germans, disgusted by the West and fearful of the Rightists in their midst, have realigned themselves with a revamped Communist Party that has itself become a voice against McWorld. With civil society's third way out of the question, and the second (capitalist) way so disappointing, they are renegotiating the first (communist) way. In the June 1994 German local elections (as in Hungary, Latvia, and a number of other nations) Communists running on the renamed Democratic Socialist Party ticket emerged as the most powerful entity in a number of localities and won the mayoralty campaign in the Saxon town of Hoyerswerda (which had experienced skinhead violence against foreigners earlier in the year).[26]

Where the old Left is regrouping around opposition to the vices of capitalism, the new Right, resentment transformed into pathology, is waging an antiforeign, antimaterialist Kulturkampf. Today, most neo-Nazis and skinheads seem well beyond the ministrations of either McWorld or the democratic socialist opposition to it. To those who are East Germans, impoverished and increasingly nostalgic, with unemployment at 16 percent or worse (over double the national norm, and far worse still among the young), it is easy to regard West

Germans as an "other"—aggressive agents of McWorld and traitors to the real Germany (rather like the Jews were made out to be in the 1920s). Up to 25 percent of East Germans under twenty-five are thought to harbor right-wing sentiments. And for those unwilling to revile their West German cousins, Germany's labor minions (foreign workers from Turkey and points east and south) give to "otherness" a distinctively alien character—different habits and mores, a foreign accent, darker skin tones—as well as a corporal embodiment that invites violent retribution.[27] Poverty roughens the already jagged edges of alienation. We can again turn to the Right's rancorous rock lyrics (cited above) to hear the economic side of the story:

> *Times are tough for the German people*
> *Foreign troops still occupy our land*
> *Forty years of calamity and corruption . . .*

The hostile warriors are blackshirt Greens—"lust for profits poisons our environment," they groan—and though their own taste is teen tawdry and calculated more to shock their peers than to embrace their forebears (no traditional lederhosen shorts or student fraternity caps here!), they know McDonald's is "a dump" and resent the incursions of global culture that to them are perhaps most paradoxically evident in their own inability to resist them.

The real foreigners (as against the symbolic foreigners: rich West Germans, Yanks, the merchants of McWorld) are another matter. "Foreigners Out!" is an easier slogan to sell than "McDonald's Out!" There are nearly 2 million Turks in Germany, 140,000 in Berlin alone, and they can be not only resisted but trashed, assaulted, and incinerated in their squalid barracks.[28] In 1990 there were a few hundred attacks; two years later there were several thousand—1,636 "rightist crimes" from January through October 1992 alone.[29] There are probably not more than 50,000 right-wing extremists of whom not more than 6,500 are neo-Nazis in Germany today;[30] but as the guerrilla swims in the sea of the people, so the radical Right in Germany gives voice to repressed resentments shared by many Germans (though, to be sure, only a minority). Indeed, there are far more intermarriages between Turks and Germans than assaults.[31] Still, the German weekly *Der Spiegel* offered a survey showing that 73 percent of Germans thought foreigners were a "problem" on which the country had to "get a grip,"[32] even though 85 percent of Germans consistently deplore violence against guest workers. Not all of the assailants are skinheads, and not all of the victims are foreigners. Jews, reporters, and liberals have also been attacked.

The assaults on Turkish hostels in eastern towns like Magdeburg, Solingen, Moelln, or Rostock are a means to an end. Just as Poland has managed to cultivate a new antisemitism without Jews, German skinheads are capable of nurturing their resentment of foreigners without Turks, who are only obvious and vulnerable underclass symbols of the McWorld overclass (and in particular the West German overclass) that has sold them out. And because they are not just frustrated adolescents, but political warriors, their ultimate target is not really Turks or Greeks at all but Germany: the Germany that has surrendered to McWorld.[33] Germany in turn reacts to its assailants not just by talking about justice and human rights: instead, it confirms a part of the right-wing critique by worrying about its image and its attractiveness to investors and wondering whether violence will jeopardize its Olympian (or, better, McWorldian) bid for the Olympic Games in the year 2000.[34]

I am not among those who think the Germans are peculiarly vulnerable to the worst that is in their history and I suspect that the hundreds of thousands of German citizens who have marched in candlelight processions in condemnation of rightist violence and racism will win the struggle for the postmodern German soul. But I am less sanguine about the capacity of the Germans (or anyone else) to contain McWorld—or to render it democratic. And it may be the struggle against McWorld that will give Germany's teen fascists and rock Nazis their most significant and dangerous following.

12

China and the Not Necessarily Democratic Pacific Rim

IN AREAS OUTSIDE of Europe and North America that have been relatively successful in both economic and political terms, what is most offensive about McWorld to local protagonists of Jihad is its cultural aggressiveness. Indeed, in many Asian nations Jihad proceeds without fear of offending democrats since democracy has had little to do with modernization. The trick in that part of the world has been to figure out how to exploit the benefits of economic modernization and capitalist markets without capitulating to either the political values (openness, rights, liberty, democracy) or the cultural habits (suburban, materialist, consumerist) attached to them. On the whole it has been easier to counter the West's political ideas than McWorld's seductive lifestyles. The authoritarian experiments, Communist and non-Communist alike, in Vietnam, Singapore, Korea, and China are proof of how easy it is to sever free markets from free political institutions. Democratic India and Japan are proof of how difficult it is to sever free markets from McWorld's way of life.

In nondemocratic Asia, markets have been cautiously welcomed in the setting of a prudent, background mercantilism where governments first establish and then try to control the inchoate but productive forces markets unleash. The democratic institutions that (Westerners argue) are necessary to the operation of markets remain wholly unwelcome. Market liberals of Milton Friedman's or Jeffrey Sachs's persuasion have assured us that the two cannot be uncoupled in the long run, but the long run here may be several lifetimes—far too long to sustain the credibility of their argument.[1] Indeed, there is no better refutation of the libertarian argument than the wildly successful controlled capitalist economies of Vietnam, China, Singapore, and Indonesia. "China's dream," says a Western diplomat in China, "is to become another Singapore," where the attraction is "that it has achieved Western living standards without being infected by Western political standards."[2]

China has had the fastest growing economy in the world in recent years, despite—or is it because of?—the brutal repression of individual rights and political liberty during the horrendous events at Tiananmen Square and ever since.[3] China, like its neighbors, struggles against Westernization at the same time it struggles for economic market productivity and for trade with the rest of McWorld. Understanding the priorities of its trading partners in Japan and the United States, as well as the logic of markets, which demands autonomy from politics and is thus indifferent to state organization, it refuses to budge on political rights. For rights, along with their accompanying ideology of political individualism, are seen as appurtenances of the resistible culture (easily separable from the irresistible market) and China's successful pursuit of the latter without yielding to the former is proof of the accuracy of its leaders' perceptions. As Perry Link describes it, the happy bargain Deng Xiaoping offered the Chinese was basically "Shut up and I'll let you get rich,"[4] a formula that worked not only for his own subjects but with the American State Department as well.[5] In the spring of 1994, China won extension of its Most Favored Nation status with the United States (without which its exports to the United States would be subject to tariffs at least twice as large as they are) without it having to make a single significant political concession. Ironically, it was only its obstreperousness with respect to intellectual property rights (it refused to shut down pirate video and cassette operations) that finally elicited American trade sanctions and a clamp-down on the pirates in 1995.

China specialist Thomas B. Gold is probably right to believe that "the Communist Party is going to concentrate on the things it thinks it can do best—presumably political control, media, education—and allow the economy to function by some of its own logic."[6] Yet ironically, while the struggle against democracy has so far succeeded, the struggle against lifestyle and culture is failing, precisely because the economy's "own logic" is the logic of McWorld and seems far more likely to bring with it the vices of the West (its cultural imagery and the ideology of consumption as well as a "logical" tolerance for social injustice and inequality)[7] than its virtues (democracy and human rights). Russia has acquired a Mafia well before it has established a free press. Vietnam is still governed by a hegemonic Communist Party, but also sports a five-star Hilton Hotel and seven golf courses to which its ranking members receive free memberships. You can buy almost anything in the world you want in Singapore other than a fair trial. The one thing that can be said with certainty about post-Deng China is that KFC will continue to open franchises at a record pace; there are twenty-eight in place in over a half dozen cities already.

The struggle for partisans of cultural autonomy within ruling circles and among cultural elites beyond it, then, cannot just be against a democracy that has made few inroads but must be against a foreign culture that has made many. The real threat of the "barbarians"—the term the Chinese have used for foreigners for hundreds of years—is less their explicit campaign for democracy than their stealth program for McWorld. The Great Wall built millennia ago to keep the barbarians out now swarms with their heirs, the ever more ubiquitous tourists who are becoming the basis for a vital Chinese industry. The Chinese have responded to the challenge of McWorld with what the Chinese like to call "market socialism," what the former *New York Times* Beijing bureau chief dryly calls "Market-Leninism."[8] Leninist political institutions can initially coexist very nicely with market capitalism, and the thirty or forty Rolls-Royces imported in each of the last few years have not shaken Communist rulership. However, Chinese-Communist and pre-Communist Chinese cultural values are vulnerable to the messages played in the CD players and to the images conveyed by the internal appointments of the Rolls-Royces (and Land Rovers and Mercedeses) being brought in. The Chinese hope to make foreign cultural imports their own, welding together the artifacts of McWorld and the images of traditional Chinese communism—as artist Wang Guangyi has done in his canvases integrating Western advertising logos into revolutionary posters or Feng Mengbo did in his Video End Game Series in which Mao's revolutionary-model operas appear on canvas as video games.[9]

Soap operas too are popular, so the Chinese have begun producing their own with considerable success. In 1991 the fifty-part series *Aspirations* created a sensation and gave serious competition to the Hong Kong, Taiwanese, and Mexican soap operas already on the air. In boom cities like Shanghai, there are few signs of the local culture that fuels Jihad, subtle or otherwise. Shanghai is not "like" Hong Kong and Singapore: it *is* Hong Kong and Singapore, except the traffic is worse. Chu Chia Chien has returned from her New York exile to the city of her youth and says of her new neighbors: "They are very fashion-conscious, but now they like to have a name brand—it is very important because it says 'I have money.' "[10] Meanwhile, the *China Culture Gazette,* official organ of the Ministry of Culture, has gone slick and fashionable, featuring busty Western nudes and sincere discussions of sexuality and eroticism. Editor Zhang Zuomin uses Red Guard language of the cultural revolution to advance the interests of the market. "I believe we must smash open Chinese culture, and apply 'the great fearless spirit' to our newspaper work," he says.[11]

With such developments made rampant by official support for markets, it is not hard to appreciate why Asian authorities in Communist and non-Communist countries alike insist on state control over information and the media, though for the most part in vain. Indonesia has shown a radical intolerance toward its independent media in recent years, in the main to forestall political opposition. But the government clearly also feels some need to use media control in its struggle against foreign culture. The cola companies, after all, have declared war on Indonesian tea culture. And while free-market philosophy urges freedom for advertising, it is agnostic about intervention via censorship against the kind of free cultural lifestyles advertising promotes.

China, no less culturally defensive than France, is tightening control over the production and screening of films with even more fervor than the French. It has restricted foreign films to 30 percent of the total market. Yet though the government tries to retain absolute control over political ideas, in leaving cultural images and commercial information to the marketplace it flails at mosquitoes with a butterfly net. In the long run the cultural mosquitoes are more likely to bring down the regime than the political butterflies that are captured. Artists have learned to use irony in place of anger, while publications like the *Cultural Gazette* make sure that between the nudes and gossip no political criticism slips in. The authorities understand that what they keep out via locks and bars on the front door labeled politics often creeps in through the wide-open back door labeled markets, but what is to be done? For example, aware of how ubiquitous McWorld's satellite transmissions have become, they have dutifully banned the use of satellite dishes to receive anything other than Chinese signals without, however, banning the dishes themselves— everywhere visible atop the sooty apartment blocks of Beijing and Shanghai. This is about as effective as making it illegal to look at pinups but licensing the sale of *Playboy*. They might of course have banned the sale and use of the dishes altogether, but that would have disrupted a highly profitable industry in which the Ministry of Electronics manufactures dishes and the Army General Staff Department as well as the Ministry of Radio, Film, and Television sell them to the general public. And so while government officials rant against corrupt Western culture, their colleagues are busily selling the instruments of corruption. Economic success for the fledgling industry—a dish in every home—will signal cultural failure: McWorld in every home.

Hot wars are conducted by force of arms; the Cold War put propaganda and images to the direct service of political ideas in a struggle for the hearts and minds of men. McWorld's war proceeds by inadvertence, circumventing heart and mind in favor of viscera and the five senses, seducing peoples with the siren call of self-interest and desire where the self is defined wholly by want, wish, and the capacity to consume. Chinese spectators in the aftermath of Tiananmen Square "ought" to be interested in truthful journalism, but, exposed to McWorld's videology, they avow to being far "more interested in sit-coms or cops-and-robbers shows than in news programs." According to Zhang Zedong who runs a state-owned satellite-dish shop, "what people want is entertainment. They're not so interested in BBC, but rather in MTV . . ."![12]

China has another problem as well: how to enforce its ideologically motivated centralist edicts on regions with a great deal of geographical autonomy that (as instructed) are motivated more by economics than ideology and that often ignore political edicts in favor of market edicts, since the two come from the same central government, but stand in sharp contradiction. In boom regions in South China, Shanghai and the Yangtze River, and Manchuria, the central government's Jihad against Westernization is largely ineffective. Like Catalonia or Lombardy, such regions achieve some independence from the Chinese centralist regime through direct engagement in world trade. Orders handed down in Beijing commanding banks to stop speculating are flat-out ignored; orders to limit oil consumption enforced by local production controls are simply circumvented by increasing imports from abroad. A family-planning clinic run by the government recently reversed the ideological polarity (one child per family) set by the authorities when it discovered it could earn more as a fertility clinic.[13] Some predict that regions on the extreme periphery like Tibet or oil-rich Xinjiang Province may try a Chinese-Quebec and secede from China altogether, although the brutal repression in Tibet suggests how committed the leadership is to retaining control.[14] As in the West, the breakdown of a centralist Communist government can mean anarchy—an argument officials have been all too ready to use to oppose democracy since the time of the emperors. According to one official: "All the time in Chinese history, when you don't have strong rule, you get chaos and warlords. If we try to get too much democracy, it'll all fall apart again. China will disintegrate, and it'll be worse than in the Soviet Union."[15]

Of course no perspicacious observer would want to argue that China faces an internal Jihad against central, modernizing rule on the scale found in Eastern Europe and the regions of the former Soviet Union; less than 10 percent of the population (less than 100 million people) count as members of the fifty-five ethnic minorities of China, and they are concentrated in the West. Yet there are fears that even as the Chinese nation struggles against Westernization, traditionally remote regions like Xinjiang, Tibet, and Inner Mongolia will step up their own struggle against "Chinafication." In predominantly Muslim Xinjiang, for example, ethnic Uighurs have more in common with neighbors across the former Soviet border than with cadres in Beijing. The central government has relied on force in the past in places like Tibet and will no doubt do the same again, especially in underdeveloped regions. In the south, however, where economic success coupled with regional autonomy is creating a natural catalyst for greater independence, the situation may be harder to contain. Moreover, the fear of "falling apart again" is deeply rooted in China's pre-Communist history of warlordism and clan feuds, and the feuding has risen again in the provinces as Communist Party control has been loosened.[16] The triple threat of secession by remote regions, clan feuds at the village level, and relative economic independence in the prospering provinces can only make the central government exceedingly anxious—whether or not it uses the language of Jihad to describe its potential adversaries.

China is of course a very special case: huge, ancient, highly civilized, Communist, traditionally hostile to foreigners and their barbarian cultures, and, though historically decentralized with a strong village culture, never at any moment in its long history really democratic. Its variations on both Jihad and McWorld are likely to have a distinctive look. What is striking is that even here where a native culture might be thought to have its greatest chances against the children of the Western Enlightenment, McWorld seems irresistible. Like Catalonia and Quebec, the provinces waging the most successful struggle for autonomy from central government interference and Communist Party busybodiness are those that have joined McWorld rather than those that fear it. Suzhou comes to look like Nanjing, Nanjing like Shanghai, and Shanghai like Hong Kong. And so, day by day, China looks more and more like it is fulfilling what the diplomat cited earlier called its dream: to become some elephantine version of Singapore where, as long as you keep your mouth shut and your politics neuter, you can do anything you want, above all make money by the boxcar.

Certainly China has been more successful in containing both internal Jihad and external McWorld than, say, Sri Lanka, where the government of what was once the island paradise of Ceylon has been kept busy by a revolt of ethnic Tamils in the north (the so-called

Liberation Tigers) and by an extremist counter-Jihad among its own Sinhalese majority;[17] or Indonesia, a simmering Asian Yugoslavia where 350 distinct ethnic groups, most with their own language, occupy thirteen thousand islands in an archipelago held together primarily by the military force of an authoritarian regime under the command of its founder, Suharto.[18] Suharto is the efficient dictator known equally for his early liquidation of a half million Communists in the 1960s, his bloody military invasion of East Timor in the 1970s (which has been compared to Iraq's takeover of Kuwait), and his remarkable success in jump-starting the Indonesian economy in the 1980s. While perhaps best known as a site for the cheap-labor manufacture of Western apparel and shoes (workers make $700 a year), under B. J. Habibie, the German-trained minister for research and technology, Indonesia has also decided to pursue the high-tech end of McWorld. It already manufactures small commuter planes and helicopters, and is hoping to leapfrog other industrialized nations by stepping smartly into twenty-first-century high-technology domains. With its disparate multicultures, Indonesia is less worried about McWorld's cultural values than about Western multicultural and democratic political ideals. Demography and topography favor fragmentation so that for Suharto the struggle is to hold the parts together by economic progress and military force.

The Asian democracies Japan, India, and (recently) Korea are special cases for a different reason than China. As committed democracies, they have already acknowledged the power of Western ideology, whose ideals they prize—if only because they were once colonial subjects of or defeated in combat by the West. Their struggle is exactly the reverse of China's. They distrust not Western political ideas but the kind of Western culture advanced by aggressive commerce and the kind of laissez-faire economics fostered by liberal markets. India faces an internal Jihad from both Hindi and Muslim fundamentalists who detest one another perhaps even more than they fear the encroaching McWorld, as well as from separatists in Assam.

Japan would seem to be the Asian nation that has succeeded best in first modernizing its economy and then assuming a position of global economic leadership without succumbing to wholesale Westernization. Democracy has been inflected with a Japanese accent and even the economy has been nurtured with policies that temper crude Western market capitalism with a careful mixture of mercantilist state support and corporatist paternalism. Indeed, the more communitarian, consensual, even familial character of Japanese corporate style has been imitated in the West by bemused admirers of the Japanese economic miracle that once was. Though not quite as ethnically homogenous as some imagine, Japan has also managed to avoid even the gentler forms of Jihad we have seen in France or Italy or China. As James Fallows has persuasively shown, its powerful and insular culture has diminished the impact of economic theory and created a distance from the cultural artifacts of McWorld seen nowhere else.[19]

Yet Japan is not wholly exempt and the case for its supposed immunity to McWorld may reflect Western fears of Japanese superiority rather than a realistic assessment of its cultural autonomy. After all, Japan has been assimilating American culture at least since the long and influential post–World War II American occupation. Karl Taro Greenfeld offers a stunning portrait of "gangsters, rock musicians, hostesses, porn stars, junkies, computer hackers, nightclubbers, drug dealers and bikers," which suggests that Japan's current Generation X—Greenfeld calls them the Speed Tribes—may represent a dividing point between a traditional and insular Japanese past and a startlingly assimilationist global (McWorldian) future.[20] Japanese rock bands (with names like S.O.B. and the Blue Hearts) are multiplying, but in music critic Neil Strauss's gloss they are "cultural sponges, soaking up Brazilian bossa nova, British hard core and American rockabilly . . . borrowing pop idioms from everywhere except Japan."[21] It should be left to those with a keener knowledge of Japan to judge how pervasive the changes signaled by recent Japanese music, literature, and pop culture really are, and to assess whether the behavior modification resulting from the climb of McDonald's and KFC into (respectively) first and second place in Japan's restaurant industry will trickle down into Japan's cultural bedrock and rot out the ancient stone.[22]

Like so many nations facing McWorld with a suspicion that impels them to struggle diplomatically (a kind of soft Jihad) against its cultural encroachments, Japan faces its own internal protests from minorities hoping to detach themselves from it. It appears to them as

McWorld appears to it, and McWorld becomes their ally against it. Okinawa, for example, annexed by Japan in 1879 and returned to it by the United States (who had taken it in World War II) in 1972, has aroused anxieties in Japan with its attempts at reviving the Okinawan language and the practice of local customs. The Okinawan movement follows those peculiarly feudal dynamics we have seen elsewhere in cases where an ethnic fragment of a plural nation-state uses world culture and global economics to make its own claim for self-determination against a mother country that in the name of its own autonomy may be opposing world culture and global economics. In their struggle for an identity apart from Japan, Okinawans have turned to a hybrid form of rock music, drawing on Bob Dylan, John Lennon, and Bob Marley to "jack up" a local folk music "into a band context."[23] In marching resolutely backward into its own history, little Okinawa seems to be marching brazenly forward into McWorld. Such are Jihad's ironies.

What the general case of Japan suggests, even to casual observers, is that in the Japanese context Jihad—with or without its ironies— denotes not simply an internal struggle of minorities against a majority Japanese culture, but the struggle by official Japan itself against the corrupting influences of the global culture into which its economic success has thrust it. But what is true for most peoples struggling ambivalently against McWorld is particularly true for the Japanese: the carriers of corruption are finally neither outsiders nor barbarians but Japan's own youth, who even as the indigenous culture works to socialize them as native Japanese, have proved themselves adept apprentices of the global practices of McWorld.

Indeed, as we complete this brief tour of the struggle against McWorld *within* the nations where capitalism has been most successful, what becomes apparent is that the confrontation of Jihad and McWorld has as its first arena neither the city nor the countryside, neither pressured inner cities nor thriving exurbia, but the conflicted soul of the new generation. Nations may be under assault, but the target audience is youth. In Okinawa, in Tokyo, in every country around the world the young generation is being fractured by the contrary pulls of past and future. For it is the young who carry the guns for the I.R.A. and the Serbian militias and the young who wear the headphones of the Sony Corporation and Nintendo. It is the young who rock to the hard music of MTV and Star Television and the young who roll to the still harsher siren song of ethnic identity and other-hatred. They run to do battle with corrupting commercial colonialists on swift synthetic cushions manufactured by Nike and Reebok. They pause amidst the tribal carnage to refresh themselves with a world beverage like Pepsi or Coke. They shake their local folk zithers at a centralist and encroaching French or German or Japanese culture they despise, and then hammer out the tunes of an even more centralist and encroaching global culture on their quaint instruments. They hatch plots against immigrant foreigners via laptop computer modems made by foreigners and assembled by immigrants in their own land. They yearn for the collective intimacy of the tribe and the gang yet groove on the anonymity and solitude of cyberspace. Fascinated equally by the blood that binds them and the blood they spill, they nevertheless navigate the bloodless world of promotion and product as if they were born to it (they were). Whether they hang with South Central L.A.'s Bloods or Cripps, belong to Berlin's neo-Nazi National Alternative, or run with Tokyo's Speed Tribes, whether they shoot at teens trying to get out of the Bosnian dead zones or are the teens being shot at, whether they are Hutu minors murdering Tutsis or twenty-year-old French paratroopers trying to come between the murderous brothers, they will be the twenty-first century's makers—and its victims. They hold Jihad and McWorld suspended in rent souls that can neither eject one or the other nor accommodate both. Dragged reluctantly from a past defined by culture and tribe into a future where velocity is becoming an identity all its own, they are accelerating toward the limits of nature—the speed of light that defines the interactions of cyberspace—in quest of a palliative to (or is it a catalyst for?) their restlessness. The outcome inside their struggling souls will likely condition the outcome for global civilization, whose prospects, consequently, do not seem terribly promising.

13

Jihad Within McWorld: "Transitional Democracies"

THE PARADOXICAL INTERFACE of Jihad and McWorld is nowhere more in evidence than behind the crumpled iron curtain in the "transitional" or "emerging democracies"—which though they most certainly are emerging from communism and in transition to somewhere, are for the most part neither democratic nor very likely to become so any time soon. If anything, they are regressing rather than progressing. Dragoslav Bokan, an editor and film director who became a leader of the Serbian private militia known as the White Eagles, confesses: "I don't believe in democracy because I don't believe any group at any time can change the course and goals of their ancestors by their own free will."[1] Another spent local academic concludes: ". . . too much history in too little room. There are no liberals here, there are only nationalists. We are victims of a long-lasting nationalist idea, impossible to get rid of."[2] The nationalist idea so many Eastern Europeans manage at once both to fear and to cherish is not the nineteenth-century ideal of integration and nation building. Yugoslavia, insists Zarko Domljan, Croatia's Assembly president elected in 1991, "is not a nation—it is a mixture of ancient tribes," and newspaper headlines regularly feature the region in terms of a "whirlwind of hatreds."[3]

Within the developed world, to which these jagged middle European shards of the ex-Soviet empire affect to belong, there is no region in which Jihad has an uglier or more disintegral presence. Both as a struggle against multicultural nation-states, states that once managed to sublimate ethnicity such as Yugoslavia, Czechoslovakia, and the Soviet Union once were, and as a battle to contain the cultural inroads of McWorld's implacable markets, Jihad has found its natural home in Central Europe and Western Asia. Its compass is described by that great arc of warring tribes that rises off the Adriatic through Albania and Yugoslavia, and—flanked by Bulgaria to the south and Hungary to the north—pushes northeast through Romania and Transylvania to Moldavia and Bessarabia and into the Ukraine and the Crimea, wrapping itself around the Black Sea and finally dropping down again into Transcaucasia, where Azerbaijanis and Armenians do battle right up to the edge of the Caspian Sea as Europe gives way to Asia. This bloody crescent has always been the heartland of Europe's zone of tumult. Above it there is a secondary arc, scarcely less bloody, whose trajectory runs from Czechoslovakia and Poland up through the Baltic nations of Lithuania, Latvia, and Estonia in the north, and then plunges down into Belarus, Great Russia proper, and the Ukraine, which features its own multicultural nightmares.

Under the great empires of the Ottomans, the Austro-Hungarians, and the Russians, these tribally supersaturated regions were neatly segmented into pluralistic zones of tolerance where local culture flourished under the watchful eye of monarchies that would brook no bloodshed other than the bloodshed that emanated from their own policies. The neo-imperial Communists also enforced a nationalities doctrine that was repressive and intolerant of parochialism. Today this imperial handiwork has come wholly unraveled, leaving behind two rabid versions of Jihad—antipluralist and antimodern—that have turned the rout of Communist imperialism into a victory for irredentism and genocide and left democracy out in the cold.

In this bloody arc, McWorld is both the target and the cause of irrepressible Jihad. Widespread criminality, sometimes indistinguishable from anarchic new markets, is providing anti-Western hotheads and new/old breed Communist-nationalists with powerful ideological ammunition. The free market in Russia has become associated with bankrupt pyramid schemes that have sucked up the savings of millions of people and turned them forever against what they perceive as an unregulated and depraved—what Solzhenitsyn calls "wild"—capitalism.[4] In the Ukraine, according to one estimate, up to one-half of "all economic activity is illegal."[5] Crime has become so pervasive in the ex-Soviet lands that at least one commentator has suggested that it be legitimized at the highest levels since "Russians are used to firm control from the top. If domination by a mafia bureaucracy offered a return to the relative order enjoyed by many under the Communist rule, many would embrace it."[6]

Still unwilling to entrust their government to private-sector criminals, many newly "free" peoples have turned the reins back over to public-sector criminals: ex-Communists and nationalists who ruled in the *ancien* Communist *régime* and, having cashed in their commissar's chips for a privileged place in the new capitalist order and supplanted old Leninist with still older tribalist dogmas, were more than ready to reinstate the heavy hand that an exasperated and weary electorate has now come to crave. The new political arithmetic equates crime and McWorld (and sometimes crime and democracy), and thereby gives the tribal Jihad against it the status of a war on behalf of decency and honesty. Lithuania, Belarus, the Ukraine, Poland, Hungary, Serbia, Croatia, Bulgaria, and Mongolia are among the countries where frustrated citizens in the second wave of free elections elected "new" governments composed of old Communists wedded to nationalist and ethnic doctrines of one kind or another. Where even they are too moderate, radical right nationalists and antisemites—like Istvan Csurka in Hungary and those in the Romanian parliament who recently voted to honor Romania's wartime fascist leader Ion Antonescu—stalk both the moderates and their parliamentary system as Hitler once stalked Weimar.[7] They wait for popular impatience to overcome frail and unrooted political institutions, often because there is no civil society to root and secure them.

The most notorious of the new old world bigots, Vladimir V. Zhirinovsky, hits exactly the right note in harmonizing the parochial interests of fanatic Russian nationalism and a struggle against McWorld that seems almost prudent when he shouts: "It was all the same to them [the Western powers] who ruled Russia, czars or Communists, their goal was to destroy Russia." Whereas in two previous world wars, Zhirinovsky thunders, the Germans came with brute force and blitzkrieg, the new aggressors invade with "pretty slogans about democracy and human rights. . . . The Americans are clever." On this point, surely he is right: "They know it is better to come here with chewing gum, stockings and McDonald's."[8] He's a little out of date in his World War II allusion to nylons and sweets; but leave McDonald's and replace chewing gum and stockings with Macintoshes and Nikes, and the advance guard of McWorld is accurately named.

There is no country in Eastern and Central Europe or the republics of the old Soviet Union that has proved immune to Jihad's contagion, and that has not suffered politically and economically for it.[9] Spawned by fear and insecurity and driven by the failure of clumsy and foolhardy attempts to impose Western economic and political institutions wholesale on societies wholly unprepared to accommodate them, a variety of small but toxic Jihads have flourished, leaving the region with no really convincing success stories. Not the Czech Republic despite its bloodless (if not quite "velvet") revolution and its poet president who, for all his dissident legitimacy, could not thwart the divorce of his country from Slovakia; not Hungary, though it comes close to being ethnically monocultural and is thus supposedly immune to the ravages of tribalism;[10] not Poland, notwithstanding its relative economic success and its traditions of Catholicism and unionism (Solidarity) that tie it to the West; certainly not Russia. In each of these countries, ethnic tensions, reawakened bigotries, separatist rumblings, or nationalist zealotry stalk governments committed in theory to the West's constitutions and McWorld's markets.

For tragic irony, no country can rival Yugoslavia, whose very name conjures the full meaning of Jihad within the domain of McWorld more eloquently than a library of books could ever do. Here was the only Communist nation to be admired at least a little by left democrats and idealists in the West, a state brave enough to reject Stalin, imaginative enough to federalize its socialist system and empower its workers, resourceful enough to bring its hostile ethnic fragments to heel, prudent enough to forge a pluralist army strong and loyal to Yugoslavia.[11] Its failure—the conquest of imagined history over actual achievement—has been the shame of the West ever since. The promise of the future in Belgrade was traded for reconstructed memories of nineteenth-century Pan-Slavic dreams like those of Nikolai Danilevsky, who postulated an Orthodox Russian soul at odds with the Catholic West, firing the imagination not only of Russians but of Bulgars, Macedonians, and Serbs. Czarist Russia actually dispatched volunteers in 1877 to support the uprising of Serbs and Montenegrins against the Turks, and (to oversimplify) Serbia returned the favor in 1914 by dragging Russia into World War I in the cause of its independence from the Austro-Hungarian Empire. Serbia today justifies its ethnic outrages in the region by appeal to anti-Vatican and anti-German sentiments and sulks about being "betrayed" by Russia (though a group of Russian volunteers called the "Czar's Wolves" were involved in the Serbia campaign in Bosnia).[12]

I will not, however, try to do justice to the tragic narrative of carnage that quickly has become Yugoslavia's destiny. That story has been in the headlines nonstop for the last three or four years. A quick glance at the absurdist maps drawn by desperate would-be peacekeepers trying to stay out of the conflagration without completely surrendering to brute force will show just how far back poor Yugoslavia has fallen into a brutal and fractious if also largely imaginary past. It is hard to tell which smacks of greater cynicism: the spirit of self-delusion and appeasement with which spineless "concerned" outsiders draw their successive maps; or the hypocrisy and deceit with which the protagonists within toy with and ultimately reject them. Perhaps it doesn't matter. For in the end, the cynicism of all negotiations in the region is an apt response to their sheer futility.

To give even Yugoslavia, let alone the dozens of emerging tribal fragments, their due here would require that I compile a Middle European encyclopedia of ethnicity and civil war that would surely run to dozens of volumes. There simply is no efficient way to do justice to the multiple Jihads that have sprung up within but against McWorld from a region that is within McWorld's borders without being of McWorld. Let me offer just one case, an instance centered on a nation in the very middle of the middle in which, despite a strong nation-state, nearly every toxic attribute of disintegral Jihad is present or threatening: the Ukraine. This largest and most powerful of the ex-Soviet Union's newly autonomous non-Russian nations, to many "the sick man of the region,"[13] boasts nuclear weapons (supposedly to be dismantled), a fleet (supposedly to be bartered off to Russia in return for fuel and gas credits), and the status of a major power (in negotiation).[14] The Dnieper River, on which the Ukrainian capital of Kiev lies, divides the country between an eastern region heavily populated with Russians (nearly 11 million or more than 20 percent of a total Ukrainian population of 52 million) and firmly attached to Russia, especially in the Crimea, which is over 60 percent Russian; and a western region with its "capital" at Lvov, where ethnic Ukrainians cherish their autonomy even as they confront ethnic rivals in Romania across the Dniester River to the west and in Hungary, Slovakia, and Belarus to the northwest. The Ukraine's big power status conceals a civic fragility: for not only is it in conflict with most of its neighbors, but it is also deeply divided from within. A senior Western diplomat has warned: "If Ukraine ruptures the whole of Central Europe and the Black Sea region goes up with it."[15]

Ukraine thus faces dual risks from Jihad: rupture from within and conflict with neighbors. Its first post-Soviet president was Leonid M. Kravchuk, an ideological Communist who, much like Milosevic in Yugoslavia, converted to lethal nationalism following independence, thereby arousing the suspicion and fear of the 11 million Russians living primarily in the east and on the Crimea peninsula in the Black Sea. Under his regime, inflation grew at as much as 40 percent a month (in a period where critics assailed a 25 percent rate in Russia), and despite the Ukraine's formidably educated workforce and natural and manufacturing resources, industrial production dropped by a third to a half (between 1991 and 1993) in what World Bank officials called a "hyperdepression."[16] In 1994, reformer Leonid D. Kuchma ousted Kravchuk and, to the consternation of ethnic Ukrainians in the west, seems to be cozying up to the Russians again. Nationalist Ukrainians have not forgotten how Stalin, after an initial period of "Ukrainization" when Ukrainian culture was celebrated and the language officially recognized by the Soviet Union, turned on the nationalists, murdering millions of them and exterminating intellectuals wholesale.

Hence, though Kuchma was Kravchuk's prime minister (breaking with him eventually), he is now distrusted both in Western Europe (he has had second thoughts about signing the nuclear proliferation treaty and seems likely to elicit a powerful anti-Russian reaction) and in the western Ukraine—which was brought into the Soviet Ukrainian Republic only after World War II and has even less use for the government in Moscow than the part that underwent Stalinist antinationalist excesses. There he has earned the epithet of traitor; how easily the language of treason comes to the warriors of Jihad! On the other hand, some have estimated that nearly half of all Ukrainians now disapprove of Ukrainian independence, and Kuchma's rapprochement with Moscow has strong support in the east, above all in the Crimea.

Once the home of Tatars, the Crimea underwent a Russian ethnic cleansing in 1944 when Stalin murdered or relocated its Turkic population to Tatarstan along the Volga River (which with nearly 5 million Tatars today is the largest of the Russian Republic's semi-autonomous regions), leaving the Crimea entirely Russian. But after the breakup of the Communist empire, a quarter of a million Tatars returned to the Crimea where they reside today, three-quarters of them unemployed, complicating the Crimea's uncertain status under Ukrainian sovereignty. The majority of Crimean Russians would probably favor reunion with Russia, but the Tatar minority, with historical claims to a Crimean homeland, favor neither Ukrainian nor Russian suzerainty. What has ensued has been an ever more inscrutable Eastern feudal (that is, Byzantine) politics. The current Crimean regional president Yuri Meshkov is followed everywhere by Kalishnikov-carrying guards (at least a half dozen politicians in the region have been gunned down), and though he leans to Moscow, probably does so because he has so few viable options.

On the other side of the Ukraine, where there are few Russians and where native Ukrainians face west, another conflict brews, this one with Romania. The Romanians and the Ukrainians have feuded over the region called Moldavia (including Bessarabia) for centuries. In World War II, after a brief interlude in 1940 (the Stalin-Hitler Pact) when it lost Transylvania to the Hungarians and Romanian Moldavia to the Soviets, the Nazi-supported Romanian regime wrested away both Bukovina in the north and Bessarabia in the east (where Romanian was spoken) once again joining all of Moldavia to Wallachia; it also took control of the purely Ukrainian trans-

Dniester region including Odessa. After the war, the Ukraine was restored but Moldavia was established again as an independent Soviet Republic, a buffer between the Ukraine and Romania but also a sore point. Its independence in 1989 exacerbated tensions, especially after Ukrainians on the east bank of the Dniester shelled Romanian-speaking Moldavians on the west bank. The campaign for a trans-Dniester autonomous region continues, leaving both Romania and the Ukraine in a state of agitation. Although President Ion Iliescu of Romania insists, "Our priority is full integration into the Western and the world economy," Romania seems even more focused on ethnic rivalries than its rival, the Ukraine.[17] In the northwestern Transylvania region, a million and a half Hungarian speakers (of a total Romanian population of 23 million) represent a potential army in Csurka's campaign for a "greater Hungary." Although they have recently been appeased by new laws permitting them to use their own language, they still are called Mongolian Vandals by nationalist Romanians.[18]

The Romanians have also continued to persecute gypsies, who suffered as much as Jews from Romania's wartime profascist racial policies. Romania is hardly the only country to oppress gypsies or "Romani" ("Roma")—a Times Mirror poll suggests "the one sentiment that unites Western and Eastern Europe is hatred of Gypsies"[19]—but it is the only one where official opinion seems to support popular prejudice. *Romania Mare*, Romania's largest weekly, recently demanded the expulsion of all gypsies from the country (there are 2½ million) and a number of gypsy dwellings have been burnt down and several gypsies murdered.[20] Unlike the Free Democrats in Hungary, which includes a statement about fair treatment of gypsies in its party platform, Romania's political parties are eloquently mute on the subject.

Prime Minister Roman (like ex-Ambassador to the United States Sylviu Brucan) is Jewish, but President Iliescu's National Salvation Front party does nothing to disavow Romania wartime leader Ion Antonescu whose Iron Guard of the Legion of Saint Michael assisted the Nazis in exterminating gypsies and Jews alike.[21] Indeed, Romania was the only power outside Germany to set up and run extermination camps. In the western Ukraine, Antonescu's minions buried children alive to save bullets and finally drew the ire of

Adolph Eichmann [*sic*], who was appalled by the inefficient and clumsy brutality of the Romanian camps.[22] Late in the war, with the writing on the wall, Antonescu changed his stripes, but not soon enough to avoid execution by the Russians in 1946. But today his reputation has been refurbished (he appears as "the great Patriot"), while Jews are again accused of betraying Romanian national interests by siding with the Soviets during the Holocaust and thus made responsible for precipitating their own liquidation! Revisionist history places blame for the mass murders in the Ukraine on the Russians and their allies the Jews.

Bram Stoker, the author of *Dracula,* wrote of this tumultuous region of a hundred inextricably entangled, intermarried, warring peoples: "Every known superstition in the world is gathered into the horseshoe of the Carpathians, as if it were the center of some sort of imaginative whirlpool . . . political life is characterized by a peculiar mysticism and theatricality."[23] What imagination has contributed is an often mythic history that makes variety the occasion of antagonism and gives to subtle, changing, and often unperceived differences the murderous force of other-hatred. Eric Hobsbawm seems to be echoing Stoker when he observes that "history is not ancestral memory or collective tradition. It is what people learned from priests, schoolmasters, the writers of history books, and the compilers of magazine articles and T.V. programs."[24]

The hatreds of the region are as often learned as remembered, more frequently inspired by hate-mongering ethnic radio programs than inherited from ancient feuds. Actual identities are more commonly multicultural. "It is perfectly common for the elderly inhabitant of some central European city," writes Hobsbawm, "to have had the identity documents of three successive states. A person of my age from Lemberg or Czernowitz has lived under four states, not counting wartime occupation; a man from Munkacs may well have lived under five."[25] Unfortunately, such tolerance-breeding genealogical uncertainties are today contrived away by terrorist rhetoric. Loosed of the imperial bonds that under the Austro-Hungarian and Ottoman empires dissolved particularist identities, today's subnationalist fragments seek a reduction to minimalist forms where local dialect, sectarian religion, and ethnic identity can merge and, courtesy of a constricting logic of ethnic self-determination, can forge a narrow nationality grounded—if not in history—in a carefully suckled hatred of "others." A Serbo-Croat–speaking Bosnian who, however, has a great-great-grandfather who became a Muslim under the Ottomans, becomes a deserving subject of expulsion. A common religion and an efficient economic partnership are not enough to keep Czechs and Slovaks aroused by rekindled "historical" passions from annihilating all they share. After all, "if there is no suitable past, it can always be invented."[26] The stories of the regions outlined here all suggest reinvented pasts employed to make war on the present in a manner that can only haunt the future.

Pessimists gave up on the region almost before it had emerged from communism. Janos Vorzsak, vice president of the Democratic Union of Hungarians in Romania, exclaimed back in 1990: "The majority of Romanians are not prepared for democracy. They have lived so long in an infernal darkness, that they are easily led. They have a primitive psychology."[27] But this is only true because leaders want it to be true, because the electronic and digital machinery of McWorld is put to work on behalf of Jihad, because memory is chained to resentment. Which means, as I shall suggest below, that it can be unchained. For if Jihad undermines the conditions for democracy, so democracy can undermine the conditions for Jihad. Or can it?

14

Essential Jihad: Islam and Fundamentalism

Nowhere is the tension between democracy and Jihad more evident than in the Islamic world, where the idea of Jihad has a home of birth but certainly not an exclusive patent. For, although it is clear that Islam is a complex religion that by no means is synonymous with Jihad, it is relatively inhospitable to democracy and that inhospitality in turn nurtures conditions favorable to parochialism, antimodernism, exclusiveness, and hostility to "others"—the characteristics that constitute what I have called Jihad.

While *Jihad* is a term associated with the moral (and sometimes armed) struggle of believers against faithlessness and the faithless, I have used it here to speak to a generic form of fundamentalist opposition to modernity that can be found in most world religions. In their massive five-volume study of fundamentalisms, Martin E. Marty and R. Scott Appleby treat Sunni and Shiite Islam but pay equal attention to Protestantism and Catholicism in a variety of European, and North and South American forms, to Hinduism, to the Sikhs, to Theravada Buddhism, to Confucianist Revivalism, and to Zionism. Marty and Appleby take fundamentalist religions to be engaged in militancy, in a kind of permanent *fighting:* they are "militant, whether in the use of words and ideas or ballots or, in extreme cases, bullets."[1] They fight back, struggling reactively against the present in the name of the past; they fight for their religious conception of the world against secularism and relativism; they fight with weapons of every kind, sometimes borrowed from the enemy, carefully chosen to secure their identity; they fight against others who are agents of corruption; and they fight under God for a cause that, because it is holy, cannot be lost even when it is not yet won. The struggle that is Jihad is not then just a feature of Islam but a characteristic of all fundamentalisms. Nevertheless, *Jihad* is an Islamic term and is given its animating power by its association not just with fundamentalism in general but with Islamic fundamentalism in particular and with the armed struggles groups like Hamas and Islamic Jihad have engaged in. There are moderate and liberal strands in Islam, but they are less prominent at present than the militant strand.

As a religion, Islam has universalist tendencies and while hardly ecumenical, it has displayed considerable tolerance for other religions, even when practiced by minorities dwelling in Muslim countries. Historically, it has shown a greater reluctance to proselytize than Christianity. It has had its empires, but nothing to rival the Crusades or the colonial empires of Britain and France. Yet Islam posits a world in which the Muslim religion and the Islamic state are cocreated and inseparable, and some observers argue it has less room for secularism than any other major world religion. Thus, while there are fundamentalist tendencies in every religion, in Islam, such tendencies have played a leading political role since the eighteenth century. This has created special problems for democracy and human rights in predominantly Muslim countries throughout the Middle East, North Africa, and Asia. Moreover, in such countries the struggle of Jihad against McWorld has been much more than a metaphor for tribalism or a worried antimodernism. It has been a literal war on the values, culture, and institutions that make up liberal society. Even Arab friends of the West feel constrained to raise doubts about Western values. In an advertisement intended to allay the worries of Americans about its Saudi Arabian ally, Ambassador Prince Bandar Ibn-Sultan nonetheless felt compelled to write: "Foreign imports are nice as shiny or high-tech 'things.' But intangible social and political institutions can be deadly."[2] An official of the Iranian Ministry of Culture and Islamic Guidance can afford to be less oblique. About satellite programs being beamed in to Teheran, he says: "These programs, prepared by international imperialism, are part of an extensive plot to wipe out our religious and sacred values."[3] With *Dynasty, Donahue, Dinky Dog,* and *The Simpsons* being beamed in courtesy of Star TV to compete with what Iranian skeptics call "the man on the balcony" (the late revolutionary leader Ayatollah Khomeini delivering interminable speeches), it is hardly surprising that the Iranian state believes "the satellite is exactly against the honorable Prophet" and is trying to ban the import, manufacture, and use of satellite dishes.[4]

Jihad has been a metaphor for anti-Western antiuniversalist struggle throughout this book. The question here is whether it is more than just a metaphor in the Muslim culture that produced the term. An empirical survey of existing governments in Islamic nations certainly affirms a certain lack of affinity between Islam and democracy. In nearly all Muslim nations, democracy has never been tried or has been pushed aside after unsuccessful experiments. In Algeria, following elections that, because fundamentalists triumphed, were annulled, it is in deep peril; in Egypt, where democracy has not really been fully tried, minimal liberties are being eroded by a fearful government trying to track down fundamentalist enemies; in Kuwait, even after the war to "liberate" it from the Iraqi oppressors, democracy is invisible. Nations like Pakistan and Afghanistan and Sudan have become or seem likely to become even less democratic than they were as Islamic fundamentalists become more powerful, while American allies like Saudi Arabia, Jordan, and the oil emirates are hard-pressed to keep up the pretense of being democratic as they pursue their antifundamentalist struggle, even though it is in the name of democracy that they do battle.

Indeed, fundamentalism may have a better record as an enemy of despots in the Middle East than have had the secular systems constructed to put down fundamentalism and to realize Western aspirations. Yet though fundamentalism has often stood against tyranny, it has never created democracy. The historical record is poor enough to have led some observers like John Waterbury to credit an "exceptionalist" thesis: that Islam creates an exceptional set of circumstances that disqualify Islamic countries from becoming democratic and fates them to an eternal struggle against the Enlightenment and its liberal and democratic children.[5] Hilal Khashan says simply, "All of the . . . democratic prerequisites are lacking in the Arab world. Arab democracy along Western terms is wishful thinking."[6]

Yet as one might expect, there are rival interpretations of Islam within the Islamic world, and no single monolithic argument goes unchallenged. Although Islam has no word for democracy and uses the Greek term (but then, as it happens, so do we) and though it often regards democratic political systems as unique to the West—what in Arabic is denominated as the strange, dark, fear-inspiring "Gharb" where the sun sets on the home of alien and aggressive peoples—it is not without its own Islamic Enlightenment sources. In at least one version of its history, Islam too is a story of the struggle between reason and belief, between consent and authoritarianism, between resistance to tyranny and tyrants. The Moroccan sociologist Fatima Mernissi insists that "throughout its history Islam has been marked by two trends: an intellectual trend that speculated on the philosophical foundations of the world and humanity, and another trend that turned political challenge violent by resort to force." The first trend offered a meditation on reason akin to Western humanism; the second "simply thought that by rebelling against the imam and sometimes killing him they could change things."[7] Both traditions "raise the same issues that we are today told are imports from the West," issues of resistance and accountability—that is to say, of democracy.

There is thus a sense in which Islamic fundamentalists are genuine resisters against corrupt worldly political authority, much as the early Christians were. The zealots who assassinated Anwar Sadat in 1981 were members of a group called literally "Jihad" and when, their bloody deed done, they shouted, "I have killed Pharaoh, and I do not fear death," they were speaking the language of martyrs of liberation.[8] In Algeria, fundamentalists came to power by the ballot in 1991 and it was the secular party of national liberation under the tutelage of the army that shut down democratic institutions rather than turn them over to its adversaries, who had vanquished them in the polls. Observers thus continue to believe that Islam and democracy have a future together. At a 1992 conference held by the United States Institute on Peace, conferees spoke of a "new synthesis" in which the "clash of opinions on the relationship between Islam and democracy could yield a new synthesis view in which Islamic notions enhance and give new meaning to democratic concepts beyond their current western-dominated usages."[9]

How real is this promise? Is democracy in Islamic countries more a victim of colonial repression and postcolonial exploitation than of indigenous Islamic forces, as critics like Edward W. Said contend?[10] Or is Islam an "exception" that rules out a free civil society and thus precludes real democracy? If democracy means Western democracy and modernization means Westernization, there would seem to be little hope for reconciliation since Islam regards Western secular culture and its attending values as corrupting to and morally incompatible with its own. But if democracy takes many forms, and is an ancient as well as a modern manifestation of the quest for self-governing communities, then perhaps it can be adapted to notions found in the Koran such as *umma* (community), *shura* (mutual consultation), and *al maslaha* (public interest). As other Islamic scholars have argued, understood this way, Islam may not be "antithetical to the telos of democratic values."[11] Islamic fundamentalists may insist that since Allah's will is sovereign, the people's will cannot be, but moderates point out that this still leaves ample room for the majority to exercise political authority as long as it does so within a framework that acknowledges the ultimate hegemony of divine power. Neither France nor Italy has a formal constitutional separation of church and state and both have constructed relatively viable democracies. Ultimate obedience to God can act as a brake on authoritarian and licentious worldly government, while affording a moderate people, constrained by faith, room to govern themselves democratically in the manner of Calvinist Geneva or Puritan Massachusetts before the Revolution.

The trouble with this path to reconciliation is that fundamentalist Islam is not first of all opposed to democracy but to modernization, particularly as manifested in Westernization. Democracy has ancient antecedents and in its premodern and preliberal forms is not necessarily at odds either with fundamentalist Islam nor with fundamentalist Christianity. The City of God for Christians and Muslims alike is constituted by brother believers who are equal in their filial posture vis-à-vis God. But unlike democracy, which can be compatible with religion (Tocqueville actually thought it depended on religion), modernity is tantamount to secularism and is almost by definition corrupting to all religion, above all to that religion that assumes the "*comprehensive* and *universal* nature of the message of God as presented in the Qur'an."[12] This comprehensive and universal sovereignty of God creates thorny problems for Islam that Christianity circumvented by postulating a "two swords" doctrine in which God ruled in His domain and Man, through kingship, ruled in his own. Pope Gregory's use of the New Testament accommodationist maxim, "Render unto God those things that are God's and unto Caesar those that are Caesar's," represented a preconstitutional separation of church and state that has no analog in Islam, which prefers that men render everything unto Allah, ecclesiastic and worldly, spiritual and temporal alike. Such a monolithic arrangement may discomfit democrats, although it also discomfits kings (since neither have a domain exclusive of Allah's in which to practice their sovereignty or their despotism; Allah does not tolerate rivals).

Nevertheless, democracy has always found a way to accommodate religion, and Jihad's war has been less with democracy than with McWorld. In the 1920s, Hasan al-Banna, founder of the Muslim Brotherhood, was railing against "the wave of atheism and lewdness" engulfing Egypt, a wave that "started the devastation of religion and morality on the pretext of individual and intellectual freedom."[13] Al-Banna could be reproaching Rupert Murdoch or Barry Diller when he assailed Westerners for importing "their half-naked women into these regions, together with their liquors, their theaters, their dance halls, their amusements, their stories, their newspapers, their novels, their whims, their silly games, and their vices." He had taken the measure of McWorld long before McWorld had jelled sufficiently to take the measure of itself. Grasping the superior corrosiveness of knowledge over arms and of communications over armies, he warned in the 1920s that the culture of the West "was more dangerous than the political and military campaigns by far." Where colonial empires failed, he seemed to prophesy, McWorld would succeed.

Al-Banna's indignation goes to the very heart of Jihad's campaign against the modern, the secular, and the cosmopolitan. It captures the essence of fundamentalism as it has existed since the seventeenth century, growing up alongside the devil modernity to which it has played angel's advocate for Puritans and Muslims, Buddhists and born-again Baptists alike. Compare al-Banna's fiery rhetoric with the mad sermonizing of the British Puritan Prynne. In his nearly hysterical genealogy of theatrical vices called "Histriomastix," Prynne condemns stage plays as "the very pompes of the Divell which we renounce in Baptisme . . . sinfull, heathenish, lewde, ungodly spectacles, and most pernicious Corruptions," and then goes on to asperse as "wicked, unChristian pasttimes" a host of modern pursuits including "effeminate mixt dancing, Dicing, lascivious pictures, wanton Fashions, face-painting, health-drinking, long haire, love-lockes, Periwigs, womens curling, pouldering and cutting of their hair, Bone-Fires, New-yeares gifts, Maygames, amorous Pastoralls, lascivious effeminate Musicke, excessive laughter, luxurious disorderly Christmas keeping . . ." and a dozen other amusements that together compose a catalog of McWorld's progenitors.[14] Is there a single item here a fervent mullah could not also condemn? We can also hear al-Banna's outrage in Jean-Jacques Rousseau's calculated rant against capital cities as coffins of true justice and morals, cities full of scheming, idle people without religion or principle.[15] Rousseau's complaints are the complaints of Provence peasants against effete Parisian courtiers and modernizing Parisian Jacobins; they are the bitter remonstrances of Alabama farmers against the cultural elites in Hollywood and New York and the out-of-touch "pols" playing special-interest games "inside the beltway." For the revolt against modernity is a rebellion against cosmopolitanism and its urban culture and urbane entertainments. Not without good reason, the anticosmopolitan animus that drives all fundamentalist reaction has come to distrust Enlightenment: for economic growth brings burgeoning worldly needs and an obsession with gratification while the arts and sciences undermine simplicity and the natural faith of simple women and men. Enlightenment breeds secularism and secularism destroys not just formal religion but the morals on which it is based and thus the social fabric that holds communities together.

Finally, al-Banna is not so far from Pat Robertson and Pat Buchanan and the Christian Right's campaign for a return to nineteenth-century family values—family values understood as direct emanations of church going, school prayer, and a Protestant Christian America. As the Muslim Brotherhood saw in Christianity a crusading corruptor, Know-Nothing American Protestants back in the 1880s saw in Mediterranean Catholic immigrants a grave peril to the American Republic, just as nervous Californians today worry about illegal Latino immigrants as a burden not only on their pocketbooks but on the moral order of their unraveling communities. To Americans, Jihad is often taken to be a foreign phenomenon, a feature of Middle Eastern politics and the Holy War between Muslim diaspora and Zionist settlers mutually obsessed with holy turf. But we can today also speak of an American Jihad. Not the American Jihad promulgated by the media focused on the World Trade Center bombers or on Arab-American supporters of Hamas—the American Jihad about which Stephen Barboza wrote his recent book.[16] The American Jihad that counts is rather the antiestablishmentarian fundamentalism of the Christian Right, the Jihad of profoundly antimodern fundamentalist Protestants who rebel against the culture of disbelief generated by the McWorld that is in their midst;[17] the McWorld they unearth on their prime-time television programming and rebury on their talk-radio rants; and in the secular public square where despised "liberal" politicians undermine their belief systems with textbooks that preach evolution and schools that bar prayer.

Modernity has enemies other than Islamic Holy War, then, some of them on McWorld's own American home turf. At least since the 1730s, when America experienced its first "Great Awakening" in Protestant fundamentalism, this country has periodically felt the zeal of reactive religion. Mainstream Christian Coalition leaders today offer what is relatively speaking a moderate version of Jihad. Jerry Falwell, the president of the Moral Majority, thus sermonizes against a Supreme Court that has "raped the Constitution and raped the Christian faith and raped the churches" and implores followers to "fight against those radical minorities who are trying to remove God from our textbooks, Christ from our nation. We must never allow our children to forget that this is a Christian nation. We must take back what is rightfully ours."[18] Pat Buchanan tells the Republican National Convention in 1992 that the country faces a cultural war for its very survival and victorious Republicans following the 1994 elections accuse President Clinton of countercultural and un-American attitudes. Less conventional warriors such as Randall Terry, the antiabortion crusader, are far more blunt: "I want you to just let a wave of intolerance wash over you. I want you to let a wave of hatred wash over you. Yes, hate is good. . . . Our goal is a Christian nation. We have a biblical duty, we are called by God, to conquer this country."[19] These Christian soldiers bring to their ardent campaign against time and the modern world all the indignation, all the impatience with moral slackness, all the purifying hatred, of the zealots in Teheran and Cairo. They indulge McWorld only in order to use its high-tech communications to organize voters or its rock music to sugar-coat salvation lyrics. Groups like Gospel Gangstas and A-1 S.W.I.F.T. press drive-by shootings into the service of Jesus:

> *In this scrap the Word of God's my A-K*
> *Pointed at your Dome*
> *'Cause my aim is straight, hey . . .*
> *You wanna be set free*
> *Then you gotta be saved*
> *Better do it now*
> *Move with the quickness*
> *Or else I'll hit you with the*
> *Drive by Witness.*[20]

They may not be angels,[21] these pious gospel cowboys, but they are not madmen either: they are winning local elections and helped win Congress for the Republicans in 1994, and they are continuing to push the Republican Party further and further rightward. They raised millions for Colonel Oliver North's senatorial campaign in Virginia and nearly won. They are astute not merely in their political tactics but in their judgment on McWorld. There is much in McWorld that is sickening, much that outrages elementary justice and morals, much that demeans religion and religious belief, much that belittles both human beings and the larger spirit to which—if they are to feel human—they feel they must belong. The yearning of American suburbanites for the certainties of a literal New Testament are no less ingenuous than the yearning of Arabic martyrs for the certainties of a literal Qur'an. They both want to be born again so as to be born yesterday, born into a former epoch before Nietzsche tried to persuade us that God had died; they want martyrdom before Weber's prophecy that rational men and bureaucratic governments will disenchant the world can come true. Some join fundamentalist collectives, others cultivate a pioneer solitude, going "off the grid" to combat the "new world order" they believe is endangering the antimodern values they cherish.[22] They may break their heads against time itself, but time has not been a friend to either religion or morals in recent centuries. Even the pragmatists who are prepared to live with what history delivers may seek deliverance from the lives they are bequeathed.

Moreover, there is a new breed of American pragmatist: a fearsome pragmatist of holy war who acts out the rage he has carefully cultured from seeds of deeply felt resentment. He may be a veteran but not necessarily, and he probably belongs not just to the National Rifle Association but to a hate group like the White Aryan Resistance or the Order or one of the rapidly spreading "militias" that are forming in nearly every state in America. He is fascinated by the destructive technology of McWorld—its assault weapons and explosives—even as he identifies McWorld's globalism with the loss of his own American style "ancient" liberty. His anger reflects a kind of studied perversion of the civil religion. To him, the constitution means the second amendment (the right to bear arms), liberty means the law stops where his property begins (federal officers are agents of totalitarianism), and government is a demon "it" fronting for communists and the United Nations against which a defensive war must be organized and waged to prevent it from taking over the country. As befits the paranoid style, his heroes are driven loners like Robert Jay Matthews, a leader of the Order who back in 1984 murdered Denver talk show host Alan Berg and was himself killed in a subsequent firefight; Randy Weaver, a white supremacist whose wife and son were killed in a shootout with the authorities in 1992; David Koresh, the Davidian "martyr" whose immolation in Waco in the 1993 government raid has become a call to vengeance for thousands of McWorld castoffs; and Richard Wayne Snell, a self-styled Nazi who murdered a black Arkansas state trooper and was executed on April 19, 1995.

April 19, 1995: that was the same day—exactly two years after the Waco tragedy—a handful of zealots "honoring" these predecessors blew up the federal building in Oklahoma City in what was the most costly terrorist episode in American history. The authorities immediately suspected Jihad. They were right, although mistakenly they thought Jihad meant foreign: Islamic or Arab or Iranian. But Jihad had come home to America in all its native ferocity. Home-grown, it stalks the heartland.

If McWorld in its most elemental negative form is a kind of animal greed—one that is achieved by an aggressive and irresistible energy, Jihad in its most elemental negative form is a kind of animal fear propelled by anxiety in the face of uncertainty and relieved by self-sacrificing zealotry—an escape out of history.[23] Because history has been a history of individuation, acquisitiveness, secularization, aggressiveness, atomization, and immoralism it becomes in the eyes of Jihad's disciples the temporal chariot of wickedness, a carrier of corruption that, along with time itself, must be rejected. Moral preservationists, whether in America, Israel, Iran, or India, have no choice but to make war on the present to secure a future more like the past: depluralized, monocultured, unskepticized, reenchanted. Homogenous values by which women and men live orderly and simple lives were once nurtured under such conditions. Today, our lives have become pulp fiction and *Pulp Fiction* as novel, as movie, or as life promises no miracles. McWorld is meager fare for hungry moralists and shows only passing interest in the spirit. However outrageous the deeds associated with Jihad, the revolt the deeds manifest is reactive to changes that are themselves outrageous.

This survey of the moral topography of Jihad suggests that McWorld—the spiritual poverty of markets—may bear a portion of the blame for the excesses of the holy war against the modern; and that Jihad as a form of negation reveals Jihad as a form of affirmation. Jihad tends the soul that McWorld abjures and strives for the moral well-being that McWorld, busy with the consumer choices it mistakes for freedom, disdains. Jihad thus goes to war with McWorld and, because each worries the other will obstruct and ultimately thwart the realization of its ends, the war between them becomes a holy war. The lines here are drawn not in sand but in stone. The language of hate is not easily subjected to compromise; the "other" as enemy cannot easily be turned into an interlocutor. But as McWorld is "other" to Jihad, so Jihad is "other" to McWorld. Reasoned communication between the two is problematic when for the partisans of Jihad both reason and communication appear as seductive instrumentalities of the devil, while for the partisans of McWorld both are seductive instrumentalities of consumerism. For all their dialectical interplay with respect to democracy, Jihad and McWorld are moral antinomies. There is no room in the mosque for Nintendo, no place on the Internet for Jesus—however rapidly "religious" channels are multiplying. Life cannot be both play and in earnest, cannot stand for the lesser gratification of a needy body and simultaneously for the greater glory of a selfless soul. Either the Qur'an speaks the Truth, or Truth is a television quiz show. History has given us Jihad as a counterpoint to McWorld and made them inextricable; but individuals cannot live in both domains at once and are compelled to choose. Sadly, it is not obvious that the choice, whatever it is, holds out much promise to democrats in search of a free civil society.

Should would-be democrats take their chances then with McWorld, with which they have shared the road to modernity but that has shown so little interest in them? Or try to reach an accommodation with Jihad, whose high moral purpose serves democracy's seriousness yet leaves but precious little space for its liberties? As it turns out, neither Jihad nor McWorld—and certainly not the quarrel between them—allows democracy much room.

PART III

Jihad vs. McWorld

15

Jihad and McWorld in the New World Disorder

THE TALK AMONG quarreling nations is about a new world order, but the clash of Jihad and McWorld foments a new world disorder in which democracy is occluded. The nation-state certainly has not in and of itself guaranteed a democratic civil society, and is probably something less than an indispensable condition for the flourishing of free women and men. After all, democracies of one kind or another arose in small city-state polities—for which they seem ideally suited—before there were nation-states, as well as under empires that had swallowed up nation-states. However, in the last several hundred years, democratic and egalitarian institutions have for the most part been closely associated with integral nation-states, and citizenship (democracy's sine qua non) has been an attribute of membership in such states. The twin assault on democratic citizenship from the fractious forces of Jihad and the spreading markets of McWorld in effect cuts the legs out from under democratic institutions. Whether or not they can secure new foundations either in the parochialism of ethnic identity (and its accompanying politics of resentment) or in the universalism of the profit motive (and its accompanying politics of commodities) is the crucial question.

The bare bones answer, on which I hope presently to put some flesh, is simply this: neither Jihad nor McWorld promises a remotely democratic future. On the contrary, the consequences of the dialectical interaction between them suggest new and startling forms of inadvertent tyranny that range from an invisibly constraining consumerism to an all too palpable barbarism. The market's invisible hand is attached to a manipulative arm that, unguided by a sovereign head, is left to the contingencies of spontaneous greed. Tyranny here is indirect, often even friendly. Alexis de Tocqueville first captured its character 160 years ago when he wrote: "Fetters and headsmen were the coarse instruments that tyranny formerly employed; but the civilization of our age has perfected despotism itself. . . . Monarchs had . . . materialized oppression; the democratic republics of the present day have rendered it as entirely an affair of the mind. . . . [T]he body is left free, and the soul is enslaved."[1] The ideology of choice seems to liberate the body (you can choose sixteen brands of toothpaste, eleven models of pickup truck, seven brands of running shoes) but fatally constricts the possibility of real freedom for the soul (you cannot choose *not* to choose, that is, you cannot choose to withdraw from the market or reject the demands of the body).

McWorld's markets surrender judgment and abjure common willing, leaving public goods to private interests and subordinating communities and their goods to individuals and their interests. The apparent widening of individual consumer choices actually shrinks the field of social choices and forces infrastructural changes no public community ever consciously either selects or rejects. For example, the American's freedom to choose among scores of automobile brands was secured by sacrificing the liberty to choose between private and public transportation, and mandated a world in which strip malls, suburbs, high gas consumption, and traffic jams (to name just a few) became inevitable and omnipresent without ever having been the willed choice of some democratic decision-making body—or for that matter of individuals who liked driving automobiles and chose to buy one. This politics of commodity offers a superficial expansion of options within a determined frame in return for surrendering the right to determine the frame. It offers the feel of freedom while diminishing the range of options and the power to affect the larger world. Is this really liberty?

Internationally, much the same thing is occurring. McWorld speaks the language of choice but severs the "freedom" to buy and sell from the right of women and men to choose in common their common goods or the social character of their shared world. The IMF and the World Bank promote markets but are interested only prudentially if at all in promoting democracy. Indeed, they have shown themselves willing to sacrifice civic equilibrium and social equality for purely economic goals like privatization and free trade. They impose on fragile new would-be democracies economic crash plans that, while they suit the investment strategies of their member nations (and, more important, their member banks), also guarantee popular resentment and generate a nostalgia for the old Communist safety nets. Neo-tribalism and Jihad are often the final beneficiaries. In the near run, agreements like GATT may seem to have a regulative impact since they place power in collectivities of nations—the new World Trade Organization created by GATT, for example—and impose an internationalist majoritarianism on individual nations. Although this compromises the capacity of individual states to regulate their own economies, it supposedly does so in the name of global distributive justice and transnational public goods.[2] In the long run, however, as national sovereignty weakens, the new arrangements actually cede power to markets susceptible to no democratic supervision whatsoever and shrink the global possibilities for public choosing on behalf of fundamental social values.

Jack Heinkman, president of the Amalgamated Clothing and Textile Workers Union, has complained that the GATT agreement legitimizes the exploitation of up to 200 million children, while the insidious environmental consequences of the surrender of sovereignty have been widely denounced in Europe and in America.[3] Further down the road, however, it is not increasingly less sovereign nations quarreling among themselves but multinational firms and their global markets that will dictate to America and other countries what is and is not possible: whether or not five-year-olds will work thirteen-hour shifts in Pakistan for 20 cents a day, whether or not scrubless on-the-cheap smokestacks in one Asian country will be allowed to undo the good work of conscientiously (and expensively) built facilities in another.[4] Even responsible American firms like Levi Strauss and Company, which has developed voluntary "Global Sourcing Guidelines" for its overseas facilities, are driven by competition and profits to seek cheap labor markets, where exploitation is endemic and regulation mainly a public relations afterthought.[5]

Jihad does little better. It identifies the self by contrasting it with an alien "other," and makes politics an exercise in exclusion and resentment. It promotes community but usually at the expense of tolerance and mutuality and hence creates a world in which belonging is more important than empowerment and collective ends posited by charismatic leaders take the place of common grounds produced by democratic deliberation. Jihad speaks the language of self-determination, but severs collective independence from the active liberty of individual citizens. Bosnian Serbia buys a certain version of "self-determination" by forfeiting the liberties of its people.

In Central Europe and Asia, the fall of the iron curtain opened myriad peoples at once both to Jihad and McWorld. The end of Marxism did not spell the end of history, but only the end of Soviet imperialism. In the ragged cohort of states of the ex-Communist empire, it has naturally opened some doors. For as a political practice, Marxism functioned to suppress the liberty in whose name its revolutions were conducted. But the end of Marxism also represented a victory for some of the Enlightenment's more hollow values—materialism, solipsism, and radical individualism—over certain of its nobler aspirations: civic virtue, just community, social equality, and the lifting of the economic yoke from what were once known as the laboring classes. These aspirations had arisen out of the Age of Reason's faith in the emancipatory power of economics and the progressive democratic thrust of history; they had inspired social revolutions in France and later Germany and Russia, none of which proved notably successful. To the extent that the failure of Marxism's revolutions (which began with the failure of Marxism's parent revolution in Jacobin France) is a failure of the Enlightenment, the fiasco has tainted Enlightenment idealism and its faith in progress, leaving us today in a more cynical and selfish world where our aspirations have shrunk to match the diminutive scale of our petty greed and the foreshortened grasp of our visible consumer's hand. The public faith of democracy sometimes seems to have been lost in the baggage thrown overboard when the public faith of socialism was jettisoned.[6]

By democracy, I understand not just government by, for, and of the people, but government by, for, and of citizens. Citizenship is power's political currency and is what gives democracy its civic solvency. Neither Jihad nor McWorld cares a fig about citizens. Thomas Friedman, in a version of the McWorld argument, has suggested that the fratricidal warriors facing one another in Ireland, South Africa, and the Middle East may have been lured from their intractable internecine struggles by the global marketplace, all of them "compelled to beat their swords into plowshares simultaneously by economic forces."[7] But peace is not democracy. McWorld's denizens are consumers and clients whose freedom consists of the right to buy in markets they cannot control and whose identity is imposed on them by a consumerism they scarcely notice. Palestinians and Zulus and North Ireland Catholics will be freer to do business in and outside of their stabilized countries, but they will not necessarily be any freer.

Not long after World War II, Victor Lebow recognized that "Our enormously productive economy . . . demands that we make consumption our way of life, that we convert the buying and selling of goods into rituals, that we seek our spiritual satisfaction, our ego satisfaction, in consumption."[8] Today, as Alan Durning remarks, "the words 'consumer' and 'person' have become virtual synonyms. The world economy," Durning concludes, "is currently organized to furnish 1.1 billion people with a consumer life-style long on things but short on time. . . . High consumption is a precondition to neither full employment nor the end of poverty."[9] It is this world that the consumers of Ireland and Palestine and South Africa are now free to join. But full employment and social justice, or a lifestyle that leaves time to enjoy the goods wealth and education produce, are the concerns of citizens, not consumers, and the release from Jihad will not automatically make them citizens. Until McWorld finds a way to nurture citizens as successfully as it nurtures buyers and sellers, such aims will be systematically neglected, whatever innovative transnational institutions are introduced. Not that citizenship flourishes under conditions of nationalist civil war or ethnic fratricide.

Jihad in fact has little more use for citizens than does McWorld. Its denizens are blood brothers and sisters defined by identities they also are not permitted to choose for themselves. It is possible to be both a sister and a producer, a brother and a consumer, but neither identity affords individuals any real sovereignty over their life plans, which are busily arranged for them by roots and blood on the one hand, or production and consumption on the other. Sovereignty is the provenance of citizenship. The sovereignty of democratic states, which gives politics a regulative function with respect to all other domains, is nothing other than the sovereignty of citizens who, in their civic capacity, make advertent common decisions that regulate the inadvertent consequences of their conduct as private individuals and consumers. In a future world where the only available identity is that of blood brother or solitary consumer, and where these two paltry dispositions engage in a battle for the human soul, democracy does not seem well placed to share in the victory, to whomsoever it is delivered. Neither the politics of commodity nor the politics of resentment promise real liberty; the mixture of the two that emerges from the dialectical interplay of Jihad versus McWorld—call it the commodification of resentment—promises only a new if subtle slavery.

Nonetheless, for all my skepticism about the dialectic of Jihad and McWorld, I do not think that democracy is impossible in an era after the eclipse of the nation-state. Democratic success stories suggest that democracy is a slow, developmental process that comes into being not through a single magical moment of founding, but through a long evolution in which the founding is usually only a culminating symbolic moment. Those who would construct some form of global democracy require patience. They also require stubbornness, however, for to preserve, let alone extend, democracy under these rapidly evolving conditions will require acts of bold political imagination and self-conscious political willing that cannot in themselves be expected to emerge from the dialectical interplay of Jihad and McWorld. Patience, political will, and boldness: not an easy combination of traits to cultivate, above all when democracy is under duress.

Traditional Global Institutions in the New World Disorder

THE EASY ANSWER to the hard question of how to order a supranational world has often been: globalize law!—establish new international institutions or fortify traditional ones like the United Nations and the World Court. From the nineteenth-century faith in the Concert of Powers and its balance of power politics, to Woodrow Wilson's Fourteen Points and the League of Nations (which America never joined) that grew from its following World War I, and on down to the United Nations established after World War II as a manifestation of the cooperation of the Allies in overcoming fascism, the hope has been that sovereign states will somehow overcome their national interests and sectarian policies; that they will cede a degree of their sovereignty to supranational bodies capable of ensuring peace and cooperation among them. Although law speaks the voice of sovereign authority, the quest for world order has placed its faith in a global law whose voice will not be muted by the absence of a global sovereignty. Unhappily, however, while law is power's solemn voice that legitimizes its brute force, power is law's indispensable condition without which its legitimacy has no muscle. Consequently, the law has always been the destitute camp follower of the itinerant armies of transnationalism—earlier, the armies of imperialism, communism, international commerce and markets; today, those of telecommunications, ecology, financial and currency markets, and global pop culture. It facilitates rather than constrains the powers it serves. As go the fortunes of nation-states, so go the fortunes of international law.

Ironically, this linkage cripples law when states are strong since they refuse to allow global law to curb their sovereignty. Yet when they are weak, it leaves international law without an enforcer. Law does not lead but stumbles along behind real power in a manner that belies its claims to transnational regulatory competence. Fans point to the law of the seas, human rights conventions, space treaties, and the new thrust toward global environmental regulation (the Montreal or Rio treaties for example); they boast with some reason about the role the European Court of Justice has played in fostering European integration. Yet events in Europe since Maastricht—indeed, since the founding of the League of Nations[10]—suggest the continuing priority of power over law, whether it is the power of national sovereignty to obstruct and negate international law, or the power of international markets to deflate and circumvent international fishing or environmental regulations.

Where positive international agreements are concluded, they reflect either a rare consensus of interests among signatory nations (as on the Law of the Seas) or the overriding interests of transnational entities like global firms that have persuaded their patron states to support them. The General Agreement on Tariffs and Trade, to take a recent example, actually utilizes its treaty provisions to prevent nations from taking environmental measures that interfere with trade, using "law" as a screen for the advancement of raw economic interests to which the treaty compels sovereign nations to acquiesce. The law is at best utilitarian—handmaiden to the interests of nations or markets—and at worst, a mere rationalization for covert force. Hobbes's great lesson remains true today: "Covenants without the sword" are still but words, of no use at all to secure men or nations. International organizations have no swords but those of their sovereign members, and thus no capacity to enforce law against the more powerful among them. Multinational corporations are not armed, but operate under conditions of transnational political anarchy where economic force is force enough.

Law has, in any case, moved beyond the Hobbesian imagination, primarily because international relations are no longer primarily a matter of relations among nations. International law journals today are at pains to emphasize how nations and their boundaries are being rendered permeable by ecological, commercial, and technological forces that, even as they call out for international regulation, necessarily defy it. Maurice F. Strong, for example, writes: "What is needed is recognition of the reality that in many fields, especially environmental issues, it is simply not feasible for sovereignty to be exercised unilaterally by individual nation-states."[11] As issues move beyond the competence of nation-states, there are no effective regulatory bodies to replace them. Oscar Schachter complains that environmental law has remained entirely "soft—composed of principles and standards of conduct not clearly accepted as obligatory and uncertain in application."[12] Geoffrey Palmer is more despairing still: "We lack the institutional and legal mechanisms to deal effectively with transboundary and biospheric environmental degradation. . . . As matters stand, we lack many of the necessary rules and the means for devising them, we lack institutions capable of ensuring that the rules we have are effective."[13] The appeal to traditional international institutions is an appeal on behalf of the weak to the goodwill of the powerless.

What is true of environmental issues, where transnationalism and subnationalism threaten anarchy, is even more true in other domains. New telecommunications technologies cross borders at will without being technically susceptible to transnational regulation of any kind—even were there effective international regulators on the scene. The virtual networks such technologies create in stocks, bonds, and currencies are likewise beyond the rational control of any entity, national or international. If totalitarian command states like the Soviet Union and Albania were unable to control pirated videos, ubiquitous computer networks, multiplying photocopy and fax machines, and satellite television transmissions (all of which helped bring them down), are weakly motivated market-subordinated states like Britain or Canada likely to do so? And should we expect the still more anemic entities that pass as international organizations and are often little more than special interest trade and market promoters to fill the gaping breech pusillanimous sovereign states have left behind?[14]

The conundrum on which the very idea of a transnational or international institution is founded is that the truly global institution depends on the cooperation of sovereign states whose sovereignty necessarily circumscribes its every move; yet its capacity to act internationally is radically undermined by the passing of the very national sovereignties that constrain it, because it has no alternative source of political legitimacy or executive enforcement. International institutions are consequently impotent as autonomous entities because of national sovereignty but are also impotent in the absence of national sovereignty; for without the agency, the goodwill, and, most critically, the capacity for armed intervention of the hegemons on which they depend, they cannot operate at all. International organizations can neither live with nor live without their obstreperous sovereign members, as the contrapuntal paralysis of the United Nations and NATO in Bosnia demonstrates.

In his compelling book urging an end to laissez-faire ideology in global economics, Robert Kuttner calls for a "true world central bank" that "would require the ceding of a substantial degree of monetary sovereignty, which in turn would mean giving up a good deal of policymaking sovereignty as well."[15] But *to whom* is sovereignty to be ceded? The cohort of nations that funds the bank? Member national banks (which actually do the funding)? Individual bankers, who are natives of some country or other and have both interests and ideologies of their own? Kuttner speaks of the need for regulatory international institutions, but never addresses the question of democratic legitimacy. Who do such entities actually represent? To whom are they accountable? Whose interests are they supposed to advance? It is not even clear to whom such formed collective entities as the new "Europe" are to report. To member national governments? Or to the individual citizens national governments represent? Or, as the German Laender and other powerful regional entities like Lombardy and Catalonia are insisting, to provincial and confederal fragments of nation-states?[16]

As presently organized, the European Union is accountable to elites: through the Council of Ministers, to the governments of its member states and through its burgeoning bureaucracies to technocrats and other professionals with norms and interests of their own. The European parliament may eventually come to represent people directly, but it is currently the product of highly politicized local elections in which elites and ideological parties continue to play a crucial role. A few maverick members have been chosen who represent a distinctive democratic viewpoint (usually Green rather than red or black)—for example, Eve Quistorp from Berlin, who works as a local Green movement organizer and has won a seat in the European parliament. But at this stage her case is the exception rather than the rule. Ultimately, a transnational form of sovereignty will have to spring from a transnational form of group identity and patriotism, but there is no appropriate form of international civil society in which such a citizenship, whether Green or communitarian or world federalist, might thrive at present. If, at the national level, citizenship comes first, and civic institutions only thereafter, where is the global citizen capable of struggling for a global democracy? Stoic cosmopolitanism has yet to fire the imagination or elicit the affections of ordinary women and men, making proposals for global government seem clever pipe dreams at best.[17] Many local activists in Europe have set their democratic sails against the winds of integration.

More than twenty years ago, James Tobin proposed a tithe on international currency transactions that could be applied to the development of disadvantaged nations. More recently Robert Reich, now secretary of labor, advanced a brilliant proposal for a "kind of GATT for direct investment" that would regulate bidding by individual nations for "high-value added investments by global corporations," and develop "fair tactics" that barred "would be threats to close the domestic market unless certain investments were undertaken within it."[18] But to succeed, these proposals would have had to have been supported by the very nations that benefit from today's unfair practices. These practices reward with fat contracts the nations willing to sacrifice the most in the way of cheap labor, high subsidies, low taxes, and environmental laissez-faire, and in effect compel peoples to barter away social justice and the common good for a stake in the international economy. Reich's fair practices would preclude such competition but to work would have to be secured by an international institution capable of execution and enforcement. It was hard enough for the national government of the United States under the two Roosevelts to contain and regulate America's early monopolies in oil, coal, steel, and railways. Where might we find political support and a mobilized citizenry for comparably muscular international organizations to contain and regulate, say, Microsoft or AT&T or Coca-Cola (which does 80 percent of its business outside of the United States) in their international ventures? Germany's post-War Basic Law, like Denmark's constitution, actually provides for the orderly ceding of certain sovereign competences to international institutions, but this provision certainly has not exempted Germany from the messy politics of the sovereign German state on matters affecting the German relationship with Europe. Nor has it given the European Union any distinctive power over German decision makers.[19]

What is required by justice and the global public good is transparent enough: among other things, peace and protection from genocide and human rights violations, full employment within a fair wage structure, globally sustainable development policies within specified ecological limits, and an even playing ground among nations with different natural resources and in different stages of economic development. Enabling treaties like the ones Tobin or Reich offer are also not hard to envision. The problem is political will and that in turn depends on active citizenship and the civic and educational infrastructures (civil society and civic education) that sustain them. After all, the nations that are signatories to the Genocide Convention include all the Western countries that have sat by and dithered while genocide is being committed in places like Rwanda—itself also a signatory nation! Their compact, which might better employ the acronym KEGFAC ("Keep an Eye on Genocide From Afar Convention"), is not devoid of understanding; everyone knows what genocide looks like and affects to know it is wrong. But as a piece of parchment, the Genocide Convention cannot forge the will and the capacity to enforce much of anything at all.[20]

In the countries where the United Nations currently has stationed troops—most often fronted by big powers like the United States and France—successes have been few and far between, with cases like Somalia and Bosnia all too typical. U.N. Secretary General Boutros Boutros-Ghali notes that most of the world's local problems today could be solved by significant United Nations intervention, at a fraction of the cost of yesterday's Cold War, but he is realist enough to admit "there is not the political will to do so."[21] The U.N. intervention in Somalia, like the parallel American operation ("Operation Restore Hope"), would have been downright comical in its futility had the tragedy not been so pervasive. American leaflets, translated into pidgin Somalia by inept exiles and dropped prior to the American intervention identified the United Nations as the "Slave Nation." Understandably, the only part of Somalia where relative peace and order have been secured are in the northeast and northwest where there was no significant foreign presence of any kind.[22]

Finally, the task of traditional international institutions trying to intervene in crisis situations is still further complicated by the absence, in many cases, of any clear pressure point. Where the culprits in need of remonstrance are neither nations nor tribes, the crisis may be real but the perpetrators are invisible. Genocide at least offers a target in the form of the slaughtering army or its surrogate irregulars. But with terrorists it is not so simple. And in the international markets to which Robert Kuttner directs his attention, where are the leverage points? Many of the transnational forces eroding national civil societies are not susceptible to interdiction at all. What just a few years ago Robert Reich called "the coming irrelevance of corporate nationality," is not coming any more.[23] It is here.

Thomas Jefferson's warning that merchants have no country has become a literal truth for the multinational corporations of McWorld. And the markets they ply nowadays are more anonymous still. How are nations to control the market in pirated software or smuggled plutonium? Who can police the world currency exchange? Has it even got an address? In order to confront Jihad, to whom does one write? And in what tone? "Dear nuclear terrorist, perhaps-covertly-supported-by-Iran, perhaps-trained-in-Ireland (or is it Libya?), probably-buying-in-Russia-or-Ukraine, possibly-associated-with-Hamas, but then again maybe not . . . ? Please cease and desist or we will . . ." Then there remains the embarrassing question of what exactly it is we can or will do. While the corporations that pollute the global environment have addresses, their handiwork is hard to identify or specify and depends on biological interactions with the products of others so that responsibility cannot really be attributed or sanctions imposed.

There does not finally seem to be much hope for traditional international institutions as saviors of democracy on a transnational scale in an era poised between Jihad and McWorld. Europe, which has achieved significant economic integration organized around regional councils, parliaments, and courts, still lacks democratic credibility with the citizens of its member countries. Most of them neither participate in its fledgling politics nor feel anything like a European civic identity to match their well-felt transnational commercial and commodity identities, let alone their identity as Bavarians or Walloons or Basques or Lombardians. Our question then becomes whether Jihad and/or McWorld can *themselves* promise to safeguard common liberty in a postnational era. Can they provide subnational or transnational political solutions to the subnational and transnational dilemmas they raise? The answer would seem to be that while ethnicity and parochialism on the one hand, and markets on the other, are nurtured by conditions that need not always be antagonistic to democracy and under some circumstances may even encourage democracy, neither is synonymous with democracy and each in its own way obstructs the global path to human liberty.

Jihad in the Global Disorder

WE HAVE UNDERSTOOD Jihad as the struggle of local peoples to sustain solidarity and tradition against the nation-state's legalistic and pluralistic abstractions as well as against the new commercial imperialism of McWorld; as such, it is not necessarily inhospitable to conditions that support democracy, which is after all much older than the nation-state. Ancient Greek democracy rested on a politics of the homogenous polis—small city-states tied together by common language, religion, and history. European democracy emerged from the Middle Ages in Helvetic cantons and Italian and German commercial towns with a local, even clannish character well before it found a home in larger national states. The tribal clan manifests a fraternal solidarity and devotion to assembly-style debate that points forward to an elementary direct democracy. Jefferson's imagined "ward republics" were utopian democratic models organized around local government and, some thought, echoed organization drawn from the Iroquois Federation, while the original Russian *soviet*, prior to its takeover by the Bolsheviks, was a local council representing diversified worker interests. The New England town also was rooted in the participatory predilections of parochialism.[24] In his beguiling account of civic tradition in Italy, Robert Putnam discovers a relationship between traditional choral societies in Italian villages and their later propensity for democracy, showing that with the appropriate civic institutions, small, homogenous communities are more than capable of developing democratic forms of life.[25]

In short, the limited scale and relative homogeneity of the entities whose antistatist and antimodern struggles incline them to Jihad can potentially incline them to local participatory democracy. Even their toxic exclusivity, based on rejection of "others," can contribute to the internal consensus necessary to forging a common will. As modernity has created institutions on a scale too large to sustain face-to-face deliberation and community interaction, the antimodern forces associated with Jihad hold out the promise of a scale of communal life more conducive to democracy.

Yet in facilitating a reduced scale for political life, Jihad in fact can simultaneously destroy the mind-set that allows democracy to function. The villages of Switzerland and Italy notwithstanding, traditional *Gemeinschaft* communities were for the most part rigorously undemocratic: closed, conformist, and hierarchical. Their exclusivity meant they were sealed against outsiders and intolerant of diversity; their ascriptive basis in a "given" identity (blood, race, religion) inured them to voluntary identities and held in check any notion that women and men might freely choose their social relations or join contrived social groupings at will; the hierarchical structure and dependency on charismatic leadership of traditional communities rendered them inegalitarian and resistant to social mobility; and their personalistic, noncontractual mode of relations rendered them prone to prejudice, gossip, argumentativeness, and corruption. Rural villages in Wisconsin too easily become havens of suicide, incest, and death while Vermont towns celebrated for their New England freedoms become coffins of conformity.[26]

Jihad's parochialism also limits its access to real power in a centralized, interdependent world. The Hutus can massacre Tutsis, but cannot deal with Pan-African environmental despoilation. Bosnian Serbs can unilaterally make war on Muslims but they cannot unilaterally increase VCR imports. In the world of McWorld, like it or not, though participation remains local, power is ever more central. The Green adage "think globally, act locally" is contradicted by the reality that local action rarely can impinge on truly global problems. Tribes pursuing NIMBY tactics ("not in my back yard!") with respect to regional policies (where do we put the petroleum refinery? the drug rehabilitation center? the refugees?) are themselves the impotent victims of other organizations' regional, national, and international policies over which local community or tribal institutions, even when democratic, provide them little control.

Ethnic tribes and religious clans are not then without democratic possibilities, but Jihad is unlikely to provide the kinds of democratic values and institutions that traditional democratic nation-states of the sort they help undo once offered. Is there today a single entity that has been created by the breakdown of nation-states associated with Jihad's multiple ethnicities, fratricides, and civil wars that looks remotely democratic? Even where they import democracy's political structures—say, a multiparty, parliamentary system or an independent judiciary or regular elections or a nominally free press—they lack the attitudinal resources to build the kind of democratic civil society that in turn makes democratic citizenship possible and lets democratic political institutions function effectively. Tribalism is little less hostile to civil society than consumerism. Without civil society, there can be no citizens, and thus no meaningful democracy.

We can admire the efforts of Western constitutional lawyers to export their own legalistic traditions to fledgling postnational countries in Eastern Europe and the ex–Soviet Union. The Center for the Study of Constitutionalism in Eastern Europe housed at the University of Chicago Law School and Central European University (which was initially funded by financier and philanthropist George Soros and has campuses in Prague and Budapest) has put constitution building at the center of its work. It offers a welcome contrast to the economic reductionism of those who think free markets and privatization are all there is to democracy. But a purely legalistic approach is no more likely to succeed than a purely economistic approach. A thin layer of parliamentarianism laid over a raging neo-tribal society cannot produce democracy.

Stephen Holmes, a principal at the Center for the Study of Constitutionalism in Eastern Europe, understands these limits, acknowledging that among the impediments to democratization is the "underreported obstacle" of "current-day Western advice," presumably including his own. Holmes proposes that Eastern Europe might benefit from a certain degree of "constitutional postponement" in which flexibility and adaptability to local conditions are favored over the formulaic applications of abstract constitutional principles.[27] However, while he regrets the passing of spontaneous local movements like Solidarity and Civic Forum, he still believes civil society can be established top-down by appropriate if supple and deliberate constitutional innovation, slighting the need to establish a bottom-up foundation in schools, voluntary associations, foundations, and other communal institutions that might in turn support a democratic constitutional edifice. Westerners either regret the absence of or simply ignore civil society in Russia, oblivious to the proliferating nongovernmental organizations that have sprung up and constitute the glimmering of a new post-Soviet "third sector."

The media have focused on the explosive relationship between President Yeltsin's reform-minded executive and the nationalist-conservative-Communist parliament: how would interested observers know then that dozens of nonprofits now dot the landscape and problematize the bipolarity of party rivals? These nonprofits include not only well-publicized foreign ventures like Big Brother/Big Sister but (to name only a few) such domestic institutions as the Rainbow Pedagogical Association, the Man's Soul Charitable Foundation, the all-Russia Foundation for Social and Legal Protection of the Disabled, the Social Ecological Union, the International Bank of Ideas, the Christian Mercy Charitable Society, the Foundation for International Diplomacy and Cooperation, ANIKA (the Association of Civilian Women in the Military Establishment), the Russian Human Rights Association "Fathers and Sons," the Independent Women's Forum, the Association of Parents of Deaf Children, the Social Development Charitable Center and Interlegal: An International Foundation for Political and Legal Studies.[28]

The emergence in Russia of this new nongovernmental infrastructure suggests that local organization and parochial community are capable of generating not just local Jihad but new local forms of civil society. However, such developments do not happen spontaneously. Left to its own devices, Jihad neither generates its own democracy nor permits others to democratize it merely by importing the constitutional mechanisms devised by others over many centuries in nation-states with long-standing and historically well-developed civil societies. On the contrary, it tends to undermine the fledgling institutions of the young civil society Russia has just begun to nurture.

16

Wild Capitalism vs. Democracy

A WKWARD AS IT may be to tease democratic potentialities out of the debris of nation-states left behind by Jihad, it is still more difficult to grasp how democracy is to be won by campaigning single-mindedly for the liberated markets of McWorld, what Solzhenitsyn aptly has called "savage capitalism." For markets do not appear in any obvious way to be ideal instruments for the regulation and control of public goods, and would-be democrats who look to them as a source of regulatory norms and democratic values would at first glance seem to have lost their marbles. Historian John Pocock asks "whether the subordination of the sovereign community of citizens to the international operation of post-industrial market forces" is a "good or bad step in the architecture of a post-modern politics."[1] My answer here is: bad. No, not bad, disastrous.

This is not to suggest that market forces and the ideology of libertarianism are not intellectually in fashion among postindustrial postmoderns or that they do not serve long-term productivity and wealth creation. Yet as advanced by pre-postmoderns such as Friedrich Hayek and Milton Friedman, the laissez-faire ideology assumes an endless "battle between collectivism and individualism" in which "any expansion of government," whether by a Stalinist autocracy or a democratic town, is "collectivist" and thus, a priori, an assault on liberty.[2] Government, including democratic government, is in this view always suspect, whereas markets are always benign. For libertarians, the extension of democracy can only mean the limitation of government and is understood to depend less on the establishing of an independent civil society than on the extension of markets via the dismantling of government, the privatization of industry, and the widening of free trade. When economistic reformers think about government at all, it is in terms of negative constitutionalism—politics as antipolitics, law as a set of limits on popular rule rather than as a set of populist enabling principles.[3]

Serious students of the market who distinguish between totalitarian collectivism and the democratic search for common goods will want to dispute these quasi-anarchist libertarian dogmas.[4] Notwithstanding the renewed popularity of the laissez-faire creed in England and America over the last few decades, amplified by a deeply felt repugnance for politics and politicians, there is a long and respectable tradition that is neither collectivist nor even welfare statist that disputes the putative sufficiency of markets and challenges their vaunted capacity for economic self-regulation.[5] Contemporary critics like Andrew Bard Schmookler and Robert Kuttner are fierce critics of the social costs of applied laissez-faire policies in the Reagan-Thatcher era, but not even Adam Smith thought the market could do everything.[6]

Market relations are simply not a surrogate for social relations, let alone for democratic social relations, and it is only the zealous proponents of capitalism in its extreme laissez-faire version (what Robert Kuttner calls its utopian incarnation) who pretend otherwise. Although there is a discernible historical correlation between democracy and capitalism, it is democracy that produced capitalism rather than the other way round. A seventeenth-century mercantilist England was in the course of the eighteenth century democratized; only in the nineteenth century did a democratized England embark on policies of full-scale industrialization, free trade (the revocation of the Corn Laws in 1846), and economic empire. To this day, the economies of capitalist nations depend on activist democratic governments, which not only play a vital countervailing role in checking market excesses and attending to common and civic values in which capitalism quite properly has no interest, but which continue to nurture markets as well. The most successful "capitalist" states with well-advertised miracle economies have in truth laced their markets with a thin but sinewy mercantilism.

Under cover of their post–World War II "free market" revolutions, both Japan and Germany actually pursued aggressive national economic policies. Franklin Delano Roosevelt's New Deal did as much to save capitalism from self-annihilation as it did to save the American people from capitalism's social ruthlessness. Neither Reagan's America nor Thatcher's England could have pursued the illusion of a return to pure laissez-faire without all of the benefits of several generations of an interventionist government and a mixed economy (as Reagan learned when he toyed briefly with a revision of the Social Security system). Truly free economies in this century have always been mixed economies in which democratic governments have balanced the interests of economic utility and social justice. Norman Birnbaum portrays the West German economy of the economic miracle as, in actuality, a market "inextricably bound to the state. Subsidies and tax incentives, a substantial public sector, considerable state support for research, a large state role in occupational training, the provision of export credits, were coordinated elements of national economic policy. The major private banks . . . the government and the Federal Bank worked together. . . . [Much of all of this was merely] a continuation of welfare state traditions modernized by Bismarck."[7]

What was true for the Germans, was true for all of the successful postwar capitalist nations. For they understood well enough that a pure laissez-faire economy quickly breaks and then self-destructs along the fissures introduced by labor strife, unemployment, trade cycles, and monopoly. Only the new transitional democracies have been talked by foreign advisors or bullied by international banks into thinking that laissez-faire capitalist economics is a self-sufficient social system. Predictably, the results have been catastrophic. As we will see below, what Aleksandr Solzhenitsyn calls "savage capitalism"—a system "fraught with unproductive, savage and repulsive forms of behavior, the plunder of the nation's wealth"—has turned the new Russia into a place where "the brazen use of social advantage and the inordinate power of money" (the very problems the collapse of communism was supposed to cure!) are today worse than ever.[8]

Even under ideal conditions, where the depredations of wild capitalism are controlled and the economy achieves a certain self-regulation, markets have a limited capacity to generate what a society needs.[9] Ideal conditions only mean that sellers and buyers interact in accord with prices whose fluctuating levels keep goods, consumers, and laborers interacting productively. At best, this only secures maximum economic efficiency in producing and distributing hard (durable) goods. Nothing else. Advocates of laissez-faire as a political strategy claim far more, however. And therein lies the problem.

There is today a disastrous confusion between the moderate and mostly well-founded claim that flexibly regulated markets remain the most efficient instruments of economic productivity and wealth accumulation, and the zany, overblown claim that naked, wholly unregulated markets are the sole means by which we can produce and fairly distribute everything human beings care about, from durable goods to spiritual values, from capital investment to social justice, from profitability to sustainable environments, from private wealth to the essential commonweal. This second claim has moved profit-mongering privateers to insist that goods as diverse and obviously public as education, culture, penology, full employment, social welfare, and ecological equilibrium be handed over to the profit sector for arbitration and disposal.[10] It has also persuaded them to see in privatization not merely a paring knife to trim the fat from overindulgent state bureaucracies but a cleaver with which democracy can be chopped into pieces and then pulverized.

In America, the confidence in the omnipotence of markets has been transformed into a foreign policy that assumes internationalizing markets is tantamount to democratizing them and that human freedom is secured the minute nations or tribes sign on to the dogmas of free trade. The Friedmans called their celebration of markets *Free to Choose,* as if choosing brands or trademarks and choosing lifeplans or common cultural norms were kindred activities.[11] More recently, Jeffrey Sachs, a zealous Friedman clone and the ambitious first consul of capitalist reform in transitional societies, has argued that Eastern Europe "shed the communist system" not to create an open society but "to adopt capitalism." That being the case, its goal must be "economic harmonization with Western Europe"—something requiring radical economic reform (a "Big Bang" as the Poles called it) and ongoing economic "shock therapy."[12] Laissez-faire doctrines can imperil the nation-state, but at least the nation-state possesses a sovereign power capable of countering raw capitalism's materialistic, privatizing consequences. In the international economy, laissez-faire doctrines are fatal, for here sovereignty vanishes and aggressive transnational bodies pursue market strategies in the absence of any countervailing regulatory bodies whatsoever. Kuttner notices that "as the ethic of laissez-faire gained ground, it did so almost in lockstep with the relative decline of its prime sponsor"— the United States.[13] While earlier incarnations of international institutions like the International Monetary Fund and the World Bank permitted the flexing of American muscle in a world arena, America's diminishing power leaves such institutions at the mercy of the true multinationals of our epoch, the transnational corporations and thousands upon thousands of nongovernmental interest groups and associations that constitute the international market.

Public relations aside, the World Bank, for example, is less concerned to create a sustainable environment or forge sustainable national economies in the debtor nations it services than to assure an open (though by no means level) playing field for international business. Its loans often bankrupt its clients: Poland's total debt in 1993 was over 60 percent of its annual GDP, while Hungary's approached 80 percent of its GNP;[14] Uganda owes 62 percent of its foreign debt to the bank while Guatemala's controversial World Bank–financed Chixoy Dam accounts for 40 percent of its external debt. The bank has also been known to impose population resettlement on peoples who have had no part in deciding on the irrigation or transportation projects being undertaken in the name of "their" development.[15]

Those who believe in the continuing vitality of the nation-state may not worry. Robert Kuttner, for example, still thinks that although "the global intelligentsia may think of itself as stateless, and global capital may see nation-states as anachronistic encumbrances . . . the state remains the locus of the polity" that "remains the structure best suited for counterbalancing the excesses of the market."[16] The state is certainly "best suited" to balance wild capitalism, but the question is whether it is any longer capable of doing so or willing to try. The reality seems to be, as Stanford University economist Paul Krugman has noticed, that "governments have consented to a regime that allows markets to boss them around."[17] The new government of the Czech Republic boasts that it wants to create "a level playing field for investors, both domestic and foreign" and is actively "preaching minimum government interference."[18] Those new states that, "as civil society has been progressively colonized by organized crime," have been led slowly to discover the "positive uses of power," must contend both with the old state-hating victims of imperious communism and their new state-hating laissez-faire advisors who urge them to turn the very state institutions by which they might control rapacious markets into their primary adversary.[19]

Even where states weigh in on behalf of civil society, there is no surrogate for the polity in the international domain—certainly not the state's weak supranational imitators—that has the clout to countervail multinational corporations and the markets in which they operate. Business leader Walter B. Wriston observes that governments no longer can even "measure" capital formation because so much new capital is intellectual.[20] How then can they regulate or control such capital? As he wryly suggests, a computer wizard with a bold new program in his mind can walk across a border untithed and untariffed, carrying more capital assets with him in his head than might be contained in a thousand cargo ships. As we saw earlier (in Part I), the new goods are virtual rather than durable, and their producers—Robert Reich's "symbolic analyst professionals"—represent a new transnational class pretty well beyond the purview of particular national sovereignties. The Senate banking committee can look over the shoulder of the nation's banks (if not very wisely or very well), but who has the power (or the vision) to look over the shoulders of international bankers and currency dealers? Or of the programmers and analysts who make banking and currency markets function? Currency markets trade up to a trillion dollars a day: no national bank, no collection of national banks, can have much of an impact on them. When in the summer of 1994, seventeen of the world's largest central banks (including America's Federal Reserve) tried to prop up the dollar, they could come up with only $5 billion.

Their effort had (in Thomas Friedman's charming image) all the impact of "a zoo keeper trying to calm a starved gorilla by offering it a raisin for lunch."[21]

Free-market advocates like Wriston boast about the failure of the Bretton Woods Treaty (by which sovereign nations tried to govern the international currency exchange after World War II)—proof that "Big Brother" (his caricature of all states, democratic as well as autocratic) has been forced out of business. Unfortunately, Big Brother's role as a guardian of social justice has also been superseded and the many junior siblings who have displaced him turn out to be both more intimidating and far less accountable. National regulatory commissions can curtail in-country labor exploitation with minimum wage laws, unemployment insurance, and safety regulations, but who can set and enforce such standards for the global market where unrooted companies can chase low-wage labor from country to country as they please? Far more today than in the nineteenth century, the workers of the world need to unite to offset the exploitative consequences of monopoly capital on a global scale. Yet never has there been less likelihood that they could do so.

Multinationals cannot be blamed for promoting high profits at the price of high unemployment or sacrificing the local environment to the economic benefits of free trade. It is the job of civil society and democratic government and not of the market to look after common interests and make sure that those who profit from the common planet pay its common proprietors their fair share. When governments abdicate in favor of markets, they are declaring nolo contendere in an arena in which they are supposed to be primary challengers, bartering away the rights of their people along the way.

Markets simply are not designed to do the things democratic polities do.[22] They enjoin private rather than public modes of discourse, allowing us as consumers to speak via our currencies of consumption to producers of material goods, but ignoring us as citizens speaking to one another about such things as the social consequences of our private market choices (too much materialism? too little social justice? too many monopolies? too few jobs? what do *we* want?). They advance individualistic rather than social goals, permitting us to say, one by one, "I want a pair of running shoes" or "I need a new VCR" or "buy yen and sell D-Marks!" but deterring us from saying, in a voice made common by interaction and deliberation, "our inner city community needs new athletic facilities" or "there is too much violence on TV and in the movies" or "we should rein in the World Bank and democratize the IMF!" Markets preclude "we" thinking and "we" action of any kind at all, trusting in the power of aggregated individual choices (the invisible hand) to somehow secure the common good. Consumers speak the elementary rhetoric of "me," citizens invent the common language of "we."

Markets are contractual rather than communitarian, which means they stroke our solitary egos but leave unsatisfied our yearning for community, offering durable goods and fleeting dreams but not a common identity or a collective membership—something the blood communities spawned by Jihad, reinforced by the thinness of market relations, do rather too well. Cybernetic and automatic rather than deliberative and genuinely voluntary, markets produce collective consequences that cannot be foreseen in the simple feedback loops established by consumers making individual choices and markets responding to them. What Ludwig von Mises blithely called the "daily plebiscite in which every penny" gives consumers the right to "determine who should own and run the plants, shops and farms" is a charming fraud; for the self-interested motives on the basis of which consumers spend their pennies have nothing to do with who runs anything, let alone with the kind of civil society these same consumers hope to live in or the civic objectives they forge together as citizens in democratic political arenas in order to control the public and political consequences of their private consumer choices.[23] Recall Felix Rohatyn's warning that markets entail "a brutal Darwinian logic . . . They are nervous and greedy (and) . . . what they reward is not always our preferred form of democracy."[24]

Democracies prefer markets but markets do not prefer democracies. Having created the conditions that make markets possible, democracy must also do all the things that markets undo or cannot do. It must educate citizens so that they can use their markets wisely and contain market abuses well; it must support values and a common culture in which the market has no interest and does not try to reward; it must deploy mechanisms that prevent the market from self-destructing via anarchy or via monopoly; and it must secure an alternative form of choice that permits common choosing as a remedy to the inadvertent social consequences of individual choosing.

Take the transportation debate raised earlier. When I choose to buy a car, I choose to get from here to there efficiently and perhaps pleasantly; however, among the consequences of my choice may be air pollution, resource depletion, the disadvantaging of public transportation, pressure on hospital facilities, and the despoilation of the natural environment by a highway system. As a consumer, the only way I can avoid these consequences is to refuse to buy a car—an irrational act from the narrow economical perspective and one that throws a wrench into the market economy. So I play the consumer and buy the car. Capitalism is served and so am I—as a consumer. But in a democratic society, I am not just a consumer, I am a citizen. And as a citizen, I can act in common with others to modify the untoward public consequences of my private choice. As a citizen I can join with others and redress the ill effects of my car purchase: we can outlaw leaded gas, fund electric engine research, subsidize public transportation, mandate hospital insurance for drivers, and limit highway construction in scenic regions. These civic activities do not curb our market freedom, they facilitate it. Democracy makes markets work by allowing us the freedom of our consumer choices in the knowledge that we can counteract their accompanying vices. To do so, however, we must have alternative nonmarket institutions, and in the international arena such democratic tools are entirely absent.

Even within nation-states, we are eschewing the tools we have. The dogmas of laissez-faire capitalism that have suffused the politics of America and Europe in the last few decades have been reinforced by the resentments of an alienated electorate that has lost confidence in its own democratic institutions; together, they have persuaded us that our democratic governments neither belong to us nor function usefully either to limit markets or to help them work. The expiration of Marxist and command economy dogmas has breathed new life into free market and laissez-faire dogmas and forced us back into Friedman's choice of radical collectivism or radical individualism. We condemn politicians as if they were not chosen both by us and from among us, and turn on governments as if we still lived under the absolute monarchs of the eighteenth century—as if constitution building were aimed exclusively at curtailing tyranny and not also at facilitating common democratic action. Citizens abjure the common "we" and allow it to be identified exclusively with corrupt politicians or totalitarian despots. Democratic authority and the abuse of democratic authority become synonymous.

When peoples emerging from communism become frustrated by wild capitalism, they turn not to discredited parliamentary institutions but back to the tougher party apparatchiks who have survived the passing of the very Communist regimes whose legacy has delegitimized parliamentarianism.[25] These developments have meant that democracy has had an increasingly hard time inside nation-states afflicted with radical market ideology. Western analysts have pushed so hard for the liberation of markets that they have "thrown out the state-controlled baby with the bath water."[26]

If laissez-faire ideology has made it this difficult to conjure up a noncollectivist democracy, how can a transnational democratic polity ever be imagined? Even if we could overcome our political diffidence, which mechanisms might afford us the chance as citizens to undo the inadvertent evils of global markets? The eclipse of the national "we" in the shadows of both Jihad and McWorld is trouble enough. Now we face their consequences in the absence of any global civic "we," prepared to act beyond national boundaries. When the only transnational "we" available has to be drawn from anarchic congeries of greedy "me's," the market ultimately fails on its own terms. We get the goods but not the lives we want; prosperity for some, but despair for many and dignity for none. McWorld's twenty-six thousand or more international nongovernmental associations are no match for its *Fortune*'s top five hundred multinational corporations. Cartels show little hospitality to citizens. McWorld is not and cannot be self-regulating. Nor is it likely to produce the kinds of democratic civic bodies it needs to stay in business. This is McWorld's paradox. It cannot survive the world it inevitably tends to create if not countered by civic and democratic forces it inevitably tends to undermine.

Now these defects may not be defects at all by the standard of macroeconomics.[27] They are only defects by the standards of politics. They become the defects of markets, however, when macroeconomics and markets are allowed to usurp the role of politics. The disastrous consequences that follow from patterning political reforms

on macroeconomic theories are patently visible in countries throughout Latin America and Africa where "as the private sphere flourishes . . . the public sphere crumbles." To Guillermo O'Donnell, a
leading Latin American political scientist, the matter is simple: "privatization is not democratization."[28] Period.

I cannot begin to do justice to the havoc wrought by the attempt
to impose an economic solution to the problems of democracy on
the world's developing regions, but I do want to offer brief portraits
of two post-Communist lands where—in confounding privatization
with democratization—wild capitalism has become the primary
arbiter of civic values for the last five years and where as a consequence an older democracy (in the newly unified Germany) and a
new would-be democracy (in old Russia) are each facing hard challenges to their democratic aspirations.

17

Capitalism vs. Democracy in Russia

THERE IS AMPLE empirical evidence to justify the shrill criticism by observers like Solzhenitsyn of Russia's experiment with overnight democratization via capitalism-in-a-hurry. There are few participants in the process who are not today deeply worried about the impact of "shock therapy" capitalism both on Russia's constitution—"a document of very limited legitimacy, and thus authority"[1]—as well as on the future of Russian democracy, "which has never been more uncertain."[2] John H. Fairbanks, Jr., believes that "many of the preconditions of fascism are now or will soon be present in Russia: hyperinflation, mass unemployment, seething status resentments, disillusion with democracy, a society that is 'De-Christianized' but still craves 'spirituality,' bitter border conflicts, constant fighting waged not by state armies but by *freikorps*-like volunteer groups and residual socialist and nationalist feelings."[3] Not every observer is so dramatic, but even sober economists such as Padma Desai have concluded that the shock strategy "hasn't worked—and won't."[4] He estimated a decline in Russian GNP of 19 percent and a further fall of 11 percent in 1993, along with inflation of 2,500 percent in 1992 and a continuing inflation thereafter of 25 percent a month. Elsewhere in Eastern Europe, even the economies that have been advertised as "successful" have nonetheless sustained a radical decline in industrial output (over 50 percent in Hungary, the Czech Republic, and Slovakia [similar to Russia], and more than 75 percent in Bulgaria), and a costly surge in retail prices, continuing inflation, and unemployment between 10 and 20 percent in nations that had none.

In Russia itself where advisors including the conservative Hoover Institution, investment bankers like Goldman, Sachs and Company, and radical free-market economists such as Jeffrey Sachs have been pushing shock tactics, in the first two quarters of 1994 industrial production fell a further 25 percent per quarter (faster than during the Great Depression in America), with agricultural production stalled at a thirty-year low.[5] Some estimates classify a full one-quarter of the Russian population as impoverished with an additional 40 percent living below the subsistence line.[6] While the rich buy cellular phones, Maine lobster, and illegal drugs, the average industrial wage remains somewhere between $40 and $70 a month, just a little more than what it takes to rent a car at a good hotel for an hour.[7] Stretch limousines at $150,000 and $30,000 Cartier watches sell out in what are usually all-cash transactions in boutiques that once targeted foreigners but now cater primarily to Russians—about a million of whom (from a population of 150 million) can afford luxury goods. By the end of 1993, nearly forty thousand foreign-make cars had been registered in Moscow.[8] At the Exhibition of Economic Achievement fairgrounds that once paid tribute to the wished-for wonders of Soviet industry and science there stands today a massive shopping arcade: a tribute to McWorld, where "Muscovites cart off newly bought Sony and Panasonic Televisions so fast it looks like a looting spree" and where a Russian visitor exclaims: "I am in shock, I am in shock, I think we have become the 51st state of America."[9] *Naglost* (a term meaning "anything goes" with particularly brazen and insolent undertones) has replaced *glasnost* as the working cry of the new capitalism, where pyramid schemes pass as investment opportunities, gut-burning moonshine is sold in Chivas Regal bottles, and protection money and security guards have become the ante of playing in any business at all.

Meanwhile, more than 15 million are unemployed (as compared with less than a million in the old Soviet Union) and critics—not all of them conservatives or nationalists or sulking Communists—argue that shock therapy has become shock without therapy. Conservative editor Aleksandr Prokhanov laments, "The economy is dying, social links are breaking apart. At some point soon society will become ungovernable."[10] Viktor Chernomyrdin, Yeltsin's new prime minister installed after radical reform failed, announced: "The period of market romanticism is over," but he must still figure out how to deal with $2.5 billion in rescheduled foreign debt, most of it favoring foreign investors who received investment credits.[11] The $11 billion in bilateral assistance promised by Western nations in 1993 and 1994 is also aimed at helping Western exporters while the $4.5 billion in real aid promised by international organizations has been forthcoming only in dribs and drabs—as has been the case throughout Eastern Europe, where Western promises have yet to pay off.[12]

New York Times reporter James Sterngold, reporting on the 1993 economic summit in Japan, wrote that the Russian aid package negotiated there "clearly amounted to less than met the eye . . . just a reallocation of funds committed" earlier.[13] While Russia awaits serious investors in its own economy, McWorld is moving in. The world's largest McDonald's is now in business near Red Square—although it caters to the well off, with a Big Mac lunch (which can be ordered in English or Russian) costing a week's wages. Ben and Jerry's has come to the provinces, although unlike Pizza Hut, it is prudently holding off on Moscow. Avon is hawking cosmetics to housewives whose vanity is being assiduously stroked by the new media, which feature Western gangster films, soap operas, and game shows; and every electronic and software firm in the world is staking out a position in what is hoped will be a primary consumer growth market in the new century.

The old creaking collectivist and statist monoliths are slowly disappearing, but in their place, alongside struggling new Russian businesses, are American-style takeover firms riding shotgun for Russian companies that buy raw materials for rubles and resell them at exorbitant dollar prices abroad. Western observers celebrate unfriendly takeovers as if they were crucial blows in the struggle for democratization. Joseph Blasi, a Rutgers University economist, happily retells the story of the Vladimir Tractor factory near Moscow where "a Russian businessman with a Harvard M.B.A. unseated the plant's chief executive with the help of a New York investment group that owned one-sixth of the stock."[14] What is greed in New York counts as economic modernization in Moscow where perhaps greed really *is* good. Many indigenous Russian investment firms trade in the vouchers given early on in the privatization process to every Russian as a marker for their piece of the old Soviet collectivist rock, taking advantage of the fact that most Russians, desperate for cash to pay rent and subsistence, cannot afford to hold on to their vouchers and are willing to sell them cheaply to speculators. Like their American counterparts, these companies manufacture nothing except unearned profits. Other firms like the notorious MMM that went into a dizzying tailspin in 1994 are little more than pyramid schemes through which gullible grandmothers are hustled out of their life savings, the proceeds of which are used to lure others into buying a stake in an outfit that neither owns nor produces anything other than the misplaced hope of its duped investors.[15] For those rich enough to want to gamble directly, there are a dozen new casinos in Moscow, while for the less well-heeled, Harrah's ruble slot machines are available in almost every neighborhood workingman's grocery store.[16]

Wild capitalism has made business and crime kissing cousins and no one is quite sure where one ends and the other begins. Street crime and mafia-style executions are only the tip of an infrastructural iceberg that lurks below the water of business and government. Often the same people who once ran state-owned enterprises are now their "private" owners, while other former Communist managers help liquidate the businesses they were supposed to privatize, leaking goods abroad on the black market and smuggling oil and nickel and scandium out of the country for profits from which neither Russia nor Russian voucher holders profit.[17] Amateur speculators lurk in the Moscow subway with signs saying I BUY VOUCHERS while enthusiastic professionals, unhindered by a centralized securities exchange, an FTC, or SEC, or regulations of any kind, exclaim: "We are making money out of air!"[18]

Money is not made out of air, however, but snatched from the pockets of Russians whose incomes do not permit them the luxury of speculation. What Robert Reich condemned as the "secession of the rich" from America's public sector is a growing issue in Russia as well: two societies are emerging, one rich, private, and insulated, the other, poor, public, and exposed to the trials of the Russian nation (that is, the Russian market) at large. As the first society succeeds, with the collusion of investors from abroad—individual and institutional—the second (including the 40 percent who are technically "impoverished") is abandoned to a bankrupt public sector incapable of offering social security, employment, or a decent wage. Even advocates of privatization now acknowledge that wage subsidies might have protected workers from what they rather charmingly call the "labor-shedding" practices of privatizers wishing to make state firms look more attractive to investors who might not have the political gumption to fire half the staff of newly acquired companies.[19] In practice, however, a large percentage of the new class that makes up the second sector of the poor, the indigent, and the unemployed are flotsam and jetsam on the tides of privatization: workers who have been sloughed off by a system that is more profitable to its new private owners without them. The real story of democratization in Russia and elsewhere in Eastern Europe will likely unfold as a product of the tensions between these two oppositional sectors.

The story of the societal malaise occasioned by Russia's precipitous embrace of raw capitalism can perhaps best be told by narrating in brief what has become a dual attack on the Russian body (and body politic) and the Russian soul. The body politic's decline is evident both in plummeting rates of political participation and the resurgence of nationalist and neo-Communist anti-Western demagogues among whom Vladimir Zhirinovsky is only the most notorious. The peril to the literal Russian body is still more startling: population statistics reveal a precipitous decline both in birth rates and life expectancy—reflecting a grueling present and a despairing future—while crime has come to stand as a metaphor for both crooked government and corrupt markets and the troublesome relations between them. The Russian soul is at risk because Russian culture and history are being infected by McWorld's tawdry pop culture and pervasive materialism, the progress of which seems to be the marker of success for the new Russian postindustrial capitalism. Let me say a word about each of these before concluding my review of the Russian example.

The economics of the cold shower has left Russian politics wet and shivering. In the milestone elections held at the end of 1993, the electorate expressed its frustration with the economy first of all by staying away in droves: over half did not vote at all, achieving in their first outing a dismal participation rate it took America two centuries to achieve. Those who did vote vented their resentments by pummeling Yeltsin's reform party, Russia's Choice, for which Yeltsin prudently declined to campaign and which received only 15 percent of votes cast. They chose rather to give nearly half of their votes to Yeltsin's most radical critics: 23 percent to Zhirinovsky's ultranationalist "Liberal Democratic" party, over 12 percent to the newly revived Communist Party, and 8 percent to the Agrarian Party.[20] That the Communists should win thirty-two seats so soon after Yeltsin set his tanks on the White House and drove Communist leaders like Rutskoi into the wilderness might seem astounding if it were not for the fact that Communists have either retaken or secured a share of power in all but five of the countries of the ex–Soviet Empire.[21] Markets may liberate but what they have liberated in the East has been reactionary resentment.

The Zhirinovsky phenomenon has been sufficiently exploited in the media to merit just a few comments here. Russia's Choice economic reformer Yegor Gaidar has compared him to Hitler, and there seems considerable evidence for the charge in Zhirinovsky's autobiographical epic-ette *The Last Thrust to the South*. Bookstands associated with his party's office sell Goebbel's *Diaries* and *Mein Kampf*, and both in his writings and speeches he indulges in inflammatory rhetoric on the order of "I may have to shoot a hundred thousand people, but the three hundred million others [in revived greater Russia] will live peacefully."[22] Some observers think he is a symbol of the menace of Russian fascism but not himself a danger (he supposedly has some Jewish ancestors and is a political opportunist of the first order). Too foolish and outspoken, isolated now in a parliament that has been marginalized by Yeltsin and his government, he seems a somewhat less likely candidate for the 1996 presidential race than he once did. But he stands for the possible stillbirth of Russia's democratic political life, and as such is a warning to optimists. He cannot be said to be a product of markets but he certainly is buoyed up by their devastating effects on many Russians.

The damage wrought by the frenzied transition to capitalism is clear in the body politic, but still more obvious in the vulnerability of the actual Russian body. Environmental depredation, ruinous under communism, continues unabated.[23] The people who live in the deteriorating environment are even worse off. Actuarial tables now give Russian men slightly less than sixty years to live, a male life expectancy lower than that of Indonesia or the Philippines. Meanwhile, Russian women are bearing children at a calamitous rate of 1.4 per person (down from 2.17 during the recent Soviet period and comparable today to the disastrously low rates in the eastern part of Germany.[24] A society with Third World mortality rates and First World–weary birth rates is a society skeptical not only about democracy but about its very future.[25]

Soaring crime rates underscore the dangers to the Russian body. The most pessimistic observers have estimated that up to 40 percent of the Russian GNP is crime-related and up to forty thousand shops and small enterprises are reputedly owned or infiltrated by a thousand or more crime syndicates. Of several thousand crime families, 150 or so boast prominent international connections. According to Yeltsin himself, 80 percent of banks and private enterprises are paying tribute to the new Russian mafia[26]—a term Russian criminals have chosen for themselves as they dress and act the part of the gangsters they encounter on Western videos of *The Godfather* and *Goodfellas,* as well as films noires from the 1930s featuring the strutting criminal portraits of Capone and others by James Cagney and Edward G. Robinson (more testimony to the intersection of Jihad and McWorld).[27]

Moscow's First City Hospital treats forty serious mugging victims daily, and the victims are not just casualties of street violence.[28] Between 1989 and 1992, more than a thousand Russian policemen were killed in crime-related violence, while in 1993 alone ten directors of Russia's largest commercial banks were murdered.[29] In 1994, Yeltsin's government moved frontally against what it called "criminal filth," but the remedy appears no more conducive to democracy than the disease since it includes provisions to suspend civil liberties, to detain suspects without bringing formal charges for up to a month, and to legitimize nonconstitutional search and seizure procedures.[30]

In figures like Zhirinovsky, Jihad continues to stalk Russian society. But for the Russian soul, Slavophile and nationalist sentiments may seem necessary fires to warm the long cold winter of McWorld. Nationalist folk songs are regularly pushed off the radio by Western rock music, and not even native Russian rock musicians can withstand the onslaught. Boris Grebenshchikov once sold rock albums in the millions: exposed to the competition of the "real thing," he does well nowadays if he sells fifteen thousand.[31] Is it a wonder then that even cosmopolitan Russians express a certain nostalgia for yesterday's Greater Russia? Or that this nostalgia must compete with and is a distant second to the grasping desire for tomorrow's greater markets? Nationalists resist Western culture, but slogans appear everywhere on behalf of the popular new cigarette West screaming, "Test the West!" What playwright Janusz Glowacki says about Poland applies to the sinking high culture of Russia and every other ex-Communist state: "Today, theaters close one after another. Warehouses are filled with books people used to risk their freedom to read. Weekly literary magazines are going bankrupt. Harlequin books are omnipresent, as are movies starring Schwarzenegger or Stallone."[32]

Russia today sells more Barbies than babushkas and more Veronikas (a Russian imitation of Barbie) than Russian bears.[33] Does this mean more or less choice? Traditional wooden toys are pushed off the shelves by Legos, plastic warriors, and Gameboys. The Gameboys are stealth cultural networks reaching into Russian homes and children's minds with a steady diet of Western games, comic characters, and attitudes about competition, violence, consumption, and winning that are indispensable to McWorld's marketing strategy. Russia's famed Ministry of Culture, now the Ministry of Culture and Tourism, is well on the way to turning the nation's artistic heritage into a theme park—to be sure, in the name of preserving a domain that can no longer depend on state subsidies. Six teams with names like the Swans and the Bears play in an American-style football league in Moscow and Coca-Cola is using its monopoly contract to make Coke, Fanta, and Sprite Russia's national drinks.[34] Zhirinovsky still attracts press attention, but a true Slavophile conservative like the author of *One Day in the Life of Ivan Denisovich* is ridiculed or ignored by the general public. Solzhenitsyn's return to Russia in 1994 attracted more attention in the Western media than in the Russian press, although he now appears on his own television talk show. So much for the Russian soul.

It is of course finally exceedingly tricky to measure fairly the costs to Russia's democracy, in the currencies of body or soul, of its precipitous entry into McWorld's domain of capitalism and markets. Societies in rapid transition are always subject to stress, and seventy-five years of Bolshevism had left the Russian nation crippled in ways for which its people will pay a price for a long time to come, whatever successor system they manage to establish. Moreover, creating a democracy itself exacts costs and is often accompanied by violence, disorder, and a period of uncertainty, even chaos. It would thus be unfair to blame every current Russian malady on the economic travails of its transition to markets. Nonetheless, markets have proved themselves incapable in Russia of producing social adjustments to compensate for the hurtful public consequences of private market choices. This means the democratic outlook is much less promising than it might be. Skeptics who have witnessed the virtues of patience in forging democratic constitutions and understand the relationship between public authority and evolving liberty may wonder whether China will not succeed in realizing a genuinely democratic civil society before Russia does.

Certainly there is little to suggest that the abrupt transformation of Russia from a command economy into a radical market economy is itself doing much to nurture democracy. Civic attitudes corrupted by crime, complacency, and despair yield to what anthropologist David Lempert has suggested may be the emergence of a "cargo cult" mentality in the new Russia with "natives" looking over the ocean for exotic and godlike foreigners to bring them the magic spoils of Western markets and American pop culture.[35] Lempert's metaphor is extreme, perhaps even insulting, but the reemergence in Russia not just of organized religion but of what he describes as faith healers, television hypnotists, UFO cults, and media-driven political extremism in which the West is blamed for every old and new Russian sin suggests a deadly fatalism. One Russian sociologist has warned: "There are more completely passive people in this country than in the rest of the world put together. If they aren't planning to kill themselves, it's because they're too passive to bother."[36]

The sordid state of Russian society is not then just a matter of nationalist complaints or dispossessed apparatchik resentment, and the views of a Zhirinovsky or a conservative mystic Slavophile like

Solzhenitsyn need not be taken as benchmarks. When Aleksandr G. Nevzorov, a thirty-six-year-old television personality from liberal St. Petersburg, cries, "Reform has meant nothing but bandits, beggars and blood, nothing to the pensioner living next to shops selling your imported food!" and is elected as a nationalist to the new parliament (in 1994), his remarks can perhaps be written off as election hyperbole and right-wing propaganda—though we may be a little surprised to see such hyperbole rewarded in the most bourgeois and pro-Western district in Russia.[37] But even exiled dissidents friendly neither to the Soviet regime nor to radical nationalist critics of the present regime are anxious. Here is Nikolai Petradov, a radical economist under Gorbachev, who complained recently: "We need reform with a human face. If reforms stay as cruel to people as they have been, Zhirinovsky will waltz into the Kremlin."[38] Or listen to Edward Limonov, a dissenter in Paris known for his cosmopolitan views, who returned to Russia in 1992 to oppose Yeltsin:

> I am a nationalist despite myself . . . because though I love the cosmopolitanism of high culture, I have no choice; to be nationalist today in Russia, it is to forget egoism and assist one's family . . . [as I did when I traveled to Siberia and saw] the municipal libraries closed for lack of funds, the orchestras reduced to silence, the misery which has become a national tragedy. The democratic pretenders in power are risking nothing short of the suicide of a civilization."[39]

This looks like Jihad by default. Limonov worries that as "69 years of party dictatorship has discredited communism," so "Yeltsin has discredited Western democracy. Democracy must not be allowed to violate people." When cosmopolitans begin to believe democracy is the demon, and when Yeltsin's own new postreform Prime Minister Viktor Chernomyrdin insists "the period of market romanticism is over . . . the mechanical transfer of Western economic methods to Russian soil has done more harm than good," capitalism has exacted a very high price.[40] Perhaps that is why even Boris Yeltsin has asserted that "Russia is simply not suited for [capitalism]. Russia is a unique country. It will not be socialist or capitalist."[41]

The story, however, is not over, and the question is not whether Russia will be socialist or capitalist but whether it will be democratic. So dismal have Russian fortunes become, that some supposedly sympathetic observers are suggesting that the de facto sovereignty of crime over government and market be made de jure! Michael Scammell, professor of Russian literature at Cornell University, scolds us for being "squeamish" about "the decline or collapse of publishing houses, journals, theater and artists clubs and the impoverishment of academic institutions, as state subsidies are reduced or withdrawn," for such institutions were overbloated in Soviet times. We should not shrink from what after all is only an echo of the "rough and tumble of America a century ago," with a "new class of businessmen, entrepreneurs and adventurers answerable to no authority but themselves" running the show for the benefit of all. To Scammell, "the existence of a mafia is an unmistakable barometer of the degree of democratization of a given society. . . . When the mafia goes, so will Russia's new found freedom."[42] In a similar vein, Nikolai Zlobin has argued that criminals of the higher sort in Russia along "with corrupt officials who are genuinely interested in evolution towards democracy and a free market economy . . ." with whom they are in league, cannot be said to be "interested in haphazard plundering of their country. Rather, they want to create an organized system from which they can control events and thus be in a strong position in the long run." Zlobin concludes that since "in many ways control in Russia has already shifted to the new criminal network, which has replaced the old communist structure" and since "after a transition . . . they would presumably have less and less need for violent tactics and more investment in controlling anarchy," one might as well make a virtue of necessity and let the mafia rule.[43] There is no need to choose between the mafia and democracy or the mafia and the free market: the mafia *is* the free market. The mafia *is* democracy.[44]

Fortunately, neither McWorld nor its fellow-traveling criminals are the only forces at work in the new Russia. There are other important factors, including the emerging outline of a new civil society and civic infrastructure focusing on associations that belong neither to the state nor to the marketplace (see the list, page 235); a young professional class of academics, lawyers, and civic professionals dedicated to civil society and the rule of law; a growing interest in a "third sector" that cannot be folded into capitalism or state socialism; a concern for constitutional issues that go beyond politics; and a growing sense of the need to support the legislature (even when it is in the "wrong" hands) against the arbitrary prerogatives of the executive (even when it is occupied by Westernizing market enthusiasts).

In his official address to the Federal Assembly in 1994, under a section entitled "The Person in a Democratic State" and in a subsection called "State Support for the Institutions of a Civil Society," Boris Yeltsin actually uttered these words—more important than anything else he has said about democracy: "Without a developed civil society state power inevitably takes on a despotic, totalitarian character. Only owing to a civil society is this power subject to serving the individual and becomes a protecting mechanism for freedom."[45] With such sentiments on the official record, and institutions that embody them in the making, it would be a self-fulfilling error to write off Russia as a potential home for democracy. But as the evidence assembled here suggests, it would also be an error to think that markets alone, especially as advanced by the aggressive Western investors who profit from them, offer a shred of real support for such civic institutions or the democracy at which they aim.

Stephen Cohen, one of the more astute observers of the new Russia and a scholar singularly unimpressed by the argument for an economistic road to democracy, wonders whether there is actually more or less democracy in the new Russia. He worries that Yeltsin's assault on the White House and his penchant for ruling by ukase— the executive decrees commissars and czars alike once employed to circumvent their own popularly elected peoples' assemblies and dumas—reinforce an all-too-Russian tendency to exalt executive power at the expense of the legislature, which is always democracy's primary residence even when we dislike the occupants elected to inhabit it. He poses the crucial and quite nearly taboo question: "Should everything created during the Soviet period be rejected as criminal or unworthy, and therefore everything built from scratch?" which, of course, is pregnant with an answer in the negative.[46]

By marking the years of Bolshevism "off limits," the Russians and their friends have left them with a grim choice between the skulking Slavophile nationalism shrouded in ancient mists that proclaims

"Vsegda Rossia!" (always Russia) and the new slogan plastered all over Moscow following "Cokefest '94" celebrating the opening of the first Coca-Cola bottling plant that proclaims "Vsegda Coke!" (always Coke!). That, of course, is precisely the joke—an impossible choice between Jihad and McWorld, which if Russia is to survive as a democracy it must elude.

The market in theory may or may not be free. The market in practice, at least in one nation trying to escape the shadows of Bolshevism overturned, has been less a path to freedom than a road to new and subtle forms of dependency. The same tune, sung in a different key, can be heard if we listen in on the story of East Germany's "integration" into a reunified "democratic" Germany.

18

The Colonization of East Germany by McWorld

I N THE MONTHS preceding the demolition of the Wall in Berlin as well as the abrupt collapse of the government whose despotism the wall symbolized, a surprising collection of East German intellectuals, students, religious leaders, and even some workers—some but by no means all of them dissidents—collaborated to establish a loose opposition group to the crumbling rule of the German Democratic Republic called *Neues Forum*. The group's signature was a courageous opposition to "people's democracy." Bertolt Brecht once said in his sly fashion that to the Communist Party democracy meant it was time to dissolve the people and elect a new one. The dissidents hoped to put the relationship right again, which did not, however, mean simply importing institutions from the West. Tied to its bold dissent was an equally firm skepticism about facile Western alternatives. Its objective was a novel civic order in which certain of social democracy's unrealized ideals might be rescued from the Stalinism of the failing regime and grafted onto a genuinely open civil society based on the not always fully realized ideals of the West. Under its new civic forum name, the group not only led (though by no means constituted by itself) a popular movement that did not so much over-throw the East German Communist regime as orchestrate its spontaneous collapse. Simultaneously, and perhaps more significantly, it strove as it did so to cultivate an embryonic new way for East Germany in which deliberative assemblies, local media, populist broadsides, a resuscitated civil society and an active intelligentsia trying (if not always succeeding) to cooperate with industrial workers, would establish a democratic society with a distinctive leftist German flavor. Reunification would have to wait until East Germany could offer a more equal partnership and insist on its own distinctive democratic institutions.

There is no reason to glamorize Neues Forum. It had serious flaws, among them a typically intellectual underappreciation of the yearning of East Germans for the material goods of the West that were being advertised as the benefits of instant reunification. It also suffered from a romanticized view of the working class that never fully shared important aspects of its program, and a deadly naïveté about the power of what was the German version of McWorld: extremely well-oiled West German political parties, powerful German and international media corporations, eager bankers and managers to whom the East was the equivalent of what centuries ago would have been a newfound lost continent, and opinion makers and mind menders capable of packaging the ambitions of all the others in the seductive wrappings of market democracy.

What followed was the king of all no contests. The Wall came down on November 9, 1989: only four months later, on March 18, 1990, a coalition of conservative West German political parties led by Chancellor Helmut Kohl's Christian Democrats rolled to a victory so complete that the Social Democrats—projected as winners just a few months earlier but as things turned out far too cautious about reunification—were soundly thrashed, securing only 22 percent of the vote.[1] More significantly, the remnants of Neues Forum had formed a coalition under the banner "Alliance 90" with other indigenous democratic and Green groups including Democracy Now and the Initiative for Peace and Human Rights organized by former dissident Marxist Robert Havemann. But Alliance 90 had stubbornly refused to constitute itself as a conventional political party, and it captured less than 5 percent of the vote.

In retrospect, it is clear the outcome was never in doubt: Alliance 90 was selling a difficult and demanding Third Way, an alternative to capitalist consumerism and Communist dictatorship that would preserve an East German democratic identity. Kohl's Christian Democrats were giving away beer, bananas, and bratwurst at political rallies promising instant reunification and instant gratification. As Neues Forum leader Jens Reich put it, "The West German hippopotamus trampled the tender shoots of East German democracy." Another disillusioned voter said: "All my life I dreamed of the day when the wall would come down, but the minute they opened it, I knew the revolution was over."[2] In Berlin's daily newspaper, the *Tageszeitung*, the editor lamented, "The Germans are succeeding in turning a great historical opportunity into an experience of hopelessness, fear and deprivation."[3] Who, he wondered, would pay for the fiasco?

More or less everyone. For what followed was a victory neither for the vanquished Neues Forum democrats nor for the lumbering hippopotamus of western German market capitalism. Reunification was embarked upon so precipitously that before anyone could blink, the West had swallowed up the East whole. Five years later, Germany still suffers from chronic economic indigestion. At the same time, a series of deep cleansings and wholesale scourings aimed at purifying ex–German Democratic Republic universities, courts, and the civil service of all Communist taint were carried out with a punitive thoroughness that made the de-Nazification program after World War II look like a sponge bath. Had cooperators with Hitler's regime been rooted out with the same efficiency as cooperators with and fellow travelers of the German Democratic Republic's regime, postwar Germany would have been stripped of its professional and business classes altogether.[4] Had Germany done without such servants, it would have had to import juridical, political, and managerial cadres from abroad, especially since most of the antifascist Germans who had combatted Hitler and might have constituted an untainted cohort for the postwar West German government had joined the new Communist regime in the East—the regime whose children and grandchildren are being exiled from their posts today.[5]

East Germany also underwent the economic acid bath of privatization, which is why with Russia it offers important lessons about the shock therapy's destabilizing impact. Under the direction of a specially constituted trust agency (Treuhandanstalt), West Germany radically trimmed down or closed much of East Germany's industrial plant—a radical deindustrialization that eventually cost more than 3 million out of the 4.5 million jobs that had existed in the German Democratic Republic. Women who had come to expect equal treatment and equal pay as laborers and special consideration as mothers under communism (which for all its tyranny did manage to make good on a few of its boasts) found themselves at the mercy of a market that had no particular interest in gender equality.

By the time it closes down its operations sometime in 1995, Treuhandanstalt will have sold or liquidated close to fifteen thousand companies, including all of East Germany's top newspapers and magazines, taken over by their western competitors and turned into outlets for West German–style journalism and opinion. Only a few properties remain on the block, including the Saxony town of Amerika (population one hundred), which Treuhand—clearly conscious of the theme-parking potential of McWorld—is pushing as a perfect site for a Wild West Park. The buyers for nearly all of East Germany's industrial plant were almost exclusively from western Germany or abroad and will pay more than $122 billion for their new properties, but Treuhand had $217 billion in costs, leaving the taxpayers of Germany with an enormous debt.[6] Some estimate that the deficit will soar to $275 billion before privatization is finished.[7] That, along with the socially destabilizing job deficit, is likely to further inflame the politics of resentment that has already turned East against West, young against old, and German against foreign worker in the new unified Germany.[8]

Unified Germany's tax system actually discriminates against the five eastern Laender whose municipalities get only 85 percent of what comparable districts in the west receive. Under federal guidelines, the western Laender can actually prevent eastern Laender from sharing in redistributed state revenues.[9] This sounds like a German version of Reich's middle-class politics of secession, where the public sector is left bankrupt by the withdrawal of the wealthy from civic responsibility.

Given this somber record, you did not have to be an ex-Communist to agree with the claim of the Party for Democratic Socialism that "Never in peacetime has so much social wealth been destroyed." Enough Germans agreed to propel this relaunched East German Communist Party to a surprising showing in the German local elections in 1994, when 40 percent of East Berlin voters saw and voted Red and a Communist, Horst-Dieter Brahmig, was elected mayor of Hoyerswerda against the combined forces of all the other parties.[10]

Two years before these startling elections results, many non-Communists had joined with ex-Communists to form a Committee for Fairness, whose platform proclaimed: "The destruction of our industry and agriculture, mass unemployment, unbearable rent increases, unfairly low wages, the closing of social, scientific, cultural and athletic organizations, the selling off of what was once 'people's' property, rejection of our right to occupy apartments, houses and land and the demoralization of people in the East, especially women, have destroyed many hopes that were raised by German unification."[11] Although the committee included Democratic Socialists (former Communists) like Gregor Gysi, it also featured Christian Democratic leader Peterm Diestel, former mayor of West Berlin Heinrich Labertz, and *Berlin Tageszeitung* editor Michael Sontheimer, as well as such former East German dissidents as writer Stefan Heym and rock singer Tamara Danz.[12] Artist Barbel Bohley, called the "mother of revolution" at the time of the collapse of the East German regime, did not join the committee but still protested: "For a half century we have not been allowed to decide for ourselves what we want. In the old days whenever we asked why things had to be done a certain way, we were told 'Because that's the way they are done in the glorious Soviet state.' Now, since reunification, we're told that we have to do everything the way it was done in West Germany."[13]

East Germans who clambered over the wall in the heady days of 1989 now stay in East Berlin in the neighborhoods where the Western bistros and boutiques have not yet signed leases. There the old working class bars and groceries remain largely unchanged, except for the gambling machines near the doors and the too expensive Western goods that are gradually driving cheaper local products off the shelves. As has happened elsewhere in the land of McWorld where the expansion of the private sector has drained political support for the public sector, public monies are not available for projects of real reunification. The great empty space at Potsdamerplatz that once anchored the Wall and its shooting zones near the Brandenburger Tor has been turned over to private multinationals like Sony and Mercedes-Benz for purely commercial exploitation and development, public uses shoved aside. Taxi drivers talk about a new "Mauer im Kopf" (a wall inside people's heads) that divides East and West more effectively (because without any visible coercion) than the physical wall ever did. Smug westerners boast they can "spot a former East German just by his or her gait," and are buying up old two-cycle Trabent cars that look like toys for their nostalgia collections.[14]

Nostalgia—renamed "ostalgia" (nostalgia for the East)—has made a provocative comeback in the eastern part of Germany, as is evident in Frank Georgi's nutty plan for an East German theme park ("Ossipark"). Many East Germans are feeling a kind of nationalist sentimentality about local goods, however shoddy when compared to their western counterparts; 80 percent claim to prefer traditional products. Beverages from Communist times like Club Cola and "Beer from Here" are taking on the products of McWorld's behemoths, their ads proclaiming, "Hurrah, I'm still alive. Club Cola: Our Cola!" Shops in the East are featuring German Democratic "East-made" cigarettes (F-6's) that retain their earlier packaging and taste formulas.[15] Ironically, however, F-6 is owned by Philip Morris, one of McWorld's giants anxious to compensate for the declining American market in tobacco. In a marketing memo for F-6 permeated by the commodification of identity politics, Philip Morris executives remind their employees that the brand is "a piece of East German cultural history and constitutes a meaningful part of the formation of identity."[16]

Even the "Jugendweihe" has made a comeback: this anticlerical rite of passage ceremony by which young Communist pioneers once celebrated their coming of age has been revived by popular demand. In the first half of 1994 over seventeen thousand fourteen-year-olds participated in the confirmation process. Against the trends elsewhere that permit Hollywood to drive local fare off the screens, East German movies like the 1973 *Legend of Paul and Paula* are being shown again. Much of this revivalist mentality represents a reaction to perceived Western arrogance akin to the resentment typical of Jihad's angry tribes. A market research firm warned that "the picture that

East Germans have of West Germans is so negative that the word disapproval really doesn't describe it. Hatred would be more like it."[17] Is it really any surprise that in 1991 when the *Frankfurter Allgemeine* ran a now notorious survey asking which was the best form of government, while eight of ten West Germans answered democracy, only three of ten East Germans did so? A stunning 82 percent of the easterners said they regarded themselves as second-class citizens in their new democratic fatherland.

West German biases and aggressive commerce combine to undermine both dissident and traditional East German culture. In the summer of 1990, shortly after the elections and only six months after the collapse of the East German regime, reporters called to the little town of Kommlitz near Leipzig discovered a vast biblio-bonfire. Ten million books had been torched, including volumes by such dissident authors as Christa Wolf, Stefan Heym, Hermann Kant, and Anna Seghers—not as an act of political repression but in a kind of instant and terminal remaindering of a stock of books that publishers did not wish to deal with. The old books were cheap and serious. The new are expensive and frivolous. New stores in the east carry more Stephen King than Stefan Heym, and prefer travel guides, tax advice, and language texts to classical authors. Books that could once be had for $4 now cost $30 (a month's rent in the former East Germany).[18]

In place of the radical broadsides and political magazines published by samizdat writers, the new western-owned magazines avoid political subjects altogether. Lubos Beniak, the editor of *Mlady Svet,* a Czech weekly, describes changes that are common throughout central Europe: "People are sick of politics. They want to be entertained, they want snappy journalism, they even want trash."[19] Hungary's most prestigious radical paper, *Reform,* with a circulation of over 400,000, was purchased by Rupert Murdoch in 1990. In 1992, its editor Peter Toke admitted: "It was exciting under the Communists, and it was easier because it was obvious what to attack. Since the revolution we've been in an identity crisis, and Mr. Murdoch is not happy at all." New German editors are looking for "readable rock critics, witty headlines, good crossword puzzles . . . classified advertisements."[20] That should placate Mr. Murdoch.

The persistence of the East-West rift within Germany along with the costs privatization has imposed on the East, where official unemployment rates hover at 16 percent and the real rate is above 30 percent, is of grave concern. So are plummeting birth rates, even more precipitous than those of Russia. In eastern Germany between 1989 and 1993, the rate per thousand people fell 60 percent while mortality rates surged, leading demographer Nicholas Eberstadt to warn that the transition from a planned economy to a liberal market order entails "far-reaching, often traumatic adjustments."[21] Yet these grim statistics do not tell the whole story. Privatization will eventually improve industrial output, and markets will offer those who never had goods the chance to get them. Reunification will gradually impose a reality that resentment cannot resist. But what the German case suggests is exactly what the Russian case establishes: that McWorld's markets, tied here to the West German political and economic leviathan, have not and probably cannot produce a democratic civil society; indeed, in East Germany, they helped destroy one in its infancy. McWorld is the problem, not the solution.

19

Securing Global Democracy in the World of McWorld

THE EVIDENCE FROM Russia and Germany highlights the short-comings of markets as vessels of democratization, but markets are only part of the story. McWorld has also brought with it techno-logical innovations in the infotainment telesector that are less inimi-cal to democracy. The old Baconian dictum that knowledge is power and that through science we can command the world, the belief that the improvement of men's minds and the improvement of his lot are finally the very same thing, was at the heart of the Enlightenment's conviction that reason embodied in science and technology could liberate the human race from prejudice, ignorance, and injustice—could eventually liberate all women and men and democratize their social institutions. Walter B. Wriston is only the latest of a host of Enlightenment-infused panglossian futurologists from Condorcet to Alvin Toffler who have composed odes to the emancipatory, demo-cratic powers of the startling new technologies that drive McWorld and have transformed capitalism from a system that serves needs into a system that creates and manipulates them. In *The Twilight of*

Sovereignty, Wriston calls his final chapter "Power to the People." Apparently believing his own mythology, he goes on to argue that "the information age is rapidly giving the power to the people . . ." speeding us along on "our journey toward more human freedom."[1]

To be sure, technology's mandarins are correct in seeing improved information and communication as indispensable to improving democracy. From the time of the Greeks, who believed Prometheus's theft of fire from the Gods lit the way to human civilization (if also to tragedy), technical gadgets have been made to support democratization. In ancient Athens, small machines that randomized the selection of white and black balls were used for jury selection. During the Renaissance (as Bacon noticed), movable type, gunpowder, and the compass transformed society by democratizing literacy (when everyone could read, neither priests nor princes could maintain their monopoly over the sovereign word); by equalizing combat (the aristocratic knight's armor was no longer a guarantee of domination over the common man, now that everyman had his musket); and by opening up a new world of exploration to all (navigation offered everyman an exit visa from indentured servitude and political persecution). In the fullness of time, long after Bacon was dead, radio and television and finally mass-produced computers offered an ongoing technically enhanced democratization of the Word that spread literacy and political knowledge and strengthened the competence and will of the well-established democratic electorates.

In the same tradition, the proposed information superhighway can potentially offer to every woman and man on the globe access to endless data banks and worldwide opinion exchange. Electronic bulletin boards can link like-minded individuals around their common interests and offer formats for community debates among those lacking common values. Video teleconference capabilities allow local town meetings to interact with similar meetings across a region, a nation, or the world, breaking down the parochialism of face-to-face interaction without sacrificing its personalism. Interactive television transforms a passive medium aimed at complacent consumers of entertainment and advertising into an active theater of social discourse and political feedback, opening up the possibility of universal multichoice-vote-at-home referenda. Satellite dishes the size of a dinner plate put a global ear at the disposal of peoples imprisoned in the most despotic regimes, and have proved their worth in places like China and Iran where, despite an official government ban, they continue to spread—and as they do, to spread unfettered images to information-starved consumers.[2]

In combination, these technologies potentially enhance lateral communication among citizens, open access to information by all, and furnish citizens with communication links across distances that once precluded direct democracy or, indeed, interaction of any kind. If the scale of ancient democracy was bounded by the territory a man could cross on foot in a day on his way to the assembly, telecommunications at the speed of light turn the entire globe into a wired town of potential neighbors—McLuhan's global village. Of course, if democracy is to be understood as deliberative and participatory activity on the part of responsible citizens, it must resist the innovative forms of demagoguery that accompany innovative technology. Home voting via interactive television could further privatize politics and replace deliberative debate in public with the unconsidered instant expression of private prejudices. Democracy calls not only for votes but for good reasons, not only for an opinion but for a rational argument on its behalf. Talk radio and scream television have already depreciated our political currency, and newer technologies are as likely to reinforce as to impede the trend if not subjected to the test of deliberative competence.

Futuristic idealism must then be treated with a certain skepticism. The history of science and technology is at best a history of ambivalence. In each of the instances explored here, we can speak only of potentiality, not of actuality. The double edge of technology's sword has been well known to us at least since Mary Shelley first told the story of Dr. Frankenstein's monster, and our technologies today possess potentialities as monstrous as any she imagined.

Telecommunications technology has the capability for strengthening civil society, but it also has a capacity for unprecedented surveillance and can be used to impede and manipulate as well as to access information. Left to the market, which is where McWorld leaves technology, monsters may end up with a free and mightily profitable reign. As we have already noticed, the market has no particular interest in the civic possibilities of technology—unless they can generate a respectable profit (generally they cannot). When profitability is the primary object, technological innovation is likely to reinforce extant inequalities, making the resource-and-income-poor information-poor as well. Computer literacy has become as important as language literacy and numeracy in the job market, and is likely to be vital to civic literacy as well. The division of labor into symbolic analysis workers and more traditional durable goods and service sector workers has actually accelerated the growth of social inequality in America.

Robert Reich has drawn a disturbing American portrait in which privileged information/communication workers increasingly withdraw public support from the larger society. His grim analysis portrays them moving to insular suburbs and buying private recreational, schooling, security, and sanitation services for their own gated communities, which the public at large cannot afford. They are then positioned to refuse to pay taxes for the declining public services they no longer need. Their withdrawal (Reich labels it the politics of secession) leaves the poor poorer, the public sector broke, and society ever more riven by economic disparities.[3] A similar pattern of "secession" by the new symbolic elites can be discerned on a global scale where elite nations secede from their global public responsibilities as fast as elite professionals secede from *their* public responsibilities within elite nations. The Third World becomes a series of urban ghettos within every First World society as well as a series of poor nation ghettos within international society. The "restructuring" of the global economy to meet the demands of the new age information/entertainment sector further reinforces the boundaries between the privileged and the rest.

Even when we set social and class issues aside, the market in technology can have untoward consequences. Technology can as easily become an instrument of repression as of liberation. Thoreau worried about how easily we become the "tools of our tools"; the new tools of the post-Gutenberg age of electronics confirm his fear. Interactive television is a powerful surveillance instrument: as consumers tell shopping networks what they want to buy and tell banks how to dispense their cash and tell pollsters what they think about abortion, those receiving the information gain access to an extensive catalog of knowledge about the private habits, attitudes, and behaviors of consumers. This information may in turn be used to reshape those habits and attitudes in ways that favor producers and sellers massaging the marketplace. The current antiregulatory fever means that the new information banks being compiled from interaction and surveillance are subject neither to government scrutiny nor to limitation or control (such as a sunset provision that would periodically destroy all information). The Federal Communications Act of 1934 promised to "encourage the larger and more effective use of radio in the public interest," but the multiplication of broadcast channels across the electronic spectrum has led the government to withdraw its regulatory presence.

Fred Friendly has been calling for an "electronic bill of rights" for a number of years, but government has been moving in the opposite direction, with the Clinton administration, despite its apparent belief in open access, committed to letting the market make the moves with a minimum of regulation. The "public airwaves" are still auctioned off to private vendors who sell them back at exorbitant rates to the public during election campaigns—increasing the costs of democracy and the dependence of elections on money at the very moment when government has backed away from regulation. The 1984 Cable Act gives local franchisers (cities and towns) rather than the federal or state government control over cable, in effect abandoning it to market forces that have shown scant regard for public needs.[4] In 1994, Senator Inouye introduced a bill into Congress directing the Federal Communications Commission to require the "reservation for public uses of capacity on telecommunications networks." His aim was to guarantee the public some voice in development of the Information Superhighway. His bill received little press attention and expired without action at the end of the 103rd Congress. Fear of government has incapacitated the public's only agent in diverting the new technologies into public channels. The model of Channel One, a classroom network (started by Whittle Communications and now controlled by K-III Corporation) that extorts classroom advertising time from needy schools in return for desperately wanted hardware, suggests that the public is likely to be served by the new technologies only in as far as someone can make serious money off it.[5]

It may be a cause of satisfaction, as Walter Wriston insists, that nowadays it is the citizen who is watching Big Brother and not the other way around. To be sure, in most post-Communist societies, as in our own market societies, Big Brother is no longer watching you; but neither is he watching those who *are* watching you, and even adversaries of regulation may find reason to be disturbed by that omission. If the classical liberal question used to be who will police the police, the pertinent liberal question in today's McWorld ought to be who will watch those who are watching us? Who will prevent the media from controlling their clients and consumers? Who will act in lieu of a government that has demurred from representing the public's interests?

There would perhaps be less cause for concern if technology and telecommunication markets were truly diversified and competitive. But as we have seen, the conglomeration of companies focused on programming, information, communication, and entertainment suggests that government's erstwhile big brother has been dwarfed today by Ma Bell and her overgrown babies, who are currently buying up the cable market and trying to purchase entertainment and software production companies as fast as they can. Their aim is to stay competitive with infotainment companies like Time Warner. Thus US West bought a significant minority interest (along with Toshiba and C. Itoh) in Warner Brothers film studio and Home Box Office only to have Time Warner acquire Cablevision ($2.2 billion) and Houston Industries ($2.3 billion) in 1995, and thereby regain control. The harder the American government tries to stay out of the development of a free market information highway, the harder corporate multinationals are trying to get in; and if they cannot effect a total takeover of the digital thoroughfare, they aspire at least to gain control of its gateways and tollbooths.

Democrats should not be the Luddites Jihad's anxious tribal warriors have become; they cannot afford to make technology and modernity enemies of self-determination and liberty. Technology is a neutral tool: allied to democracy it can enhance civic communication and expand citizen literacy. Left to markets, it is likely to augment McWorld's least worthy imperatives, including surveillance over and manipulation of opinion, and the cultivation of artificial needs rooted in lifestyle "choices" unconnected to real economic, civic, or spiritual needs.

Not so long ago, the prescient historian J. G. A. Pocock suggested that

> [today we find] ourselves in a post-industrial and post-modern world in which more and more of us were consumers of information and fewer and fewer of us producers or possessors of anything, including our own identities. When a world of persons, actions, and things becomes a world of persons, actions, and linguistic or electronic constructs that have no authors, it clearly becomes easier for the things—grown much more powerful because they are no longer real—to multiply and take charge, controlling, and determining persons and actions that no longer control, determine or even produce them.[6]

The world Pocock describes is McWorld—what Neil Postman, another savvy critic of the tyranny of technology over its makers, calls technopoly. Technopoly suggests "the submission of all forms of cultural life to the sovereignty of technique and technology."[7] Postman is not a technological determinist and recognizes that technology can be both friend and enemy. But liberated from our common democratic choices and left to the market, we are more likely to confront the enemy than the friend. Which is perhaps why John Pocock thinks the key to living in the postindustrial, postmodern world is finding "means of affirming that we are citizens . . . that we are persons and associating with other persons to have voice and action in the making of our worlds."[8]

Many who are skeptical of McWorld have assailed in particular its pervasive materialism. These include traditionalist advocates of the moral Jihad against the West's consumer culture, like Aleksandr Solzhenitsyn or his more militant Islamic brethren as well as some of Jihad's harshest critics like Zbigniew Brzezinski, who has blamed the temptations of tribalism on the West's "permissive cornucopia" that breeds materialist self-gratification and a "dominant cultural reality" defined by the "dynamic escalation of desire for sensual and material pleasure."[9] American kids from small towns in the farm belt with ears cocked to the siren song of urban shopping districts and suburban malls hundreds of miles away are no different than Russian veterans of communism succumbing to the insistent commercial jingles that come tumbling from their new Japanese TVs. "My dad won't even let us get MTV," complains a teen from Nebraska, whose friends "see the shopping mall as the great hangout of the rest of the nation, and they don't have one."[10] So, the kid from Nebraska and the kid from Smolensk end up in L.A. or St. Petersburg where whatever distinct culture that may have attached to their youth is stripped away and replaced with the videology of a McWorld utterly indifferent to diversity or democracy.

Such attitudes and behaviors are as much the product as the cause of McWorld's strategies, and make understandable the alliance against McWorld's global culture forged by Jihad's warriors—an alliance that leads premodern tribalists and postmodern Puritans to make common cause. Are these aroused and zealous camp followers of Jihad then really so nutty in their censuring of materialism and their call for modes of living more commensurate with the needs of the human spirit? How different is their rhetoric from the more austere and secular argument advanced so fervently by Vaclav Havel, who has not permitted his reputation as an ironist to obscure his unselfconscious commitment to forging a strong connection between politics and service to others? Havel calls for an awareness of "the secret order of the cosmos" that makes "genuine conscience and genuine responsibility . . . explicable only as an expression of the silent assumption that we are observed 'from above.' "[11]

The complaint against McWorld represents impatience not just with its consumption-driven markets and its technocratic imperatives, but with its hollowness as a foundation for a meaningful moral existence. These absences translate into profound civic alienation that disconnects individuals from their communities and isolates them from nonmaterial sources of their being. Citizenship is not a cure for spiritual malaise but spiritual malaise is a roadblock to citizenship because it impairs the capacity to create the community institutions on which a civil society and a democratic culture must rest.

As Robert Putnam has wisely suggested, "The norms and networks of civic engagement also powerfully affect the performance of representative government," so that when people start bowling alone instead of together in leagues, even so pedestrian an activity as this may signal trouble for democracy.[12] That is why Harry C. Boyte and other supporters of renewed citizenship have argued that we learn to be citizens not first in politics but in the "free spaces" of school, church, 4-H club, and YMCA.[13] A culture of advertising, software, Hollywood movies, MTV, theme parks, and shopping malls hooped together by the virtual nexus of the information superhighway closes down free spaces. Such a culture is unquestionably in the process of forging a global *something:* but whatever it is, that something is not democracy. For democracy rests on civil society and citizenship, and while the new telecommunications technologies are not necessarily averse to either, they produce neither unless directed by citizens already living in and dedicated to a civil society.

A Global Civil Society?

AS A FRAMEWORK for democracy, the nation-state is twice impaired: the challenges of global McWorld and regional Jihad are not susceptible to its interventions; and the ideology of laissez-faire that accompanies McWorld and has become the mantra of its proponents within national government undermines whatever residual capacity it might have for action in the name of public good. Sovereignty is indeed in a twilight, condemned to a shadow world by government's myriad postmodern detractors—ex-Communist and postindustrialist alike. In the post-Communist East, government is too closely associated with totalitarian despotism: to speak of citizens still evokes the language of comrades and faithful party hacks. In the democratic West, government remains too identified with bureaucracy, inefficiency, and a professional political class in whom peoples everywhere have lost confidence, if in part because they have lost confidence in themselves. Until we retrieve our public institutions and reclaim their powers as surrogates for our own, government and its communication technologies will be part of the alien world we confront—part of "it"—rather than a tool with which we can confront "it." To make government our own is to recast our civic attitudes, which is possible only in a vibrant civil society where responsibilities and rights are joined together in a seamless web of community self-government.

At the same time, democracy demands new post-nation-state institutions and new attitudes more attentive to the direct responsibility people bear for their liberties. To be sure, global government, above all democratic global government, remains a distant dream; but the kinds of global citizenship necessary to its cultivation are less remote. Citizenship is nurtured first of all in democratic civil society. A global citizenship demands a domain parallel to McWorld's in which communities of cooperation do consciously and for the public good what markets currently do inadvertently on behalf of aggregated private interests. This is no easy task. More than sixty years ago, John Dewey had already suggested that the problem was to identify a democratic public. "Not that there is no public, no large body of persons having a common interest in the consequences of social transactions," he wrote. "There is too much public, a public too diffused and scattered and too intricate in composition. And there are too many publics, for conjoint actions which have indirect, serious and enduring consequences are multitudinous beyond comparison."[14] How much more elusive than Dewey's national "public" is a global "public"—not just a network of NGOs, but a civic nexus across all boundaries; not just groups like "Doctors without Frontiers" (*Médecines sans frontières*) but a world of citizens without frontiers?

The creation of a public is the task of civil society. Only there are attitudes likely to emerge that favor democracy and counter the siren song of McWorld. Only there are communities possible that answer the human need for parochial interaction in ways that remain open to inclusion and to cosmopolitan civic sentiments. But how can civil society be constructed in an international arena? Those wishing to try—not just in Russia and Germany where patience and civic cunning are imperative, but in an America and Western Europe that have grown complacent about the civic domain—need both to recall the story of democracy's founding, and at the same time to invent new institutions appropriate to novel global conditions. Old democrats often suffer from their civic longevity. They forget the lessons of their own history, forget how violent and disruptive democratization can be, how long it takes to construct a foundational free society before a democratic constitution can ever be raised up upon it. Like the cautious senator who cannot remember the risk-taking boy he once was, the modern democrat represses the memory of revolution and tumult in which he first reached his own uncertain majority, pretending that he was forever a prudent sage and that it did not take a prolonged and painful childhood to learn the arts of liberty (if they were learned at all).

Specialists seem persuaded that to construct a new democracy, whether for Russia, Somalia, or for the whole planet, requires nothing more than the export of prefabricated constitutions and made-to-order parliamentary systems. Joshua Muravchik is a perfect exemplar whose problems begin with the very title of his new book: *Exporting Democracy*.[15] Fed Ex the Federalist Papers to Belorussia; send a multiparty system to Nigeria by parcel post; E-mail the Chinese the Bill of Rights; ship the U.N. a civilian-controlled, all-volunteer, obedient but conscience-sensitive peacekeeping force from a country with a high tolerance for casualties and no interests of its own . . . and in the flash of a laser beam: democracy! For global government, do exactly the same thing, globally.

Not quite. Democracies are built slowly, culture by culture, each with its own strengths and needs, over centuries, which is why the West Germans might have taken more care before expunging the novice civil institutions of the East German resistance movement like Neues Forum; and why the Russians might want to pay more attention to native institutions like the Russian mir (village commune) or soviet (council) and a little less to import Western institutions. For the lesson of Western democratic history is patience and self-reflection. Between Magna Carta's first assertion of rights by the English king's vassals and the "Glorious Revolution" of 1688 that ushered in the era of parliamentary supremacy, stretched 450 long, war-filled years; and it would be 150 years more before Parliament became even nominally "democratic." Switzerland's proto-democratic federal system took its first steps in 1291 but acquired a fully democratic constitution only in 1848 (totally revised in 1874), more than five hundred years later. France initially experimented with aristocratic regional parliaments hundreds of years before its revolution in 1789, and it required still another century for something resembling a workable democratic republic to come into being.

In the 150 years between the foundings at Jamestown and Plymouth Rock and the founding of the United States of America in 1789, colonial Americans had a half-dozen generations of experi-

ence with royal charters, commonwealth government, town meetings, and a frontier wilderness society that sharpened their sense of
autonomy and fashioned talents for self-government that would be
indispensable to the working of the federal constitution. Moreover, it
took the young democratic republic another seventy-five years and
a bloody civil war to confront the issues of slavery and state
sovereignty left unresolved by the 1789 constitution.[16]

A people corrupted by tribalism and numbed by McWorld is no
more ready to receive a prefabricated democratic constitution than a
people emerging from a long history of despotism and tyranny. Nor
can democracy be someone's gift to the powerless. It must be seized
by them because they refuse to live without liberty and they insist on
justice for all. To prepare the ground for democracy today either in
transitional societies or on a global scale is first to re-create citizens
who will demand democracy: this means laying a foundation in civil
society and civic culture. Democracy is not a universal prescription
for some singularly remarkable form of government, it is an admo-
nition to people to live in a certain fashion: responsibly, auton-
omously yet on common ground, in self-determining communities
somehow still open to others, with tolerance and mutual respect yet
a firm sense of their own values. When John Dewey called democracy a way of life—it is the idea of community life itself, he
insisted—rather than a way of government, he called attention to its
primacy as an associated mode of living in a civil society. A global
democracy capable of countering the antidemocratic tendencies of
Jihad and McWorld cannot be borrowed from some particular
nation's warehouse or copied from an abstract constitutional template. Citizenship, whether global or local, comes first.

These lessons would not be so hard for the complacent denizens of
McWorld and the angry brothers of Jihad if the idea of civil society
had retained its currency among those who call themselves
democrats today. But battered by history and squeezed between two
equally elephantine state and private market sectors, civil society has
fairly vanished both as theory and as democratic practice. Even in
America, where the heritage of John Locke ought to have kept it
supple, the idea of civil society has petrified and crumbled—its dry
remains easily pushed aside in favor of a set of simple interlocking
oppositions: the state versus the individual, government versus the

private sector, public bureaucracy versus free markets, corrupt politicians versus angry voters. Politically alienated and consumption-weary people, equally uncomfortable with what they see as a rapacious and unsympathetic government and a fragmented and self-absorbed private sector, find themselves homeless. Neither the market nor the state bureaucracy seems to speak to them or serve them in their public identity. Although it is ultimately accountable to the people in their capacity as voters, the government is regarded by them as an almost foreign body: a threatening sphere of quasi-legitimate coercion managed by unresponsive representatives, professional politicians, and bureaucratic managers who have lost much of their authority as authentic voices for the public they supposedly represent. Voting, at best, is reduced to an act of spite or retribution against outlaws disguised as candidates.

On the other hand, the private sector, representing commercial markets, and comprising private individuals and corporations, speaks for the public only inasmuch as it aggregates the desire of individuals and companies—private prejudices and special interests given a "public" status they do nothing to earn. The "public corporation" does nothing to deserve its legal sobriquet. It is private in everything but its name. Not only is the actual public left voiceless and homeless, but those in government who still try in good faith to receive counsel from the now-phantom public do not really know where to turn, since so-called public opinion polls canvass private prejudice and since special interests represent themselves and only themselves. In America and most other democracies, politicians who were once citizens temporarily holding office are metamorphosed by power into "professionals" out of touch with their constituencies, while citizens are reduced by their impotence to whining antagonists of the men and women they elect to office or to sulking clients of government services they consume without being willing to pay for. For peoples so cynical about their own democratic institutions to recommend democracy to cousins in transitional states or to conceive of a global democracy in the world beyond sovereign borders is problematic at best. For today's half-baked citizens recommend democracy without trusting it: they abdicate their own majority powers in favor of term limits, constitutional amendments, and supermajorities. Likewise, they recommend markets without believing in them: without being persuaded for an instant that markets can secure citizenship or civic liberty or much of anything beyond the material goods that no longer satisfy their yearning spirits.

To envision a democratic civic entity that empowers citizens to rule themselves is then necessarily to move beyond the two-celled model of government versus private sector we have come to rely on. Instead, invoking the traditional language of civil society, we need to begin to think about the domains people occupy as they go about their daily business as having at least three primary arenas, whether within tribal enclaves, nation-states, or a global society: the government and the private sector to be sure, but also the civil domain, civic space or what Eastern Europeans and Russians regularly referred to as civil society before they became "democratic" and were persuaded by their Western handlers that local participatory institutions were unsuited to democracy's market ambitions.

Civil society, or civic space, occupies the middle ground between government and the private sector. It is not where we vote and it is not where we buy and sell; it is where we talk with neighbors about a crossing guard, plan a benefit for our community school, discuss how our church or synagogue can shelter the homeless, or organize a summer softball league for our children. In this domain, we are "public" beings and share with government a sense of publicity and a regard for the general good and the commonweal; but unlike government, we make no claim to exercise a monopoly on legitimate coercion. Rather, we work here voluntarily and in this sense inhabit a "private" realm devoted to the cooperative (noncoercive) pursuit of public goods. This neighborly and cooperative domain of civil society shares with the private sector the gift of liberty: it is voluntary and is constituted by freely associated individuals and groups; but unlike the private sector, it aims at common ground and consensual (that is, integrative and collaborative) modes of action. Civil society is thus public without being coercive, voluntary without being privatized. It is in this domain that our traditional civic institutions such as foundations, schools, churches, public interest and other voluntary civic associations properly belong. The media too, where they take their public responsibilities seriously and subordinate their commercial needs to their civic obligations, are part of civil society.

Unhappily, civil society has been eclipsed by government/market bipolarities and its mediating strengths have been eliminated in favor of the simplistic opposition of state and individual: the command economy versus the free market. This opposition has forced those wishing to occupy noncoercive civic space—whether in traditional democracies, new democracies, or the global civic domain—back into the private sector where they reappear, quite improperly, as "special interest" advocates supposedly unmarked by common concerns or public norms. We are compelled to be voters or consumers in all we do; if we wish to be citizens, if we want to participate in self-governance rather than just elect those who govern us, there is no place to turn.

Throughout the nineteenth century, in Tocqueville's America and afterwards, American society felt like civil society. Without trying to romanticize the social conditions of that decentralized period, we can see how they allowed liberty a more local and civic aspect, while a modest governmental sphere and an unassuming private sector were overshadowed by an extensive civic network tied together by schools, granges, churches, town halls, village greens, country stores, and voluntary associations of every imaginable sort. It was these "municipal" institutions that fired Tocqueville's imagination. Government, especially at the federal level, was a modest affair (probably too modest for some of the tasks it needed to accomplish) because the constitution had left all powers not specifically delegated to it to the states and people. Markets were also modest affairs, regional in nature and dominated by other associations and affections.

It was only when individuals who thought of themselves as citizens began to see themselves as consumers, and groups that were regarded as voluntary associations were supplanted by corporations legitimized as "legal persons," that market forces began to encroach on and crush civil society from the private sector side. Once markets began to expand radically, government responded with an aggressive campaign on behalf of the public weal against the new monopolies, inadvertently crushing civil society from the state side. Squeezed between the warring realms of the two expanding monopolies, statist and corporate, civil society lost its preeminent place in American life. By the time of the two Roosevelts it had nearly vanished and its civic denizens had been compelled to find sanctuary under the feudal tutelage of either big government (their protectors and social servants) or the private sector, where schools, churches, unions, foundations, and other associations could assume the identity of corporations and aspire to be no more than special interest groups formed for the particularistic ends of their members. Whether those ends were, say, market profitability or environmental preservation, was irrelevant since by definition all private associations necessarily had private ends. Schools became interest groups for people with children (parents) rather than the forges of a free society; churches became confessional special interest groups pursuing separate agendas rather than sources of moral fiber for the larger society (as Tocqueville had thought they would be); voluntary associations became a variation on private lobbies rather than the free spaces where women and men practiced an apprenticeship of liberty.

Paradoxically, once civil society had been privatized and commercialized, groups organized in desperate defense of the public interest found themselves cast as mere exemplars of plundering private interest lobbies. Unions, for example, though concerned with fair compensation, full employment, and the dignity of work for all became the private sector counterparts of the corporations, and in time learned all too well how to act the part. When they tried to break the stranglehold of corporations over labor, they were deemed another "special interest" group no better than those against whom they struck, and perhaps worse (since the companies struck were productive contributors to the wealth of America). Environmental groups have undergone the same transmogrification more recently. Although pursuing what for all the world looks like a public agenda of clean air for all including the polluters, they are cast as the polluters' mirror-image twin—another special interest group whose interests are to be arbitrated alongside those of toxic-waste dumpers. The media surrendered their responsibility to inform democracy's proprietors and became sellers of gossip and wholly owned subsidiaries of private sector proprietors with no responsibilities at all other than to their profit margins. Under such conditions, the "public good" could not and did not survive as a reasonable ideal. Its epitaph was written by David B. Truman, who in his influential 1951 primer *The Governmental Process*, a book that helped establish the dominant paradigm in social science throughout the 1960s and 1970s, wrote summarily that in dealing with the pluralist pressure system of private interests that is America, "we do not need to account for a totally inclusive interest, because one does not exist."[17] McWorld has only dropped an exclamation point into Truman's assertion.

We are left stranded by this melancholy history in an era where civil society is in eclipse and where citizens have neither home for their civic institutions nor voice with which to speak, even within nation-states nominally committed to democracy. Be passively serviced (or passively persecuted) by the massive, busybody, bureaucratic state where the word *citizen* has no resonance; or sign onto the selfishness and radical individualism of the private sector where the word *citizen* has no resonance. Vote the public scoundrels out of public office and/or vote your private interests into office by voting your dollars for the scoundrels willing to work for you: those are the only remaining obligations of the much diminished office of citizen in what are supposed to be the best established democracies.

If these cheerless observations are at all well grounded, and democracy suffers from the polarizing effects of a vanished civil society in America and other Western democracies, surely those looking to create new democracies under the conditions either of Jihad or of McWorld face formidable challenges. Their first priority surely must be the reconstruction of civil society as a framework for the reinvention of democratic citizenship, a mediating third domain between the overgrown but increasingly ineffective state governmental and the metastasizing private market sectors. Our choices need not be limited by the zero-sum game between government and commercial markets in which growth for the one spells encroachment for the other: a massive statist bureaucracy or a massive McWorld. Although that is precisely the choice that has been offered to peoples in Russia and East Germany, we need not opt either for some caricatured Big Brother government that enforces justice but in exchange plays the tyrant, or for some caricatured runaway free market that secures liberty but in exchange fosters inequality and social injustice and doggedly abjures the public weal. For this leaves us only with the choice between McWorld or tyranny. Indeed, as the nation-state loses its sovereignty, it is not so much the choice between tyranny and McWorld but the tyranny *of* McWorld itself that becomes our destiny. Only some version of a global civil society can hope to counter its inadvertent despotism.

Civil society grounds democracy as a form of government in which not politicians and bureaucrats but an empowered people use legitimate force to put flesh on the bones of their liberties; and in which liberty carries with it the obligations of social responsibility and citizenship as well as the rights of legal persons. Civil society offers us a single civic identity that, belonging neither to state bureaucrats nor private consumers but to citizens alone, recouples rights and responsibilities and allows us to take control of our governments and our markets. Civil society is the domain of citizens: a mediating domain between private markets and big government. Interposed between the state and the market, it can contain an obtrusive government without ceding public goods to the private sphere. At the same time it can dissipate the atmospherics of solitariness and greed that surround markets without suffocating in an energetic big government's exhaust fumes. In the international domain, where states are weak and markets dominant, civil society can offer an alternative identity to people who otherwise are only clients or consumers—or passive spectators to global trends they can do nothing to challenge. It can make internationalism a form of citizenship. Within national states, both government *and* the private sector can be humbled a little by a growing civil society that absorbs some of the public aspirations to self-government, without casting off its liberal character as a noncoercive association of equals. Because they tend to their own affairs and take more responsibility on themselves, citizens inhabiting a vibrant civil society worry less about elections and leaders and term limits and scandals; and they simultaneously free themselves from the "free" markets that otherwise imprison them in a commercial mentality that leaves no room for community or for spirit.

To re-create civil society on this prescription does not entail a novel civic architecture; rather, it means reconceptualizing and repositioning institutions already in place, or finding ways to re-create them in an international setting.[18] In the United States, for example, this suggests turning again to schools, foundations, voluntary associations, churches and temples and mosques, community movements, and the media, as well as myriad other civil associations and removing them from the private sector, repositioning them instead in civil society. It suggests helping citizens to reclaim their rightful public voice and political legitimacy against those who would write them off as representing only hypocritical special interests. In Russia and other transitional societies it means supporting the new civic infrastructure and worrying more about getting people involved in local civic associations than about the outcome of elections or the vicissitudes of competing nationalist, socialist, capitalist, and reformist parties playing at parliamentary politics. For McWorld, it means seeking countervailing institutions not in international law and organization but in a new set of transnational civic associations that afford opportunities for nationally based civil societies to link up to one another and for individual citizens of different countries to cooperate across national boundaries in regional and global civil movements. Civil society needs a habitation; it must become a real place that offers the abstract idea of a public voice a palpable geography somewhere other than in the twin atlases of government and markets.

More than anything else, what has been lost in the clash of Jihad and McWorld has been the idea of the *public* as something more than a random collection of consumers or an aggregation of special political interests or a product of identity polititcs. The public voice turns out to be the voice of civil society, the voice of what we can call variously an American civic forum, a Russian civic forum, or a global civic forum—civil society's own interactive representative assembly. We have noted that the democratic citizen must precede the democratization of government. It now becomes clear that civil society offers conditions for the creation of democratic citizens. A citizen is an individual who has acquired a public voice and understands himself to belong to a wider community, who sees herself as sharing goods with others. Publicity is the key to citizenship. The character of the public voice is thus essential in defining the citizen. For a public voice is not any old voice addressing the public. The divisive rant of talk radio or the staccato crossfire of pundit-TV are in fact perfect models of everything that public talk is *not*.

Much of what passes for journalism is in fact mere titillation or dressed-up gossip or polite prejudice. The media have abandoned civil society for the greater profits of the private sector, where their public responsibilities no longer hobble their taste for commercial success. How long a journey it can be for women and men nurtured in the private sector and used to identifying with one another only via a cash contract on the one hand, or in terms of Jihad's blood fraternity on the other, to find their way to civil society and speak in its measured public voice, particularly if that voice must also have a transnational or international resonance. "Public" inflects "voice" in a remarkable fashion that turns out to hold the key to civil society and citizenship. A genuinely public voice—the voice of civil society—can empower those who speak far more effectively than either the officially univocal voice of government or the obsessively contrary talk of the private sector's jabbering Babel. The voice of civil society, of citizens in deliberative conversation, challenges the exclusivity and irrationality of Jihad's clamor but is equally antithetical to the claim of McWorld's private markets to represent some aggregative public good. Neither Jihad nor McWorld grasps the meaning of "public," and the idea of the public realized offers a powerful remedy to the privatizing and de-democratizing effects of aggressive tribes and aggressive markets.

If civil society is one key to democracy, then global strong democracy needs and depends on a methodical internationalization of civil society. Civil society in turn must again discover adequate incarnations at the national level to become susceptible to globalization. For a historical model we might look back at the American Committees of Correspondence founded in the Revolutionary War era by citizens without legitimate political outlets (the British controlled the formal institutions of government); these committees allowed them to gather together informally in bodies that were neither governmental nor private but that together forged the civic matériel by which the new Republic was first fought for and won and then established and constituted. Are virtual committees of correspondence possible on the Internet? Can citizens log on to a civic bulletin board across national boundaries? Here is a starting point for a genuinely civic telecommunications.

Not so long after the Committees of Correspondence inaugurated their successful revolution against English tyranny, Thomas Jefferson had proposed local civic assemblies as a continuation of direct and decentralized self-government: "Where every man is a sharer in the direction of his ward-republic," he had written, "and feels that he is a participator in the government of affairs, not merely at an election one day in the year, but every day; when there shall not be a man in the State who will not be a member of some one of its councils, great or small, he will let the heart be torn out of him sooner than his power be wrested from him."[19] Only at the local and regional levels where Jihad plays out its game can an alternative form of identity be won that can ultimately contain McWorld at the global level. Neither the tribal circle nor the traffic circle, neither the clan nor the mall, offers adequate public space to the kind of democratic community that can provide citizens both identity and inclusion. The affinities that spring from local association must not barricade the way to regional affections, national identification, and global alliances, as tribes and clans (whether historical or invented) too often do. Technology may permit us to reconstruct electronic wards and teleassemblies linking together distant neighbors. But this will happen only if markets are not left to determine how these technologies will be developed and deployed, and if global communication is disciplined by prudent deliberation and civility. How civil society can be forged in an international environment is an extraordinary challenge. Recognizing that it *needs* to be forged is, however, the first step toward salvaging a place for strong democracy in the world of McWorld.

There is a second, more institutional step as well. The parts may become more civil and participatory, their members more civic; yet they must be aligned by some form of global organization that permits cooperation without destroying their autonomy. A global civil society is a foundation for but not yet the same thing as a global democratic government.

Democracy and Confederalism

How is a world integrated by markets but otherwise utterly disintegral to be held together if not by global government and unmediated international law—neither of which, I have suggested, hold out realistic promise? The primary form of reorganization in recent years, thanks to the politics of Jihad, has been partition. What is the alternative? Federalism is probably too aggressive and centralist a solution for countries as fractured as Croatia or Afghanistan and cannot even guarantee the integrity of, say, Switzerland, India, or Germany. Confederalism offers a more promising strategy, for it permits the nation-states already in existence to create, bottom-up, a global association. The alternative, a centralized, top-down governing frame, requires an international sovereign—some global legislator—to establish it; and the international sovereign is the very entity that is missing.

The Federalist Papers have been required reading for desperate governments seeking to slow the pace of partition and civil disintegration. The *Articles of Confederation* make far more relevant reading. Article III of the *Articles,* in conjunction with a revitalization of civil society locally, provides a modest framework for holding rival national fragments together in a loose alliance rather like the one that "united" the three original cantons of Switzerland in 1291 at the Rütli. Article III provides for the full autonomy of the member states and honors their independence (indispensable to those pursuing a politics of identity), but also declares that:

> The said states hereby severally enter into a firm league of friendship with each other, for their common defense, the security of their liberties, and their mutual and general welfare, binding themselves to assist each other against all force offered to, or attacks made upon them, or any of them, on account of religion, sovereignty, trade or any other pretense whatsoever.

This would seem to offer a starting place to defend against the depredations both of Jihad and McWorld. The Article assumes a certain root citizenship within each of the states, and probably would be effective only under conditions where civil society had set down such roots. Article IV provides that "the free inhabitants of each" state "shall be entitled to all the privileges and immunities of free citizens in the several states, and the people of each state shall have ingress and regress to and from any other state, and shall enjoy therein all the privileges of trade and commerce." Ethnic cleansing and involuntary refugees would be barred, equal citizenship and free movement enjoined.

Similar provisions held together the Helvetic Confederation that made the Swiss such an extraordinary example of democratic association (if not of inclusive citizenship) long before parliamentary institutions elsewhere had found their way to genuine representative government. The splintered factions of many a ruptured nation could do worse than reconceive themselves in terms of a "firm league of friendship" around their common liberties (if they have any!). Quebec and the Anglophone provinces of Canada may well be compelled to such a solution if they are to avoid a costly struggle. Confederalism is no panacea but it may offer a viable alternative to more centralist, coercive, and thus futile solutions to national disintegration. Modeled not on the American Federalist constitution but its confederalist predecessor, which gave the colonies sufficient time to live together to discover the need for more integrative remedies— and to acquire the trust and tolerance on which such remedies depend—this solution offers a gradualist, voluntary, trust-building strategy of supranationality. Like democracy itself, such inclusive forms of confederal association are evolutionary in nature and depend on the success of ties that are initially much looser. The model is Switzerland prior to 1800 rather than the European Union, for Switzerland assured the civic vitality of the parts before crowding them into a larger whole; it took citizenship as a set of local attributes (to become a Swiss one must still acquire communal citizenship first, the national passport comes only afterwards) and by securing them in participatory institutions guaranteed that the confederal whole would be democratic.

The new Europe has in fact seemed most democratic not in its rigid representation of national states and their governments and certainly not in its technocratic dependence on market forces, but rather in its representation of the regions. We have seen how German Laender and Spanish provinces have striven for a European membership that has a strongly confederal feel to it. Closer to their own peoples, their potential association with Europe (if it ever is permitted by their own national governments) can effect ties that their member citizens may regard as relevant to them.

. . .

The problem of democracy under modern conditions is immensely complicated. In the context of the dialectical interplay of Jihad and McWorld, reformist arguments tend to chase their own tails. Strong democracy needs citizens; citizens need civil society; civil society requires a form of association not bound by identity politics; that form of association is democracy. Or: global democracy needs confederalism, a noncompulsory form of association rooted in friendship and mutual interests; confederalism depends on member states that are well rooted in civil society, and on citizens for whom the other is not synonymous with the enemy; civil society and citizenship are products of a democratic way of life. Yet the circle of democracy *is* unbroken, and perhaps the first and last and only lesson this book can teach is that until democracy becomes the aim and end of those wrestling with the terrors of Jihad and the insufficiencies of McWorld, there is little chance that we can even embark on the long journey of imagination that takes women and men from elementary animal being (the thinness of economics) to cooperative human living (the robustness of strong democracy). Thus, in Rwanda or in Bosnia or in East Timor or in Haiti, we perhaps misconceive the challenge when we ask how to partition or internationalize or pacify a disintegrating country; perhaps the real challenge is how to make it democratic. Democracy is to be sure already the sought-after final outcome for those trying to rescue the planet: but it must also be the guiding principle going in.

If the democratic option sounds improbable as a response to Jihad (it is!), think of the "realist" solutions currently being debated—peace and stabilization through foreign invasion, expulsion, partition, resettlement, United Nations Trusteeship, military intervention, or simple dismemberment. Will they contain the spreading global fires of Jihad? And if the democratic option sounds utopian as a response to the infotainment telesector with its infectious videology and its invisible electronic fingers curling around human minds and hearts wherever satellite transmissions can be received, think of the alternative: surrender to the markets and thus to the least noble aspirations of human civilization they so efficiently serve; and the shrinking of our vaunted liberty to

Regis Debray's wretched choice between "the local Ayatollah and Coca-Cola."[20]

In a nation at war, Abraham Lincoln saw in democracy a last and best hope. On our paradoxical planet today, with nations falling apart and coming together at the same moment for some of the very same reasons, and with cowering national governments and toothless international law hardly able to bark, let alone bite, democracy may now have become our first and only hope.

Afterword

A YEAR AFTER the publication of *Jihad vs. McWorld*, both Jihad and McWorld are alive and well. The ironies that tie them together—for Jihad needs McWorld as shadows do the sun—continue to deepen. India has just elected a Parliament dominated by the Hindu nationalist Bharatiya Janata Party. It also has its first Hindu nationalist Prime Minister in history (Atal Bihari Vajpayee) who, amidst fears of Hindi extremism, avows that his favorite movie is Walt Disney's *The Lion King*. America's anti-internationalist, corporation-baiting, Nafta-detesting right wing has made Patrick Buchanan, a former television pundit who has spent his entire life inside the Washington beltway establishment, its noisy antiestablishment candidate. Buchanan, in turn, like some mad apostate of the class that created him, decries the "myth of Economic Man (that) believes economics drives the world, politics is about economics, and money drives politics" and pledges his leadership on behalf of "conservatives of the heart"—seemingly launching a new American Jihad to conduct the latest skirmish in a cultural war he first promulgated in 1992.[1]

President Rafsanjani of Iran is continuing to reach out to the West for renewed trade ties, but militants are setting cinemas on fire and assaulting women on bicycles to display their attachment to the culture in whose name he rules. The Olympics are coming to Atlanta, yet it is not the common Olympic spirit but common consumption that Olympic sponsors such as Budweiser appear to be selling. Budweiser's tie-in commercial features a McWorldian Bud Blimp (a frog writ large?) that appears in a close encounter with a dozen different ethnic cultures whose distinctiveness is lost in the Blimp's friendly intrusiveness.[2]

Like the Bud Blimp, the signs of McWorld's spreading empire are everywhere. Internet users can now participate in "cyber seders" (try http://www.emanuelnyc.org); Coke has successfully purchased the once civic-minded song "We Are the World," on the way to "eliminating the very concept of a 'domestic' and 'international' Coca-Cola beverage business;"[3] and Disney is founding "schools" and study "institutes" in Florida while building whole new towns like "Celebration" to promote its multiplying wares, soft and hard.[4] Bill Gates, CEO of Microsoft, has begun to buy up the world of culture, having already purchased the electronic rights to the photographs of Ansel Adams, the art images of the Barnes Collection, and one intact Washington pundit (Michael Kinsley, erstwhile *New Republic* editor and *Crossfire* anchor) to inaugurate a new internet magazine called SLATE and give Gates's internet business instant legitimacy.[5]

It is then hardly surprising that when Klaus Schwab and Claude Smadja, respectively the founder and managing director of the Davos Forum—a preeminent global market think tank—turn to look in the mirror, they are startled by what they see and become inadvertent prophets of the struggle between McWorld and the zealous populist reaction to it:

> Economic globalization has entered a critical phase. A mounting backlash against its effects, especially in the industrial democracies, is threatening a very disruptive impact on economic activity and social stability in many countries. The mood in these democracies is one of helplessness and anxiety, which helps explain the rise of a new brand of populist politicians. This can easily turn into revolt.[6]

Or, better, turn into Jihad's deeply felt counterrevolution: recent elections in "transitional democracies" in the countries of the old Soviet bloc have brought back into office many old communists, often retooled as new nationalists. Democracy has been unsettled in these countries by the deep disillusion that has followed the conflation of markets and liberty, giving the words of Schwab and Smadja their resonance. The world continues then to fall apart and come together; and, however newsworthy the disintegrative forces may seem, the integrative forces still seem poised to overwhelm them. Hezbollah is no match for Wal-Mart.

If my fundamental analysis of the dialectics that bind Jihad and McWorld together continues to be validated by current events, there are, nonetheless, issues raised by critics that merit some reply. Because I assail both Jihad and McWorld for their indifference (if not outright antipathy) to democracy, it might seem to some that I loathe them without qualification. In fact, I argue quite explicitly that next to their vices both have intrinsic advantages, even virtues. McWorld's modernization has created a healthier, wealthier world in which at least the conditions for greater equality are present. I am neither a nostalgic dreamer after earlier Golden Ages nor a Luddite antagonist of technology and its improvements. Capitalism and the science from which it arises constitute a system of power and control that generates wealth and progress with unprecedented efficiency. It is not capitalism but unrestrained capitalism counterbalanced by no other system of values that endangers democracy. My criticism of McWorld is aimed at what may be called economic totalism. If the political totalism of the fascist and communist world once tried, at horrendous human costs, to subordinate all economic, social, and cultural activity to the demands of an overarching state, the economic totalism of unleashed market economics seems now to be trying (at costs yet to be fully reckoned) to subordinate politics, society, and culture to the demands of an overarching market. As once political totalism rationalized *its* dominion by reference to its supposed association with freedom—the government of the proletariat was to usher in a communist age of pure freedom—so today markets rationalize their dominion over every other sector of life by appealing to the supposedly manifold liberties of consumer choice.[7]

But the lesson of modern pluralism that undergirds the concerns of this book is that humankind depends for its liberty on variety and difference. We are governed best when we live in several spheres, each with its own rules and benefits, none wholly dominated by another. The political domain is "sovereign" to be sure, but this means only that it regulates the many domains of a free plural society in a fashion that preserves their respective autonomies. The usurping dominion of McWorld has, however, shifted sovereignty to the domain of global corporations and the world markets they control, and has threatened the autonomy of civil society and its cultural and spiritual domains, as well as of politics. The alternative to McWorld I detail in Part III of this book is not a state-dominated society in place of a market-dominated society, but a many-sectored civil society in which the autonomy of each distinctive domain—the economic market included—is guaranteed by the sovereignty of the democratic state. Only a democratic polity has an interest in and the power to preserve the autonomy of the several realms. When other domains wrest sovereignty away from the state, whether they are religious or economic, the result is a kind of totalitarian coordination—in the Middle Ages it was theocratic; in this age of McWorld it is economistic.

These considerations will suggest why the sallies of critics who cannot distinguish consumerism from democracy are so peculiarly off base.[8] For them, consumer society in a market world *is* democracy, and those who assail McWorld are surreptitious elitists, however "democratic" their rhetoric. Like Edward Shills, who once tried to skewer Dwight MacDonald, Irving Howe, and Theodore Adorno as "aristocratic" twins of the likes of Wyndham Lewis and Ortega y Gasset because they too were intolerant of mass culture, so these new stalwarts of unbridled capitalism insist that a critic of McWorld's consumerism, democracy incarnate, cannot by definition count himself a democrat. By whose definition?

Admirers of Milton Friedman's version of unrestrained capitalism would like us to think that markets are surrogates for democratic sovereignty because they permit us to "vote" with our dollars or D-Marks or yen.[9] But economic choices are private, about individual needs and desires; whereas political choices are public, about the nature of public goods. As a consumer, one may buy a powerful car that can make 130 miles per hour, yet without contradiction the very same person may as a citizen vote for speed limits in the name of public safety and environmental preservation. The problem with Disney and McDonald's is not aesthetics, and critics of mass taste such as Horkheimer and Adorno (and me) are concerned not to interfere with the expression of private taste or public judgment, but to prevent monopoly control over information, and to interdict that quiet, comfortable coercion through which television, advertising, and entertainment can constrict real liberty of choice. It is not too little faith in democratic man and woman but a great deal of faith in the power of the mind machines of McWorld's software producers that leads me to suspect the "autonomy" of consumer choice. It is hard not to be skeptical when recalling the last line of *Quiz Show,* the film account of the game show scandals of the 1950s. Said a representative of the great plunderers of public trust in what at the time was an innocent television medium, "We're not exactly hardened criminals here—we're in show business!" Those who invest billions in advertising, promotion, packaging, and cultural warfare in the name of selling products that nobody can be said to "need" are hardly criminals either: but their kind of show business is directed precisely at liquidating anything that smacks remotely of consumer autonomy, let alone democratic liberty. Hucksterism and snake oil swindles are not what Jefferson had in mind when he envisioned an educated citizenry or a civic republic.

The push toward concentration in the infotainment telesector that is rooted in this show business mentality, which is a primary focus of Part I of this book, has accelerated since it was published in the summer of 1996, almost at the same moment that the Disney company acquired ABC. In the year since, a half dozen new major mergers and acquisitions have further narrowed ownership in this vital sector.[10] Combined with a telecommunications bill that further deregulates the industry and removes traditional barriers preventing mergers between carriers, broadcasters, and cable operators as well as between local and long distance companies, this move toward concentration has had a potentially devastating effect on the variety and liberty of civic communication. In the nineteenth century, the great monopolies in oil, steel, coal, and the railways were finally dismantled by vigorous government anti-trust regulation. But Michael

Eisner is no Rockefeller and Bill Gates is no Vanderbilt and Steven Spielberg is no Carnegie. Eisner, Gates, and Spielberg are far more powerful, for theirs is power not over oil, steel, and railroads—mere muscles of our modern industrial bodies—but over pictures, information, and ideas—the very sinews of our postmodern soul.

McWorld has virtues then, but they scarcely warrant permitting the market to become sovereign over politics, culture, and civil society. Jihad too has virtues which, I acknowledge, may be less than easily discernible in light of my harsh criticism of parochialism's abuses. Nonetheless, as Robert Bellah and his colleagues demonstrate in their study of America's yearning for community (*Habits of the Heart*), and as Michael Sandel shows with acute historical insight in his recent tribute to *Democracy's Discontents*, the fractious, material forces of our time leave us seeking forms of communion and fraternity that ethnic, religious, and civic communities once gave us. The success of the Communitarian movement suggests how deep the yearning runs.

Yet though there is a deep human need for community, and though democracy itself flourishes most richly when it is founded on the consensual will of tightly knit communities (city states and rural republics are its natural ground), the conditions of community present democrats with a conundrum. For the great dilemma of community is that those forms of communal association that yield the highest degree of intimacy, membership, solidarity, and fraternity are those rooted in strong communal ties of the sort that arise out of blood, narrow belief, and hierarchy: the demonization of outsiders. By the same token, democratic communities—community in its only safe form—become increasingly less fraternal, solidaristic, and satisfying as they become more open, egalitarian, and voluntary. "Democratic community" is thus something of an oxymoron. Defined rigidly, above all by reference to their enemies, communities can fasten people together into a body that no one can tear asunder. Defined with imaginative artifice by achieved values, common work, and chosen ends, communities remain open and egalitarian but are often more fragile. The hope of civil society, which is the hope of this book, is that the love of liberty and the imperatives of equality will lend to democratic communities the necessary centripetal impetus that less open communities have by nature.

My discussion of Jihad—indeed the very use of the word in the title—has drawn other criticism as well. For although I made clear that I deployed Jihad as a generic term quite independently from its Islamic theological origins, and although I insisted that Islam has itself both democratic and nondemocratic manifestations and potentials, some readers felt the term singled out Islam and used it in pejorative ways to criticize non-Islamic phenomena. While extremist groups like Islamic Jihad have themselves associated the word with armed struggle against modernizing, secular infidels, I can appreciate that the great majority of devout Muslims who harbor no more sympathy for Islamic Jihad than devout Christians feel for the Ku Klux Klan or the Montana Militia might feel unfairly burdened by my title. I owe them an apology, and hope they will find their way past the book's cover to the substantive reasoning that makes clear how little my argument has to do with Islam as a religion or with resistance to McWorld as the singular property of Muslims.

I have much less sympathy for those who read only one or another section of the book and concluded, lazily, that I must be writing either about McWorld alone or Jihad alone. Some critics have simply lumped *Jihad vs. McWorld* in together with Pandemonium prophets like Robert D. Kaplan (*The Ends of the Earth*) and Samuel P. Huntington ("The Clash of Civilizations"), dismissing us all as Pandoric pessimists.[11] But as must be clear to anyone who reads the book cover to cover, it is finally about neither Jihad nor McWorld but about democracy—and the dangers democracy faces in a world where the forces of commerce and the forces reacting to commerce are locked in struggle.

No one grasped that more clearly or prophetically than President Bill Clinton, who has said: "Mr. Barber is arguing that democracy and the ability to hold people together . . . is being threatened today by the globalization of the economy . . . (and by) a world people think they cannot control." Hence, it is "more important today for . . . democracy to work, for the basic values (of democracy) to work, to be made real in the lives of ordinary citizens."[12]

President Clinton understood what many critics overlooked: that the struggle between Jihad and McWorld, for the ordinary women and men caught between them, is a struggle to preserve democracy and to extend civil society. In this sense, the struggle for democracy is the real subject of *Jihad vs. McWorld*. My concern is not with capitalism but with civil society and what capitalism does to it, not with religion or ethnicity but with citizenship and how fundamentalist zealotry can undermine it. We need markets to generate productivity, work, and goods; and we need culture and religion to assure solidarity, identity, and social cohesion—and a sense of human spirit. But most of all, we need democratic institutions capable of preserving our liberty even in parochial communities; and capable of maintaining our equality and our precious differences even in capitalist markets. With mediating civic institutions firmly in place and democracy once again the sovereign preserver of our plural worlds, Jihad can yield to healthy forms of cultural difference and group identity while McWorld can take its rightful and delimited place as the economic engine of a world in which economics is only a single crucial dimension. With McWorld's excesses under control, communities of blood and spirit will not have to make war on it and, beyond the homogenous theme parks of commerce, we may rediscover the free spaces in which it is possible to live not only as consumers but as citizens.

June 1, 1996
Piscataway Township

APPENDIX A

Justice-of-Energy-Distribution Index

It is not a central concern of this study's examination of energy usage, but there is a radical injustice in patterns of production, distribution, and usage of energy resources that undermines the kinds of global integration toward which McWorld is supposed to tend. Using just two indices (based on statistics in *The Economist Book of Vital World Statistics: 1990,* New York: Times Books, 1990), we can see clearly the extent of this injustice among nations.

If we compare the amount of energy a nation uses as a percentage of world usage to that nation's percentage of world population, we get a justice-of-energy-distribution index (JEDI-A) that, if greater than 1, suggests injustice pure and simple (see Table 1. Energy Usage and Population). The forty-seven nations surveyed represent a cross section of First, Second, and Third World countries, some of which are producers and exporters, and some merely importers of fossil fuels.

JEDI TABLE 1. ENERGY USAGE AND POPULATION (1990)

Ranking	Country	World Population (percent)	World Energy (percent)	JEDI-1
1.	Chad	.11	.001	.009
2.	Ethiopia	.94	.01	.01
3.	Mozambique	.29	.005	.02
4.	Bangladesh	2.06	.07	.03
5.	Zaire	.66	.02	.03
6.	Sri Lanka	.33	.02	.06
7.	Iraq	1.02	.12	.12
8.	Pakistan	2.07	.27	.13
9.	Bolivia	.14	.02	.14
10.	India	15.67	2.24	.14
11.	Indonesia	3.44	.49	.14
12.	Philippines	1.15	.16	.14
13.	Thailand	1.07	.28	.26
14.	Egypt	1.02	.36	.35
15.	China	21.71	8.49	.39
16.	Brazil	2.84	1.13	.40
17.	Zimbabwe	.17	.07	.41
18.	Albania	.06	.04	.67
19.	Malaysia	.33	.22	.67
20.	Cuba	.20	.15	.75
21.	Vietnam	1.26	1.08	.86
22.	Mexico	1.63	1.43	.88
23.	South Korea	.82	.76	.93
24.	Argentina	.63	.63	1.00
25.	Hong Kong	.11	.11	1.00
26.	Mongolia	.04	.04	1.00

↑
M
O
S
T

J
U
S
T

ENERGY USAGE AND POPULATION (1990) (*continued*)

	Ranking	Country	World Population (*percent*)	World Energy (*percent*)	*JEDI-1*
	27.	Spain	.77	.85	1.10
	28.	Yugoslavia	.46	.59	1.28
	29.	Puerto Rico	.07	.09	1.29
	30.	North Korea	.43	.60	1.40
M	31.	Israel	.09	.13	1.44
O	32.	South Africa	.58	.85	1.47
S	33.	Libya	.08	.12	1.50
T	34.	France	1.10	2.15	1.95
	35.	Hungary	.20	.42	2.10
U	36.	Japan	2.41	5.12	2.12
N	37.	U.K.	1.12	3.03	2.70
J	38.	Sweden	.16	.44	2.75
U	39.	Denmark	.10	.29	2.90
S	40.	Belgium	.19	.57	3.00
T	41.	Saudi Arabia	.28	.90	3.21
↓	42.	U.S.S.R.	5.58	19.56	3.51
	43.	Australia	.33	1.16	3.52
	44.	Norway	.08	.30	3.75
	45.	Kuwait	.04	.18	4.50
	46.	U.S.A.	4.84	24.24	5.01
	47.	Canada	.51	2.65	5.20

If we compare the amount of energy a nation uses as a percentage of world usage to that nation's percentage of world Gross Domestic Product, we get a justice-of-energy-distribution index (JEDI-B) that, if greater than 1, suggests economic inefficiency that is also a form of injustice (see Table 2. Energy Usage and Gross Domestic Product). The standard here is not absolute justice; it asks only that if a nation consumes more than its fair share by population, it justify that usage by its economic productivity.

JEDI TABLE 2.
ENERGY USAGE AND GROSS DOMESTIC PRODUCT (1990)

Ranking (most to least just)	Country	World GDP (percent)	World Energy (percent)	JEDI-2
1.	Chad	.86	.001	.001
2.	Ethiopia	.03	.01	.33
3.	Japan	16.00	5.12	.32
4.	Hong Kong	.30	.11	.37
5.	Iraq	.30	.12	.40
6.	France	5.30	2.15	.41
7.	Sweden	1.00	.44	.44
8.	Spain	1.90	.85	.45
9.	Denmark	.60	.29	.48
10.	Mozambique	.01	.005	.50
11.	Sri Lanka	.04	.02	.50
12.	Zaire	.04	.02	.50
13.	Brazil	2.00	1.13	.57
14.	Bolivia	.03	.02	.67
15.	Israel	.23	.13	.57
16.	Norway	.51	.30	.59
17.	Belgium	.86	.57	.66
18.	U.K.	4.60	3.03	.66
19.	Bangladesh	.10	.07	.70
20.	Philippines	.22	.16	.73
21.	South Korea	.96	.76	.79
22.	Libya	.14	.12	.86
23.	Thailand	.32	.28	.88
24.	Australia	1.30	1.16	.89
25.	U.S.A.	27.30	24.24	.89
26.	Puerto Rico	.10	.09	.90
27.	Canada	2.70	2.65	.98
28.	Cuba	.15	.15	1.00

↑
M
O
S
T

E
F
F
I
C
I
E
N
T

ENERGY USAGE AND GROSS DOMESTIC PRODUCT (1990)
(*continued*)

MOST INEFFICIENT ↓

Ranking (most to least just)	*Country*	*World GDP (percent)*	*World Energy (percent)*	*JEDI-2*
29.	Indonesia	.46	.49	1.07
30.	Malaysia	.19	.22	1.16
31.	Pakistan	.23	.27	1.17
32.	Argentina	.49	.63	1.29
33.	Mexico	.97	1.43	1.47
34.	India	1.50	2.24	1.49
35.	Kuwait	.11	.18	1.64
36.	South Africa	.49	.85	1.73
37.	Yugoslavia	.30	.59	1.97
38.	Albania	.02	.04	2.00
39.	Egypt	.17	.36	2.12
40.	Saudi Arabia	.42	.90	2.14
41.	Zimbabwe	.03	.07	2.33
42.	Hungary	.16	.42	2.63
43.	Mongolia	.01	.04	4.00
44.	North Korea	.11	.60	5.45
45.	U.S.S.R.	3.27	19.56	5.98
46.	China	1.19	8.49	7.13
47.	Vietnam	.06	1.08	18.00

In a perfectly just world, a nation would consume a percentage of the globe's energy equivalent to or less than its share of the world's population and would require no more of the world's energy to sustain its GDP than its proportionate share of global GDP. In an imperfectly just world, nations might consume more than their fair share as measured by population but would at least consume no more than their fair share as measured by GDP. But as the JEDI tables for population and for GDP indicate, most of the world's developed nations and not a few of its less developed nations consume radically disproportionate quantities of energy as measured by population; and some also score badly on the efficiency rating and are hence doubly unjust. Saudi Arabia, despite its enormous reserves (or because of them?) uses more than three times its fair share as measured by population, and is inefficient to boot, using more than twice its fair share as measured by GDP. The United States and Canada are horrendously unjust in their usage by population (five times what they deserve and ranked 46th and 47th out of the 47 nations surveyed), but are at least efficient and thus fair in their usage as measured by GDP. Likewise Japan consumes too much by population but is extremely efficient (ranking third) by GDP.

Among the seven nations that are unjust on both scales, the ex-Soviet Union (as it was constituted when these 1990 statistics were compiled), is the global energy villain, using three and a half times more energy than its population warranted and nearly seven times as much as its GDP warranted. Some of Russia's former allies, like ex-Yugoslavia and Hungary, did little better, and overendowed Saudi Arabia and Kuwait were not far behind. South Africa and North Korea round out the group of seven that are both unjust and inefficient. Of course nations like ex-Yugoslavia and Russia that are today in transition would score better in 1995 than they did earlier, not because their efficiency has grown but because—as a result of anarchy, civil war, and rapid privatization (the twin evils of Jihad and McWorld being experienced simultaneously)—their GDPs have plummeted.

China is a nightmare waiting to happen on energy usage. At present, it uses far less than its population warrants; but its radical inefficiency of usage (46th of 47) suggests that as its GDP continues to grow at better than 14 percent a year and as it realizes its plan to make automobile manufacturing a key to its development, it will not only use a radically disproportionate percentage of the world's energy, but may threaten to tap out global resources completely. Would that it might imitate Hong Kong, which uses only a third of what it deserves by the measure of its GDP, and uses an exactly fair share (one to one) by the measure of its population!

The story of the West is mixed. Although almost all of the Western democracies are fair with respect to GDP, there are significant differences among them, with France and Sweden ranked sixth and seventh, and the United States and Canada (though still "efficient" with a JEDI of less than 1) ranked 25th and 27th. Yet while France is extremely efficient, using less than half of what its GDP warrants, it still consumes twice what its population warrants. Spain is Europe's energy saint, using just a tiny bit more energy than its population warrants (best among the Western nations at number 27) and less than half of what its GDP warrants (ranked eighth). Worldwide, Chad is saintly beyond all reason, proving perhaps only that poverty is the primary predicate of justice on these indices, where so many of the world's poorest nations are compulsory practitioners of energy altruism.

Our indices suggest that Jihad tends to impair economic efficiency, lowering a nation's ranking on the GDP scale, but that it also diminishes overall energy usage, improving the nation's ranking on the population scale. The forces of McWorld increase energy usage, lowering the ranking on the population scale; but they can improve efficiency, increasing the ranking on the GDP scale. Finally, neither Jihad nor McWorld has any intrinsic interest in the fairness question and here, as in other domains, the poorest nations with neither energy reserves nor a productive economy do the worst. They are "good energy citizens" by default, because in the cruel competition of McWorld they are not citizens at all.

APPENDIX B

TWENTY-TWO COUNTRIES' TOP TEN GROSSING FILMS, 1991

Country	1	2	3
Argentina	*Terminator 2*	*Dances/Wolves*	*Godfather III*
Austria	*Dances/Wolves*	*Home Alone*	*Robin Hood*
Brazil	*Terminator 2*	*Dances/Wolves*	*Robin Hood*
Chile	*Terminator 2*	*Dances/Wolves*	*Wild Orchid*
Denmark	*Dances/Wolves*	**The Crumbs**	*Robin Hood*
Egypt	*Dances/Wolves*	*Ghost*	*Lethal Weapon 2*
Finland	**Mr. Numbskull**	*Naked Gun 2½*	*Terminator 2*
France	*Dances/Wolves*	*Terminator 2*	*Robin Hood*
Germany	*Home Alone*	*Dances/Wolves*	*Robin Hood*
Greece	*Hook*	*Silence/Lambs*	*Robin Hood*
Hungary	*Look Who's Talk 2*	*Terminator 2*	*Kindergarten Cop*
Iceland	*Dances/Wolves*	*Home Alone*	*Naked Gun 2½*
Italy	**Johnny Stecchino**	*Robin Hood*	**Women in Skirts**
Japan	*Terminator 2*	*Home Alone*	*Pretty Woman*
Malaysia	*Terminator 2*	**The Banquet**	**Armor of God II**
Mexico	*Terminator 2*	*Robin Hood*	**Pelo Suelto**
Netherlands	*Dances/Wolves*	*Robin Hood*	*Kindergarten Cop*
Poland	*Dances/Wolves*	*Robin Hood*	*Pretty Woman*
Spain	*Dances/Wolves*	*Terminator 2*	*Robin Hood*
Sweden	*Pretty Woman*	*The Little Mermaid*	**The Gas Station**
Switzerland	*Dances/Wolves*	*Home Alone*	*Robin Hood*
U.K.	*Robin Hood*	*Terminator 2*	*Silence/Lambs*

Bold face = Domestic film

SOURCE: *Variety International Film Guide, 1993*

Country	4	5	6
Argentina	*Robin Hood*	*Sleeping/Enemy*	*Naked Gun 2½*
Austria	*Terminator 2*	*Naked Gun 2½*	*Not w/o Daughter*
Brazil	*Predator*	*Mutant Turtles*	*Silence/Lambs*
Chile	*Mutant Turtles*	*Dogs go to Heaven*	*Robin Hood*
Denmark	*Home Alone*	*Sleeping/Enemy*	*Kindergarten Cop*
Egypt	*Godfather III*	*Total Recall*	*Robin Hood*
Finland	*Dances/Wolves*	*Home Alone*	*Robin Hood*
France	*Silence/Lambs*	*White Fang*	*Alice*
Germany	*Terminator 2*	*Not w/o Daughter*	*Naked Gun 2½*
Greece	*Terminator 2*	*Cape Fear*	*Naked Gun 2½*
Hungary	*Hot Shots!*	*Naked Gun 2½*	*Dances/Wolves*
Iceland	*Silence/Lambs*	*Robin Hood*	*Three Men/Lady*
Italy	*Terminator 2*	**Christmas Vacation**	*Dying Young*
Japan	*Total Recall*	**Omoide Poroporo**	**Doraemon**
Malaysia	*Robin Hood*	*Dances/Wolves*	**Oper. Scorpio**
Mexico	**V. Peligroso**	*Dances/Wolves*	**Vacaciones 2**
Netherlands	*Terminator 2*	*Naked Gun 2½*	*Silence/Lambs*
Poland	*Indiana Jones 3*	*Look Talking 2*	*Gremlins 2*
Spain	*Silence/Lambs*	*Home Alone*	**High Heels**
Sweden	*Dances/Wolves*	*Home Alone*	*Die Hard 2*
Switzerland	*Terminator 2*	*Not w/o Daughter*	*Green Card*
U.K.	*Three Men/Lady*	*Home Alone*	*Dances/Wolves*

7	8	9	10
Home Alone	*Ghost*	*Tie Up/Down*	*Awakenings*
Kindergarten Cop	*Silence/Lambs*	*Sleeping/Enemy*	*Look Talking 2*
Dying Young	*Sleeping/Enemy*	*Kindergarten Cop*	*Kickboxer*
Silence/Lambs	*Home Alone*	*Doors*	**La Frontera**
Look Talking 2	*Silence/Lambs*	*Naked Gun 2½*	*Terminator 2*
Terminator 2	*Wild at Heart*	*Weekend at Bernie's*	*Mutant Turtles*
S. M. Kormy	*Silence/Lambs*	*Kindergarten Cop*	*Hudson Hawk*
Une Epoque	*Hot Shots*	**Op Corned Beef**	*Thelma/Louise*
Pappa Portas	*Silence/Lambs*	*Green Card*	*Look Talking 2*
L'Amant	*Dbl Life/Veronica*	*Prince of Tides*	*Thelma/Louise*
Home Alone	*Oscar*	(only 8 listed)	(only 8 listed)
Sleeping/Enemy	*Terminator 2*	**Child/Nature**	*Misery*
Thought Love	*Hook*	*JFK*	**Damn/Met**
Dragon Ball	**Torajiro**	**Kyujitsu**	**Dragon Ball**
Dances/Wolves			
(tie)			
Tricky Brains	**Fist/Fury**	**Top Bet**	**Fruit Punch**
Silence/Lambs	*Bronco*	*Three Men/Lady*	**Como Fui**
Sleeping/Enemy	*Home Alone*	*Look Talking 2*	*Little Mermaid*
Flatliners	*Ghostbusters 2*	*Cinderella*	*Hunt Red October*
Kindergarten Cop	*Regarding Henry*	*Cyrano Bergerac*	*Ghost*
Silence/Lambs	*Three Men/Lady*	*Hunt Red October*	*Sleeping/Enemy*
Naked Gun 2½	*Kindergarten Cop*	*Little Mermaid*	*Silence/Lambs*
Sleeping/Enemy	*Naked Gun 2½*	*Kindergarten Cop*	*Commitments*

Notes

Introduction

1. Francis Fukuyama, in *The End of History and the Last Man,* (New York: Free Press, 1992), although he is far less pleased by his prognosis in his book than he seemed in the original *National Interest* essay that occasioned all the controversy; and Walter B. Wriston, *Twilight of Sovereignty* (New York: Scribner's, 1992).

2. See Georgie Anne Geyer, "Our Disintegrating World: The Menace of Global Anarchy," *Encyclopaedia Britannica, Book of the Year, 1985* (Chicago: University of Chicago Press, 1985), pp. 11–25. Daniel Patrick Moynihan, *Pandaemonium: Ethnicity in International Politics* (New York: Oxford University Press, 1993); and Zbigniew Brzezinski, *Out of Control: Global Turmoil on the Eve of the Twenty-First Century* (New York: Scribner's, 1993). Also see Tony Judt, "The New Old Nationalisms," *The New York Review of Books,* May 26, 1994, pp. 44–51.

3. Two recent books, the one by Zbigniew Brzezinski cited above about the "global turmoil" of ethnic nationalism (Jihad), the other by Kevin Kelly about computers and "the rise of neo-biological civilization [McWorld]" both carry the title "Out of Control." See Brzezinski, *Out of Control;* and Kevin Kelly, *Out of Control: The Rise of Neo-Biological Civilization* (Reading, Mass.: Addison-Wesley, 1994). The metaphor is everywhere: for example,

in Andrew Bard Schmookler's *The Illusion of Choice* (Albany: State University of New York at Albany Press, 1993), Part III on runaway markets is also entitled "Out of Control."

4. In its "new tack on technology," writes *New York Times* reporter Edmund L. Andrews, the Clinton administration wants only to avoid doing anything "to spook investors with heavy-handed regulatory brow-beating," hoping rather to reduce "the regulatory barriers that have prevented competition." Edmund L. Andrews, "New Tack on Technology," *The New York Times,* January 12, 1994, p. A 1. At the end of the 1994 congressional session, a Communications Bill that would have imposed some controls on the information superhighway expired quietly.

5. Rohatyn cited by Thomas L. Friedman, "When Money Talks, Governments Listen," *The New York Times,* July 24, 1994, p. E 3.

6. Steiner writes that the new Eastern European democratic revolutions of recent years were not "inebriate with some abstract passion for freedom, for social justice." Consumer culture, "video cassettes, porno cassettes, American-style cosmetics and fast foods, not editions of Mill, Tocqueville or Solzhenitsyn, were the prizes snatched from every West[ern] shelf by the liberated." George Steiner, in *Granta,* cited by Anthony Lewis, "A Quake Hits the Summit," *International Herald Tribune,* June 2–3, 1990.

7. Cited by Aleksa Djilas, "A House Divided," *The New Republic,* January 25, 1993, p. 38.

8. In February 1994 there were about eighty thousand U.N. troops deployed in eighteen countries; a handful are on the borders between Israel and its hostile neighbors (Syria and Lebanon) and on the frontiers dividing India and Pakistan and Iraq and Kuwait. But in their greatest numbers, they can be found trying (unsuccessfully) to separate rival factions in Somalia (over twenty-six thousand) and former Yugoslavia (over twenty-five thousand) as well as in Georgia, Cyprus, Liberia, Angola, Mozambique, Rwanda, the western Sahara, Haiti, El Salvador, and Cambodia. For a report see Brian Hall, "Blue Helmets, Empty Guns," *The New York Times Magazine,* January 2, 1994, pp. 18–25, 30, 38, 41.

9. David Binder, "Trouble Spots: As Ethnic Wars Multiply, U.S. Strives for a Policy," *The New York Times,* February 7, 1993, p. A 1.

10. Muslim users at times intentionally obfuscate the difference between meanings; thus, speaking to an Arab audience in mid-1994 just as the accord over Jericho and Gaza went into effect, Yassar Arafat spoke militantly to a Palestinian audience of a Jihad to recapture Jerusalem—only to "explain" later to agitated Israelis and Westerners that he meant only to call for a peaceful struggle.

11. See Arthur Schlesinger, Jr., *Disuniting America* (New York: Norton, 1993).

12. A minimalist's list would include the Netherlands, Denmark, Iceland, Luxembourg, Norway, and Portugal representing less than 1 percent of the world's population. Japan is sometimes also included in the list, which brings the number to under 5 percent.

13. *The Washington Post,* National Weekly Edition, December 21–27, 1992, p. 28.

14. Cited by David Binder, "Trouble Spots." Of course Lansing was no friend of Wilson's vision, and actually worked to undermine aspects of his policies. Daniel Patrick Moynihan is persuaded that Wilson himself came to see the dangers of self-determination, since toward the very end Wilson admitted he had developed the rhetoric of self-determination "without the knowledge that nationalities existed" and thus without foreseeing the destructive forces the idea could unleash. Moynihan, *Pandaemonium,* p. 85.

    Even Amitai Etzioni, an ardent American supporter of communitarianism, worries about the "evils of self-determination." Amitai Etzioni, "The Evils of Self-Determination," *Foreign Policy,* No. 89, Winter, 1992–93, pp. 21–35.

15. The map on which the warring parties settled for a brief time in 1994 was still more egregious in its surrender to the Serbian aggressors, though it at least tried to connect the isolated ethnic dots with lifelines of contiguity. At this writing, both NATO and the United Nations appear to have surrendered to the logic of force altogether.

16. British diplomat and historian Harold Nicholson gives a notoriously tragi-comic account of one of those 1919 post–World War I meetings in which the Balkans were carved up, during which Prime Minister David Lloyd George mistakes the standard geographer's colors green (for valleys) and brown (for mountains) for Greeks and Turks and, pointing at Scala Nova, colored green, tells the Italian delegates, "You can't have that—it's full of Greeks!" Full of green valleys, Nicholson tells his boss, but very few Greeks. The negotiations continue to their melancholy conclusion, which, both "immoral and impractical," are to doom Europe to another war. Harold George Nicholson, *Peace-Making: 1919* (New York: Harcourt and Brace & Co., 1939).

17. In *Blood and Belonging,* his recent book on nationalism that accompanied the affecting television series, Michael Ignatieff looks not only at the obviously fratricidal spectacle of Eastern Europe but at Ireland, Quebec, and Germany as well, aware that the most toxic cases may simply be advanced instances of a disease infecting healthy nations too. Michael Ignatieff, *Blood and Belonging: Journeys into the New Nationalism* (New York: Farrar, Straus & Giroux, 1994).

18. Günter Grass cited by Marla Stone, "Nationalism and Identity in (Former) East Germany," *Tikkun,* Vol. 7, No. 6, November/December 1992, pp. 41–46.

19. See Orlando Patterson, "Global Culture and the American Cosmos," Paper No. 2 in the Andy Warhol Foundation for the Visual Arts Paper Series.

20. This is the theme of Walter B. Wriston, *Twilight.* "How does a national government measure capital formation when much new capital is intellectual?" Wriston asks (p. 12). The answer: they don't. Wriston, who is the former chairman of Citicorp, is a little too much of a technological Pangloss, however, and his tendency to think it will all turn out in the end, as long as

we recognize the new realities, detracts a little from his careful analysis of those realities. He relies heavily on earlier books on the information revolution and its effect on nationhood, like Ithiel de Sola Pool's *Technologies Without Boundaries* (Cambridge: Harvard University Press, 1990); Peter Drucker's *The New Realities* (New York: Harper & Row, 1989); and George Gilder's *Microcosm* (New York: Simon & Schuster, 1989). An early study is F. A. Hayek's *Denationalisation of Money* (London: Institute of Economic Affairs, 1976).

21. Former Secretary of State George Shultz as cited by Wriston, *Twilight*, p. 10.

22. The return of the Democratic Party to executive power in the United States thus changed nothing with respect to this market ideology. President Clinton was closely associated with the Democratic Leadership Council whose research arm was keen to put aside traditional democratic antibusiness rhetoric and make markets and government serve one another. In a widely discussed major foreign policy statement for the Clinton administration, National Security Advisor Anthony Lake indulged in a veritable celebration of the marriage of markets and democracy, using the phrase *market democracy* as if it were some ur-original formulation that could be found in the Magna Carta or the *Federalist Papers*. To an academic audience at Johns Hopkins University, he said "we contained a global threat to *market democracies*." America must "consolidate new democracies *and* market economies . . ." and "help democracy *and* market economics take root in regions of greatest humanitarian concern" [emphasis added]. These "liberating forces" are what "create wealth and social dynamism." On the other hand "backlash states" that resist these forces "tend to rot from within both economically and spiritually." "Verbatim: A Call to Enlarge Democracy's Reach," *The New York Times*, September 26, 1993, Section 4, p. 3.

23. President Clinton's secretary of state thus avowed in 1993 that his meeting with Boris Yeltsin had to be regarded as "an endorsement of democracy and free-market reform in Russia." Warren Christopher, cited in Elaine Sciolino, "Clinton Will Visit Yeltsin," *The New York Times*, October 23, 1993, p. A 1.

24. *The New York Times* ran a front-page business section article by Philip Henon urging the Clinton administration to open the Vietnamese market under the unambiguous title: "Missing Out on a Glittering Market," September 12, 1993, Section 3, p. 1. Subsequently, that happened.

25. Aleksandr Solzhenitsyn, "To Tame Savage Capitalism," *The New York Times*, November 28, 1993, p. E 11.

26. The Czech Republic boasts that its velvet revolution transformed "a totalitarian regime [in]to a democratic system and a profit-based economy," but who exactly will profit remains to be seen. Cited from a Czech Republic advertising supplement in *The New York Times* (January 7, 1994) just prior to President Clinton's meeting with President Havel in Prague in January 1994.

27. Robert McIntyre, "Why Communism Is Rising from the Ash Heap," *The Washington Post*, National Weekly Edition, June 20–26, 1994, p. 24.

28. Brzezinski is properly exercised by what he calls our modern world's "permissive cornucopia," though unlike Allan Bloom, he spends more time sounding the tocsin than examining the causes of the threat. His vague remedy is a Freudian reimposition of "self-restraint" that will curb a Western world as "out of control" in its own way as the Third World it faces.

29. IRAN FIGHTS NEW FOE: WESTERN TELEVISION and FOR CLERICS, SATELLITES CARRYING MTV ARE DEADLIER THAN GUNS, scream *Wall Street Journal* headlines; *The Wall Street Journal*, August 8, 1994, above an article by Peter Waldman citing an Iranian cleric who complains that satellite dishes spread "the family-devastating diseases of the West," p. A 10.

30. Jon Pareles, "Striving to Become Rock's Next Seattle," *The New York Times*, July 17, 1994, Section 2, p. 1.

31. Of McDonald's nearly 15,000 restaurants, nearly forty-five hundred, or one-third, are abroad; there are over one thousand in Japan alone. Gary Hoover, *Hoover's Handbook of American Business* (Austin: Reference Press, 1994), pp. 746–747.

32. Jack Lang, the culture minister of the socialist government deposed in 1993, was especially ambivalent, personally leading the campaign on "franglais" and its mangling of authentic French and calling for legislation to protect the French language (passed under the successor conservative government) as well as the fight to protect the French film industry against Hollywood in the GATT round, yet also proclaiming his affection for Americans and their culture.

33. National Public Radio, *All Things Considered*, December 2, 1993, from the broadcast transcription.

34. Slavenka Drakulic, "Love Story: A True Tale from Sarajevo," *The New Republic*, October 26, 1993, pp. 14–16.

35. There is also a Michael Jackson babushka that gradually turns into a panther and a chimpanzee.

PART I. THE NEW WORLD OF MCWORLD

Chapter 1. The Old Economy and the Birth of a New McWorld

1. He adds: "We decided not to tailor products to any marketplace, but to treat all marketplaces the same." Cited in Louis Uchitelle, "Gillette's World View: One Blade Fits All," *The New York Times*, January 3, 1994, p. C 3.

2. The population of Greece is about 10 million, of Ireland 3.5, and of Switzerland 6.5 million. McDonald's currently has nearly 15,000 restaurants in over seventy countries, and earns 45 percent of its profits outside the United States. Andrew E. Serwer, "McDonald's Conquers the World," *Fortune*, October 17, 1994, pp. 101–116.

3. GM employed 775,000 in 1989, down from a high of 876,000 in 1986. Its workforce today is still in the 700,000 range even after the cost-cutting job cutbacks of recent years.

4. Government expenditures from the latest available figures (1985–88) were, for Senegal, $686 million, for Uganda, $327 million, for Bolivia $619 million, and for Iceland $867 million, for a total of 2.5 billion. *The Economist Book of Vital World Statistics* (New York: Times Books, 1990), p. 136. Domino's figures are from Gary Hoover, *Hoover's Handbook of American Business* (Austin: Reference Press, 1994), p. 243. Portugal's government expenditures were $17.4 billion and Indonesia's were $17.2 billion.

5. For 1985–88, Argentina's spending averaged $27.5 billion; *Vital World Statistics,* p. 137.

6. Reebok, 1992 Annual Report. With international headquarters in Bolton, England, selling shoes manufactured in six Asian countries including Thailand, China, and the Philippines and sold in 140 countries around the globe, this formerly British company is only as American as its U.S. shoe sales make it in any given year (just $1.3 billion of over $3 billion in global sales in 1992).

7. The engine and drive trains are still Japanese. The same trends are visible throughout the industry: in 1993, the Japanese car-maker Honda reported that where its first-generation 1977 model Accord (made in Marysville, Ohio) had no American parts, the 1982 model already was 50 percent American while the new fifth-generation Accord currently in production will have more than 80 percent American parts. Doron P. Levin, "Honda Star Gets Another Sequel," *The New York Times,* August 27, 1993, p. D 1.

8. James Bennet, "Want a U.S. Car? Read the Label," *The New York Times,* September 18, 1994, p. E 6. In its American advertising campaign, Mitsubishi boasts that its cars are "made in America," and sold through "a full-fledged American corporation—Mitsubishi Motor Sales of America, Inc.," and that it employs thirty-seven hundred Americans at its U.S. Diamond-Star plant—all part of its "tradition of Americanization"!

9. Robert Reich points out that when an American buys a $20,000 Pontiac Le Mans from General Motors, $6,000 goes to South Korea for labor and assembly operations; $3,500 to Japan for engine and transaxle; $1,500 to Germany for design engineering; $800 to Taiwan, Singapore, and Japan for small parts; and $600 to Britain, Ireland, and Barbados for services. This leaves just $8,000 for GM stockholders and the American lawyers, insurance, and health services involved. See Robert Reich, *Work of Nations* (New York: Alfred A. Knopf, 1991), pp. 113–114.

   Other industries have had the same experience: Boeing, perhaps the American corporation of which Americans are proudest, is currently planning production of its 777 Twinjet with which it aspires to dominate the mid-sized aircraft market into the twenty-first century. Yet 20 percent of the aircraft will be built by Japanese firms in Japan (Mitsubishi, Kawasaki, and Fuji Heavy Industries), engines will come from Rolls-Royce (as well as two American companies), wing flaps are to be manufactured by Alenia in Italy, Brazil's Embraer will make the fin and wingtip assemblies, while literally hundreds of other companies in Korea, Singapore, Northern Ireland, and elsewhere will be involved in smaller ways. Harvey Elliot, "Flying Foreign," *The Economist: The World in 1993*, special edition of *The Economist*, London, December 25, 1993/January 7, 1994, pp. 6–7.

10. Asahi Glass of Japan owns 49 percent of the Corning subsidiary, and Nippon Electric Glass owns Owens-Illinois; these are the two American firms that produce the majority of television tubes. Keith Bradsher, "In Twist, Protectionism Used to Sell Trade Pact," *The New York Times*, November 7, 1993, Section 1, p. 26.

11. More parochially, however, those who prophesied doom for the American car industry in the 1970s and 1980s—closely tracked by historians like Paul Kennedy anticipating the decline of the United States as an economic power—have had to eat their words. Detroit is back and Japan is now the complacent "leader" being compelled to play catch-up. See Paul Ingrassia and Joseph B. White, *Comeback: The Fall and Rise of the American Automobile Industry* (New York: Simon & Schuster, 1994).

12. The place of the car in America has been recently monumentalized in Alliance, Nebraska, where a replica of Stonehenge executed in junked cars and called "Carhenge" is now drawing tourists; Carhenge postcards are available at the local McDonald's. See "Fossil Fuels," in *U. Magazine*, September 1994.

13. "Mondialisation et ségrégations," *Le Monde diplomatique: Les frontières de l'économie globale*, May 1993, p. 7.

14. Robert Kuttner, "Brave New Corporate 'Workplace of the Future,' " *The Berkshire Eagle*, August 1, 1993, Section E, p. 1. Kuttner was reporting on an Aspen Institute Conference on "Tomorrow's Corporation."

   In *Liberation Management*, an example of new age corporate utopianism, Tom Peters writes "the definition of every product and service is changing. Going soft, softer, softest. Going fickle, ephemeral, fashion. . . . [A]n explosion of new competitors . . . and the everpresent new technologies are leading the way." Tom Peters, *Liberation Management: Necessary Disorganization for the Nano-second Nineties* (New York: Alfred A. Knopf, 1993), p. 6.

15. William Gibson, with his trilogy of works in the early eighties (*Neuromancer, Count Zero,* and *Mona Lisa Overdrive*), introduced the notion of cyberspace (from Norbert Wiener's classic study of interactive communications technology and cybernetics in the late forties) into general parlance. Technically, the term refers to the invisible electronic information space between the computer keyboard (input) and the computer screen (output). *The New York Times* devoted nearly an entire issue of its *Book Review* to computer-generated books and the literary culture of cyberspace in 1994, and since then it has reviewed CD-ROM "books" as well.

16. Julie Edelson Halpert, "Technology: One Car, Worldwide, with Strings Pulled from Michigan," *The New York Times*, August 29, 1993, Section 3, p. F 7.

17. IBM plans on a massive restructuring that will liquidate over sixty thousand jobs; although it will cost nearly $9 billion, it is supposed to save over $4 billion a year in the long run. IBM was hemorrhaging (a second-quarter 1993 loss of $40 million on revenues of 15.5 billion), but Procter & Gamble was perfectly healthy when roughly at the same time in the summer of 1993 it announced the elimination of thirteen thousand jobs or 12 percent of its workforce (a third of them in the United States). Other corporations including General Electric, AT&T, Johnson & Johnson, the Chubb Group, Eastman Kodak, and Raytheon have made job elimination a key to future competitiveness. An end to maritime subsidies in 1997, planned by the Clinton administration, will if it occurs mean the loss of twenty thousand maritime jobs. Don Phillips, "Pulling the Plug on American-Flag Ships," *The Washington Post*, National Weekly Edition, May 24–30, 1993, p. 33.

18. Iraq acquired its capacity from countries such as the United States, Germany, France, Britain, and Saudi Arabia, all of which presumably had a vital national interest in preventing nuclear proliferation. Robert J. Samuelson, "The Global Village Revisited," in *Vital World Statistics*, p. 4.

19. West Germany with 102 deals was the chief culprit, but the U.S., Switzerland, and Britain had nearly two dozen deals each, while Brazil, Italy, Austria, France, and Japan had five to fourteen deals each. Douglas Jehl, "The World: Who Armed Iraq? Answers the West Didn't Want to Hear," *The New York Times*, July 18, 1993, p. E 5. However, it is not the countries but the firms nominally flying country flags that are doing business; and as Middle East expert Anthony Cordesman has observed, "One major foreign order is incentive enough for some of these firms to turn a blind eye to the law," as well as, one surmises, to the conflicting security interests of their "mother" nations. Ibid.

20. See Uchitelle, "Gillette's World View."

21. Lester Brown et al., eds., *Vital Signs 1993: The Trends That Are Shaping Our Future* (Washington, D.C.: Worldwatch Institute, 1993), pp. 74–75.

22. Andrew Pollack, "Honda Set to Increase U.S. Output," *The New York Times*, September 20, 1993, p. D 1.

23. Andrew Pollack, "Today's Corporate Game Plans Know No Boundaries: Mabuchi Motors; an Un-Japanese Model for Japan," *The New York Times*, January 3, 1994, p. C 1.

Chapter 2. The Resource Imperative: The Passing of Autarky and the Fall of the West

1. Outside of the OECD nations and South Korea (whose Samsung Group is number 18 in the world), there are only a tiny handful of other nations with top 500 corporations on the list, and the 17 corporations in question in those countries (as ranked in 1992) are almost all petroleum companies like Venezuela's PDVSA (at number 56), Mexico's PEMEX (at number 57), Indian Oil (at number 188), and Malaysia's Petronas (at number 226); or mining outfits, which comprise the only sub-Saharan companies on the

list—a couple of South African companies and Zambia's Industrial & Mining (the only black African company on the list at number 457). *Fortune,* July 26, 1993, pp. 191–204.

2. Starting in 1950, fertilizer rather than land has increasingly been the indispensable factor in feeding the world's burgeoning population. While per capita grainland shrank as population grew, per capita use of fertilizer has grown steadily, staying well ahead of population growth until just a few years ago. These trends have favored advanced agricultural economies and disadvantaged those economies in the nations where population was growing.

    The role of agriculture in the overall economy and the number of workers in the agrarian sector are not correlated with gross agricultural output. The OECD devotes less than 3 percent of its GNP to agriculture yet manages to produce 28 percent of the world's cereals. *The Economist Book of Vital World Statistics* (New York: Times Books, 1990), p. 56.

    American farms employ less than 2.5 percent of the workforce, but America remained in 1988 the world's number two grain producer (behind China with nearly 70 percent of its labor force in agriculture), the number two fruit producer (behind Brazil with a quarter of its labor force in agriculture), and number four vegetable producer (behind China, India, and the former USSR). *Vital World Statistics,* ibid., pp. 62–66. The key statistic here is "agricultural efficiency, as measured by fertilizer and tractor use": ibid., pp. 58–59; and *Vital Signs 1993: The Trends That Are Shaping Our Future,* (Washington, D.C.: Worldwatch Institute, 1993), p. 19.

3. *Vital World Statistics,* pp. 36–38.

4. There are a few odd cases like Albania, which have fallen from Second to Third World status as a consequence of the collapse of communism.

5. Paul Kennedy, *Preparing for the Twenty-First Century* (New York: Vintage Books, 1994), p. 193.

6. Christopher J. Schmitz, *World Nonferrous Metal Production and Prices: 1700–1976* (Totowa, N.J.: Frank Cass & Co., Ltd., 1979), pp. 48–53. France had been the number one producer in the early years of industrialization, and more recently Jamaica, Surinam, and Guyana, and then Australia, took the lead.

7. *Historical Statistics of the United States: Colonial Times to 1970,* Parts 1 and 2 (Washington, D.C.: U.S. Department of Commerce, Bureau of the Census), 1975.

8. Post-1970 statistics are from *Metal Statistics Annual Reports (1993–1960),* (Frankfurt: Metallgesellschaft AG, 1993), and are calculated not in metric tons but in ti's, units of one thousand tons.

9. Schmitz, *World Nonferrous Metal,* p. 53. Three American firms are thus still among the six dominant global aluminum companies. However, environmental concerns and high labor costs are slowly driving processing plants abroad as well, increasing American dependency still further. For more on American companies, see Steven Kendall Holloway, *The Aluminum Multinationals and the Bauxite Cartel* (New York: St. Martin's Press, 1988); for more

detailed statistical information on American production, see U.S. Bureau of Mines, *Aluminum, Alumina and Bauxite Annual Reports* (Washington, D.C.: Department of the Interior, Bureau of Mines, 1994).

10. The story is the same for most metallurgical refining; e.g., "The cost of complying with federal environmental regulations is about six cents per pound of lead and between nine and fifteen cents per pound of copper— about 20 percent of the price of each metal in 1986, although rising metal prices have reduced this fraction to more like 10 percent today." National Research Council, Committee on the Competitiveness of the Minerals and Metals Industry, 1990, p. 14.

    Recycling can make a difference. Over half the trash in many community dumps can be incinerated (after sorting) and used to produce energy (see Barry Meier, "Finding Gold, of a Sort, in Landfills," *The New York Times,* September 7, 1993, p. A 14). In their use of minerals, Americans have in recent years secured as much as 25 percent of consumption from recycled materials. But in many cases, as with lead, environmental and safety considerations make recycling difficult. See *Lead Annual Review: 1993* (Washington, D.C.: Department of the Interior, Bureau of Mines, 1994).

11. Rocco Michael Paone, *Strategic Nonfuel Minerals and Eastern Security* (Lanham: University Press of America, 1992), p. 57.

12. Clyde S. Brooks, *Metal Recovery from Industrial Wastes* (Chelsea: Lewis Publishers, 1991), p. 5. There are limits, however. Manganese, for example, essential to iron and steel production, cannot be recovered from waste; nor have viable substitutes been found. See *Manganese Annual Report: 1991* (Washington, D.C.: U.S. Department of the Interior, Bureau of Mines, 1992), p. 3.

13. Where once only precious metals were recycled, today we recycle copper and copper alloys, chromium, cobalt, cadmium, nickel, manganese, molybdenum, lead, titanium, and zinc, though in vastly different amounts. With cadmium, manganese, and molybdenum, for example, the amounts are negligible, while for titanium (crucial for major aerospace structural elements such as wing skins and supports, compresser blades, and rotor parts for helicopters) up to 80 percent of the metal form is recycled. In its mineral form, where it is used to produce pigments that appear in a wide diversity of goods including paints, papers, plastics, textiles, and such common commodities as Twinkies and toothpaste, no recycling is possible and as a result we are totally import-dependent. See Paone, *Nonfuel Minerals.*

14. Aluminum, whose story of diminishing returns we told above, has in recent decades become something of a recycling success. As recently as 1975, we derived significantly less than 10 percent of our consumption from recycling. Today the figure is up to 42 percent of consumption, mainly as a consequence of garbage recycling. It turns out that 2 million tons of aluminum show up annually in municipal waste so that the excessive consumption habits that produced our dependency are happily producing byproduct wastes that are reducing the costs of that dependency. See Brooks, *Metal Recovery.*

15. Paone, *Nonfuel Minerals*, p. 227. Of course, substitution is not always a simple matter. Chromium and cobalt, for example, are metals absolutely essential to modern technology. Stainless steel (corrosion-resistant steel) can be made without nickel, but not without chromium, and efforts for chromium have yet to produce results. Although it takes "years of intensive research and development to discover replacements and produce them on meaningful levels," research and development efforts in the United States, Japan, and other advanced industrial nations are producing synthetic metals, high-performance plastics and ceramics, and advanced alloys and other composites that may eventually replace traditional natural metals in the world's new technologies.

16. Estimates suggest the nodules lying on the Pacific Ocean floor alone contain 359 times more cobalt, 83 times more nickel, and 9 times more copper than the world's other known reserves. Deep-sea diving, high-pressure-withstanding submersibles are being developed by several national teams, and a consortium of Japanese companies including Hitachi, Sumitomo, and Mitsubishi expects to have its deep-sea robotic vacuums in place by 1996. Tony Emerson with H. Takayama, "Into the Challenger Deep," *Newsweek*, July 5, 1993, pp. 62–63.

17. The precise figures are offered with a useful narrative in *Vital Signs*, pp. 46–63.

18. The United States, for example, derives nearly 75 percent of its electricity from coal, oil, and gas, 17 percent from nuclear, 9.5 percent from hydroelectric, and only 0.5 percent from geothermal. Only a handful of nations derive the majority of their electricity from nonfossil fuels. France and Belgium are heavily dependent on nuclear (over 60 percent each), while New Zealand, Canada, Austria, and Switzerland all derive a majority from hydroelectric. Meanwhile, literally dozens of countries (especially in Africa and the Middle East) derive virtually 100 percent of their electricity from fossil fuels (see *Vital World Statistics*, pp. 80–81).

19. Until recently, bikes outnumbered cars in China 250 to 1; however, although it continues to use bicycles as a primary transportation vehicle, reducing dependency on petroleum, steel, rubber, aluminum, and matériel and at the same time sparing the planet additional environmental pollution, it is now planning to expand automobile production radically. *Vital Signs*, p. 21.

20. C. A. S. Hall, C. J. Cleveland, and R. Kaufmann, *Energy and Resource Quality: The Ecology of the Economic Process* (New York: John Wiley and Sons, 1986), p. 161.

21. The Energy Information Administration, *Annual Energy Review: 1991* (Washington, D.C.: Department of the Interior, 1991).

22. Figures from R. Samuelson, "The Global Village," introductory essay to *Vital World Statistics*, no page.

23. The Energy Information Administration, *Annual Energy Reports* (Washington, D.C.: Department of the Interior, 1992).

24. In 1989, Qatar, the United Arab Emirates, Bahrain, Kuwait, and Oman ranked, respectively, numbers one, two, three, eight, and nine in per capita

energy consumption in the world; whatever else their bad consumption habits bred, dependency was not among them.

25. Some Western nations without fossil fuels have moved to alternative sources: alpine nations like Switzerland and Austria get most of the energy they use (other than in their autos) from hydroelectric and the rest from nuclear (37.7 percent). France, with the most developed nuclear industry in Europe, derives 64.2 percent of its domestic energy production from nuclear fuels, and Belgium is not far behind. South Korea (49 percent) and Japan (27.2 percent) are also significantly nuclear. *Vital World Statistics,* p. 81.

26. About seven-eighths of its total energy consumption derives from imports—the French too love to drive! Despite its nuclear production, because it exports much of what it produces it must still import to satisfy domestic demand.

27. See Appendix A.

28. *International Petroleum Encyclopedia* (Tulsa: Penwell Publishing, 1993), pp. 284–285.

29. Jane Perlez, "Ukraine Miners Bemoan the Costs of Independence," *The New York Times,* July 17, 1993, pp. A 1,5.

Chapter 3. The Industrial Sector and the Rise of the East

1. Paul Kennedy, *The Rise and Fall of Great Powers* (New York: Random House, 1988); and Kennedy, *Preparing for the Twenty-First Century* (New York: Vintage Books, 1993); David P. Calleo, *Beyond American Hegemony: The Future of the Western Alliance* (Brighton: Wheatsheaf, 1987).

2. Along with China, *The Economist*'s favorites for 1993 as reported in *The World in 1993.*

3. *The Economist Book of Vital World Statistics* (New York: Times Books, 1990), p. 39. The list might also include nations like Puerto Rico, Cuba, Sweden, Portugal, Uruguay, Zimbabwe, Mexico, Brazil, and Turkey that devote at least a quarter of their GNPs specifically to manufacturing. I have not included Eastern European nations in the eighties, even though they rank high, because the importance of the industrial sector there is overstated by virtue of the fact that services (mostly undertaken by the state under communism) are excluded.

4. Joseph Nye, paraphrasing Stephen D. Krasner's *International Regimes* (Ithaca, N.Y.: Cornell University Press, 1983) in Nye's *Bound to Lead: The Changing Character of American Power* (New York: Basic Books, 1991), p. 33.

5. Nye and Huntington and others believe that the prospects for American decline have been overstated. If the emergent service economy in its new age information/communication contours—the infotainment telemarket—is to be the new standard for growth, then countries like China and Japan are less threatening than they seem. In Nye's portrait, Japan is a "one-dimensional economic power" despite its industrial might. It lacks the global cultural and institutional resources—the soft power resident in the new service sector—to maintain its current leadership. Nye, ibid., p. 166.

6. It is important to remember, in gauging America's twentieth-century journey, that its wartime hegemony in world manufacturing and industrial production represented an artificially heightened profile as a result of the rest of the world's artificially diminished potential. Nye suggests that with 1938 rather than 1945 as the historical marker, there is *no* American decline even in the manufacturing sector—only a decline from the artificially high wartime prominence. See Nye, ibid., pp. 5–6. Today the top eight banks are Japanese and the United States has only two in the top fifty—Citicorp at number 25 and Chemical at number 42.

7. The heavy industrial sectors remain important, of course. American steel production, which as recently as 1970 was still 20 percent of the world total, had fallen to 11 percent by 1985, but has remained stable or risen slightly since then. *Statistical Abstract of the United States—1992*, (Washington, D.C.: U.S. Bureau of the Census), p. 751, table 1266.

8. IBM is at number 7 and General Electric at number 9. Thirty of the top 100 remain American. Japan is next with 128 of the top 500, followed by Britain with 40, Germany with 32, and France with 30. *Fortune*, July 26, 1993, p. 188.

9. *Business America*, April 6, 1992, p. 5.

10. These figures are all from Gary Hoover, *Hoover's Handbook of World Business* (Austin: Reference Press, 1994), pp. 158–161.

11. Just as America conducts the bulk of its trade with its immediate NAFTA neighbors, so the Common Market and the Pacific Rim countries conduct over 60% of their trade within their own blocs. *Vital World Statistics*, p. 152. These figures for intra-European trade have increased regularly since the early seventies.

12. The historical time comment is by former Nigerian President General Olusegun Obasanjo and the others are from reports also cited by Kennedy, *Preparing for the Twenty-First Century*, p. 210.

13. *Forbes*, July 19, 1993, pp. 182–184.

14. All the figures in this section are from Gary Hoover, *Hoover's Handbook of American Business* (Austin: Reference Press, 1994), and the *Hoover's Handbook of World Business*.

15. Richard W. Stevenson, "IKEA's New Realities," *The New York Times*, April 25, 1993, p. F 4.

Chapter 4. From Hard Goods to Soft Goods

1. Bill Keller, "Transition in Africa," *The New York Times*, September 25, 1993, Section 1, p. 1.

2. *Fortune*, July 26, 1993, pp. 188–204. Estimates vary so widely because they reflect different media—print, broadcast, billboard, and direct mail.

3. Ben H. Bagdikian, *The Media Monopoly*, fourth edition (Boston: Beacon Press, 1992), p. 246.

4. Lewis Cole, "Screenplay Culture," *The Nation*, November 4, 1991, pp. 560–566.

5. Bernard Weinraub, "Ovitz Firm Gets AT&T Executive," *The New York Times*, June 17, 1994, p. D 1.

6. Lester Brown et al., eds., *Vital Signs 1993: The Trends That Are Shaping Our Future* (Washington, D.C.: Worldwatch Institute, 1993), pp. 80–81.

7. Ibid. Also see Jackson Lears, *Fables of Abundance: A Cultural History of Advertising in America* (New York: Basic Books, 1994).

8. *Fortune*, July 26, 1993, pp. 188–204. The loss in prestige of a traditional brand name can devastate a company, as the recent history of Ovaltine, White Cloud bathroom tissue, Old Gold cigarettes, or Lavoris mouthwash suggests.

9. Luciano Benetton in an interview "Krieg ist Realität" [War Is Reality], in *Der Spiegel*, September 1994, p. 127. He adds that honesty has not cost Benetton any market share.

10. In fact, this HIV ad was the first salvo in a campaign to introduce a new magazine being published under Benetton's logo called (naturally) *Colors*. Why is an apparel company publishing a hip international magazine? For the same reason Sony has put *Sony Style* on the newsstands: to exploit a new merchandising strategy, the magalog. "Part life-style book, part catalog, there are now more than 100 of these hybrids whose strategy is to reach customers directly and treat every page as a marketing opportunity." Charles Lee, "Trends: Advertisers Move into Publishing," *Newsweek*, November 1, 1993, p. 69.

11. Roddick has been compelled to back off on some of her environmental claims recently.

12. Quantum Systems Inc. in Ramsey, New Jersey, has patented a system that replaces telephone ringing sounds and busy signals with fifteen-second ads. Theresa Riordan, "Patents," *The New York Times*, June 27, 1994, p. B 2.

13. "A major uproar followed the announcement last month that Space Marketing Inc. of Roswell, Ga., in cooperation with Lawrence Livermore National Laboratory in California and the University of Colorado, planned to launch a one-mile-wide display satellite into orbit around Earth. The spacecraft, made of thin plastic film, would reflect sunlight to Earth from aluminized letters or symbols." Malcolm W. Browne, "City Lights and Space Ads May Blind Stargazers," *The New York Times*, May 4, 1993, p. C 1.

14. Quoted by Donella Meadows, "The Global Citizen," *The Berkshire Eagle*, July 5, 1993.

15. "Buy this 24-year-old and get all his friends absolutely free," reads the MTV ad for advertisers. "If this guy doesn't know about you, you're toast. He's an opinion leader. He watches MTV. Which means he knows a lot more than just what CDs to buy and what movies to see. He knows what car to drive, what clothes to wear and what credit card to buy them with. And he's no loner. He heads up a pack." Reproduced in *Adbusters*, Vol. 3, No. 2, Summer, 1994. *Adbusters* is an extraordinary Canadian quarterly "journal of the mental environment," devoted to deconstructing the advertising industry.

16. A Nike ad from a few years ago offered women's magazine readers a steamy twelve-page "passion play in six acts" called "Falling in Love," with scenes entitled "lust," "euphoria," "fear," "disgust," and "the truth" in which shoes were definitely (at best) bit players.

17. Annetta Miller and Seema Nayyar, "Ads of Our Lives," *Newsweek*, September 26, 1994, pp. 48–50.

Nintendo, a cowboy hero on the cyberspace frontier, knows this very well. In a new 1994 ad campaign aimed at its primary market of teenagers, it sells not its game machines and software but the kids themselves back to the kids so that, according to Nintendo advertising manager Don Coyner, they will know Nintendo speaks "kidspeak" in "a way they can totally relate to." Nintendo's "Play It Loud" commercials are "wild and frenetic, mocking a mother who yearns for 'a doctor in the family' and a security guard who intones, 'No running, no spitting, no loud music, no skateboarding, no skating.' " A kid screams, "We want to be free to do what we want to do," and a voice tells viewers to "hock a loogie at life" (spit at it) and "give the world a wedgie" (bunched-up underwear). See Stuart Elliot, "The Media Business: Advertising: Nintendo Turns Up the Volume," *The New York Times*, July 1, 1994, p. D 15.

18. Stuart Elliot, "In Search of Fun for Creativity's Sake," *The New York Times*, January 3, 1994, p. C 19.

19. *Time* magazine as cited by Stuart Elliot, "Advertising," *The New York Times*, June 1, 1994, p. D 15.

20. "The LOOK," BBC special on the fashion industry.

21. Sallie Hofmeister, "In the Realm of Marketing, the Lion King Rules," *The New York Times*, July 12, 1994, p. D 1. It is this logic that has led Disney to buy into Broadway (having refurbished the Forty-second Street theater where *Beauty and the Beast* is breaking records; and to seek a historical venue for a new American theme park—no longer in Virginia, which scotched its plan for a civil war theme park next to Manassas, but somewhere between Orlando and cyberspace.

22. See Frank Deford, "Running Man," *Vanity Fair*, August 1993, p. 54. Also see Donald Katz, *Just Do It: The Nike Spirit in the Corporate World* (New York: Random House, 1994).

23. Christine Brennan, "The Athletic Shoe Company That Won't Tread Softly," *The Washington Post*, National Weekly Edition, May 31–June 6, 1993, p. 20.

24. Nike 1992 Annual Report.

25. Among the companies he endorses, General Mills (Wheaties), Wilson Sporting Goods, and Sara Lee (which puts him in Hanes briefs *and* puts Ball Park Franks in him) pay him a million each, Gatorade $2 million, and Nike—his big contract—$20 million a year. Is Nike crazy? Probably not: Air Jordan is a $200 million-a-year brand, which accounts for 5 percent of Nike's 1992 revenues. Curry Kirkpatrick, "Up, Up, and Away," *Newsweek*, October 18, 1993, pp. 65–67. His 1995 late season return to basketball can only inflate these figures.

For a brilliant account of advertising's history see Jackson Lears, *Fables of Abundance;* for an account more in the spirit of advertising itself, see Randall Rothenberg, *Where the Suckers Moon: An Advertising Story* (New York: Alfred A. Knopf, 1994).

26. Nike's Annual Report thus boasts that "people anxiously await the debut of new advertising, and are equally enthusiastic in their response. The U.S. women's print campaign [of which the passion play is presumably a part], for instance, has garnered acclaim for its message of honesty and self-empowerment." The aim is "creating emotional ties with consumers, giving them an opportunity to believe in the products and motivations of Nike."

27. Michael Lev, "Store of Future: It Also Sells Shoes," *The New York Times,* June 17, 1991, p. D 1. According to P. K. Anderson, editor of *Visual Merchandizing and Store Design,* "There is less leisure time today so people need to have fun. You have to use every trick in the book to keep those shoppers lingering longer."

   In addition to its Portland store, Nike plans to build fourteen similar Nike Towns by the end of the decade. It has also installed ten mini–Nike Towns—"presentation stores"—in America, and plans eighty more worldwide. Nike recently opened a Vienna office with a view to East European sales possibilities. Ken Hamburg, "Nike Planning Lay-offs Globally," *The Oregonian,* September 21, 1993, p. B 18.

28. "There is a crisis in America right now," says CEO Knight, and Nike wants to help. Reebok has its own version of P.L.A.Y. called The Reebok Foundation, which sponsors a Human Rights Awards Program that aspires to "make a difference in the larger world." (Paul Fireman, Reebok CEO, in the Reebok 1992 Annual Report.)

   Corporate philanthropy by moguls who have sucked markets dry is of course an old American tradition. Today's efforts are novel only in the causes to which they are devoted—ideally both politically correct *and* aimed at creating new consumers for their products (women, kids). Carnegie built libraries, he did not subsidize new generations of steel buyers.

29. PepsiCo's new 1993 ad campaign dumped "Gotta have it!" in favor of "Be young, have fun, drink Pepsi," presumably because visionary executives believe consumers will reverse the order of words and the logic words convey in their soft-drink-softened brains and drink Pepsi *in order to* have fun and become young. "We want to keep the notion alive that Pepsi is for people who want to feel and be young," says Phil Dusenberry, the advertising executive responsible for the new campaign. Patricia Winters, "Pepsi Harkens Back to Youth," *Advertising Age,* June 25, 1993, pp. 3, 43.

30. Coca-Cola 1992 Annual Report.

   Earl Shorris discusses the general impact of advertising on culture in *A Nation of Salesmen: The Tyranny of the Market and the Subversion of Culture* (New York: Norton, 1994).

31. As Mark Pendergrast tells the story in his *For God, Country and Coca-Cola* (New York: Scribner's, 1993), Coke has been doing whatever it takes to

penetrate markets ever since accommodating the Nazis (who were claiming Coke was a Jewish-American company because it sold Kosher-stamped bottles) by passing out samples at Hitler Youth rallies, and accommodating Stalin by decaramelizing "White Coke" and shipping fifty cases in clear bottles with red-star-embossed white caps for his approval. Coke was also there recently when the Berlin Wall came down, handing out six-packs. Pendergrast sums it up unsentimentally: "In World War II, Coke was an American imperialist symbol, a kosher food, a fake Communist beverage and the drink of Hitler Youth. Most people thought the war was about good, evil, competing ideologies and so on, but for Coca-Cola the issue was simpler: more Coke or less Coke." See Mark Pendergrast, ibid., and his short piece "A Brief History of Coca-Colonization," in *The New York Times*, August 5, 1993, p. F 13.

32. Take an example from another consumer area: are microwave ovens "necessities"? In the United States, 44 percent of the population think so; in Mexico, only 19 percent think so. If another 25 percent of Mexicans can be persuaded that they "need" microwaves, the market for American microwaves—especially in the era of NAFTA—is dramatically enhanced. Figures from Anthony de Palma, "Mexico's Hunger for U.S. Goods Is Helping to Sell the Trade Pact," *The New York Times*, Week in Review, November 7, 1993. Section 4, pp. 1–2.

33. In the 1992 Coca-Cola Company's Annual Report entitled appropriately to our theme here "Worlds of Opportunity."

34. *The New York Times Magazine*, December 25, 1994, pp. 36–37. It is perhaps in the name of the ideology of fun that "junior toiletries" and "infant fragrances" like Jacadi's "l'eau des petits" are being marketed by all the major parfumeurs. Shao Ko of Paris has fragrances aimed at juveniles named after Babar, Celeste, Mickey, and Minnie—the theme-parking of perfumes. See "L'esprit du Bébé," *The New Yorker*, February 6, 1995, p. 28.

35. See Edward C. Banfield with the assistance of Laura Fasano Banfield, *The Moral Basis of a Backward Society* (New York: The Free Press, 1958).

Chapter 5. From Soft Goods to Service

1. Figures from Bill Orr, *The Global Economy* (New York: New York University Press, 1992), p. 101.

2. Ibid., p. 99.

3. John Holusha, "The Risks for High Tech," *The New York Times*, September 5, 1993, p. F 7. Much of the decline results from cutbacks in public sector spending, but even private sector spending has remained flat.

4. *Fortune*, August 26, 1991, pp. 165–188.

5. *Fortune*, August 23, 1993, pp. 160–196.

6. Figures and quotes from D. J. Connors and D. S. Heller, "Viewpoints: The Good Word in Trade is 'Services,' " *The New York Times*, September 5, 1993, Section 3, p. 9.

7. *Fortune,* May 31, 1993, pp. 206–208.

8. Pat Cadigan, "Pretty Boy Crossover," *Synners* (New York: Bantam, 1993) as cited in John Leonard, "Gravity's Rainbow," *The Nation,* November 15, 1993, pp. 580–588.

9. Quoted by Bernard Weinraub, "Robert Altman," *The New York Times,* July 29, 1993, p. B 1.

10. Roger Cohen, "Aux Armes! France Rallies," *The New York Times,* January 2, 1994, p. H 1.

11. Ibid.

12. Cited by Daniel Pipes, "The American Conspiracy to Run the World," *The Washington Post,* National Weekly Edition, Nov. 14–20, 1994, p. 25.

13. Corporations are especially fond of this language: thus General Electric Chairman Jack Welch called Sony founder Akio Morita (felled recently by a cerebral hemorrhage) "spiritually global." Jolie Solomon with Peter McKillop, "We Have Lost a Very Important Player," *Newsweek,* December 13, 1993, p. 50.

14. In a special issue of the *International Political Science Review* (Vol. 14, No. 3, July 1993) on "The Emergent World Language System" [the title already makes the point!], Abram de Swaan writes: "In the midst of this galaxy there is one language that is spoken by more multilingual speakers in the supranational language groups than any other and that is therefore central to all central languages. This supercentral language is, of course, English," p. 219. David D. Daitin goes further in an argument that corresponds to the battle between Jihad and McWorld when he writes, "The logic of globalization suggests that world languages such as English will begin to challenge national vernaculars in such a way as to threaten their existence as living languages." "The Game Theory of Language Regimes," ibid., p. 226.

15. Even the first time around, in the 1930s, the public interest ultimately was undercut by the compromises won by commercialism: see Robert W. McChesney, *Telecommunications, Mass Media, and Democracy* (New York: Oxford University Press, 1993).

16. This is not exactly a new story. As William Leach tells it in his *Land of Desire: Merchants, Power and the Rise of a New American Culture* (New York: Vintage Books, 1994), the rise of consumerism from the 1890s through the Depression more or less parallels the rise of American capitalism.

17. The absence of government interest in America is startling, given the implications of the new media merger mania for freedom of information, equal access to knowledge, and issues of monopoly. A private coalition of sixty nonprofit, consumer, labor, and civil rights groups has convened a Telecommunications Policy Roundtable that hopes to provide public debate about the public interest in these new technologies, but it is unlikely to be an adequate counterbalance to the multibillion-dollar deals currently being struck by private corporations.

Chapter 6. Hollyworld: McWorld's Videology

1. Jeff Miller, "Viewpoints: Should Phone Companies Make Films?" *The New York Times,* January 2, Section 3, p. 11.
2. Roger Cohen, "Europeans Back French Curbs on U.S. Movies," *The New York Times,* December 12, 1993, Section 1, p. 24.
3. Cited by Roger Cohen, "Aux Armes! France Rallies," *The New York Times,* January 2, 1994, p. H 1.
4. Marselli Sumarno, "Indonesia," in the *Variety International Film Guide* (Hollywood: Samuel French Trade, 1993), p. 210. The United States demanded easier access for American film exports to Indonesia in return for guaranteeing it would not encumber Indonesian textile imports into the United States.
5. Roger Cohen, "Europeans Back French Curbs," p. A 24.
6. Alan Riding, "French Film Industry Circles the Wagons," *The New York Times,* September 18, 1993, Section 1, p. 11.
7. Thus, a local hit like *Les Visiteurs* can still outearn a megahit import like *Jurassic Park.*
8. Bernard Weinraub, "Directors Battle Over GATT," *The New York Times,* December 12, 1993, Section 1, p. 24.
9. Paul Chutkow, "Who Will Control the Soul of French Cinema?" *The New York Times,* August 9, 1993, Section 2, p. 22.
10. Roger Cohen, "Barbarians at the Box Offices," *The New York Times,* July 11, 1993, Section 9, p. 3.
11. In a piece of doggerel called "The GATT in the VAT," Stuart Elliot captures the mood of ridicule with which Americans view the French anxieties:

> *They note with delight GATT's roiling the French,*
> *The folks who make teeth around the world clench.*
> *The French claim our movies, TV and such,*
> *Will put their own film makers in Dutch.*
> *They clamor their culture's in peril, The French,*
> *Terrified Spielberg will make them retrench.*
> *Overshadowed by "Jaws" and "Terminator 2,"*
> *How will Gerard get his Depar-dieu?*

Stuart Elliot, "GATT in the VAT," *The New York Times,* December 12, 1993, p. E 5.
12. Germany is more typical of Europe than France. It has offered much less resistance to Hollywood. In the late 1950s, it had over seven thousand screens available and sold over 750 million tickets, with German films counting for nearly half of the business done. America took in only one-quarter of the revenues, while French and Italian films were each earning 10 percent of the market. Germany offered its people a genuinely diversified, culturally heterogeneous culture market. By 1975, however, television

and rising prices had driven ticket sales down to only 128 million, while the number of screens available had been reduced to around thirty-two hundred. Meanwhile, the American share had crept up to over 41 percent while the German share of revenues was down to only 13 percent. During the 1980s the German share skidded erratically to and fro between 10 and 20 percent of the market, but American imports climbed inexorably through 53 percent in 1981 to 66 percent in 1984 up to 83 percent in 1992, a year in which nine of Germany's ten top-grossing films were American, with *Basic Instinct, Hook, Beauty and the Beast, Home Alone,* and *JFK* occupying the top five spots. (All figures are from information provided by the Statistical Department of the Spitzenorganisation der Filmwirtschaft e.V. in a letter dated June 28, 1993.) As in other countries, Germany still is home to a great deal of filmmaking, as many as three thousand productions each year. But only 10 percent of these represent serious productions with real budgets and a far smaller percentage actually find their way to a commercial screening.

13. David Stratton, "Gone with the Wind," *Variety International Film Guide,* p. 14.

14. Figures from the Statistical Department of the Spitzenorganisation der Filmwirtschaft e.V.

15. "Sleeping With the Enemy: Europe's Film Industry," *The Economist,* October 26, 1991, p. 91. Limiting the number of American films cannot prevent the successful megahits from reaping disproportionate percentages of overall revenues.

16. French film director Alain Corneau warned "Think of a world in which there is only one image." Cited in Riding, "French Film Industry."

17. Uma de Cunha, "India," *Variety International Film Guide,* p. 205.

18. Deborah Young, "Iranian Cinema Now," in *Variety International Film Guide,* p. 30.

19. In *Dances with Wolves,* Kevin Costner documents the conquest of Native American Indians by the new Americans; will Islam fare any better against Kevin Costner? *Dances with Wolves* turns out to have made more than half its revenue from foreign screenings. This is true for more and more American films, including such seeming "American" hits as *JFK, Pretty Woman,* and *Robin Hood.*

20. Quoted in David Hansen, "The Real Cultural Revolution," *Newsweek,* November 1, 1993, p. 74.

21. Cited by Andrew Horton, "Russia," *Variety International Film Guide,* p. 324. What is getting made in Russia is tawdry genre films with titles like *The Little Giant of Big Sex, Violence, Whorehouse,* and everybody's favorite, *Even KGB Agents Fall in Love.* For the rest, traditional studios like Mosfilm and the Gorky Studio are now principally engaged in servicing foreign productions like the American-made *Russia House* to earn foreign currency.

22. Hollywood's domination of the global market is evident not only in its revenues and ticket sales, but also in its increased share of imports in every importing market. A survey of the "Best Ten" list of foreign films in Japan published by *Kinema Jumpo* starting in 1924 offers a revealing picture of the

growth and decline of national cinema in countries like India, Sweden, France, and Italy that once supplied Japan with high-quality imports. After an early monopoly by Hollywood in the late twenties and thirties when (from 1924 through 1934) 77 (or 73 percent) of the top 106 foreign films were American, America became only one among many importers. From 1935 to 1940 only 27 (or 45 percent) of 60 top imports were American. After the war, from 1948 through 1968, 59 (or just 28 percent) of imports were American. In 1960, for example, only Charlie Chaplin's *The Great Dictator* made the top ten, while three Italian, four French, and two Russian films completed the list. As late as 1967 only *In the Heat of the Night* was on the list, the other nine top foreign films coming from a variety of Swedish, Soviet, and other European coproductions. But starting in 1969, between four and seven of the top ten imports were American (70 or 54 percent of 130 top films between 1969 and 1988), and in the last five years the American lock has meant eight or nine of the top ten imports as well as top-grossing films measured against domestic production. All statistics are from the Japanese film magazine *Kinema Jumpo* Best Ten: 1924–89.

23. Coproduction makes it harder to identify product by a single national culture, but it has been more about financing films internationally than creating them that way artistically, and although coproduction has certainly given an international flavor to films like *The Crying Game* and *The Lover,* its main impact has been to regionalize and thus denationalize what were once specifically French or Swedish or Indonesian or Chinese pictures.

"The 'new democracies' of East Europe are learning some bitter lessons as the air is let out of the cushion of state funding, driving them into unlikely partnerships which threaten 'national character'; in East Asia, long time enemies China and Taiwan are both depending on the dominant Hong Kong film industry to pump life into their own film cultures; and in Scandinavia, multi-Nordic co-productions have all but obliterated the concept of a film's 'nationality'." David Stratton, "Gone with the Wind," *Variety International Film Guide,* p. 20.

24. As Derek Elley, editor of *Variety International Film Guide,* has written, coproducing a film in Italy and Yugoslavia probably means planning the film in a Roman bistro, a cheap and quick shoot in what was Yugoslavia, and then . . . "An American star who hasn't worked in Hollywood for some months is signed up for a male lead, a British character actor who has been holidaying in Rome agrees to play the 'heavy' for modest terms . . . an Italian actress who can mumble a few words of English . . . An American director who is in-between TV series is signed on as director, though it is vaguely explained to him that he will not be credited as director in Italy. The producer now books his studio and pays the expense to Yugoslavia. The Yugoslavs will pay the expenses there and probably leave a lot of the company with useless dinars in their pockets." Derek Elley, "Coproductions: Who Needs Them?" *Variety International Film Guide,* p. 19.

25. Another French strategy is to call for the dubbing of French films into English (imitating the dubbing of American films into French, which has

helped Hollywood capture French audiences), but dubbing has the side effect of slightly "Americanizing" French films and enhancing the sovereignty of English. The French resort to the strategy to prevent the even more destructive Hollywood habit of remaking French films—as happened with *Three Men and a Baby* and *Point of No Return*, originally *La Femme Nikita*.

26. Germany's Volker Schlöndorff, Australia's Peter Weir, Canada's Bruce Beresford, and Holland's Paul Verhoeven are only a few of the directors who have taken their big talents to Hollywood where those talents have been tailored to its diminutive needs and tastes. Along with Wim Wenders and other European directors, England's David Puttnam, who tried Hollywood and went home, is calling for an extension of French quotas and French-style subsidies to all of Europe. But if there is any venue from which "you can't go home again" it is probably Hollywood, and most directors from abroad are trying to figure out how to make the journey the other way.

27. See Philip Weiss, "Hollywood at a Fever Pitch," *The New York Times Magazine*, December 26, 1993, p. 22. He auditioned (interviewed) for a job with people like Scott Rudin, the equally celebrated young producer of the *Sister Act* and *Family Values* movies.

28. Report on France, *Variety International Film Guide*, p. 163.

29. Movies are about marketing and marketing means deferring judgment to the DAT—the digital audiotape of audience response at the special previews producers arrange to test-market their films. When forced to choose between a Chen Kaige insight and a DAT report on audience response, producers like Scott Rudin will tell you that DAT wins every time.

30. All Indonesian figures and quotes from Philip Shenon, "Indonesian Films Squeezed Out," *The New York Times*, October 29, 1992, p. A 19.

31. For all the fears abroad, America's global film sovereignty is still just gearing up. As John Marcom, Jr., notes in his *Forbes* essay "Dream Factory to the World," "Hollywood is already one of the world's most powerful suppliers of consumer products. Yet it has scarcely begun tapping foreign markets." John Marcom, Jr., "Dream Factory to the World," *Forbes*, April 29, 1991, p. 98.

32. Despite their success, American producers actually complain that the world is radically underscreened. Although half of American film revenues now come from abroad, constituting a $3.5 billion surplus, the United States still has a movie screen for every 10,333 people (24,000 screens for 250 million people), while Japan has only one screen for every 61,500 people. Italy's film houses are not air-conditioned, and most of the world has not yet seen the lucrative magic of multiplex cinemas—although they are on the way, with Time Warner, for example, scheduled to construct thirty in Japan alone in 1993–94. Alan Citron, "American Films Boffo Overseas," *International Herald Tribune*, March 31, 1992.

33. Not literally, of course. There are limits to the direct influence of films. Bosnian and Serbian assassins wear Adidas, sport Walkmans, and know all

about Michael Jordan but still manage to slaughter their neighbors with brutal zest. Saudi Muslims watch Western consumer films without seeming to give up their religion. Both Hitler and Stalin were notorious film buffs while P.L.O. chairman Arafat apparently is enamored of American Westerns, but this is not to suggest that *High Noon* or *Gunfight at the OK Corral* either deterred him from or led him to his fateful handshake with Israeli Prime Minister Rabin in Washington in 1994.

Chapter 7. Television and MTV: McWorld's Noisy Soul

1. For background on the role of television and advertising in American life see the older books by Marie Winn, *Plug-In Drug* (New York: Grossman Publishers, 1977); Frank Mankiewicz and Joel Swerdlow, *Remote Control: Television and the Manipulation of American Life* (New York: Ballantine Books, 1979); Jerry Mander, *Four Arguments for the Elimination of Television* (Brighton: Harvester Press, 1980); and Todd Gitlin, *Inside Prime Time* (New York: Pantheon, 1983).

2. Geraldine Fabrikant, "Bell Atlantic's Acquisition," *The New York Times,* October 14, 1993, p. C 7.

3. I will not try here to rehearse the thoughtful critique of television that has been offered by social critics such as Marshall McLuhan, Neil Postman, or Todd Gitlin. But, as an encapsulation of our themes here, John Berger's comment that "publicity turns consumption into a substitute for democracy" is worth citing. Berger, Ways of Seeing (London: Penguin, 1972), p. 149.

4. Steven Daly, "London Is Dead: Invasion of U.S. Pop Culture," *The New Republic,* June 14, 1993, p. 12. Daly cites Morrisey's lyric "We look to Los Angeles for the language we use/London is dead/London is dead."

5. Miklos Vamos, "U.S. Cultural Invasion: Hungary for American Pop," *The Nation,* March 25, 1991, pp. 11–12. This was more than three years ago: things have hardly improved.

6. Other fare includes a Steppes version of *The Dating Game* called *Love at First Sight* and two hundred episodes of the Mexican American-soap-rip-off *The Rich Also Cry.* Nadeshda Azhginkhina, "High Culture Meets Trash TV," *Bulletin of the Atomic Scientists,* January/February 1993, p. 42.

7. The Poles comprise the seventh largest number of cable viewers in Europe with 400,000 more than the French. Jane Perlez, "Poland Exercises the Right to Channel Surf," *The New York Times,* November 14, 1993, p. E 18. These numbers have presumably grown considerably in the last several years. Poland's first legally approved commercial channel Polsat initiated its "indigenous" programming in 1993 by broadcasting Hollywood director Michael Cimino's Oscar-winning film *The Deer Hunter* (it has Central European ethnic pretensions) along with hard-core soap opera classics like *General Hospital* and *Dallas.*

8. Patrick E. Tyler, "CNN and MTV, Hangin' by a Heavenly Thread," *The New York Times,* November 22, 1993, p. A 4.

9. Philip Shenon, "Star TV extends Murdoch's Reach," *The New York Times,* August 23, 1993, p. C 1.

10. Seabrook continues, "The promotions department is often said to be the core of MTV. Everything on MTV is a promotion for something, and the promo department's mission, in a sense, is to promote that." Says one of MTV's employees, "You're selling a feeling about what it means to be . . . God I don't know." John Seabrook, "Rocking in Shangri-La," *The New Yorker,* October 10, 1994, pp. 64–78.

11. In Prague high schools today, official reading materials for the high school graduation exam include the Beatles' "Lucy in the Sky with Diamonds," John Lennon's "Woman," Metallica's "Enter Sandman," and Pink Floyd's "Happiest Days of Our Lives." *Harper's,* June 1994, p. 22. But then Eric Segal's *Love Story* was once on France's vaunted university examination!

12. When MTV started, the average age of management was twenty-five; today, it is closer to twenty-nine. Redstone thinks guerrillas are kids: "By the way," he adds, "this is also why freedom fighters all over the world associate themselves with MTV"! Cited by Seabrook, "Rocking," p. 76.

13. Steve Clarke, "Rock Conquers Continent," *Variety,* November 16, 1992, p. 35.

14. Helmut Fest, "MTV Europe Ignores Local Acts," *Billboard,* March 7, 1992, p. 8.

15. Uma de Cunha, "India," in *Variety International Film Guide* (Hollywood: Samuel French Trade, 1993), pp. 205–210.

16. In his *Cassette Culture: Popular Music and Technology in North India* (Chicago: University of Chicago Press, 1993), Peter Manuel thus describes how portable cassette players created cultural shock waves in Northern India, with traumatic effects on Indian popular culture. With cassette players, there was at least some listener choice: with satellites, the monopolies control taste, even while affecting to respond to local markets.

17. Cited by Peter Waldman, "Iran Fights New Foe: Western Television," *The Wall Street Journal,* August 8, 1994, p. A 10.

18. See Elisabeth A. Brown, "Music Television Turns 10," *The Christian Science Monitor,* August 6, 1991, pp. 10–11.

19. Clarke, "Rock," p. 199.

20. Celestine Bohlen, "Russia Parties Subdued by Early Vote Returns," *The New York Times,* December 13, 1993, p. A 6.

21. Cited by Azhginkhina, "High Culture," p. 193.

22. Nor is MTV really to be taken seriously when it plays bad boy, as the group Public Enemy does. The mischief starts with the group's name (so too with N.W.A. [Niggers With Attitude]) and continues in song titles such as "Fight the Power," which black filmmaker Spike Lee used in his *Do the Right Thing.* A good deal of rapper rage is all posture: impotence as porn with the volume turned up so that hard decibels and fierce scatology cover the softness underneath. Most viewers around the world do not understand English anyway, and for them the point is the sound, the style, and the feel, not the words.

23. The Nobody Beats the Wiz chain thus runs a major advertising campaign featuring the schlock-shock MTV cartoon figures Beavis and Butt-head wearing MTV T-shirts while selling their *Death Rock* album. This anthology album assembles a morbid collection of death songs aimed at self-destructive youths who are killing themselves and each other at record rates. The ad ran in major media markets before Thanksgiving of 1993 under the headline "Huh, huh, huh, This ad is cool!" with large cartoon figures of the two MTV cartoon characters Beavis and Butt-head. These blatant morons had just a month earlier been relegated to a late-night hour, after children watching the popular MTV series in prime time had set fire to their rooms in imitation of their cartoon pranks. Songs on the Beavis and Butt-head *Experience* album include "I Hate Myself and Want to Die" (Nirvana); "Looking Down the Barrel of a Gun" (Anthrax); "99 Ways to Die" (Megadeth); "Search and Destroy" (Red Hot Chili Peppers); and "I Am Hell" (White Zombie).

24. Seabrook, "Rocking," p. 75.

25. Citation from Seabrook, ibid., p. 69. A number of rap artists have had run-ins with the law, including Tupac Shakur whose 1991 album "2pacalypse Now" raps about "droppin' the cop!" He allegedly did just that in October 1993, and was himself the victim of a shooting in late 1994; the rapper Flavor Flav of Public Enemy was arrested around the same time for attempted murder after reportedly shooting at a neighbor. But the real profiteers here are not the rappers who have found in the glamorization of ghetto life a paying hustle, but the record companies and the corporations that own and quietly earn considerable profits from them. For background see, for example, Toure, "Snoop Dogg's Gentle Hip-Hop Growl," *The New York Times*, November 21, 1993, Section 2, p. 32.

26. Lyrics and reality get all mixed up in MTV's savage version of McWorld. "Gangsta rap" often is the work of authentic gangsters. In 1993 alone, in addition to the Tupac Shakur arrest for allegedly shooting two cops noted above, Flavor Flav allegedly shot at his girlfriend's lover; Snoop Doggy Dogg was charged for carrying two guns and has a murder charge pending; and assault and rape charges have been brought against sundry other denizens of MTV. For one report see Nathan McCall, "The Rap Against Rap," *The Washington Post*, National Weekly Edition, November 14, 1993, p. C 1; and the *Newsweek* cover story "Rap and Race," *Newsweek*, June 29, 1992, pp. 46–52.

27. Robert Scheer remarks that the handlers and profiteers who lived off Michael Jackson never seemed to notice that "there was something profoundly wrong with elevating someone so maladjusted to the status of universal spokesman for children in the sacred precincts of Disneyland and Pepsi commercials." "Mega-Michael," *The Nation*, October 11, 1993, pp. 376–377.

28. Michael J. O'Neill, *The Roar of the Crowd: How Television and People Power Are Changing the World* (New York: Times Books, 1993), p. 110.

29. Adrian Lyttelton, "Italy: The Triumph of TV," *The New York Review of Books,* August 11, 1994, pp. 25–29.

30. Gore Vidal, *Screening History* (Cambridge: Harvard University Press, 1992), p. 81.

31. Mark Crispin Miller, *Boxed In: The Culture of TV* (Evanston, Illinois: Northwestern University Press, 1988), p. 19.

32. Kenichi Ohmae, *The Borderless World: Power and Strategy in the Interlinked Economy* (New York: Harper Business, 1990), p. xiv.

33. Moisi is deputy director of the French Institute for International Relations; cited in Roger Cohen, "The French, Disneyed and Jurassick, Fear Erosion," *The New York Times,* November 21, 1993, p. E 2. Moisi links Jihad and McWorld (without calling them that), noting that "one minute it's dinosaurs [*Jurassic Park*], the next North African immigrants, but it's the same basic anxiety."

34. The object is to send great quantities of data, pictures, and sounds to every home on an interactive basis. The old "new" technology required fiber optics that carry thousands of signals and permit broadcasting centers to send information to everyone. Integrated Services Digital Network's new switching technology permits a particular home to get only those data it requires (just the way each home receives only the calls placed to it by phone rather than every phone conversation in America). It is this switching capacity that makes the new mergers between phone and cable broadcasting companies so potentially profitable. To rewire American homes with fiber optics would cost upwards of $400 billion; by using the ISDN system, existing wires can be employed at a fraction of the cost.

35. Formerly owned by Whittle Communications, and now in the hands of K-III, a firm specializing in education and publishing for profit whose chairman H. Kravis is also a key player in public broadcasting.

36. Colgate-Palmolive has test-marketed a teen perfume called Maniac, while Randy Pernini of Miami has created a designer fragrance for "discriminating" (not) boys between three and ten. See Chapter 4, note 34, above.

Chapter 8. Teleliterature and the Theme Parking of McWorld

1. I speak here as someone who has been engaged in a number of major educational projects for television—for example, with Patrick Watson, the ten-part series *The Struggle for Democracy* (the book accompanying the series is from Little, Brown and Company, 1988). As we achieved television success, we risked educational failure.

2. Robert Lynch, a McGraw-Hill director, quoted by Meg Cox, "Electronic Campus," *The Wall Street Journal,* June 1, 1993, p. A 5.

3. The Authors Guild, *Electronic Publishing Rights: A Publishing Statement,* October 18, 1993.

4. *User's Guide for Great Literature,* Personal Library Series, Bureau Development, Inc., 1992. English-language originals are cut but otherwise

untouched, but translations from foreign classics are ancient and the principle of selection obviously has more to do with what was available free than with scholarly or editorial judgment.

5. Cox, "Electronic Campus."

6. Stern's *Private Parts* passed the million mark in sales in its first several weeks in print.

7. See John Lahr's telling essay on celebrity, "The Voodoo of Glamour" (with Richard Avedon), *The New Yorker*, March 21, 1994, pp. 113–122.

8. Ornstein is cited in an article by Jennifer Senior, "Hollywood on the Potomac," placed ever so appropriately in the "Style" section of the Sunday *New York Times*, December 12, 1993, Section 9, p. 1.

9. English publishers buy far more books from the Americans than American publishers buy from the English. Ditto more or less every other country in the world. Japanese writers are emulating hot (cool) Americans writers like Jay McInerny, which compels them to incorporate McWorld into the fabric of their characters' nominally Japanese lives. Haruki Murakami's protagonists in *The Elephant Vanishes* smoke Marlboros and get high to Bruce Springsteen or Woody Allen while playing out story lines in high-tension rendezvouses at McDonald's—I mean the actual Honshu burger franchise, not just the metaphoric world it embodies. Murakami quotes American films like *The Wizard of Oz* as if they were pillow books of Japanese civilization on the doorstep of the twenty-first century.

10. Nadeshda Azhginkhina, "High Culture Meets Trash TV," *Bulletin of the Atomic Scientists*, January/February 1993, p. 42.

11. German Information Service, *The Week in Germany*, November 26, 1993.

12. Bagdikian tracks media monopoly but also follows an equally alarming development, "the subtle but profound impact of mass advertising on the form and content of the advertising-subsidized media." Ben H. Bagdikian, *The Media Monopoly*, fourth edition (Boston: Beacon Press, 1992), p. xxx.

13. Ibid., p. 4.

14. Ibid., pp. 21–22. The German firm Bertelsmann launched a $100 million joint venture with America Online in 1995.

15. Cited by Bernard Weinraub, "A Hollywood Recipe: Vision, Wealth, Ego," *The New York Times*, October 16, 1994, p. A 1.

16. Cited in M. Meyer and N. Hass, "Simon Says, 'Out!', Viacom Ousts Simon & Schuster's CEO," *Newsweek*, June 27, 1994, pp. 42–44.

17. Sarah Lyall, "The Media Business: Paramount Publishing to Cut Jobs and Books," *The New York Times*, January 24, 1994, p. D 8.

18. Bagdikian, *Media Monopoly*, p. 19.

19. Ibid.

20. Paramount did so well selling *Dancing with Wolves* through McDonald's that it did the same with *The Addams Family* and the *Wayne's World* series as well as *Ghost* and *Charlotte's Web*. McDonald's as a film outlet is a natural expression of its status as theme park. It's a two-way relationship: Amblin Entertainment sold commercial rights for *Jurassic Park* products to over one

hundred licensees including McDonald's. Bernard Weinraub, "Selling Jurassic Park," *The New York Times,* June 14, 1993, pp. C 11, 16. Movie critic Stuart Klawans notes the irony of the film itself, which features its own theme park and theme park store with Jurassic Park tie-in items identical to those being sold in the real world. Which world then is real? See Stuart Klawans, "Films," *The Nation,* July 19, 1993, p. 115–116.

21. 1992 *Report to Shareholders,* McDonald's Corporation, Oak Brook, Illinois. McDonald's 1992 U.S. sales were $13.2 billion; outside the United States it earned another $8.6 billion for a total of nearly $22 billion.

22. Its stock has more than doubled since 1991 and it projects earnings of nearly $9 billion in 1995, up from $7.1 million in 1992. *USA Today,* June 2, 1994, p. 3B.

23. Andrew E. Serwer, "McDonald's Conquers the World," *Fortune,* October 17, 1994, p. 104.

24. From the McDonald's Annual Report, 1992; ellipses in original.

25. The soft drink industry understands this as well as anyone: "Coke Light is trying to extend the American cultural model in its international markets," says Tom Pirko, a New York management consultant. "They're saying refreshment is a lifestyle thing and there may be kind of a reverse chic in this approach." Daniel Tilles, "Coke Light Gears Up for a Hard Sell," *The International Herald Tribune,* May 18, 1994. Randal W. Donaldson, an Atlanta Coca-Cola spokesman supporting the nationwide move to bring fast foods and soft beverages into schools, states bluntly: "Our strategy is ubiquity. We want to put soft drinks within arm's reach of desire." Robert Pear, "Senator, Promoting Student Nutrition, Battles Coca-Cola," *The New York Times,* April 26, 1994, p. A 20.

26. Prince Consort Albert, May 1, 1851, inaugural address, cited by Michael Sorkin, *Variations on a Theme Park* (New York: Noonday Press, 1992), p. 209.

27. Margaret Crawford, "The World in a Shopping Mall," in Sorkin, *Variations,* p. 4.

28. Ibid., p. 14.

29. As malls find their way to Eastern Europe and elsewhere, local investors insist with a mixture of self-interest and naïveté that what they are investing in is "American conditions without the American mentality." *The Week in Germany,* German Information Service, October 8, 1993, p. 5. The problem is, the conditions *are* the mentality. These developments have led a group of politicians, writers, artists, clergymen, and professors to form a "Committee for Fairness" that, according to its founding statement, opposes "the destruction of our industry and agriculture, mass unemployment, unbearable rent increases, unfairly low wages, the closing of social, scientific, cultural and athletic organizations, the selling of what was once 'peoples property,' rejection of our right to occupy apartments, houses and land and demoralization of people in the East, especially women, [that] have destroyed many hopes that were raised by German unification." Stephen Kinzer, "Group Is Formed to Defend East German Interests," *The New York Times,* July 12, 1992, p. A 1.

30. Cited and brilliantly analyzed in Edward W. Soja's "Inside Exopolis: Scenes from Orange County," in Sorkin, *Variations*, p. 94.

31. Linda Killian of the Renaissance Capital Corporation, quoted in Ann Imse, "Hang on for the Ride of Your Life," *The New York Times*, December 12, 1993, p. F 6.

32. William Booth, "Wayne's World," *The Washington Post*, National Weekly Edition, August 29–September 4, 1994.

33. From an article in *Der Spiegel*, summarized in *The Week in Germany*, German Information Center, November 5, 1993.

34. Coldwarland has already come to pass, according to a peculiar and droll story that came out of Russia at the end of 1993. Russian aerospace entrepreneurs, working with American counterparts, leapt out ahead of the Germans by putting into practice an idea even the inventors of Ossi Park might have found far-fetched. MIGS Etc., Inc. of Sarasota, Florida, ran ads in major print media with the offer: "Fly a MIG-29 at Mach 2.5 in Moscow . . . You Need Not Be a Pilot"! The company promotes what it might profitably advertise as Evil Empire nostalgia rides in MIG-29 fighter planes and T-80 tanks for prices approaching $100,000 (for a two-MIG dogfight). The *New York Times* not only ran the ads but published a tourism piece by someone who took a ride and editorialized on the concept, musing about whether Lenin, Stalin, John le Carré, and Tom Clancy must not be somewhere "shaking their heads in collective amazement." "Your Very Own Cold War," *The New York Times*, October 25, 1993, p. A 18.

35. Cited by Michael Sorkin, "See You in Disneyland," in his *Variations*, p. 206.

36. The Disney Annual Report, 1992, p. 14.

37. Ibid., p. 8.

38. In Florida, President Clinton delivers stirring words written by lyricist Tim Rice, the librettist for *Jesus Christ Superstar* and the Disney films *Aladdin* and *Beauty and the Beast*, the latter now a musical playing at Disney's Broadway theater in New York. Rice's script has Clinton propose that national happiness "still evolves from liberty, from property." See Jon Wiener's understandably cynical account in "Disneyworld Imagineers a President," *The Nation*, November 22, 1993, p. 620.

39. The description is Michael Wines's in "Yes, Virginia, the Past Can Be Plasticized," *The New York Times*, November 28, 1993, p. E 4. Wines's piece is less skeptical than his title, however; he cites James McPherson (Princeton University's civil war historian and Pulitzer Prize winner and avowed preservationist) as having "mixed feelings" and notes that places like Williamsburg (which in 1994 ran a highly controversial mock slave auction) have already established the precedent for Disney at Manassas.

CEO Eisner is certainly anxious not to be seen as ransacking history. In Florida, he hired Eric Foner, the DeWitt Clinton Professor of History at Columbia University and a prize-winning Civil War historian, as a packaging consultant. According to Jon Wiener's account in *The Nation*, Foner had complained about the editing and context of the speech delivered by the Lincoln robot at Disney's Anaheim Hall of Presidents, a speech that omitted any reference to slavery. Disney hired the critic. When Foner was finished, even a radical journalist had to acknowledge an "impressive" achievement: "In this park full of attractions that are calculatedly sentimental, sickeningly cute or crudely commercial, visitors to the redesigned Hall of Presidents will find a strikingly intelligent and remarkably progressive program." Jon Wiener, "Disneyworld Imagineers."

40. For an account of the sad struggle of Dexter King to build a $60 million hi-tech King amusement center in time for the Atlanta Summer Olympics in 1996, against the United States Park Service, which has to date overseen the King Historic District, see Ken Ringle, "A Dream Turned Nightmare," *The Washington Post*, National Weekly Edition, January 23–29, 1995, p. 9.

Chapter 9. Who Owns McWorld? The Media Merger Frenzy

1. Ben H. Bagdikian, *The Media Monopoly*, fourth edition (Boston: Beacon Press, 1992), p. 19.

2. Bagdikian's top twenty-three, listed alphabetically, are Bertelsmann, Capital Cities/ABC, Cox, CBS, Buena Vista Films, Dow Jones, Gannett, General Electric/NBC, Paramount (now Viacom), Harcourt Brace Jovanovich, Hearst, Ingersoll, International Thomson, Knight Ridder, Media News Group, Newhouse, News Corporation Ltd. (Murdoch), New York Times, Reader's Digest, Scripps-Howard, Time Warner, Times Mirror, and the Tribune Company. Ibid., pp. 21–22.

3. Jolie Soloman, "Hollywood and Vice: Here Comes a New Golden Age," *Newsweek*, August 23, 1993, p. 51.

4. Quoted by Cindy Skrzyki in her appropriately entitled piece, "Today, AT&T; Tomorrow, the Wireless World," *The Washington Post*, National Weekly Edition, August 30–September 5, 1993. Skrzyki comments: "It will make it possible for customers to stroll into an AT&T Phone Store and order everything from a cellular phone (which AT&T makes) to cellular service (which McCaw offers) to long-distance calling (over the AT&T network). On the technical side, AT&T switches may handle the call and AT&T software will tell the network which calls to send, hold, or put into a messaging system. And the slice of radio spectrum that AT&T would acquire as part of the deal gives it a precious commodity that is vital to launching new wireless devices that send and receive voice and data signals over the air."

5. Quoted by Ken Auletta, "The Last Studio in Play," *The New Yorker*, October 4, 1993, p. 80.

6. Calvin Sims, "Synergy: The Unspoken Word," *The New York Times*, October 5, 1993, p. D 1.

7. Ted Turner is chairman of the board and president of Turner Broadcasting, TNT, etc.; Sumner Redstone is CEO of Viacom and the feisty competitor for Paramount; for Barry Diller see text; Martin S. Davis is former president and CEO of Paramount; Michael Ovitz is chairman of the Creative Artists Agency and a key player in the MGM–Crédit Lyonnais deal;

Bill Gates is the power behind Microsoft; and John C. Malone is president of Tele-Communication, part-time chair of Liberty Media, as well as a one-quarter owner of Turner Broadcasting, which makes him a major force beyond Barry Diller's QVC Network.

For a biography of one of the great masters of communications and entertainment who set the course for many of the men here, see Connie Bruck, *Master of the Game: Steve Ross and the Creation of Time Warner* (New York: Simon & Schuster, 1994).

8. *Fortune* says Malone is now worth over a billion dollars. His sobriquet as king of cable is reported by Allen R. Myerson, "A Corporate Man and a Cable King," *The New York Times*, October 14, 1993, p. C 7.

9. The declaration is offered as an appendix in Kenichi Ohmae, *The Borderless World: Power and Strategy in the Interlinked Economy* (New York: Harper Business, 1990).

10. Cited by Ken Auletta, "Under the Wire," *The New Yorker*, January 17, 1994, p. 52. Gore genuinely believes in the role of government as a regulator and equalizer, but after the elections of November 1994, there is little to suggest he will get much support in Congress or the nation.

PART II. THE OLD WORLD OF JIHAD

Chapter 10. Jihad vs. McWorld or Jihad via McWorld?

1. See David Gonzalez, "The Computer Age Bids Religious World to Enter," *The New York Times*, July 24, 1994, Section 1, p. 1.

2. See Allan Bloom, *The Closing of the American Mind* (New York: Simon & Schuster, 1987). I have explored the ironies of Bloom's complaint elsewhere in *An Aristocracy of Everyone: The Politics of Education and the Future of America* (New York: Ballantine Books, 1993), Chapter 5.

3. The Rudolphs suggest that "Clinton and others too easily invoke 'ancient hatreds' to explain what are really contemporary conflicts. The question, in other words, is not why old conflicts are flaring up anew, but rather why traditionally harmonious mosaics have been shattered." Susanne H. Rudolph and Lloyd I. Rudolph, "Modern Hate: How Ancient Animosities Get Invented," *The New Republic*, March 22, 1993, p. 25.

4. Benedict Anderson, *Imagined Communities: Reflections on the Origins and Spread of Nationalism* (London: Verso, 1991).

5. Walter Russell Mead in a review of William Pfaff's *The Wrath of Nations* (New York: Simon & Schuster, 1993), *The New York Times Book Review*, November 7, 1993, p. 25.

6. Observers like Liah Greenfeld try to elicit some consensus by persuading us that nationalism is a question of phenomenology: simply everything and anything people we call nationalists say and do. Her broad characterization permits nationalism to encompass multiple "roads" to modernity,

certainly all of those alluded to above, new and old alike. Normative philosophers like Yael Tamir take a narrower "essentialist" view, insisting that we must first define the idea theoretically and then limit actual cases to those that conform to the normative concept. For her, "liberal nationalism" and "ethnic nationalism" are not two species of an underlying genus but rival understandings, only one of which can be tenable. Yael Tamir, *Liberal Nationalism* (Princeton: Princeton University Press, 1993); Liah Greenfeld, *Nationalism: Five Roads to Modernity* (Cambridge: Cambridge University Press, 1992). Even Greenfeld ultimately chooses to see nationalism as a forge of modernity and to this degree narrows her definition to exclude wholly reactionary visions of nationalism.

7. In his chapter on "Nationality" in *On Representative Government*. Rousseau's most eloquent argument on behalf of nationalism as a condition for republicanism comes in his essay *Considerations on the Government of Poland*, written in 1771. See *The Government of Poland*, edited by W. Kendall, (New York: Bobbs-Merrill Company, 1972).

8. G. Mazzini, *The Duties of Man and Other Essays*, chapter III (London: Dent, 1917), cited in S. Baron, *Modern Nationalism and Religion* (New York: Meridian Books, 1960), p. 49. For a full account of Mazzini's extraordinary role as a liberal revolutionary nationalist see Dennis Mack Smith, *Mazzini* (New Haven: Yale University Press, 1994).

   Anthony Smith is a neo-Mazzinian who believes there is no "alternative to the myth and ideal of nationalism as a cement and vision for large groupings of human beings, one which is both ideologically acceptable and sociologically feasible," precisely because nations alone "can ground the inter-state order in the principles of popular sovereignty and the will of the people." Anthony Smith, "Ties That Bind," *The LSE Magazine*, Spring, 1993, pp. 8–11.

9. Paul Hazard, *European Thought in the Eighteenth Century* (Gloucester: Peter Smith, 1972), pp. 471–472.

10. Eric Hobsbawm, *Nations and Nationalism Since 1780* (Cambridge: Cambridge University Press, 1992), p. 121. With the transformation, ethnicity and language became the decisive hallmarks of the new nationalism.

11. José Ortega y Gasset, *The Revolt of the Masses* (New York: W. W. Norton & Co., 1932), p. 83. Ortega hoped that the nationalist outburst of the twenties might signal its final passing: "The last flare, the longest; the last sigh, the deepest. On the very eve of their disappearance there is an intensification of frontiers." We might hope the same today, were not Ortega's hopes so dismally contradicted by subsequent history.

12. Yael Tamir, *Liberal Nationalism*, pp. 6, 14.

13. Edmund Burke, *The Works*, London, 1907, VI, p. 155.

14. Anderson, *Imagined Communities*, p. 7.

15. Joel Kotkin, *Tribes: How Race, Religion, and Identity Determine Success in the New Global Economy* (New York: Random House, 1993). "As the conventional barriers of nation-states and regions become less meaningful

under the weight of global economic forces, it is likely such dispersed peoples [as Jews, Chinese, Indians, etc.]—and their worldwide business and cultural networks—will increasingly shape the economic destiny of mankind." p. 4.

16. Eric Hobsbawm, "The New Threat to History," a lecture to the new Central European University in Budapest, reprinted in *The New York Review of Books*, December 16, 1993, pp. 62–63.

17. Tony Judt, "The Old New Nationalism," *The New York Review of Books*, May 26, 1994, p. 45.

18. Adam Michnik in " 'More Humility, Fewer Illusions'—A Talk Between Adam Michnik and Jurgen Habermas," *The New York Review of Books*, March 24, 1994, pp. 24–29.

19. Marshall Berman used Marx's phrase as the title to a perceptive book about the condition (and pathology) of urban America. See *All That Is Solid Melts into Air* (New York: Viking Penguin, 1988).

20. "Winter in the F.R.G.," by the German band *Endstufe* (Final Stage), translated by Elizabeth A. Jackson for the London magazine *Searchlight;* reprinted in Stephen Silver, "The Music of Hate," *The New York Times*, February 8, 1993, p. A 23.

21. See Silver, "The Music of Hate," ibid.

22. At least two bands, Stoerkraft and Böse Onkelz (Destructive Force and Evil Uncle) have abandoned the Right: see Stephen Kinzer, "Berlin Journal," *The New York Times*, February 2, 1994, p. A 4. See Chapter 11, note 21, below.

23. The new realities nationalism is meant to address are not, however, really very well-suited to it. John Lukacs, for example, sees in nationalism "the main political force in the twentieth century." John Lukacs, *The End of the Twentieth Century and the End of the Modern Age* (New York: Ticknor and Fields, 1993), p. 8.

24. Michael Ignatieff, *Blood and Belonging: Journeys into the New Nationalism* (New York: Farrar, Straus & Giroux), p. 5.

25. Feudalism had both an imperial and cosmopolitan moment, defined by the Holy Roman Church and the pan-German Empire and at the same time had a local and parochial moment manifested in, for example, France's prenational provinces such as Burgundy and Provence or England's prenational counties such as Essex and Dorset.

26. Under the nominal suzerainty of distant emperors, Burgandians, Normans, Ouic northerners and Oc Franconian southerners had gone their parochial ways. Jeanne D'Arc strove to unite them through blood and battle in a "France" created from fratricide. This at least is how modern atavists like George Bernard Shaw tell the story in fictional re-creations like *Saint Joan*, where the maid of Orleans appears as both a nationalist and a Protestant. In England's War of the Roses, chronicled dramatically by Shakespeare, from the corpses of feuding Dorsetmen and Lancastermen rose a new nation of Englishmen, whose clannish loyalties were replaced with the elementary obedience of subject to crown.

27. The French historian Renan wrote: "Or, l'essence d'une nation est que tous les individus aient beaucoup de choses en commun et aussi que tous assent oublie des choses." Cited, Anderson, *Imagined Communities*, p. 199.

28. The after effects of population dispersals and Russian colonization are dirtying the transition of the Baltic states to independence and democracy today. Responding to Russian colonization under communism, which had left Latvians nearly a minority in their own country and Lithuanians and Estonians with large minority Russian populations, the Baltic countries have today imposed monocultural citizenship laws that amount to a kind of constitutional ethnic cleansing that may force the Russians out.

29. For this reason, I will not try here to reproduce the graphic studies of fratricide and civil war that have been recently offered by Eric Hobsbawm, Michael Ignatieff, Daniel Patrick Moynihan, John Lukacs, William Pfaff, and Walter Connor along with many other fine historians and social scientists. In addition to the titles already given above in the notes, see Walter Connor, *Ethnonationalism: The Quest for Understanding* (Princeton: Princeton University Press, 1994) and Pfaff, *Wrath of Nations*.

 Nor do I want to reproduce the kind of detailed everyday pictures of life in the ex-Soviet world and Eastern Europe we have come to expect from discerning journalists like Timothy Garton Ash in his series for *The New York Review of Books* and Georgie Anne Geyer in her columns for the *Washington Times* and *The Wall Street Journal*. Geyer was an early and keen observer of the coming of Jihad: a decade before Daniel Patrick Moynihan and Zbigniew Brzezinski were worrying about planetary pandaemonium, Geyer had written a prescient essay called "Our Disintegrating World: the Menace of Global Anarchy," *Encyclopedia Britannica Book of the Year 1985* (Chicago: University of Chicago Press, 1985), pp. 11–25.

Chapter 11. Jihad Within McWorld: The "Democracies"

1. J. J. Rousseau, *Politics and the Arts: Letter to M. D'Alembert on the Theater* (originally published in 1758), Allan Bloom, editor, (Ithaca, N.Y.: Cornell University Press, 1960), p. 58.

2. Michael Ignatieff, *Blood and Belonging: Journeys into the New Nationalism* (New York: Farrar, Straus & Giroux), p. 5.

3. French Minister of Culture Jacques Toubon worries about "tribal" tendencies in language, with executives speaking English, immigrants speaking their own languages, ordinary people speaking "the language of television," and "in the middle the language of administration . . . and perhaps of intellectuals and professors"—all of which would result in a "catastrophe." *The Latest European News*, published by United Airlines, November 29, 1994.

4. According to Alan Riding, "Celts and Proud of It (Even if They Are French)," *The New York Times*, August 2, 1991, p. A 4.

5. Of the 2.8 million who inhabit the peninsular fragment jutting out into the Atlantic, there are perhaps 100,000 involved in the local folk movement.

Once the target of Nazis who promised them independence if they would ally themselves with the Germans, the Celts of Brittany actually forged a Brittany Liberation Front and talked revolution in 1968. Today, more intellectuals than peasants actually speak Breton, although there is a "seed" school (a "Diwan") with one thousand children enrolled, and leaders encourage local playwrights to compose Breton plays and urge academics to plan Breton dictionaries.

6. The bureau was founded in 1982 and in 1993 had a $4.2 million budget. Marlise Simons, "A Reborn Provençal Heralds Revival of Regional Tongues," *The New York Times*, May 3, 1993, pp. A 1, 8. The "conceit" here is not the importance of cultural identity, but the belief that a handful of intellectuals can revivify languages that have no practical use in schools, commerce, or the home.

7. See André Frossard, "L'Europe: une nouvelle tour de babel," Document, *Paris Match*, 1993/4.

8. The Swiss offer a particularly interesting case of multiculturalism in which the French Swiss identify with the progressive interests of France and Europe while the German Swiss (those in the country, not the Zurich bankers and Basel corporation executives) see themselves as true Swiss (not ersatz Germans) hostile to Europe and the McWorld it represents. I have written at length about the Swiss case in *The Death of Communal Liberty: the History of Freedom in a Swiss Mountain Canton* (Princeton: Princeton University Press, 1974). See also the excellent compendium on Switzerland in Europe, *Can the Confederatio Helvetica Be Imitated?* Special issue of *Government and Opposition*, Vol. 23, No. 1, Winter, 1988.

9. The 1994 version of the advertisement, paid for by the Generalitat de Catalunya, offers a blank page and a point identified as Barcelona on it: "In which country would you place this point?" it mischievously asks. Several pages later comes the answer: Catalonia is "a country in Spain with its own culture, language and identity . . . a country in which many foreign enterprises have invested and are still heavily investing . . . a country with the know-how to get the Olympic Games for its capital." An early advertisement appeared in *The New York Times*, July 17, 1992, pp. A 5, 7. The new campaign started in the spring of 1994 with an April 25 *Newsweek* advertisement. The ambivalence toward McWorld is expressed in the simultaneous focus on Catalonian separatism and the Catalonian cultural heritage *and* on Catalonia's capitalist and commercial virtues and its role as a European economic center; Barcelona's patron saint Sant Jordi and Catalan heroes like Dalí, Miró, and Casals somehow get mixed in a description of Catalan multinational corporations. The same ambivalence appears in another version of the advertisement, which begins with the headline: CATALONIA, A MODERN COUNTRY WITH CENTURIES OF TRADITION.

10. Commentators have suggested King Juan Carlos may have bested Pujol in the short run by charming the crowds with his deferential Catalan and his good manners, and by making Pujol's attempt to seize the Olympics look

clumsy and fanatic; but his performance was in effect orchestrated by the Catalan nationalists to whom he was responding and they are surely the real long-term victors.

11. Alan Riding, "The Olympics Crown a King with Laurels," *The New York Times*, August 12, 1992, p. A 5. The special privileges Pujol gained for Catalonia are now being sought by ethnic nationalists from other regions of Spain.

12. As paraphrased by Marlise Simons, "A Reborn Provençal," pp. A 1, 8.

13. The measure passed by a nearly 80 percent margin in Geneva and Neuchâtel and failed by nearly the same margin in the founding German Swiss cantons of Schwyz and Uri (approximately 75 percent).

14. "Switzerland and Europe: Time to Join the Others?" *The Economist*, November 28, 1992, p. 52. The insufficiently docile masses, perched imperturbably on their European Himalayas, managed on December 6, 1992, to once again ignore their elites. Though only a bare popular majority of 50.3 percent had said no, eighteen of twenty-six cantons had stood firmly against while only eight (all francophone) had voted yes (fourteen were needed for passage).

15. For example, see "La vieille tradition du chemin solitaire" (the old tradition of the solitary road), in the Left daily *Libération*, December 7, 1992, as well as the accompanying editorial by Gerard Dupuy, "Un Nouveau Coup Contre L'Europe" (a new blow against Europe). Dupuy wrote: " 'L'exception' suisse, sa fonction de soupape, n'a plus grand sens dans un monde en voie d'homogèneisation, en particuliere dans sa partie européenne."

16. The ban lasted only a few years, and was supported for more cynical reasons by the local railway company, but the language used to justify the ban was remarkably prescient in its predictions of economic encroachment and environmental ruin. For the details, see Barber, *The Death of Communal Liberty*.

17. On Quebec, see Michael Ignatieff, *Blood and Belonging.* Because he is Canadian by birth, his treatment of Quebec is perhaps the most convincing section of his book.

18. Joel Kotkin captures some of the ambivalence of diaspora peoples by using the term *tribe* to refer to transnational peoples operating on the new economic frontier of trade and commerce—i.e., Indians, Chinese, and Jews but also (rather oddly) Brits and Americans too. See Kotkin, *Tribes: How Race, Religion, and Identity Determine Success in the New Global Economy* (New York: Random House, 1993).

19. An Amendment to the Canadian Constitution guarantees the equality of English and French in New Brunswick, but it is a result of attempts to mollify the Quebecois. See Clyde Farnsworth, "Acadians Cling to Their Culture, and to Canada," *The New York Times*, July 5, 1994, p. A 4.

20. Perhaps it is not so surprising that some of the same weary people who reviled the Communist symbols that dominated Communist East Berlin's Karl Marx Platz should now revile the commercial symbols that dominate it (renamed Augustus Platz) today. Where the "imperialist" hammer and

sickle once flew now sits the glitzy "imperialist" logo of Mercedes-Benz—much as, in today's Budapest, the "Gold Star" logo of the South Korean electronics giant has been plastered across what was previously the apartment of Marxist theoretician George Lukacs.

21. The band Radikahl's song "Swastika." There is a powerful paradox in the use of modernity's commercial medium, rock music, by the enemies of modernity, who wear T-shirts bearing the logo: "Hitler: The European Tour."

    There has been slippage, however, and bands like Stoerkraft and Böse Onkelz have moved away from the Right. Ingo Hasselbach, a founding member and vice chairman of the outlawed National Alternative recently published a book called *The Reckoning: A Neo-Nazi Drops Out* (*Die Abrechnung: Eine Neonazi Steigt Aus*) (Berlin: Aufbau Verlag, 1994) that suggests the posturing of at least some neo-Nazis is born of economic frustration rather than deep ideological convictions.

22. The band Final Stage's "Winter in the F.R.G." asks "Will there ever be a Germany again worth living in?" (see above). Schoenhuber eschews such neo-Nazi crudities in favor of such polite one-liners as: "Me, I love the Turks, but it is when they are in Turkey I love them the most." Rather than celebrate Hitler, he speaks of the great fascist party that Hitler "betrayed." Philippe Boulet-Gercourt, "Franz Schoenhuber: un SS trés frequentable," *Le Nouvel Observateur/Monde*, April 16–22, 1992, p. 66 my translation.

23. Between July 1991 and July 1992, East German manufacturing jobs were almost halved (45.6 percent) as compared with a reduction of 2.5 percent in comparable jobs in West Germany. *The Week in Germany*, September 25, 1992. In 1991, Treuhandanstalt (the West German privatization agency) facilitated the sale of ten East German newspapers to West German publishers. *The Week in Germany*, April 19, 1991.

24. Ignatieff notes the tendency of German skinheads to borrow from the British, though he indulges in both exaggeration and a certain Canadian animus against England in quipping that: "Skin culture may just be Britain's most enduring contribution to Germany and the new Europe." Ignatieff, *Blood and Belonging*, p. 83. For Nazis on-line, see Jon Wiener, "Free Speech on the Internet," *The Nation*, June 13, 1994, pp. 825–828.

25. For an account from a critical perspective, see Norman Birnbaum's two-part essay, "How New the New Germany?" Part I, *Salmagundi*, Nos. 88–89, Fall 1990/Winter 1991, pp. 234–263; Part II, *Salmagundi*, Nos. 90–91, Spring/Summer 1991, pp. 131–178, 292–296. Also, Peter Rossman, "Dashed Hopes for a New Socialism," *The Nation*, May 7, 1990, pp. 632–635.

26. These victories occurred despite a united opposition joined by all other parties. The Democratic Socialists have a faction called "Communist Platform," which remains Marxist-Leninist, but for the most part the party depends on East German local loyalty, the politics of personality, and a party philosophy that states: "Our goal is not the revolutionary overthrow of the democratic parliamentary order and the building of some kind of dictatorship, but rather the true democratization of Germany." The party leader, Gregor

Gysi, plays directly on East German resentments: "I accept the political freedom, the legal order and the democratic possibilities that this system offers. But I also maintain that people in eastern Germany have lost important rights, and that in this society there is much social injustice and much that needs to be fundamentally changed. We are not facing the global, social, ecological and cultural challenges that confront us. So for me there are still very good reasons to be anti-capitalist." Stephen Kinzer, "In Germany, Communists Resurgent," *The New York Times*, June 29, 1994, p. A 6.

27. Next to workers from Greece, Italy, Turkey, and North Africa, are newer immigrants from Vietnam and India along with a burgeoning crowd of political refugees from Eastern Europe who make good use of Germany's liberal asylum laws.

28. Frankfurt, for example, is nearly a third foreign, and has over 140 nationalities, making it a rival of Los Angeles and New York as a center of multiculturalism. Germany's other irony is that, like Israel, it has enacted a legal right of return for all ethnic Germans. Thus, in addition to the millions of East Germans, it has dealt with 100,000 ethnic Germans from the East. To West Germans, many of these returnees, and poor East Germans as well, are seen as "foreigners." Naturally, the returnees resent the "real" Turkish and Greek "foreigners" just as much as they themselves are resented by the West Germans. Ignatieff tells the revealingly ironic story of the newly arrived ethnic German immigrant from Russia. "I thought I was coming to Germany, instead, it's Turkey," she says—in perfect Russian since she herself speaks no German (while many Turks, second and third generation, speak perfect German)! Ignatieff, *Blood and Belonging*.

29. According to the Federal Office for Protection of the Constitution. Ferdinand Protzman, "German Attacks Rise as Foreigners Become Scapegoats," *The New York Times*, November 2, 1992, p. A 1.

30. Ibid.

31. In 1991, for example, there were about 44,000 marriages between a German and a foreigner (not quite 10 percent of the total number of marriages), including 3,500 between Turkish men and German women and 880 between German men and Turkish women. *The Week in Germany*, January 29, 1994.

32. *Der Spiegel*, October 26, 1992.

33. "The nightmare of the new Germany is that its teenage gangs talk politics," writes Ignatieff, *Blood and Belonging*, p. 84.

34. The antiforeign climate "contradicts the Olympic spirit, since in the Olympic village everyone is a 'foreigner,' " worries a key player in Stephen Kinzer, "German Violence Worries Investors," *The New York Times*, January 1, 1993, p. A 3.

Chapter 12. China and the Not Necessarily Democratic Pacific Rim

1. Milton Friedman in *Capitalism and Freedom* (Chicago: University of Chicago Press, 1982) or Jeffrey Sachs in *Poland's Jump to the Market Economy*, based on

the Lionel Robbins Memorial lectures delivered at the school of economics, January 1991 (Cambridge: MIT Press, 1993).

2. Cited by Nicholas D. Kristof, "China Sees 'Market-Leninism' a Way to Future," *The New York Times*, September 6, 1991, p. 1. Also see Kristof and Sheryl WuDunn, *China Wakes: The Struggle for the Soul of a Rising Power* (New York: Times Books, 1994) for a pointed if at times overly harsh and cynical treatment of China today.

3. On the economic "miracle" in the "awakening dragon" of China, see William H. Overholt, *The Rise of China: How Economic Reform Is Creating a New Superpower* (New York: Norton, 1994). Overholt is among those who actually think authoritarianism in China, as in Taiwan and Singapore, is good for economic development since it frees the government from the need to kowtow to public opinion or interest groups. Overholt reports that "China's Guangdong Province has become second only to the United States as a market for Procter & Gamble shampoos" and is Motorola's "No. 2 market in the world for second generation cordless phones." A similarly naïve enthusiasm is found in many journalists; see for example Joe Klein's "Why China Does It Better," *Newsweek*, April 12, 1993, p. 23.

4. Perry Link, "The Old Man's New China," *The New York Review of Books*, June 9, 1994, p. 31–36.

5. Remarkable proof of the impotence of sovereign states in the face of McWorld's markets is offered by Link, who writes: "It is reliably reported that representatives of ten major US corporations, in a meeting with Chinese economic czar Zhu Rongji in Beijing early this year, actually urged Zhu to take a tough line with Clinton on MFN." Official American policy falls not to Chinese obstinacy but to unofficial American corporate meddling. Link, "Old Man's New China," p. 34.

6. Cited by Nicholas D. Kristof, "Chinese Communism's Secret Aim: Capitalism," *The New York Times*, October 19, 1992, p. A 6.

7. The Chinese economic miracle, with a growth rate over 18 percent, is increasing social inequalities and income maldistribution: a meal served to a table of friends at a fancy restaurant can cost ten times the annual wage of most workers.

8. Nicholas D. Kristof, "China Sees 'Market-Leninism' a Way to Future," *The New York Times*, September 6, 1991, p. 1.

9. The difficult position of artists in post-1989 China is described, and artwork displayed, by Andrew Solomon, "Their Irony, Humor (and Art) Can Save China," *The New York Times Magazine*, December 19, 1993, pp. 42–51.

10. Cited by Suzy Menkes, "Yuppie Shanghai Shows an Old Flair," *International Herald Tribune*, May 25, 1993.

11. Cited by Jianying Zha, "China Goes Pop: Mao Meets Muzak," *The Nation*, March 21, 1994, pp. 373–376.

12. Nicholas D. Kristof, "Satellites Bring Information Revolution to China," *The New York Times*, April 11, 1993, pp. 1, 12.

13. Ibid. By the same token, the failure to acquire the 2000 Olympic games was an economic disaster for the Beijing region that would have profited economically, and a blow to China's global image; but for officials worrying about insidious outside influences, it may have represented an inadvertent victory.

14. Dave Lindorff, "China's Economic Miracle Runs Out," *The Nation*, May 30, 1994, pp. 742–744.

15. Kristof, "China Sees 'Market-Leninism' a Way to Future," *The New York Times*, September 6, 1991, p. 1.

16. Sheryl WuDunn, "Clan Feuds," *The New York Times*, January 17, 1993, p. A 10.

17. It has responded to both provocations with a heavy-handed and brutal use of force—over sixty thousand are estimated to have been killed, including Sri Lanka's president, who was assassinated by a terrorist on May Day 1993; in 1987, India was dragged into the Tamil conflict, sending over fifty thousand troops into northern Sri Lanka to enforce its own solution. The troops went home empty-handed, and for his trouble, Indian ex–Prime Minister Rajiv Gandhi was assassinated by Tamil terrorists in 1991. In 1993 some progress was made toward resolving the dual Jihad of Tamils and extremist Sinhalese (see Edward A. Gargan, "Sri Lanka Is Choking Off Long Ethnic Revolt," *The New York Times*, March 20, 1993, p. 1). Yet most observers believe Sri Lanka's multiculturalism may yet destroy it; see William McGowan, *Only Man Is Vile: The Tragedy of Sri Lanka* (New York: Farrar, Straus & Giroux, 1993).

18. Indonesia is 85 percent Muslim, but 10 percent of the population are Christian, the rest falling into small Hindu, Buddhist, and animist minorities. Military intervention has been episodic and Suharto would like to convince his trading partners that his is a disciplinarian regime no worse, say, than Singapore's or Taiwan's. But repression is unceasing: most recently, three very influential magazines, including its best known newsmagazine *Tempo* (founded in 1971), were closed down without warning.

19. James Fallows, *Looking at the Sun: The Rise of the New East Asian Economic and Political System* (New York: Pantheon, 1994). Fallows is unpersuaded that the economic slump of 1994 is anything other than a small bump in Japan's road, and contests those like Bill Emmott (*Japanophobia: The Myth of the Invincible Japanese*, New York: Times Books, 1994) who think Japan is a country like any other (which in my terms would make it a better candidate for McWorld).

20. Karl Taro Greenfeld, *Speed Tribes: Days and Nights with Japan's Next Generation* (New York: HarperCollins, 1994). There are, Greenfeld reminds us, 25 million Japanese between the ages of fifteen and thirty. They are "the children of the industrialists, executives and laborers who built Japan Inc." and they are "as accustomed to hamburgers as to rice balls and are often more adept at folding a bundle of cocaine or heroin than creasing an origami crane."

21. Neil Strauss, "In Performance," *The New York Times*, July 23, 1994, Section 1, p. 12.

22. The most innocuous changes can signal the deepest challenges: for example, in 1994 economic pressures mounted to introduce Western-style self-service gas pumping at Japan's sixty thousand gas stations. In the ensuing controversy focusing on safety and jobs, culture was hardly mentioned. Yet while self-service may be economically efficient, it problematizes the cultural ideal of full employment (see Part III) and the traditional Japanese concern for courtesy and service. The campaign to maintain full-service pumps is hardly likely to inspire a cultural Jihad, but perhaps it ought to. For a discussion, see Andrew Pollack, "Japan's Radical Plan: Self-Service Gas," *The New York Times*, July 14, 1994, p. D 1.

23. The quote is from Kina's American producer Ry Cooder, cited by Neil Strauss in a fascinating account of the career of Shoukichi Kina, who played New York in the summer of 1994 and has made the new Okinawan hybrid a popular international sound. Cooder, who is also Kina's lead guitarist on one of his albums, says, "Kina hybridized the Okinawan folk style and the folk instruments into this sort of pop or garage band setting, like everyone does in the modern era." See Neil Strauss, "Okinawa Gives Its Flavor to Rock," *The New York Times*, July 16, 1994, p. 11.

Chapter 13. Jihad Within McWorld: "Transitional Democracies"

1. Cited by John Kifner, "The World through the Serbian Mind's Eye," in the Week in Review, *The New York Times*, April 10, 1994, Section 4, p. 1.

2. Vladimir Goati as cited in ibid.

3. Domljan cited by Milton Viorst, "The Yugoslav Idea," *The New Yorker*, March 18, 1991, pp. 58–79. "Whirlwind" citation from "A Whirlwind of Hatreds: How the Balkans Broke Up," *The New York Times*, February 14, 1993, p. E 5.

4. In the summer of 1994, Russia's largest investment company witnessed the collapse of its stock from a high of $50 a share to less than 50 cents. The so-called MMM fund was in fact "built on sand," having "reported no earnings, revealed no investments, explained no financial strategy." Its soaring share prices resulted from the sale of more and more shares, new buyers in effect providing profits for old buyers in the classic pyramid scheme strategy. The company blamed the government both for interfering and for not regulating, while the millions of Russian shareholders blamed mainly the government. See Michael Specter, "10,000 Stampede as Russian Stock Collapses," *The New York Times*, July 30, 1994, p. A 1.

5. According to Alexander Paskhaver of The Center for Economic Reform in Kiev; cited by Misha Glenny, "Ukraine's Great Divide," *The New York Times*, July 14, 1994, p. A 23.

6. Nikolai Zlobin, "Mafiacracy Takes Over," *The New York Times*, July 26, 1994, p. A 19. As surprising as the essay is *The New York Times*'s willingness to give it prominent Op Ed attention.

7. On the forty-fifth anniversary (1991) of his execution as a war criminal, Marshal Ion Antonescu, who had joined Hitler's invasion of the Soviet Union in World War II and was responsible for the death of 250,000 Jews, was honored by the new Romanian parliament. The legislative honors were unanimous and Prime Minister Iliescu, though he had expressed disapproval earlier, remained silent.

8. Celestine Bohlen, "Zhirinovsky Cult Grows," *The New York Times*, April 5, 1994, p. A 1, 12. Zhirinovsky speeches have been collected and annotated in Graham Frazer and George Lancelle, *Absolute Zhirinovsky: A Transparent View of the Distinguished Russian Statesman* (New York: Penguin Books, 1994).

9. Within a year of the collapse of communism, "GNP in every East European country has declined.... [I]ndustrial output fell 10% in Hungary, 28% in Romania, 30% in Bulgaria" and in every case ethnic tensions had augmented the impact of economic problems. Serge Schmemann, "For Eastern Europe, Now a New Disillusion," *The New York Times*, November 9, 1990, p. A 1, 10.

10. In addition to ferocious nationalist sentiments within Hungary, which often takes the form of Jew bashing, the Hungarians are making a cause of the millions who live outside of Hungary in Serbia, Romania (7 percent of the population), and Slovakia (11 percent)—outside of the Russians living beyond Russian borders, one of the largest minority groups in Europe. The cause of "greater Hungary" has become the rallying cry of internal zealots like Csurka who are calling (using the literal translation of the German term "lebensraum") for Hungarian living space. See, for example, Stephen Engelberg, "Now Hungary Adds Its Voice to the Ethnic Tumult," *The New York Times*, January 25, 1993, p. A 3. Istvan Csurka was in the Hungarian Democratic Forum (Hungary's ruling party under Joseph Antall until the 1994 elections), and led Antall's antipress campaign. Though once a friend of the dissidents, he has become distanced even from the conservatives. His media appointees did a great deal of damage, however. He's known as "an idiot, and no one has ever taken him seriously." Milos Vamos, "Hungary's Media Apparatchiks," *The Nation*, December 13, 1993, p. 725.

11. So loyal that in 1989, when tribalism first peered out from the ruins of the Stalinist empire, nearly every observer thought that the army's disciplined troops would contain its reawakened appetites inside of Yugoslavia itself.

12. Just a few years ago, the Serbian slavophile, Vasily Belov, captured the sense of historical resentment perfectly: "The so-called UN sanctions in Yugoslavia—these are sanctions of the Vatican and a Germany united by Gorbachev." Serge Schmemann, "From Russia to Serbia," *The New York Times*, January 31, 1993, p. E 18.

Popular Serb actor Nikolai Burlyaev wrote not too long ago in the Belgrade daily *Den*: "Today Serbia is alone. The whole world seems to have ganged up on it. The current Russian Government has betrayed it. It betrayed a people of the same blood and faith as the Orthodox Russian nation, it betrayed its own—Slavs, so similar to Russians . . ." Schmemann, ibid. Russia did finally give up on its Serbian friends after the Bosnian Serb legislature rejected a major power compromise that would have left the Serbs with much of the territory it conquered in Bosnia. Yeltsin had his own sentiments about the treason of the Serbs against its sponsors in Moscow.

13. Misha Glenny, "Ukraine's Great Divide," *The New York Times*, Op-Ed, July 14, 1994, p. A 23.

14. Russia has offered to cancel over $2.5 billion in debt. Meanwhile, the West voted to give $4 billion in aid (including $200 million to shut down and clean up Chernobyl). Unfortunately for Kravchuk, the vote came the day before he was ousted from office, and it is his successor Kuchman who will reap the political rewards of the prize.

15. Cited by Misha Glenny, ibid.

16. Steve Erlanger, "Ukraine Questions Price Tag of Independence," *The New York Times*, September 8, 1993, p. A 8.

17. In another of those special advertising supplements designed to seduce Western capitalists untutored in the history of Middle Europe to sink millions of dollars into the region; see "Romania: Rebuilding the Nation," 1994.

18. The accord was engineered in the spring of 1992 by a team from Princeton's Project on Ethnic Relations, following decades of repression under Communist dictator Ceauşescu. Hungary reciprocates the bloody sentiments, still calling the 1920 Treaty of Trianon that tore the Transylvanian Carpathians with its 600,000 Hungarians from it "bloody Trianon" and toying with scenarios that return the region to its sovereignty. Caryl Churchill's documentary play *Mad Forest* captures many of the tensions in Romania just before the fall of Ceauşescu, but it mostly overlooks ethnic rivalry and antigypsy bigotry.

19. Toby F. Sonneman, "Old Hatreds and the New Europe: Roma after the Revolutions," *Tikkun*, Vol. 7, No. 1, January 1992, pp. 49–52.

20. Gypsies arrived from India in the thirteenth century dispersing in two diaspora, the first in the Balkans, Moldavia, and Wallachia (Romania today) where from the fourteenth to the nineteenth century they were enslaved; the other dispersed as wanderers throughout Europe. Their Indian-based caste system kept them wholly insulated from their host countries, which in Germany, Finland, and Great Britain actually made it a capital offense to be *born* a gypsy. Nazi pogroms destroyed 70 to 80 percent of all gypsies, somewhere between a half million and a million (there was no gypsy census against which to measure the genocide).

21. Antonescu was a syphilitic cavalry officer who ousted despotic King Carol II in 1940 dubbing himself "conductor," and modeling himself after "Der Führer." Antonescu was seen as a national savior and some associate his name with that of Iliescu's party, the National Salvation Front.

22. For details see Robert D. Kaplan, "Bloody Romania," *The New Republic*, July 30 and August 6, 1990, p. 12, and Sonneman, "Old Hatreds."

23. Kaplan, "Bloody Romania." Kaplan describes his own journey through Romania this way: "I encountered a surrealistic hell of rowdy alcoholism,

with gangs of factory laborers living in dormitories away from their families and bereft of all pride, drinking medicinal alcohol and watching kung fu movies in cafés." He points out that Iliescu uses these miners as a praetorian guard against the antiregime intellectuals in the cities.

24. Eric Hobsbawm, "A New Threat to History," *The New York Review of Books*, December 16, 1993, pp. 62–64.

25. Ibid.

26. Ibid., p. 62. Hobsbawm points to a study of the Indus valley called "5000 Years of Pakistan," even though "Pakistan was not even thought of before 1932–33, when the name was invented by some student militants. It did not become a serious political aspiration until 1940. As a state it has existed only since 1947."

27. Cited in Celeste Bohlen, "Ethnic Rivalries Revive, in E. Europe," *The New York Times*, November 12, 1990, pp. A1, 12.

Chapter 14. Essential Jihad: Islam and Fundamentalism

1. Martin E. Marty and R. Scott Appleby, *Fundamentalisms Observed*, Vol. 1 of the Fundamentalism Project (Chicago: University of Chicago Press, 1991), pp. viii–x.

2. Advertisement in *The New York Times*, July 20, 1994.

3. Chris Hedges, "Teheran Journal," *The New York Times*, August 16, 1994, p. A2.

4. Leslie Planner and Cherry Mosteshar, "Bringing a Beam of Delight to the Closed World of Iran," *The Guardian*, August 5, 1994, p. 14.

5. "There is something exceptional about the degree of authoritarianism that prevails in the Middle East today. . . . Whether or not Islam and Middle Eastern 'culture' are separable phenomena, the two work in ways that do not augur well for democracy." "Democracy Without Democrats," in G. Salame, editor, *Democracy Without Democrats* (London: I. B. Tauris Publishers, 1994), pp. 32–33.

6. Hilal Khashan, "The Limits of Arab Democracy," *World Affairs*, Vol. 153, No. 4, Spring 1991, pp. 127–135.

7. Fatima Mernissi, *Islam and Democracy: Fear of the Modern World* (Reading, Mass.: Addison-Wesley, 1992), p. 21. For a remarkable portrait of Islam as seen by a photojournalist, see Abbas, *Allah o Akbar: A Journey Through Militant Islam* (San Francisco: Phaidon Press, 1995).

8. As John O. Voll suggests, "Leaders of Jihad believed that armed struggle against a wicked government was a requirement of their faith." "Fundamentalism in the Sunni Arab World," in M. E. Marty and R. S. Appleby, *Fundamentalisms Observed*, p. 345.

9. From the executive summary, *Islam and Democracy*, Timothy D. Sisk, editor, (Washington, D.C.: United States Institute of Peace, 1992), p. x.

10. See, for example, Edward W. Said, *Culture and Imperialism* (New York: Alfred A. Knopf, 1993).

11. Sisk, *Islam and Democracy*, p. 23.

12. Voll, "Fundamentalism," p. 348.

13. Cited in ibid., p. 360. Free institutions are seen as a pretext for corruption, not evil in themselves but not to be taken seriously because they are only the Trojan horse in which the West's vices are smuggled in.

14. Prynne, cited by Jonas Barish, *The Antitheatrical Prejudice* (Berkeley, California: The University of California Press, 1981), pp. 84–85.

15. Jean-Jacques Rousseau, *Letter to D'Alembert on Theater*, Allan Bloom, editor, *Politics and the Arts* (Ithaca: Cornell University Press), p. 58.

16. See Stephen Barboza, *American Jihad: Islam after Malcolm X* (New York: Doubleday, 1994).

17. Stephen Carter has written a penetrating account of the trivialization of true belief that the religious encounter in secular America: *The Culture of Disbelief: How American Law and Politics Trivialize Religious Devotion* (New York: Basic Books, 1993).

18. Jerry Falwell, founder and president of the Moral Majority, in a March 1993 sermon; cited in The Anti-Defamation League, *The Religious Right: The Assault on Tolerance and Pluralism in America* (New York: The Anti-Defamation League, 1994), p. 4.

19. Ibid. Terrell is the founder of "Operation Rescue," the antiabortion activist group.

20. From "Drive by Witness," by A-1 S.W.I.F.T., cited by Michael Marriot, "Rhymes of Redemption," *Newsweek*, November 28, 1994, p. 64. Also see Nicholas Dawidoff, "No Sex, No Drugs, But Rock 'N' Roll," *The New York Times Magazine*, February 5, 1995, pp. 40–44.

21. The scandals, sexual and fiscal, that rocked telepreacher constituencies like Jim Bakker's, continue today. The Gospel Music Association had to announce in 1994 that married Christian pop singer Michael English had gotten Marabeth Jordan, another man's wife and a singer in the trio First Call, pregnant—proving perhaps that he who uses the tools of Devil McWorld is likely to be snared by the devil.

22. Philip Weiss offers a stunning account of new age reactionary drop-outs in his "Off the Grid," *The New York Times Magazine*, January 6, 1995, pp. 24–52.

23. Charles B. Strozier has written a fascinating account of the apocalyptic side of fundamentalism; see *Apocalypse: On the Psychology of Fundamentalism in America* (Boston: Beacon Press, 1994). See also Paul Boyer, *When Time Shall Be No More: Prophecy Belief in Modern American Culture* (Cambridge: Harvard University Press, 1993).

PART III. JIHAD VS. MCWORLD

Chapter 15. Jihad and McWorld in the New World Disorder

1. Alexis de Tocqueville, *Democracy in America* (Mattituck: American House, 1838), Book I, Chapter 15.

2. Thus the U.S. Business and Industrial Council is fighting the WTO provisions of GATT, which it fears "is an official surrender by the United States to foreign governments." Advertisement in *The New York Times*, July 28, 1994, p. A 13.

3. Jack Sheinkman, "When Children Do the Work," *The New York Times*, August 9, 1994, p. A 23.

4. Ibid. As David Keppel writes in a pointed letter taking exception to *The New York Times*'s editorializing on behalf of the WTO, it is unlikely to be some small country like Benin that challenges American environmental standards as an obstruction to free trade. Rather, "only nominally will the challenger be Benin. It will really be a major global corporation, finding a friendly or desperate foreign government to help overturn regulations it is always fighting." *The New York Times*, Letters, August 3, 1994, p. A 20. Note that Article 2 of the WTO treaty prohibits governments from regulating "with the effect of creating unnecessary obstacles to international trade." Unnecessary obstacles like a ban on child labor, industrial safety standards, environmental protection regulations, and so forth!?

5. For the controversy here see Laurie Udesky, "Sweatshops Behind the Labels," *The Nation*, May 16, 1994, pp. 665–668, and the ensuing correspondence, including a rejoinder from Levi Strauss & Company in *The Nation*, August 8/15, 1994, pp. 146, 176.

6. In a recent dialogue involving the German social philosopher Juergen Habermas and the Polish reformer and editor Adam Michnik, Habermas replies to the question "What is left of socialism?" with the clear response "radical democracy." Michnik is "entirely" in agreement. But what this seems to mean is not that democracy survives, but that its idealistic possibilities (associated with socialism as a noble theory) have in practice vanished along with socialism. Michnik, " 'More Humility, Fewer Illusions'—A Talk Between Adam Michnik and Juergen Habermas," *The New York Review of Books*, March 24, 1994, p. 24.

7. Thomas L. Friedman, "A Peace Deal Today Really Is a Bargain," *The New York Times*, September 11, 1994, Section 4, p. 1.

8. Quoted by Vance Packard in his early classic on consumption, *The Waste Makers* (New York: David McKay, 1960), and cited again by Alan Durning in his excellent study for the Worldwatch Institute called *How Much Is Enough: The Consumer Society and the Future of Earth* (New York: W. W. Norton & Company, 1992), pp. 21–22.

9. Durning, ibid., pp. 22, 116.

10. The League was an abject failure; the United States was never a member and seventeen other nations out of sixty-three member states dropped out prior to its demise at the onset of World War II, which it failed to avert. See Mihaly Simai, *The Future of Global Governance* (Washington, D.C.: United States Institute of Peace, 1994), p. 27.

The attempt by the more numerous but weaker developing nations in 1974 to institute a "new international economic order" through U.N. Resolution 3201 was made a mockery of by the refusal of powerful First World nations to take an interest. The same fate befell the New World Information Order conceived in the early 1980s as a response to McWorld's communications hegemony. Not even the United Nations' powerful Security Council members have succeeded in bending the international body to the purposes of effective peacekeeping, as the charade in Bosnia makes clear.

11. Maurice F. Strong, "ECO '92: Critical Challenges and Global Solutions," *Journal of International Affairs*, No. 44, 1991, pp. 287–298. Thus, a 1994 conference explored reconfiguring international agenies like the World Bank and I.M.F. See *Rethinking Bretton Woods* (Washington, D.C.: Center for Concern, 1995). The several environmental and social "summits" that have met over the last five years have had similar objectives, but have been long on rhetoric and short on common action.

12. Oscar Schachter, "The Emergence of International Environmental Law," *Journal of International Affairs*, No. 44, 1991, p. 457.

13. Geoffrey Palmer, "New Ways to Make International Environmental Law," *American Journal of International Law*, No. 86, 1992, p. 259. Also see Benjamin B. Ferencz, *New Legal Foundations for Global Survival* (New York: Oceana Publications, 1994), which like almost everything else written about international law deploys a futile rhetoric of "must," "should," and "ought" in a domain where realists correctly talk in terms of "can't," "don't," and "won't."

14. There are a variety of international institutions—laws, conventions, agencies, and organizations—strewn about among the hulks of disintegrated nations, slaughtered tribes, homeless refugee masses, and devastated environments that constitute the history of the last seventy-five years that have some legitimacy. In limited domains where powerful nations can agree on particular agenda items, these institutions have even accomplished some good. During the postwar era when the United States could play "hegemon" to the world, most "international" institutions in fact conducted themselves as not very disguised agents of American policies and interests and helped secure a limited "pax Americana" that in turn assured a limited, Cold War kind of peace. John Gerard Ruggie introduces the term, which has become fashionable in academic international relations and economics circles among scholars like Robert Keohane, Charles Kindleberger, and Robert Gilpin.

15. Robert Kuttner, *The End of Laissez-Faire: National Purpose and the Global Economy after the Cold War* (New York: Alfred A. Knopf, 1991), p. 260. Kuttner offers a penetrating account of the illusions of laissez-faire and their devastating impact on the American economy.

16. Assembly of Regions; see discussion below, note 19.

17. For a fascinating exchange on patriotism and cosmopolitanism, see Martha Nussbaum, "Patriotism or Cosmopolitanism? Martha Nussbaum in Debate," *Boston Review*, special issue, Volume XIX, Number 5, October/November 1994, and my reply in the same issue.

18. Robert Reich, *Work of Nations* (New York: Alfred A. Knopf, 1991), p. 313.

19. Article 24/1 of the Basic Law discussing the "power of integration," states that "the Federation may by legislation transfer sovereign powers to inter-

national institutions." It was replaced by a new "Europe Article" in 1992. For a careful discussion see Charlie Jeffrey, "The Laender Strike Back: Structures and Procedures of European Integration: Policy-Making in the German Federal System," research paper prepared for the 26th World Congress of the International Political Science Association, Berlin, August 21–25, 1994.

20. Humanitarians still dream of intervention by a United Nations army not dependent on American hegemony. But a global humanitarian army without a global sovereignty is unthinkable, while a global army dependent on the participation of interested nations can be neither disinterested nor global. For a discussion, see Kai Bird, "The Case for a U.N. Army," *The Nation*, August 8/15, 1994, p. 160.

Even the venerable World Federalist Association has seemingly given up the conceit of a world government and campaigns primarily within nations on behalf of extant organizations that have already proved themselves incapable of peacekeeping, let alone of world government. A recent fund-raising flier encloses prewritten messages to be mailed to designated representatives including President Clinton, asking them to "support the United Nations and global change" but little else.

21. Cited in Stuart Elliot, "In Search of Fun for Creativity's Sake," *The New York Times*, January 3, 1994, p. C 19.

22. Joan Lewis, "UN Blues: Responding to the Crisis in Somalia," *LSE Magazine*, Spring 1994.

23. Reich, *Work of Nations*, Chapter 12.

24. Hannah Arendt brings all three together in her discussion of primary democracy in *On Revolution* (New York: Viking Press, 1963), pp. 22–24.

25. In his *Making Democracy Work: Civic Traditions in Modern Italy* (Princeton: Princeton University Press, 1993), Robert Putnam has shown how traditional choral societies have marked the Italian towns where they existed in earlier centuries with a distinctive capacity for civic engagement and democracy.

26. See Michael Lesy, *Wisconsin Death Trip* (New York: Pantheon Books, 1973), and Jane Mansbridge, *Beyond Adversary Democracy* (Chicago: University of Chicago Press, 1983).

27. Stephen Holmes, "Back to the Drawing Board," *East European Constitutional Review*, Vol. 2, No. 1., Winter 1993, pp. 21–25. It is not clear that the center is taking his advice, however, since the same issue of the journal in which his editorial advice appears is devoted to a discussion of "The Separation of Powers," while subsequent volumes have been organized around such abstract institutions as constitutional courts, the post-Communist presidency, and the "design" of electoral regimes.

28. A list of such associations and ongoing news about their activities is published in the monthly newsletter *Third Sector*, prepared by the editorial group of the Interlegal International Foundation in Moscow. (Moscow: Belka Technology Publishers, 1994). I discuss the impact of these institutions on the new Russia below.

Chapter 16. Wild Capitalism vs. Democracy

1. J. G. A. Pocock, "The Ideal of Citizenship Since Classical Times," *Queen's Quarterly*, Spring 1992, p. 55.
2. Milton Friedman, in his introduction to the new edition of Friedrich von Hayek's classic *The Road to Serfdom* (Chicago: University of Chicago Press, 1994).
3. Stephen Holmes calls negative constitutionalism "the political equivalent to libertarianism in economics" and believes it is "very likely to produce a new autocracy in the not so long run" since it refuses to act positively to contain the abuses of a market society." Holmes, "Back to the Drawing Board," *East European Constitutional Review*, Vol. 2, No. 1, Winter 1993, pp. 21–25.
4. Anarchist in the sense that the libertarians believe all government, democratic or not, is an evil, and as government grows, liberty is necessarily diminished.
5. See the long and fruitful tradition of critical political theory that can be traced back to Rousseau and John Stuart Mill—liberal democrats who worried about the excesses and abuses of private property and monopoly capital. Mill's *Autobiography* is particularly critical of certain features of the private property system—this despite Mill's celebration of liberty in *On Liberty*. Rousseau's *Second Discourse* "On Inequality" offers an early portrait of the impact of private property on natural human equality and civic virtue.

   From such early critics, the lineage extends down to Karl Polanyi, John Maynard Keynes, and John Kenneth Galbraith. See, for example, John Kenneth Galbraith, "Capitalism's Dark Shadows," *The Washington Monthly*, (July/August 1994), pp. 20–23, where Galbraith suggests there are those in the capitalist economy such as corporate managers, stockholders, professionals, retirees on social security, who actually prefer low growth and high employment despite its horrendous impact on most workers in the economy and on capitalism itself.
6. In his *Theory of Moral Sentiments*, Adam Smith offered an account of human behavior that went well beyond economic utility, and *The Wealth of Nations* leaves ample room for public authorities that retain responsibility for such public goods as education, health, welfare, public works, and control of the potentially "conspiratorial" aspects of markets (monopolies, for example).
7. Norman Birnbaum, "How New Is the New Germany?" Part I, *Salmagundi*, Nos. 88–89, Fall 1990/Winter 1991, pp. 234–263; Part II, *Salmagundi*, Nos. 90–91, Spring/Summer 1991, pp. 131–178, 292–296.
8. Aleksandr Solzhenitsyn, "To Tame Savage Capitalism," *The New York Times*, November 28, 1993, p. E 11.
9. Andrew Schmookler refuses this concession in his well-documented study *The Illusion of Choice: How the Market Economy Shapes Our Destiny* (Albany, N.Y.: State University of N.Y. Press, 1993). But laissez-faire economists appear to have learned nothing from the twenties and thirties.

10. Through the voucher movement, Americans have become familiar with the privatization of education. Fewer know that nearly 2 percent of our prison population has been turned over to private companies in the thirteen states that have surrendered their sovereign power of punishment to private vendors like the Corrections Corporation of America; or that there are currently more private security guards in America than public police. See Anthony Ramirez, "Privatizing America's Prisons," *The New York Times*, August 14, 1994, p. K 1.

11. Milton and Rose Friedman, *Free to Choose* (New York: Harcourt Brace Jovanovich, 1980).

12. Jeffrey Sachs, *Poland's Jump to the Market Economy* (Cambridge, Mass.: the M.I.T. Press, 1993), pp. 4–5 and p. 57. Although he has been relieved of his duties (or relieved himself of his duties, as he insists) in Russia, Sachs continues to be a market guru to other transitional nations. For a critique from the left, see Jon Wiener, "The Sachs Plan in Poland," *The Nation*, June 25, 1990, p. 877.

13. Robert Kuttner, *The End of Laissez-Faire: National Purpose and the Global Economy after the Cold War* (New York: Alfred A. Knopf, 1991), p. 18. Kuttner notices, of course, that "oddly enough, for a decade the U.S. has preached an ever more devout adherence to laissez-faire while practicing a perverse, unacknowledged Keynesianism"—namely its bankrupting support of the dollar as the international medium of exchange, its economy-overheating defense spending, and Reagan's deficit-enlarging tax cuts (p. 18).

14. *The Economist*, March 13, 1993, p. 21.

15. See Bruce Rich, *Mortgaging the Earth: The World Bank, Environmental Impoverishment and the Crisis of Development* (Boston: Beacon Press, 1994); also Andrew Cohen's review essay "Potemkin Environmentalism," *The Nation*, July 18, 1994, pp. 101–103. On its fiftieth birthday, the World Bank (aka, the International Bank for Reconstruction and Development) is vowing to do better on environmentalism at least. In its 1994 statement "Embracing the Future," it claims to be as interested in human development programs and the environment as in pure economic development and markets. See Thomas L. Friedman, "World Bank at 50, Vows to Do Better," *The New York Times*, July 24, 1994, p. A 4.

16. Kuttner, *End of Laissez-Faire*, p. 24.

17. Thomas L. Friedman, "When Money Talks," *The New York Times*, July 24, 1994, p. E 3.

18. Advertisement for "The Czech Republic," *The New York Times*, January 7, 1994, p. 6.

19. Holmes, "Drawing Board."

20. Walter B. Wriston, *Twilight of Sovereignty* (New York: Scribner's, 1992), p. 12.

21. Friedman, "When Money Talks."

22. It may be worthwhile citing in full Jeffrey Sachs's prescription for economic reform in Poland (which appeared as the "Balcerowicz Plan" in honor of Leszek Balcerowicz, Poland's Deputy Prime Minister for the economy in the government Sachs advised). The five "main pillars" of his

reform were, first, macroeconomic stabilization aimed at cutting the rate of credit expansion by tightening of domestic credit via monetary and fiscal measures; second, liberalization including the end of all central planning, price controls, and regulation of international trade; third, privatization with the transfer of ownership of state assets to the private sector; fourth, the construction of a social safety net including unemployment compensation; and fifth, mobilization of international finance assistance. (Sachs, *Poland's Jump*, pp. 45–46). Pillar four was never built and pillar five never provided much subsidy, so pillars one through three quickly became the essence of shock therapy. This plan, in which civil society is ignored and political reforms are taken for granted, has been a prescription for disaster almost everywhere.

23. Ludwig von Mises, *Human Action: A Treatise on Economics* (New York: Van Nostrand, 1949), p. 2. Andrew Bard Schmookler in his effective if overwrought internal critique of market economics perfectly captures the delusions of the marketeers in his title: *The Illusion of Choice*. Carl Kaysen, whom Schmookler cites (p. 37), is typical in his confounding of consumer choice with civic freedom: "People have preferences in respect to what kinds of goods they buy; where they live and work, what kinds of occupations they pursue . . . what kinds of mortgages, automobile loans, bank loans they owe. The working of the market, provided that it is competitive, makes the best possible reconciliation of these preferences with the technical possibilities of production, which in combination with these preferences . . . determine what jobs, goods, services are available." But "preferences" do not determine anything except what consumers happen to "want" at a given moment. Social and political choices are not the expression of preferences but of deliberative choices made in the setting of common debate with fellow citizens trying to figure out what their communities value and need (see below).

24. Felix Rohatyn, cited in T. Friedman, "When Money Talks, Governments Listen," *The New York Times*, July 24, 1994, p. E 3.

25. Just try to talk about citizens or comrades or neighbors or brothers in the lands that have finally rid themselves of communism. In too many of these countries, the failure of the Communist "we" has extirpated hope in the possibility of a democratic "we." Back in 1990, then mayor Gavriil Popov of Moscow, at that time an "economic reformer" under Gorbachev, wrote: "If economic transformations are to work, we must create an effective apparatus for management, yet the masses have an intense hatred of any bureaucracy." Since then, they have permitted that bureaucracy to cripple their democratic capacity to act in common to curb wild capitalism. Or, when fed up, have fallen into a nostalgia for governmental bosses who can fix everything (in return for the resurrender of recently won liberties).

26. Robert McIntyre, "Why Communism Is Rising from the Ash Heap," *The Washington Post*, National Weekly Edition, June 20–26, 1994, p. 24. Too

familiar with Stalinist government, many of Lenin's abused children have come to regard democratic government as just one more variation on totalitarianism, the more dangerous because it wears the mantle of popular legitimacy. A cartoon by Margulies hits the mark when it depicts one Solidarity veteran standing in front of a Warsaw market after the 1990 elections in which Solidarity won overwhelmingly, and saying to another: "I've had it with bread lines, food shortages, and scarce housing . . . It's time we got rid of this rotten government," only to be reminded by his comrade, "WE ARE the government!" In the days of the Solidarity government; from *The Houston Post*, reprinted in *The Washington Post*, National Weekly Edition, January 1–7, 1990.

27. Critics like Schmookler and Kuttner find markets wanting in their own right and by their own measures. Regardless of whether they are correct, it is when markets usurp political functions that they must necessarily fail.

28. Both quotes from Guillermo O'Donnell, "The Browning of Latin America," *New Perspectives Quarterly*, Vol. 10, Fall 1993, p. 50.

Chapter 17. Capitalism vs. Democracy in Russia

1. Peter Reddaway, "Instability and Fragmentation," in the aptly named symposium "Is Russian Democracy Doomed?" *Journal of Democracy*, Vol. 5, No. 2, April 1994, p. 16.

2. Michael McFaul, "Explaining the Vote," ibid., p. 4.

3. John H. Fairbanks, Jr., "The Politics of Resentment," ibid., p. 41.

4. Padma Desai, "Ease Up on Russia," *The New York Times*, December 10, 1993, p. A 35. In the same vein, Saul Estrin introduces his careful conceptual and economic analysis of privatization by admitting that "privatization of the former state sector is, however, not the only way, and may not be the best way to ensure successful transition to the market economy," although he does not raise (and could not be expected to raise) the question of whether the market economy is the only alternative to the Communist command economy. Saul Estrin, *Privatization in Central and Eastern Europe* (New York: Longman, 1994), p. 4.

5. Because so many American progressives and liberals supported Gorbachev, Yeltsin relied in the early days on more conservative advisors including the Heritage Foundation. Cold War veteran Richard Perle is currently involved in joint ventures with new Russian enterprises aimed at the conversion of military facilities! See Jim Hoagland, "The New Guest in Moscow," *The International Herald Tribune*, April 1, 1992.

6. Margaret Shapiro and Fred Hiatt, "The Agony of Reform," *The Washington Post*, National Weekly Edition, March 14–20, 1994, p. 6.

7. Michael Specter, "The Great Russia Will Live Again," *The New York Times Magazine*, June 19, 1994, p. 31.

8. Celestine Bohlen, "Russia's New Rich on a Giant Buying Spree," *The New York Times*, August 31, 1993, p. A 1.

9. AP report, "Russia's Reckless Capitalism," *The Berkshire Eagle*, August 4, 1994.

10. Specter, "Russia Will Live," p. 32.

11. David M. Kotz, "The End of the Market Romance," *The Nation*, February 28, 1994, pp. 263–265.

12. Melvin Fagen, "Russia: Shock Therapy Isn't the Way to Promote Democracy," *The International Herald Tribune*, May 12, 1992.

13. James Sterngold, "Summit in Tokyo: Yeltsin Arrives in Tokyo as Aid Plan Is Prepared," *The New York Times*, July 9, 1993, p. A 7.

14. Joseph Blasi, "Privatizing Russia—A Success Story," *The New York Times*, June 30, 1994, p. A 23.

15. See Louis Uchitelle, "In the New Russia, an Era of Takeovers," *The New York Times*, April 17, 1994, p. C 1. This is "a world of investors still more interested in buying ownership of Corporate Russia for a fraction of its value than in improving what they own."

16. Liesl Schillinger, "Uneasy Rider," *The New Republic*, April 19, 1993, pp. 9–11.

17. Michael Dobbs and Steve Coll, "The Free Market's Ugly Face," *The Washington Post*, National Weekly Edition, March 1–7, 1993. Also see "From Russia with Cash," *The Washington Post*, National Weekly Edition, February 15–21, 1993. The polite version of this phenomenon is given by Alexander Bim, D. Jones, and T. Weisskopf in their soothingly economistic account of "Privatization in the Former Soviet Union and the New Russia," where they write: "The predominance of insider control of privatized enterprises in Russia at the present time reflects not only problems in the tactics of the radical reformers . . . (but) the strong desire of a large proportion of the Russian people for stability and security." Estrin, *Privatization*, p. 274.

18. Bill Gifford, "Art of the Zdyelka," *The New Republic*, February 28, 1994, p. 12. Gifford describes how the ruble exchange rate leapt in January 1, 1994, from 1,250 a dollar to, just three weeks later, 1,800 a dollar, with the July 1994 ruble futures contract selling at 2,174 a dollar. The original Russian voucher plan offered every Russian vouchers worth 10,000 rubles each, or two weeks of a miner's salary or ten bags of potatoes or three cases of vodka or in dollars, ten cups of coffee in the West. The total voucher offer was for an estimated fixed capital of 1.4 trillion rubles divided by 150 million people. Companies with over one thousand employees or fixed capital of 50 million rubles were required to privatize. Bill Gifford, "Russian Citizens to Get Share," *The New York Times*, October 1, 1992, p. A 1.

19. See Wendy Carlin and Colin Mayer, "The Treuhandanstalt: Privatization by State and Market," Paper Presented at the National Bureau of Economic Resources Conference on Transformation in Eastern Europe, Cambridge, Mass., February 26–29, 1992. Carlin admits, for example, that Germany's office of privatization (Treuhandanstalt—see below) also shed jobs to control their own expenditures. No one seemed much interested in the impact of labor-shedding practices on the millions of East German workers who were supposed to be socialized into West Germany's democracy.

20. The results of the December 12, 1993, elections were:

Liberal Democratic (ultranationalist)	22.79%	(59 seats)
Russia's Choice (Reformist)	15.38%	(40 seats)
Communist Party	12.35%	(32 seats)
Women of Russia (Centrist)	8.10%	(21 seats)
Agrarian (Communist farmer)	7.90%	(21 seats)
Yavlinsky-Boldyrev-Lukin Reform	7.83%	(20 seats)
Russian Party of Unity and Accord (reform)	6.76%	(18 seats)
Democratic Party (Centrist)	5.5%	(14 seats)

21. Only Albania, Armenia, the Czech Republic, Estonia, and Latvia have kept their Communists completely out of their governing circles.

22. "Every Man a Tsar," *The New Yorker*, Vol. 69, December 27, 1993, p. 8.

23. For the environmental costs of the transition see Murral Feshbach and Alfred Friendly, Jr., *Ecocide in the USSR: Health and Nature Under Siege* (New York: Basic Books, 1992), pp. 565–566. The problem is less ongoing despoilation than the economic inability to clean up the mess left by the Soviet regime. Chernobyl, still operating, and Lake Baikal, among the world's largest freshwater bodies (still dead for all practical purposes), are perhaps the best known examples of the economic disincentives to ecologically sound policy produced by the new market economy.

24. Michael Specter, "Climb in Russia's Death Rate," *The New York Times*, March 6, 1994, p. A 1. Falling life expectancy reflects the reemergence of diseases like cholera and tuberculosis as well as the swath being cut by crime and alcoholism through the Russian male population. Vodka, a Russian sop under commissars and tsars alike, is the one consumer item available at a realistic price (about a dollar a bottle).

25. For a check on these generalizations, readers may wish to consult the United Nations Children's Fund's *Crisis in Mortality, Health and Nutrition,* a survey of health conditions from 1989 to 1994 in Russia, Albania, Bulgaria, the Czech Republic, Slovakia, Hungary, Poland, Romania, and the Ukraine. UNICEF director James P. Grant states: "This health crisis is unprecedented in the peacetime history of Europe in this century," and is "obviously . . . eroding political support for the reforms that are under way." Barbara Crossette, "U.N. Study Finds a Free Eastern Europe Less Healthy," *The New York Times*, October 7, 1994, p. A 13.

26. Claire Sterling, "Redfellas," *The New Republic*, April 11, 1994, pp. 19–20. Also see her new book *Thieves' World: The Threat of the New Global Network of Organized Crime* (New York: Simon & Schuster, 1994).

27. Celestine Bohlen, "Russian Mobsters Grow More Violent and Pervasive," *The New York Times*, August 16, 1993, p. A 1.

28. Serge Schmemann, "Russia Lurches into Reform," *The New York Times*, February 20, 1994, p. A 1.

29. In recent times, even foreign businesses have become targets and prudent investors have had to hire their own heavily armed security forces. Only McWorld's symbolic masters like McDonald's and Coca-Cola have been spared, not perhaps because they are totems but because the publicity

would be bad (because they are totems!). See Michael Specter, "US Business and the Russian Mob," *The New York Times*, July 8, 1994, p. D 1.

30. About measures that only Zhirinovsky's party supported in parliament, the newspaper *Isvestia* commented: "Every time Russia has tried to do something for the greater good of the state, it has ended in political terror and dictatorship and extraordinary powers in the hands of extraordinary bodies." David Gurevich is moved to ask, "Is there no third way between Vladimir Zhirinovsky and Michael Corleone?" in "The MOB—Today's K.G.B.," *The New York Times*, February 19, 1994, p. A 19. There is not yet a clear answer to his question.

31. Andrew Solomon, "Young Russia's Defiant Decadence," *The New York Times Magazine*, July 18, 1993, pp. 16–23; see also his book *The Irony Tower: Soviet Artists in a Time of Glasnost* (New York: Alfred A. Knopf, 1991).

   Michael Specter, in "Could We Tell Tchaikovsky This News?," *The New York Times*, February 20, 1994, Section 1, p. 15, writes: "Driven by advertising and money, radio here is beginning to bear a resemblance to stations in NY and LA, where classical broadcasts are under siege."

32. Janusz Glowacki, "Given the Realities It's Impossible to Be Absurd," *The New York Times*, September 19, 1993, Section 2, p. 7. Glowacki is the author of "Antigone in New York." Recalling Sartre's paradox—we were never so free as under the Nazi occupation, he mused—another writer Glowacki interviews complains: "The worst thing is there is no censorship anymore, and when everything is allowed you don't feel like writing."

33. Liesl Schillinger, "Barbski," *The New Republic*, September 20, 1993, pp. 10–11.

34. See William Schmidt, "Moscow Journal: West Sets Up Store and the Russians Are Seduced," *The New York Times*, September 27, 1991, p. A 4.

35. David Lempert, "Changing Russian Political Culture in the 1990's—Parasites, Paradigms, and Perestroika," *Journal for the Comparative Study of Society and History*, Vol. 35, No. 3, July 1993, pp. 628–646.

36. Quoted by Andrew Solomon, "Defiant Decadence."

37. "Russian Gadfly From TV to Politics," unsigned special to *The New York Times*, December 26, 1993, p. A 18.

38. Cited in Margaret Shapiro and Fred Hiatt, "The Agony of Reform," *The Washington Post*, National Weekly Edition, March 14–20, 1994, p. 6.

39. In an interview, "L'ecrivain international choisit la Grande Russie," *Liberation*, April 6, 1992. My translation.

40. Cited by David M. Kotz, "The End of the Market Romance," *The Nation*, February 28, 1994, p. 263.

41. Cited in *The Washington Post*, Weekly National Edition, April 5–11, 1993.

42. Michael Scammell, "What's Good for the Mafia Is Good for Russia," *The New York Times*, December 26, 1993, Section 4, p. 11.

43. This would be a sort of democracy since "Russians are used to firm control from the top. If domination by a mafia bureaucracy offered a return to the relative order enjoyed by many under the communist rule, many would

embrace it." Nikolai Zlobin, "The Mafiacracy Takes Over," *The New York Times*, July 26, 1994, p. A 19.

44. Along with other fans of order (if not law) at any price, Zlobin will be pleased to know that at least one high-flying member of the criminal class agrees with him: "The Mafia is what's holding this country together. We do provide structure, and when we take over a business, that business works. It's noble work." Andrew Solomon, "Defiant Decadence."

45. Boris Yeltsin, Address to the Federal Assembly, February 24, 1994, pp. 32–37; translated by Nina Belyaeva, "Rule of Law for Civil Society," paper prepared for the XVI World Congress of the International Political Science Association in Berlin, August 1994, p. 10.

46. Interview with S. F. Cohen, "What's Really Happening in Russia," *The Nation*, March 2, 1992, pp. 259–264.

Chapter 18. The Colonization of East Germany by McWorld

1. The Christian Democrat poster features slogans like "Off to the future, but not with red socks." Supporters played on Kohl's name, which means both cabbage and cash in German, by shouting "Keine Kohl ohne Kohl"—no cash without Kohl.

2. Peter Rossman, "Dashed Hopes for a New Socialism," *The Nation*, May 7, 1990, pp. 232–235.

3. *Tageszeitung*, August 4, 1990.

4. In fact, tens of thousands of tainted functionaries found their way quickly back into the new Federal Republic of Germany's bureaucracies. As Norman Birnbaum reminds us, war criminal Field Marshal Kesselring went straight from his jail term to tenure as Chancellor Konrad Adenauer's military advisor, while Dr. Hans Globke who had written an authoritative commentary on the Nuremberg Laws for the Nazis ended up as his chief of staff. Norman Birnbaum, "How New the New Germany?," Part I, *Salmagundi*, Nos. 88–89, Fall 1990/Winter 1991, pp. 234–263.

5. The pastor of Martin Luther's Castle Church in Wittenberg observed wryly that during the revenge attacks on former East German officials: "Those who were the most cowardly are now loudest in their demands for revenge." ibid.

6. Ferdinand Protzman, "Privatization in East Is Wearing to Germans," *The New York Times*, August 12, 1994, p. D 1. According to its interim report published in *The International Herald Tribune*, as of August 1994, Treuhand had sold 247 chemical companies with only a dozen remaining; 181 steel and metal fabricating firms with 25 remaining; 238 iron and nonferrous metal manufacturers with 16 pending; 1,060 machine tool and die companies with 54 pending; 490 electronics firms with 14 left to be sold or liquidated; 512 textile manufacturers with 19 to go; and 1,017 construction companies with just 7 left. The liquidations comprised mainly sales to Westerners but also included the return of companies to pre-Communist

ownership and liquidations. Most of the jobs lost came from downsizing to make companies more attractive to investors rather than from straight liquidations.

7. *The Week in Germany,* July 15, 1994. Detlev Rohwedder, Treuhand's first chairman, was assassinated on April 1, 1991, and replaced by Birgit Breuel.

8. Even sober academic accountants with no political ax to grind such as Wolfgang Siebel have warned that the Unification Treaty had a "financially flawed basis," despite the "gigantic transfer of funds to East Germany." Wolfgang Siebel, "Necessary Illusions: The Transformation of Governance Structures in the New Germany," *The Tocqueville Review,* Vol. 13, No. 1, 1992, pp. 179–199. Despite the fact that the transfers amount to roughly a third of Germany's federal budget (about 9,500 Deutsch Marks per East German), "most of these federal transfers are not destined for productive investment. Sixty-two percent is spent subsidizing social benefits such as unemployment compensation and housing subsidies." These subsidies make up nearly 70 percent of eastern Germany's GNP, and can be compared with the Marshall Plan's transfers in 1947 of roughly 800 Deutsch Marks per capita.

9. Ibid. Saxony, Mecklenburg, Brandenburg, Saxony-Anhalt, and Thuringia are the eastern Laender, based on older provinces that had been eliminated by the Communists in 1947. Siebel concludes that privatization in Germany finally "undermines the basis of healthy municipal finance. Municipalities are left with only those programs that run at a loss. This in turn tends to undermine the political and administrative credibility of local administration as a whole." Ibid., p. 187. Siebel suggests that hysteria about former Communist associations "appeared as a psychological compensation for the political incompetence to deal appropriately with the material consequences of unification." Ibid., p. 189.

10. Stephen Kinzer, "German Neocommunists Surging, Capture a City Hall," *The New York Times,* June 29, 1994, p. A 6. The Democratic Socialist party has 130,000 disciplined members of whom perhaps 90 percent were Communists earlier and 20,000 are hard-liners. Gregor Gysi, a member of parliament, is its telegenic and politically astute chief, while Hans Modrow who was East Germany's last Communist leader serves as its Honorary Chairman. The Party Handbooks insist, "Our goal is not the revolutionary overthrow of the democratic parliamentary order or the building of some kind of dictatorship, but rather the true democratization of Germany." Party leader Gysi says: "People in Eastern Germany have lost important rights, and there is much social injustice . . . we are not facing the global social, ecological and cultural challenges that confront us. So for me there are still very good reasons to be anticapitalist." See ibid.

11. Stephen Kinzer, "Group Is Formed to Defend East German Interests," *The New York Times,* July 12, 1992, p. A 11. Also see Kinzer, "In Germany, Too, an Effort to Mobilize Political Outsiders," *The New York Times,* July 19, 1992, Section 4, p. 2.

12. Stephen Kinzer, "Group Is Formed."

13. She remonstrated, "The people I worked with wanted to reform East Germany. We never thought the country would disappear and be swallowed up by the West." A woman with little patience for politics, she scorned both the trial of former East German President Honnecker by the West Germans and the Committee for Fairness. Her wholly independent voice rang clear. Stephen Kinzer, "Berlin Journal: One More Wall to Smash: Arrogance in the West," *The New York Times*, August 12, 1992, p. A 4.

14. Catarina Kennedy-Bannier, "Berliners," *The New Republic*, July 18–25, 1994, p. 11.

15. Stephen Kinzer, "Luckenwalde Journal: In East Germany, Bad Ol' Days Now Look Good," *The New York Times*, August 27, 1994, p. A 2.

16. Cited by Margaret Talbot, "Back to the Future, Pining for the Old Days in Germany," *The New Republic*, July 18–25, 1994, pp. 11–14.

17. Ibid.

18. East Germans were once voracious readers, which is perhaps why the literate leaders of Neues Forum gained such an extensive following. First printings ran to a half million volumes. Poetry volumes could expect first printings of twenty thousand. Those days are over. East Germans remain one-fifth of the total German population but buy less than 2 percent of its books. While East-zone writers saw themselves as dissidents, they were also part of a reformist socialist project, working for their country as they wished it might one day be. To Stefan Heym, a Jewish writer who fled Hitler, fought in the American army, and has been a dissident under the Communists, new writers are another breed; they "see themselves less as East Germans than as writers who live in Germany."

19. Roger Cohen, "High Hopes Fade at East European Newspapers," *The New York Times*, December 28, 1993, p. A 1.

20. Ibid.

21. Statistics and quote from "The Population Plunge That's Wracking Eastern Germany," *Business Week*, August 29, 1994, p. 20. *Business Week* noted that "such changes are unprecedented for an industrial country at peace."

Chapter 19. Securing Global Democracy in the World of McWorld

1. Walter B. Wriston, *Twilight of Sovereignty* (New York: Scribner's, 1992), pp. 170, 176. Wriston also thinks "modern information technology is also driving nation states towards cooperation with each other so that the world's work can get done," p. 174.

2. A Western diplomat in China says, "the Chinese Government has decided and I think logically that it really can't shut out satellite television entirely, whatever the threat. We're not talking about a few dissidents here. Hundreds of thousands of Chinese have now invested their life savings in these dishes, and there would be a nasty public uproar if the Government really forced the dishes down." And in Iran, the *Teheran Times* concludes that "The cultural invasion will not be resolved by the physical removal of satellite dishes." Both quotes from Philip Shenon, "A Repressed World

Says 'Beam Me Up,' " *The New York Times*, September 11, 1994, Section 4, p. 4. Note that the danger is not of political propaganda but of pop cultural contamination. Murdoch willingly took the BBC World Service off of his China service and in Iran the problem is not CNN, but *Dynasty*, which is the most popular program in Teheran today.

3. Robert Reich, *Work of Nations* (New York: Alfred A. Knopf), Chapter 23, "The New Community."

4. See Brock, *Telecommunications Policy* (Cambridge, Mass.: Harvard University Press, 1994).

5. Channel One currently is in about twelve thousand junior high and high schools. It offers free televisions, VCRs, and a satellite dish to schools (usually needy ones) willing to dish up two minutes of soft news, two minutes of commercials, and eight minutes of infotainment to its students during regular school hours. Channel One sells spots for up to $195,000 for thirty seconds, and has attracted many of the corporations on McWorld's frontier, including Pepsi and Reebok. Chris Whittle has sold it to K-III, an educational publisher, for profit.

6. J. G. A. Pocock, "The Ideal of Citizenship Since Classical Times," *Queen's Quarterly*, Spring 1992, p. 55.

7. Neil Postman, *Technopoly: The Surrender of Culture to Technology* (New York: Alfred A. Knopf, 1992), p. 52.

8. Pocock, "Ideal of Citizenship."

9. Zbigniew Brzezinski, *Out of Control: Global Turmoil on the Eve of the Twenty-First Century* (New York: Scribner's, 1993), p. 73. Solzhenitsyn thinks "the former crisis of the meaning of life and the spiritual vacuum (which during the nuclear decades had even been deepened from neglect) stand out all the more" in the new age of evaporating "self-restraint." Solzhenitsyn, "To Tame Savage Capitalism," *The New York Times*, November 28, 1993, Section 4, p. 11.

10. Quoted by Dirk Johnson, "It's Not Hip to Stay, Say Small-Town Youth," *The New York Times*, September 5, 1994, p. A 1. Meanwhile, teenage ex-subjects of the commissars, wooed by the same seductive voices of McWorld, flock to the new punk clubs like Tam-Tam and the World Jeans Festival in St. Petersburg and to Cokefest and Moscow's hot new radio stations that specialize in Annie Lennox, Cyndi Lauper, and Urban Cookie Collective. "We reach for the young adult," says the manager of Moscow's most popular radio station, "we play what people want to hear, and believe me, that is not opera." Nor even Russian rock (the Russians do not share East Germany's taste for local bands): "It wouldn't be fair to the native musicians to cram them in between UB40 and Prince. That would sound so bad." Michael Specter, "Could We Tell Tchaikovsky This News?" *The New York Times*, February 20, 1994, Section 1, p. 5. There is only one classical music station left in Moscow, and the explanations are pretty much identical to those offered in explaining a similar situation in New York.

11. Vaclav Havel, *Summer Meditations*, translated by Paul Wilson (New York: Alfred A. Knopf, 1992), p. 6.

12. Robert Putnam, "Bowling Alone: America's Declining Social Capital," *Journal of Democracy*, Vol. 6, No. 1, January 1995, p. 65.

13. Harry Boyte and Sara Evans, *Free Spaces: The Sources of Democratic Changes in America* (Chicago University of Chicago Press, 1992).

14. John Dewey, *The Public and Its Problems* (New York: Henry Holt and Company, 1927), p. 137.

15. Joshua Muravchik, *Exporting Democracy: Fulfilling America's Destiny* (Washington, D.C.: American Enterprise Institute Press, 1994).

16. Democracy requires patience and flexibility and an architect's sense of place, and cannot be delivered ready-made to peoples unprepared to make it function. Jean-Jacques Rousseau warned would-be founders that "as, before putting up a large building, the architect surveys and sounds the site to see if it will bear the weight, the wise legislator does not begin by laying down laws good in themselves, but by investigating the fitness of the people, for which they are destined, to receive them." Jean-Jacques Rousseau, *The Social Contract*, Book II, chapter 8.

17. David B. Truman, *The Governmental Process*, first published in 1951, second edition (Berkeley: Institute of Governmental Studies, 1971), p. 51.1.

18. There is a new international organization called CIVICUS dedicated to creating a framework for transnational N.G.O. cooperation. See also Peter J. Spiro, "New Global Communities: Nongovernmental Organizations in International Decision-Making Institutions, *The Washington Quarterly*, 18:1, Winter 1995, pp. 45–56.

19. Thomas Jefferson, Letter to Joseph C. Cabell, February 2, 1816.

20. Regis Debray warns that "An American monoculture would inflict a sad future on the world, one in which the planet is converted to a global supermarket where people have to choose between the local Ayatollah and Coca-Cola." Cited by Roger Cohen, "Aux Armes, France Rallies," *The New York Times*, January 2, 1994, p. H 1.

Afterword

1. Cited in David Brooks, "Buchananism: An Intellectual Cause," *The Weekly Standard*, March 11, 1996, p. 18. Buchanan, with his penchant for "cultural war" (see his 1992 Republican National Convention Speech), is as close to an official (respectable) leader of American Jihad as we have.

2. Phil Patton, "Now It's the Cars That Make the Characters Go," *The New York Times*, Sunday, April 21, 1996, H 13.

3. Glenn Collins, "Coke Drops Domestic and Goes One World," *The New York Times*, January 13, 1996, B 1.

4. "The Walt Disney Company is helping build one of the most unusual public schools in the nation—a high-tech model for the next century, a learning laboratory with fiber optic cables linking classrooms to the homes of every student. But the most unusual aspect of this public school . . . is that it is linked to an adjacent national teacher training academy that could make Disney a lot of money. Disney will use the academy and school to

develop classroom videos, software, and other educational products to be sold nationally." Mary Jordan, "This School's No Mickey Mouse Operation," *The Washington Post*, National Edition, July 25–31, 1995, p. 33. The town of Celebration (in Florida), where the school will be located, will have 800 homes, hospital, fire station, lake, inn, barber shop, churches, movie theaters, and ice cream parlors. Disney has also opened a for-profit Chautauqua called The Disney Institute. Meanwhile, through its ABC division, Disney fired controversial talk show hosts on the left and right, including Jim Hightower in 1995, and Alan Dershowitz and Bob Grant in 1996—Dershowitz because he called Grant a racist, Grant because he was a racist!

5. Kinsley drew *Newsweek* cover attention and a long *New Yorker* profile, earning back his salary almost instantly. See "Swimming to Seattle," Cover Essay, *Newsweek* Magazine, May 20, 1996. Ken Auletta, Gates/Kinsley essay, *The New Yorker*, April 8, 1996.

6. Cited by Thomas L. Friedman, "Revolt of the Wannabes," *The New York Times*, February 7, 1996, A 19.

7. Even the Nazis played this game: "Work will make you free!" (*"Arbeit macht frei!"*) was the slogan that greeted incoming "guests" of the work/death camps.

8. See, for example, Fareed Zakaria, "Paris is Burning," *The New Republic*, January 22, 1996, pp. 27–31.

9. Fareed Zakaria, ibid.

10. See my op ed essay "From Disney World to Disney's World," *The New York Times*, August 1, 1996.

11. See, for example, Philip Gourevitch, "Misfortune Tellers," *The New Yorker*, April, 1996.

12. President Clinton, in an extended critical exposition of the book's themes before a breakfast gathering of religious leaders in Washington, September 7, 1995, C-Span.

Index

© Leah Kreutzer

ABOUT THE AUTHOR

BENJAMIN R. BARBER is the Whitman Professor of Political Science at Rutgers University and the director of the Walt Whitman Center for the Culture and Politics of Democracy. He is the author of numerous books, including the political classic *Strong Democracy* as well as *An Aristocracy of Everyone*. With Patrick Watson, Barber also created and wrote the prizewinning television series and book *The Struggle for Democracy*. He writes regularly for *Harper's*, the *Atlantic Monthly*, and many other publications. He is married to the dancer and choreographer Leah Kreutzer.